GROWING TIGERS IN A TERRARIUM

THE IMPORTANCE OF MARTIAL ARTS IN AN UNRAVELING SOCIETY

WRITTEN BY WILLIAM POWELL

ART WORK BY KIMBALL PAUL

COVER DESIGN BY JOHN LESANCHE

FORWARD BY DAVID SABOE

TECHNICAL ADVISER ERICA THOMPSON

1

THIS BOOK IS DEDICATED TO THOSE WHO DARE TO BREAK THE CHAINS OF FEAR.

AND TO THOSE WHO MADE THE ULTIMATE SACRIFICE FOR GOD AND COUNTRY.

"IT WAS DARK ALL AROUND. THERE WAS FROST ON THE GROUND WHEN THE TIGERS BROKE FREE." –ROGER WATERS FROM THE FINAL CUT.

IN APPRECIATION OF MY BEST FRIEND AND MODERN VALKYRIE ERICA- WHO MADE THIS POSSIBLE.

TO MY WARRIOR CHILDREN RACHEL SAVANNAH AND NICO ALEXANDER - I LOVE YOU ENDLESSLY.

TO MY PARENTS ROBERT AND ROSEMARIE- THANKS FOR ALWAYS BEING THERE FOR ME. I LOVE YOU.

TO THE GREAT MARTIAL ARTS MASTERS AND WARRIORS THAT I'VE MET ALONG THE WAY- THANK YOU.

YOU WILL ACHIEVE ALL YOU DESIRE WITH THE HELP OF OTHERS.

HURRY TO JOIN THE HUMAN RACE BEFORE YOU DIE A HORRIBLE BLOODY DEATH WITH NO SAY IN THE MATTER AND NOTHING TO SHOW FOR THE STRUGGLE.

TRAIN. TRAIN.

TRAIN UNTIL YOU DIE.

AND WHEN YOU LEAVE

THIS WORLD YOU WILL BE

REMEMBERED AND THE

DEAD WILL BE WARNED THAT A

(KENPO)WARRIOR IS COMING.

LIFE IS NOT A DRESS REHEARSAL. YOU MAY OR MAY NOT HAVE A THOUSAND LIFETIMES TO EVOLVE, CAN'T TELL YOU. BUT I AM SURE YOU HAVE AT LEAST THIS ONE.

CONTENTS

FOREWORD

"When the student is ready, the teacher will appear" - Buddhist proverb

I first met Sensei Powell in his Chicago school some 20 years ago, seduced by a huge bruise I saw

on a friend's leg and finding out about the school only after asking him about the bruise and pleading

with him to learn more. As we were in the school's changing room, Mr. Powell walked in with a

huge smile and greeted me warmly. I scarcely understood the journey that I was about to take. As the

class started, it was time to rock. Sensei Powell unleashed incredibly powerful techniques while

explaining them so eloquently that even a newbie could understand the principles. Mind blown and

eyes open, I felt a new awakening. The sensation was akin to what Mr. Anderson must have felt after

taking the red pill in The Matrix and discovered the reality behind the curtain of what we perceive to

be real life. Who was this warrior teacher and what happened to the guy who greeted me in the

locker room? As Sensei Powell used to say, "Smile on the face, death in the hand". This school was

for me.

Built upon the traditions of samurai warriors, Shaolin monks, Vikings, and military Special Forces,

his school wasn't for everyone. One night he explained to me his popcorn principle for students.

Imagine a small flat table covered with popcorn kernels. As the kernels start popping, a teacher has

two choices: you can madly scramble to try to catch them before they fly off the table and into the

abyss, or you can let the popcorn fly and see where it lands keeping only those that managed to stay

on the table due to sheer will and tenacity. Instead of wasting energy to retain all students, he would

keep only those whose personal drive and dogged determination matched that of the school. This obviously had an effect on the caliber of students that the school produced – there are no slackers or quitters here. He developed a machine (his school) capable of developing true warriors . . . those with the knowledge, ability, and courage to act. At one point nearing the end of a tortuous and exhausting training session as sweat poured onto the floor, Sensei Powell said amusingly, "and to think you pay money for me to do this to you". Each student knew what they wanted - to reach their full potential as a martial artist and a human being. The school was a crucible in which we burned away fear, doubts, and self-consciousness. We emerged stronger in spirit and at a higher level of consciousness. Growing Tigers in a Terrarium is not just a book about one man's journey of understanding into martial arts and bushido. It is a book of personal development highlighting the importance of learning from failure and of testing your mettle as told through the recounting of actual events. It is a manual for living an ordinary life in an extraordinary manner. The sometimes disturbing and often-humorous personal "war stories" in this book provide enough remarkable real-life experiences for 10 lifetimes, yet they all happened to Sensei Powell. He now has more than 35 years' experience in the martial arts and applies the principles from his past teachings along with his real-life experience both inside and outside of the dojo to bring the "reality taught here" tagline to life. Sensei Powell's courage and ability to live in the moment allowed him to continuously test his fighting skills, find some illuminations along the Way, and use those life lessons to build something greater than himself - a school intent on teaching others real martial arts in the ancient traditions of bushido.

-David J. Saboe, GODAN-5th Degree Black Belt, Chinese Kenpo Karate
Author of *"Get Real! A Practical Approach to Personal Safety"*

TIME TO BECOME WHO YOU ARE OR LET OTHERS REMEMBER NOTHING.

AN ATTACK NEED NOT BE BY APPOINTMENT BUT CAN HAPPEN AT ANY TIME.

GROWING TIGERS IN A TERRARIUM

THE IMPORTANCE OF MARTIAL ARTS IN AN UNRAVELING SOCIETY

CHAPTER ONE

The Importance of: TRAINING WARRIORS.

Since the beginning of time, there has ALWAYS been the need for WARRIORS.

Watching the moral fabric of society seemingly ripping at the seams at every glance, it is clear that there is a growing NEED FOR EVERY MAN, WOMAN AND CHILD TO LEARN THE MARTIAL ARTS for Self Defense, Human Survival and Community Prosperity. No doubt at all.

Families going to baseball games are being attacked in broad daylight. Young kids are being killed for their sneakers, hats or cell phones on their way to school. Rape and robbery rates are up or going unreported. Children are being kidnapped, molested and murdered. Mass shooting sprees in schools, movie theaters and other soft targets are occurring around the globe. Mini-mobs of ten or more teens are attacking and beating innocent people for FUN on their way to work or jogging through the park. Bullying at school has become a 24/7 epidemic through the cyber technology of non-stop social media and responsible for increasing teenage suicides.

Is the world losing its mind?

Some say that that is just the way it is.

WE SAY NO.

REAL martial arts training allows us the Ability to Take Action. (ATTA) Whether we do or not is up to us. WE DO NOT have to be a passive victims of assault, battery, robbery, rape, or murder. And neither do our children. The importance of this book?

We can FIGHT BACK.

TRAINING is the answer. Train to achieve unity between a clear, calm mind and a strong healthy body. A cool head and swift action can be the DIFFERENCE BETWEEN SAVING YOUR LIFE OR THE THAT OF ANOTHER.

LEARN and TRAIN. LEARN and TRAIN. Then simply TRAIN. TRAIN. TRAIN until you die.

It may not only prolong your time on Earth, but enhance the quality of your life while here. Then you may become one of those rare humans called WARRIORS. Men and Women of Integrity and Purpose that Live their Life to the Fullest Without Regret or Fear.

As an American Master, I will be taking the opportunity to SHARE with you concepts and ideas on The Way of Martial Arts, in learning, training, teaching, and living them in these modern times.

It is not a book about technique, as there are an abundance of them already published. This is an autobiographical series of funny, fantastic, yet true stories of a martial journey that has spanned half a lifetime and a vast array of martial arts training from The Great Masters.

Within these stories are the secrets of The Arts and The Way; The Way of the Warrior.

Different segments of the martial arts will be discussed that may or may not be of interest to you AT THIS POINT in your training. If too esoteric, too unenlightening, or just too boring, save it for reference at a later date or take Warrior Action Now (WAN) and chuck it in the nearest trash

bin or use it to balance your kitchen table.

For what it's worth, here we go.

Here Is To Living A Life Worth Living, And Defending.

William "Billy" Powell, Shihan
Sixth Degree Black Belt

"This is what it's all about...

Growing Tigers in a Terrarium.

Little boys and girls who grow to be strong men and women

who can take...or not take action.

Warriors who believe they are so and live The Way.

That's all we promise at Kenpo School.

Nothing more."

JUMBO! (Swahili Warrior Greeting)

THE TERM "KENPO" AS USED THROUGHOUT THE BOOK IS MEANT TO REPRESENT ALL MARTIAL ARTS. THIS IS NOT JUST ABOUT KENPO.

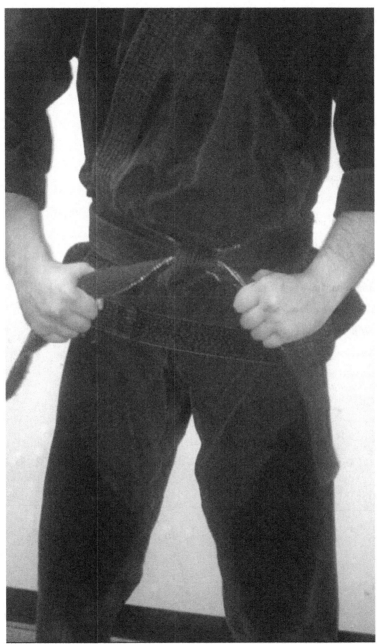

PREPARE FOR PLATEAUS DURING YOUR TRAINING AND SMASH THROUGH THEM.

CHAPTER TWO

The Importance of: UNDERSTANDING PLATEAUS.

plateau: an extensive stretch of elevated and comparatively level land; a broad low stand for table decorations; a relatively level portion in the curve indicating a subject's rate of learning; also the condition it typifies. -Wikipedia

This is one of the most important realities of your training and a guaranteed element. If you start and continue to train, you will confront the most treacherous of all your enemies "yourself" in the hidden guise of outside forces that are simply plateaus of your own creation. These plateaus are The Universe's Way of making sure only the worthy, only the tenaciously determined are gifted with the true Way of Power...the true Way of Life and to a great extent, the true Way of Death.

There are always choices. There always were. There always are. There always will be.

Things happen. But just as the Way of the Warrior begins to show you glimmers of things previously unseen, ideas thought previously foolish, and realities that have newer, less clearly defined boundaries; make sure the things that are keeping you from training are indeed real and not apparitions. Like ghosts hiding the coward or laziness in us all or let's just say the "I'm so busy" part that dogs us all.

If by some karmic fate, you are lucky enough to find a true martial arts school, see in it the power of mind, body and spirit; feel reborn and happy enough to glean new insight into the world you will become busy with success. As your schedule is filling in as your power grows accelerating your success, are you now so busy that training becomes a distraction?

17

Training is not a distraction. You are the distraction.

Attending class is not getting in your way. You are getting in your way.

DO NOT LET THIS HAPPEN.

This is very intense stuff- the concept of Bushido...The Way of the Warrior.

BE KEENLY AWARE THAT AS YOUR POWER GROWS SO WILL YOUR SUCCESS AND ASSOCIATED STRAINS ON YOUR TIME. DO NOT LET TRAINING BE THE CASUALTY.

CHAPTER THREE

The Importance of: THE GYROSCOPE OF SELF DEFENSE.

When you first learn real self-defense, you are like a baby in the woods. Hopefully you can stay hidden in the leaves or behind big trees until you have lived enough to grow, become aware, knowledgeable, strong and able to defend yourself out in the open. At any time you must be Able To Take Action (ATTA) in defense of self since "Attack need not be by appointment and can come at any time and in any manner, therefore the techniques and movements of the martial arts are naturally endless." With this base, here is the theory known at PWOK (Powell's Way of Kenpo Martial Arts School) as the Gyroscope of Self Defense:

When you first enter a real martial arts school you have brought with you various degrees of skill, courage and fear. At the most common, you are standing in the center of the room and someone is throwing a brick at you. At first, you watch helplessly as the brick hurtles toward your head and IF you respond in any manner, it's most likely to be an eye-closing-and-hands-lifting-to-protect-your-face motion. The result is you take the impact of the brick and do little else.

In classes to come and with the addition of new skills, you see the brick before thrown, watch its release and use your hands and arms in a blocking manner with eyes open. This succeeds in keeping the brick from hitting you flush in the face and merely scrapes your wrist skin. You are pleased with your progress and rightly so. Your training continues in the center of the gyroscope.

Soon, you not only easily evade any brick thrown at you, but you find that you are no longer even in the room when a brick thrower is present.

So you have learned to defend against an attack directly from the front...12:00 if you were to paint a large clock on the floor. Substituting a punch as the attack instead of a thrown brick, you now learn to develop a similar defense against that same attack (or any frontal attack for that matter) when it is launched from 1:00 or 11:00 or any "time" on the entire clock, creating a "circle of self-defense". As your skills improve, you can substitute different defensive techniques for any attack coming from a given "clock point". So you now can defend against any single-person attack from any clock point on the dial. You are at the center and the hands of the clock (or direction of attack and defense) emanate outward to a corresponding time on the "floor clock".

Now that you have attained proficiency, defending from any time on the floor clock, imagine taking the clock and standing it up on end like balancing a coin on its side. You now have the "standing clock" as an exact duplicate of the floor clock standing up before you. The standing clock is your vertical reference point for attack/defense launch points just as the floor clock is your horizontal map for proper foot movement and attack/defense directional motion. In many cases the floor clock will relate to lower body/foot movements with the standing clock utilizing upper body/arm/hand/head maneuvers. You may step to 2:00 with a right foot, pivot to 8:30 with your left then block/attack with left hand to 3:00 and right elbow strike to 8:15.

This is a generality and certainly not an absolute. For now concentrate on using the clocks as directional points of attack and defense rather than maps of individual body part movements.

Looking at the "standing clock" in front of you, you are still at the center with the 12:00 time point directly overhead, the 6:00 directly below you, and 3:00 and 9:00 to your right and left respectively. You now learn to defend against an overhead strike (more likely than a punch

20

coming from the ceiling) or a groin kick coming from below at the 6:00 time. You now replicate the technical proficiency of defensive and offensive movements learned from the "floor clock" now applied to the angles of attack along the time points of the "standing clock."

Here is the heart of the matter. After you master defense of both clocks, the clocks begin to spin both on their own axis and on a spinning axis similar to flicking a quarter on a table with your finger and watching the spinning circle it creates. In other words, the floor clock spins and the 12:00 position may move to the 4:00 point and continue on in a clockwise motion. Same for the standing clock which spins like the Wheel of Fortune. With both clocks spinning on the base axis (which is you at the center) the standing clock may tilt 45 degrees and continue to spin while the floor clock begins to rise in imitation of the standing clock to perhaps a 30 or 40 degree angle. In any event, the sphere that the spinning clocks create never stops moving until the attack is thwarted and the quarter slows down to then reveal the content of the clock angles.

As you become more comfortable with the nuances of attacks and defensive techniques coming from and going to different angles and points of flow from any and all points on the never ending spinning sphere, you will fear no attack and recognize the unpredictability and effortless destructive power of the Kenpo Warrior. What you have now designed is a near impenetrable "Gyroscope of Self Defense" allowing you at its center to attack and defend on any axis from any time point on the now spinning globe shape you have created in your expanding martial arts portfolio.

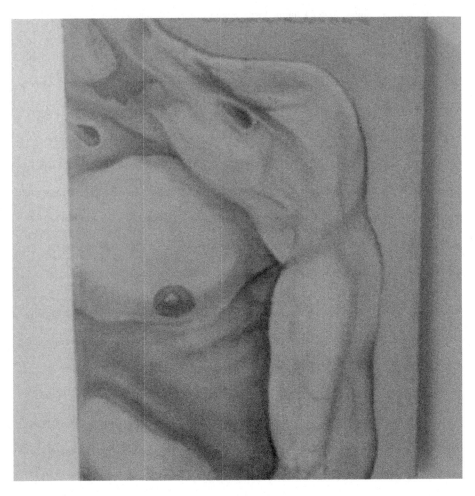

TESKA IS A CONCEPT THAT RESONATES THROUGH EVERY GREAT MARTIAL ART.

CHAPTER FOUR

The Importance of: T.E.S.K.A

All martial arts knowledge whether secretive to this day or widespread and well known for thousands of years can be explained, understood and categorized under the acronym T.E.S.K.A. A complete martial artist is well versed in all aspects of TESKA; perhaps not even aware of the word or this type of categorization of martial skill and understanding. It is a term created and used exclusively here at PWOK but holds true in any great Martial Arts School in the land.

TESKA stands for Technique. Endurance. Strength. Knowledge. Attitude.

These elements are then subdivided and studied as they relate to Mind, Body and Spirit.

As an example:

TECHNIQUE can be looked at in terms of Technique of the Mind (recognition of the proper defensive response to the attack presented); Technique of the Body (application and execution of the actual martial technique); Technique of the Spirit (increasing power effectiveness of the applied technique with meditation, Chi development/transfer, focus and KIAI! spirit yell).

As well, **ENDURANCE,** or ability to stay powerfully focused on a given task without tiring, is reflected in Mental Endurance (mental discipline); Physical Endurance (aerobic and anaerobic capacity) and Spiritual Endurance (tapping into inner strength of the human being with near superhuman results as witnessed in great endeavors like Iron man competitions, Decathlons, the Strong Man events, etc.) .

STRENGTH of the Mind (broad knowledge of Life, the Arts and Humanities, the Sciences, History and eager pursuit of higher education along with the mental conviction to survive every day). Strength of the Body (weight training, running, stretching, dieting, and nutrition) Strength of the Spirit (using personal life experiences including success and failure, victory and defeat, in becoming spiritually empowered by surviving on Earth this long in the face of life's grand tests and travails, steadied by the spiritual bond of you and God or you and the Universe).

KNOWLEDGE OF the Mind, Knowledge IN the Mind, Knowledge OF the Body and Knowledge IN the Body (the latter created through movement repetition and demonstrated in muscular memory both mental and physical leading to a "State of Grace" visible in all you do). KNOWLEDGE OF/IN the Spirit is simply knowing who you really are. What will you do at the moment of truth? Can you wait for the dust to settle? Can you remain still until the moment of action? When your life or the life of another hangs in the balance how will you react? How will you act? In combat will you surge forward or cower in fear? Knowing who you are empowers you to do what must be done at the exact moment such action is required. The Impeccable Warrior.

ATTITUDE-Mental Attitude (positive and confident). Physical Attitude (perceived demeanor exhibited during walking, sitting, speaking, eating, defecating, or stillness during preparation and subsequent execution of organized movement). Attitude of the Spirit (connection with God or the Universe and being in the moment). As the great Yoga master, Goswami Kriyananda says, "We are a part of Life, not apart from Life." See TESKA in and out of the dojo. Attitude of The Warrior can be revealed in this thought by an unknown master:

"You can tell a Tiger by its Stripes, a Crane by its Plumage, and a Warrior by his Courtesy."

THE WAY IS NOT DIRECT. THE PATH IS LONG AND THE TRAVEL TREACHEROUS. COOL

A DERANGED, MENTALLY ILL INDIVIDUAL CAN BE UNPREDICTABLE & DANGEROUS.

CHAPTER FIVE

The Importance of: KNOWING SUPREME POWER IS INDIVIDUAL VIOLENCE.

Since the dawn of time, individual violence has been the supreme form of power at the very core of civilization (as "civilized" as humans were at any given time).

Eventually individual power was magnified by the forming of groups known as friends, allies, tribes, clubs, organizations, mobs, armies, states, nations etc. to create the modern structure of international power that we see today as the basis for diplomacy. The modern way of saying "I won't kill you unless you don't do what I want" ...but in nation speak. And even nation speak is fraught with deception and potential for miscommunication. "Today, with the fluctuating, un-stable situation on the ground, and the essence of our coalition strategy being a multi-cultural assessment with preventative action being comprised of relative inertia, it may be necessary to bomb civilian targets in order to achieve a favorable outcome." What?

At the start, man walks to retrieve catch from rabbit snare. Bigger man, stronger but not as technically skilled at the hunt, waits for the snarer to collect the quarry, then jumps out of bushes overwhelming Snareman and takes the food. Snareman soon carries weapons to discourage Bigman . Bigman then also carries weapons so as not to be discouraged. After several armed encounters, Snareman moves his snare elsewhere and Bigman stops looking for and messing with Snaremen. The basis for understanding and coexistence emerges but does not yet take hold.

In evolution to groups of like-minded individuals, the story continues. In the beginning, a group of people may live close to the river and have and abundance of water ("WaterPeople"). For food they must travel away from the river to the forest to acquire it from the land of the

"ForestPeople". The "WaterPeople" approach the forest in search of food and encounter the ForestPeople who want to protect their supply of food. They are both questing for basic survival needs of food and water, and being in a primitive state of "geopolitics" they fight over it. The WaterPeople (WP) have bigger, stronger, more skilled and determined individuals acting as a single purpose unit and defeat the ForestPeople (FP) who do not resist out of fear of fighting weakness. The WP take all that they can carry and destroy whatever remains as a lesson to the FP regarding defying their needs in the future.

The ForestPeople, defeated, sit and look at what this encounter has wrought. It left many of their kind dead or injured, without food and more importantly, without the security previously afforded by the "community" regarding their "safety" being part of this particular group of humans.

The WaterPeople return home victorious and thrilled at the way they were able to expand their power, gain needed resources and provide for their own people at relatively no cost to the group as a whole. Soon the WaterPeople are regularly raiding the ForestPeople and taking more than they need because they can. As the WP are prospering, the FP are dying both figuratively, literally and quickly. Finally, the ForestPeople leaders have a choice, put up a fight or die. Well they already know how to die so it's TIME TO FIGHT BACK. When the WP again come to raid the life supply of the FP, they get a new response, a real fight.

Now the WaterPeople are still bigger, stronger and more skilled so they again prevail. But for the first time, a portion of their raiding party has been killed and they do not take "more than they need" since they simply can't carry it. They return to a surprised, concerned but still thankful and hungry base camp by the water. It didn't work out as well as it had before. The ForestPeople, defeated, but with some food left have begun to take heart. If they fight, they die in terms of the brave individuals who put up the battle against the WaterPeople, but continue to survive in that they retain previously stolen food and can now continue to feed themselves. The FP conclude that is better than before. They will continue to fight and more importantly take steps to TRAIN IN TECHNIQUES AND WEAPONRY so that they can further inflict damage on the attackers from the river in hopes of eventually preventing the attacks altogether.

Now, the WP still need food and the FP still continue to have at it, so the conflict continues. After time and with many losses on both sides, the enlightened leaders of one side or the other have an idea. Stop the bloodshed. NEGOTIATE an end to the fighting by addressing the source of the conflict and the COMMON NEEDS of both groups.

So the WaterPeople come again, but this time they bring water with them to EXCHANGE for some food of equal value. The ForestPeople, thankful that not only have the WaterPeople not come to KILL them, but rather to HELP them in their water needs, are more than eager to compromise and WORK TOGETHER.

After many such successful commercial interactions, and the mutual trust this type of cooperation builds, the ForestPeople are allowed to send "ambassadors" to the WaterPeople Camp and visa versa. They move to and fro with no checkpoints, no watchtowers and both peoples interact building a new, MORE PROSPEROUS and CIVILIZED society for all. They even decide to create a joint WaterForest Camp halfway between them to further their cooperation and requirements in feeding and watering their people. This of course leads to the inevitable propagation of procreation with the resulting WaterForestPeople as a new entity with the cultural roots of both.

This story holds true today and can be expanded upon using many historical examples from any given time period. People will take. People will take even when there are repercussions. People will take until the repercussions' pain exceeds the value of the taking. Then people will no longer just take. Instead they begin to ask.

So here we are, learned from a small fictional story the blueprint for peace by looking at the history of man, survival needs, fighting, resistance, war strategy, understanding, communication, cooperation and see hope for all humanity and the future of the world. Then it unravels.

The antithesis to this civilized concept is reflected clearly in the fact that all the nuclear might of America could not save two lost teenagers with automatic weapons from massacring innocent kids at Columbine High School in Colorado or a lone gunman's killing of First graders in the little elementary school of Sandy Hook in Newtown, Connecticut. No force on Earth, that the victims possessed at the time, could be there at that moment to at least give them a chance at survival. Maybe martial arts training could not save them all, especially the babies, but it might have saved but one precious human being...even if it was through mental discipline or calm mind at the right moment to jump out a previously unseen escape window.

As long as the authorities, all knowing and all seeing are powerless to protect any of us from indiscriminant attack from a determined perpetrator, individual violence will continue to be the most unpredictable, dangerous force on Earth and the true vessel of Supreme Power.

It's time to take Self Defense personally as the government, police and most citizens aren't able.

NO ONE HAS THE RIGHT TO PUT THEIR HANDS ON YOU WITHOUT PERMISSION.
ONCE THEY DO, THEY GIVE UP THE RIGHT TO BE HEALTHY.

HUMOR IS THE WARRIOR'S FIRST LINE OF DEFENSE.

CHAPTER SIX

The Importance of: HUMOR WHILE LEARNING.
:

One of my favorite teachers, Master Kimball Paul (so skilled in the Internal Art of Tai Chi Chuan he touches you and then decides how much internal pain you will feel and for how long) once said to me, "Don't ever become a Master, because then you can't ever make a mistake!" In fact, Master Kimball has said so many things of relevance on my Martial Quest over the years, a full entry will be devoted exclusively to his truly otherworldly wisdom later.

But now, I want you to know what it's like to goof up on "The Grand Stage" and still maintain enough Warrior Humor to keep from tossing yourself (with perfect Judo throw technique of course) out a window. If you don't quit, at least you are still in the game. Even if folks are laughing at you.

It all started when 10th Degree Black Belt, Grandmaster Shorty Mills (another full report on this amazing man to come) asked me to ride with his World Champion Karate school to Stamford, Connecticut where he was to be inducted into The World Martial Arts Hall of Fame in May of 1996. Hanshi Shorty had chartered a huge bus for the semi-cross-country trip from Sweet Home Chicago to Stamford. I forgot to mention that Hanshi is the biggest, baddest human I have ever met. He also happens to be African American. His fearsomeness is only eclipsed by the power of his heart and the benevolence of his soul. Speaking of Soul, I was about to learn an enjoyable reverse discrimination lesson during the trip as the only Great White Hope riding for 13 hours in a Black Bus of Death. There were 48 of us with me being the whitest. Being a well-trained and funny Warrior, I did not fear for my physical well-being, but rather the mental abuse my sense of style would take as I learned new elements of training that I had not been shown. Maybe this is why its called a Black Belt. This included seeing gis (martial uniforms) that were dry-cleaned, pressed and transported by hangers to Stamford. My gi was rolled up in a sick, stench filled ball in the ratty gym bag stuffed under my seat. The bus ride was a story in itself and for another time.

After we arrive in Stamford, Hanshi asks me to attend a martial arts Board Meeting to hear a presentation on a ground fighting system which the instructor wanted recognized. This would give him the authority to grant rank in terms of belts like most martial arts systems. There is no belt ranking in Wrestling, but the popularity of Gracie Jiu Jitsu in Mixed Martial Arts and the excitement caused by its success in the UFC, made the instructor's idea an intriguing request.

The Board is an unbelievable gathering of ten 10th Degree Black Belts. Let me say that again. I am in the audience looking at TEN (10)...TEN! 10th Dans from all the famous martial arts systems! I don't know of any such gathering of extremely high level Grandmasters at any martial arts event before or since. Anyway, this grappling instructor begins a full presentation of his case on the value of ground fighting in general, his system in particular and the need to give belt ranks to wrestlers. He was quite persuasive and I admired his moxie for having the stones to get up there in the first place. He was heavy into it...and I was becoming convinced of his argument being an old wrestler myself. Then it happened.

I had been looking at Hanshi periodically during the speech to gauge his facial expression in hopes of gaining insight into what he was thinking, when he looked directly at me and mouthed the words "Attack Him." Being well trained and a swift order taker when it comes to Hanshi, I immediately spring to action in preparation for a full assault on the grappling instructor. My mind has just fired the synapses that made my legs ready to propel me from my seat. Just as

I begin to act, Hanshi senses my movement (even before I move) and with his eyes pierce out and into my brain stopping me dead in mid-synaptic firing as he mouths "Not Yet." I stand down (sit down actually) and await further orders. After another 10 minutes of a very persuasive demonstration, the grappling instructor is at the pinnacle of his presentation when Hanshi unleashes the Hounds of Hell (or at least a singular Doberman from New Jersey) with the eye and mouth command "Now!" Or maybe he just nodded, it was all a blur from that point.

Hell bent for leather, I leap up like a mad demon with accompanying death yell and rapidly close the distance on the grappling instructor in a millisecond. Not bothering to inquire via eye contact or mouthed orders from Hanshi during my short flight to the GI on what he wanted me to do when I got there, I just winged it and finally land on the very large martial artist focused on how he was impressing The Board with his ideas.

That was the least of his problems, as I arrived and introduced myself via a bear hug and Greco Roman throw to which we both crashed to the ground with a loud thud as all Hell breaks loose. The sound of chairs flying, tables turning over with water glasses spilling to the buzzing audio soundtrack of what I heard to be a montage of gasps, shrieks, hurried talking, calls for help, security and more than one Grandmaster screaming "MATE!" or STOP! in Japanese.

I heard all this unimportant stimuli in a secondary kinda way until I heard Hanshi's distinctive bellow with the command of "MATE!" I freeze immediately and things begin to speed up again as I have returned from Vampire Transport Speed (VTS) to regular human movement.

What I see is ALL TEN Grandmasters standing and looking/screaming at me in outrage that I interrupted this sacred meeting. In addition, the audience is sitting in stunned amazement as they try to process whether this is part of the test for the grappling instructor or if I was just a nut ball who flipped his lid. As I am trying to process the reality of the situation and execute my next move, I notice that the sound emanating from below is the grappling instructor still underneath me growling a combination of indiscernible curses in an aggressive Eastern European dialect smattered with broken English directed clearly and heatedly at me. I catch Hanshi's eye as he is standing above me, assuring the esteemed Board that the attacking madman is indeed one of his prized Black Belts, his guest at the weekend events, and now under control. You could hear the kind of the breath release ushered when the owner finally gets the leash on a Rottweiler. They (the 9 other 10th Dans) look to Hanshi Shorty Mills in a respectful, yet inquisitive manner as he passes their curious gaze onto me with the seemingly appropriate question "What are you doing?"

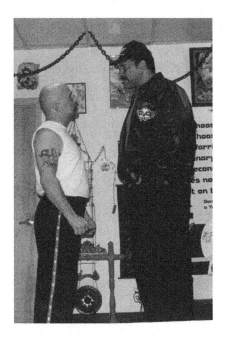

"I SAID 'TALK TO HIM." Ohhhhhhhhhh.

I look up at him with the grappling instructor still pinned facedown to the abrasive hotel carpet-over-concrete meeting room floor. With my heart pounding and my sanity definitely in question, I respond with "You said ATTACK HIM! SIR." Hanshi responds with a terse yet clear "I said 'TALK TO HIM!'" I must have had a confused look on my face because Hanshi repeated calmly and clearly for all to hear, "I wanted you to TALK to him about his grappling system and how it compares to yours."

After I got off the flattened teacher and extended a heartfelt apology, he walked out while still mumbling more anger and without finishing the presentation. Not sure he is the forgiving type. Not sure I blame him. I wonder how many hours of work, thought and preparation he must have put into that presentation. Then, the balls to get up there in front of a panel of 10th Dans and speak for a cause was very impressive. He just hadn't prepared for the possibility that a Maniac Hellion would be called to action (of one type or another) by his Grandmaster as a loyal, order following student.

The rest of the weekend I was the topic of repeated stories and jokes with Masters yelling things like "Quick watch out it's Hanshi Mills' attack dog!" or "I said TALK TO HIM...NOT ATTACK HIM!" and the like. I kept my SENSE OF HUMOR, a big smile and promised not to attack anyone while they are eating dinner at the banquet or sitting by the pool. Hanshi wasn't upset with me since I was just following orders. In fact, he invited me to Stamford for the type of excitement that I bring to simple things like a bus trip, a hotel stay or a black tie event banquet.

Good thing that I didn't attack anyone else that weekend. There were more than a few smiles, good hearted laughter and friendly chatter when my name was read as "Karate Instructor of the

Year" and the newest inductee into The 1996 World Martial Arts Hall of Fame. Thank you Hanshi for nominating me. Then again who could turn you down? Surely not with your very own Attack Black Belt at your side. By the way, the Grappling Guy did not attend the banquet.

THIS PHOTO TAKEN JUST AFTER THE GRAPPLING INSTRUCTOR LEFT THE ROOM.

Seems he checked out and flew home. Just as well, since the Board did not approve his request on awarding Belt Rank promotions to wrestlers.

Sorry man.

THERE ARE MANY PATHS TO ENLIGHTENMENT. GET ON ONE AND MOVE FORWARD.

CHAPTER SEVEN

The Importance of: UNDERSTANDING THE WARRIOR "V".

First, let's make an important distinction regarding one the most overused, misrepresented words in the English language. The word is "Warrior". It has been repeated to ear saturation levels by newscasters, sportsmen and the media as a commonly uttered description of someone with "guts"...or someone who toughed it out to overcome the odds of a particular challenge.

This is incorrect.

The fact is, unless you have been trained in the military sciences, been educated and are learned in the military ways of strategy in warfare by attending institutions like West Point, The Naval Academy, The Citadel etc., OR are Soldier, Marine, Airman, SEAL/Naval Personnel AND/OR a long-term Student and Advanced Practitioner of the Martial Arts trained in a reputable dojo-YOU ARE NOT A WARRIOR! No matter how brilliant a pro golfer's birdie shot on 18th hole, coming back from 2 strokes down, or a basketball player's amazing playoff feats of endurance and skill while playing with the flu, it does not warrant the sacred title of Warrior.

The Way of War is known in the Japanese martial arts as Budo. A Warrior is called Bushi. Bushido is the Way of the Warrior. This Warrior Ethos represent the example of living Bushido in the modern age. There are NO other Warriors. This is a simple as rain falling to the ground.

No further explanation is needed.

Now, as far as understanding the Warrior V:

Imagine that you are in a trench in the ground that is wide enough at the bottom for two to four people standing side by side and widens at the top to a width of perhaps10 ft. The depth of the trench is deep enough that you are at eye height when standing upright with your feet touching the bottom, with both parcels of high ground to your right and left. The trench goes outward toward infinity, and if you were to look behind you, it would appear as if you had come from infinity from the backside of the trench. The shape of the geology/geography is basically that of a long dugout "V" that extends in both directions endlessly from where you are standing in the trench. Sort of like a dried riverbed that wanders endlessly in the carved shape of an etched serpent in the ground. IF you are a Warrior, you are sometimes in the trench moving, standing still, looking forward or back, up or down, side to side or immobile, with eyes slammed shut frozen in fear. Sometimes you are up on the ground above you to the right. Sometimes you are up on the ground above you to the left. But MOST of the time you are IN the trench walking purposefully forward towards a destiny that appears endless and unknown.

ONCE YOU HAVE JUMPED INTO THE TRENCH, YOUR FATE IS SEALED.

You must move forward.

You may turn and try to move backward, hoping your life experience so far (represented by looking behind you down the trench of the past) will prepare you for what is to come, or maybe you just stand there and cower in fear. You can even scurry out of the trench and run away as fast as you can. It matters not. Regardless of your actions AFTER jumping in, once you have made the leap, once you have "opened the door" to the mythic, to the great mystery of The Way...The Way of Life, you are forever changed. Once you enter, you may leave, but you can never go back. For you will always know that there is something greater available to you in a parallel life that is full of wonder, joy and endless power and passion, even as you cower along in the weakened life you have chosen to live. You have glimpsed behind the thin veil that barely separates the worlds: The world of Warriors and the world of ordinary men/women.

As the great Warrior Sage Don Juan, from the Carlos Castaneda books, has stated:

"We choose only Once. We choose either to be Warriors or Ordinary men. A Second choice does not Exist. Not on this Earth."

So, as you stand in The Warrior V neck deep in terra firma, you look out in a forward direction and begin walking down the path before you. (We will use Trench, Path and Way interchangeably.) The Way is set "cast in stone" if you like, as you move purposely down the path of your life in pursuit of things not yet known, not yet experienced, not clearly defined, not readily understood and not without fear. As you walk the Path of The Way, it strikes you odd that you see no one else with you in the trench. Since The Way curves and straightens, has inclines and depressions, sharp turns and endless stretches of clearly traversable straight-aways, the trench occasionally gives you far reaching sight abilities. Then, around the next bend, the footing becomes slippery, a trench floor of jagged obstacles with grabbing fescue, causes you to pay attention to your every footstep and your sight distance shrinks to a but a few meters in front of you. Sometimes, the path is cleared by unknown benefactors who support your Warrior Quest.

While there is no one else in YOUR trench, there are people on the upper plateaus of YOUR trench. If you stop, and look up to the LEFT you will see them: hundreds and hundreds, maybe thousands of them, moving fast and with chaotic and schizophrenic purpose. They are Ordinary People, folks like you used to be. People who have jobs, get up, eat breakfast, move through life like psp-powered zombies darting to and fro between IMPORTANT things, meetings and events. The look in their faces is similar even though the bone structure and skin color are varied. The look is of suppressed fear, masked with nervous pursuit of the next task. They are woefully detached from The Way and yet somehow seem ok with that.

These people do the life experience like they shop at K Mart, picking up items for use in their daily life. They have life figured out and it sucks. Get up. Go to work. Feed the family. Do something fun for escape. Get paid. Pay bills. Pray. Go to sleep. Wake up. Rinse. Repeat. These are regular, ordinary people. They are consumed with the mundane but at least they work, live and die somewhat responsibly. They think they are happy, but yearn for more and are not sure why.

Now you pivot your head and look away from the ordinary left up to the higher ground on the RIGHT. There are people there too. A lot less of them and they appear much less harried and wired but odd at first glance. They are clearly different from the ordinary people we saw on the left side of the trench. We will call these people The Mystics. For lack of a better word, this is a term we will use to include the many non-ordinary people: a mix of warriors, witches, wizards,

43

martial arts masters, artists, clairvoyants, palm readers, fortune tellers, religious zealots and pious clerics, etc. Clearly this group is a combination of eclectic thinkers and passionate doers. There are real Mystics and fakers. Those who can and those who cannot. More likely than not they are phonies. But, there are REAL Masters within this group. REAL Artists. REAL Witches. REAL Men of God. You must look hard. YOU MUST SEE in order to tell the difference. Characteristics of the Mystics are much different, and surely more colorful than the Ordinary People on the opposite side of the trench.

The Mystics differ from Ordinary People in many ways. They often cannot hold jobs, often have trouble communicating with people and have problems with certain types of authority. They would rather practice, meditate and dwell on the mythic than work and pay the bills. Some have achieved great power. Some have done nothing but play pretend warrior. Some have ended up there through heavy drug use, alcoholism or mental problems. Some have gotten there through lifelong training and commitment. The real ones are here by choice/fate and have developed the capabilities, knowledge and powers of the Ancients and can readily demonstrate these acquired skills. Their powers can border on the amazing and can penetrate the veil separating the worlds.

As your gaze returns forward and you move down the Warrior V, the upper plateaus continue to offer the choices of these lifestyles and the corresponding human representatives. You continue to walk. At some point you stop and pop up onto the left plateau and live amongst the ordinary people and do the ordinary things expected of an ordinary person living an ordinary life on earth. You get a job, pay the bills, find a lover and live. But there IS a difference. You are a Warrior. As a Warrior you move through this type of life with confidence, joy and a vigor that separates you from most others. Most enjoy your company while others scorn your pleasant outlook and demeanor. You feel the difference and the "edge" you have over many others in most ordinary things. You live life every moment you are here and you make a regular earth existence something special. It is said "THE HIGHEST ART IS LIVING AN ORDINARY LIFE IN AN EXTRA-ORDINARY MANNER." You agree. Then you hop back down in the trench and with a knowing smile, continue your walk. Your training, your Warrior Path extends ever forward.

On you go.

All of a sudden you stop, leap up to the right to the place of The Mystics. This mythical landscape is more to your Warrior liking as you feel more at ease making your way moving amongst the colorful folk. You train with them. You learn from them. You are deceived by some. Hurt by others and disappointed by others still. After a while the mind games, alternate theories of reality and power leave you fatigued. You may or may not have been fortunate enough to know what the Masters know. More likely this is a tiring place. Fulfilling and exhausting at the same time. Back to the trench you go. Walking. Training. Learning. Moving forward.

Now as you walk your trench, you occasionally leap up to either right or left worlds. Sometimes you stay up on one side for a long time. Sometimes you jump back and forth, over the trench from right to left and back again.

The Trench keeps going. The Way keeps going. The Path keeps going.

You keep going.

After experiencing firsthand the ups and downs, rights and wrongs, truths and fantasies, excitements and boredoms of BOTH upper plateaus, you continue on your Way traveling over vast humps and straights of your trench with a keen eye to the goings on of the upper plateaus.

Soon it becomes so second nature to walk the Path while perceiving both the Ordinary People and The Mystics, that you become aware of the things that are happening IN THOSE WORLDS. It's a certain type of peripheral vision that allows you to be partly in both upper plateaus AT THE SAME TIME that you continue your steady journey on your Way. Almost like a Warrior Traveler with BOTH Mystic and Ordinary elements developing simultaneously. When you note something or someone of particular interest, that stands out from the din on either plateau, you are free to hop up and experience that which has caught your attention. Then back into the trench and on you go.

Now, as the journey winds on, you come upon a new experience in the trench. In the distance you see it for the first time, something or someone in the great distance...someone IN THE TRENCH with you! You continue to move at an alternately speedy, anticipatory pace in excitement of a meeting with someone AHEAD of you in the V and in a contrasted gait with slower, fearful mini-steps as you ponder the new trench mate.

As you move rapidly ahead, you may or may not perceive that which you are passing on the upper plateaus. However, you notice something unsettling. The image in the trench is getting bigger as you approach. Not bigger from the natural appearance of a runner catching up to and passing a competitor moving in the same direction, but rather the image growth suggesting an entity that is APPROACHING you. What is this? Someone or something is coming TOWARD you. Someone is coming BACK FROM THE WAY? Did they reach the end? What do they know? What is the truth? What happens ahead? The Stranger approaches. Closer. Closer.

Almost within speaking range...

As you are about to say something, he passes, just missing you at shoulder width.

He continues onward past you, saying nothing.

"What is Ahead?" you yell as he is almost out of earshot.

"Death" he mutters. "Anything else?" you query.

"Yes." he says.

Nothing more is offered as he begins to shrink.

Smaller. Smaller. So very small.

He's now just a dot in the distance.

YOU WALK ON.

2001 PAN AMERICAN GAMES INTERNATIONAL JIU JITSU CHAMPION.

CHAPTER EIGHT

The Importance of: GETTING YOUR ASS KICKED...
LEARNING CARLSON GRACIE JIU JITSU-AND OTHER LESSONS OF A PROPERLY PAINFUL MARTIAL EDUCATION

It seems that every decade there is the newest, baddest, MOST FEARED martial art that "comes out of secrecy" to crush any practitioners of any other system, as well as, the usual bullies, village toughs and standard strong arm robbers. In the 1950's it was JUDO, brought back by WW II servicemen that learned the art in the Pacific. Wise off to a Judo man in a bar and you'll find yourself with a dumb look on your face as the result of an exploding kidney earned by landing on the corner of the pool table from of a perfect Judo throw. So much for starting a drinking conversation with "Hey Fat man!"

In the 1960's, it was KARATE (if you wanted the board breaking bravado associated with "Registering Your Hands as Deadly Weapons") or KUNG FU (if you loved the way Kato (Bruce Lee) kicked every villain's butt as he was saving Green Hornet's ass in every episode). KUNG FU also got a huge recognition factor from the exploits of the amazing Bruce Lee and his "borrowed" hit television series "Kung Fu" starring David Carradine, winner of many Emmy ·Awards. KARATE and KUNG FU imbued the American scene in many ways with a key one being the growth of Karate and Kung Fu competitions. These bare knuckle "point fighting" tournaments yielded many superstars like Shorty Mills, Bill "Superfoot" Wallace, Ken Knudsen etc. and made celebrities of Chuck Norris, Bob Wall, Cynthia Rothrock, Judo Gene LaBelle and Angela Mao Ying to name but a few. In addition to the widespread competitions that started in Chicago and spread to the coasts, the first recognized World Champions in Joe Lewis, Mike

Stone and Bill Wallace were crowned.

THE FIRST WORLD HEAVYWEIGHT FULL CONTACT KARATE CHAMPION-JOE LEWIS.

Karate's "Golden Age" in the 60's, started in the Midwest with Grandmaster Robert Trias' 1st Open Karate Tournament at the University of Chicago in 1963 as competitions then sprung up across the country. These American martial arts pioneers also began the popular union between the martial arts and Hollywood moviemakers. This really took off with the commercially successful big budget (for the time) martial arts blockbuster ENTER THE DRAGON starring BRUCE LEE. The relationship continues to exist profitably to this day.

So, the legendary prowess and fear inspiring "KARATE MAN" was born! And don't forget singing "Everybody was Kung Fu Fighting, those Cats were Fast as Lightning...it was a Little Bit Frightening...They Fought with Expert Timing..." Admit it. You know you did.

As an offshoot of the Karate/Kung Fu fighting competitions of the '60's, the 1970's produced the new FULL CONTACT KARATE, more appropriately named and commonly referred to as KICKBOXING. Since Full Contact Fighters could not use all martial arts techniques for fear of fighter injury, the gloved hands of boxing combined with the kicks of Karate and the lack of ground fighting made Kickboxing the sports official name. Kickboxers and Full Contact Karate fighters were the new BAD BOYS of the martial arts.

The top level point fighters of Karate became the base of this new type of fighting competitor and rose to become the first Kickboxing and Full Contact World Champions like Joe Lewis. No longer were points alone the deciding factor in victory where politics in judging were responsible for more than a few disputed championships. Kickboxing was pretty cut and dry. A knock out or an outright beating is pretty clear. It was exciting to watch and more accepted as a television sport. Its ranks grew as a legitimate testing ground for the martial arts skills of the fighters.

Soon, pure kickboxers arrived trained in the special skills required of the sport. Warriors like

Dennis Alexio, Rick the Jet Rufus, Dickie "The Hammer" Hone etc. A KICKBOXER was a bad mofo and the newest torch bearer in the evolutionary chain of the Most Feared Martial Arts. On a parallel rise were the esoteric arts of Bruce Lee with his amazing JEET KUNE DO, the lethal invisibility of Stephen Hayes' NINJITSU, the gorgeously fluid, violently flowing power of Ed Parker's and The Tracy Brothers' KENPO KARATE and its offshoots like Adriano Emperado's KAJUKENBO.

The 1980's had a perfect example of "The Ultimate Martial Art" and its own movie to launch it! You only had to watch the evolutionary changing of the guard represented in the popular movie "KICKBOXER" in 1989. In it, the World Champion Kickboxer (played in the movie by real Kickboxing World Champ Dennis Alexio) would not only lose his title, his ability to walk, but the mantle of "MOST FEARED" with the emergence of the unstoppable MUAY THAI or THAI BOXING. I remember this time particularly well being heavily into the martial arts at Black Belt level. It was particularly amazing to witness the devastating effectiveness and brutal conditioning of the THAI FIGHTER.

In fact, the Bad Guy Anti-Hero in the movie named Tong Po was big, bad and bald except for a samurai-type top knot and was basically invincible. He showed the old way of Muay Thai by drenching his hands in a sticky paste then immersed in small broken shards of glass for some matches. Fists of Bloody Death for Sure. Tong Po showed the mental discipline and focused training of Muay Thai by kicking wooden poles with his shins into a mushy pulp. I have seen the paint blasted off metal poles with similar techniques here in Chicago. Tong Po was a badass of the first order and represented the newest breed of Warrior To Fear. (WTF)

Thai Boxing was now what everyone (almost everyone) wanted to learn but most were afraid to. Let's face it. Unlike most other studies in life, learning Muay Thai HURTS! I took the time and physical punishment to learn Muay Thai and can tell you that I do not like smashing my shins

into a pole any more AFTER training in the Art than before starting. But being able to drop an

opponent with a single leg kick to the thigh is VERY COOL. More regarding the brutal Art of

Muay Thai later.

In the 1990's it was all about GRACIE JIU JITSU. When the family secret was let out via "The

Gracie Challenge" the martial arts world was blown away. More than any other martial arts

arrival, the Gracie System, used as a collective name of all the various Brazilian Jiu Jitsu styles

practiced and taught by members of the Gracie Family, was this simple fact. Learn it or prepare

for the possibility to be humbled by any skinny dude with a surfer attitude. Even wearing a

Gracie tee shirt gave the biggest guys room to pause and seeing one made you feel somewhat

uncomfortable with your level of training. GRACIE JIU JITSU WAS ALL THAT AND MORE.

We'll talk extensively about my experience learning Carlson Gracie Jiu Jitsu from Carlson

Gracie Jr., his father Carlson Sr. and Master Instructor and Coach Extraordinaire, BJJ Black Belt

Jeff Neal, here in Chicago. As it turns out, I not only fell in love with the Art, but actually

became the first American to win the Pan American Games International Jiu Jitsu Gold Medal as

a member the Carlson Gracie Jr. Competition Team in 2001.

Very cool stories of my painful martial upbringing in BJJ to follow later.

In the 2000's MIXED MARTIAL ARTS (MMA) became the Art of Choice for many getting into

the martial arts or with those who now understood the importance of BOTH stand up and

ground fighting thanks to the Gracies. One reason that the United States is nearly impossible to

defeat in War is that Americans may endure a temporary defeat (like Pearl Harbor or 9/11)

but learn from its mistakes to create effective battle plans. This EVOLUTION of new strategies and tactics eventually prove victorious.

For the most part, the Brazilians were initially unwilling to alter their devastating Art as the Americans were learning it, incorporating it with Greco Roman Wrestling and using power and strength training with improved stand up skills. This cross training evolved into a mixture of different martial arts...and for a time defeating the Gracies at their own game. Now they too cross train to match the Americans in the Octagon enhancing the amazing skills and success of Brazilian Jiu Jitsu.

As world class wrestlers and other well trained Warriors of various arts emerged in bigger, stronger, more fearsome form, the ULTIMATE FIGHTING CHAMPIONSHIP demonstrated that NO ONE ART ALONE is best. It pays to be skilled in many arts and to use the best of all techniques, tactics and strategy to compete at a world class level.

What will be the ART of 2010? 2030?

We have skipped over the obvious lethality of the Philippine and Indonesian Knife and Stick Arts like Kali, Serak and Arnis. Suffice it to say they are as lethal as it gets and in league with the death dealing skills of a trained soldier with a flame thrower. It's just so hard to trace the lineage of these feared arts as most of the practitioners are dead or keep their art secret.

If your martial art is not mentioned in the above decade jumping paraphrased script, it is my fault as these are the arts that I have experience with and can speak on. No offense intended. You can see from the past that as we continue to evolve, our Arts will represent that evolution.

And of course, what we don't yet know will ALWAYS BE THE MOST FEARED.

PEE WEE, RECREATION AND HIGH SCHOOL WRESTLING CHAMPION-MOI

MY DAD AT FAR LEFT WAS AN INTENSE COACH. THAT'S ME IN 5TH GRADE WATCHING THE DISTRICT WRESTLING CHAMPIONSHIPS AND DREAMING OF MY DAY TO COME.

ME IN TIGHTY WHITEY FIGHT GEAR WITH MY FATHER'S OLYMPIC TRIALS BOXING GLOVES. A PAINTING OF MY DAD IS ON THE WALL AND MICKEY MOUSE IS WATCHING OVER ME. NO MOUTH PIECE NEEDED SINCE I ONLY HAD BABY TEETH AT THE TIME.

CHAPTER NINE

The Importance of: LEARNING WRESTLING.

I was born unto a Warrior House.

My father, Robert "Butch" Powell was a Fighter, Wrestler, Gymnast, Football Player, Boxer and United States Marine. He was the All Marine and All Service Boxing Champion who fought in the 1956 Olympic Trials Finals at the Cow Palace in CA. He earned a scholarship for Boxing to Penn State but the ring death of another collegian combined with other factors caused the sport to be dropped from college athletics in Pennsylvania. Butch is Irish Welch, built like a stone gladiator and a badass of the first order. He was also a gentleman; college educated, well-spoken and quite a father figure.

"BUTCH" POWELL USMC-1957 ALL MARINE AND ALL SERVICE BOXING CHAMPION.

I was brought up the Son of a Marine. Great swaths of the classic Robert Duvall movie "The

Great Santini" could have played on a screen on any wall of our house in New Jersey and you

Boxing Hall to enshrine 'Butch' Powell

Robert "Butch" Powell, who has been a health and physical education teacher in New Jersey for more than 30 years, will be enshrined in the Wyoming Valley Boxing Hall of Fame at the annaul induction dinner in the spring.

Powell began his boxing career while in high school at Meyers with Joe Rodano's Boys Club and after receiving a scholarship to Penn State, he went 5-0 as a freshman.

However, the next year he enlisted in the U.S. Marines and promptly won the welterweight championship during basic training at Camp LeJeune. He later won the LeJeune Open Boxing Championship before finishing second in the AAU championships in 1955 as a welterweight.

The following year he finished second at the All-Merine Championship at 139 pounds and later won the 139-pound South Western Regional Olympic Championship before losing in the Olympic Trials at 139 at San Francisco.

In 1957, Powell became the All-Marine Corps champion at 139 pounds as well as the 1957 all Service championship.

After his discharge he matriculated to East Stroudsburgh University, graduating in 1962. For the last 34½ years, he has been a health/phys ed teacher at the Bridgwater-Raritan Regional School in Bridgewater, N.J.

Robert 'Butch' Powell
circa 1955

could watch either version (reality or cinema) with equal interest. I was taught discipline,

manners and to take zero shitola from the "boobs and knuckleheads". And no one was allowed

to make fun of my name by calling me "Pow Wow" or "Willie" without a crease to the teeth.

In fact, the name Powell is sacred to our family and anyone with it is expected to give it their all in everything. Whether it's my Kenpo School jacket, my daughter Rachel's Cross Country shirt or my son Nico's football jersey, if it says Powell, its 100% pure smashmouth effort to come. I remember the time I had to bring Rachel a different set of spikes since the freezing sleet and pouring rain had made the hilly, wooded X country track slippery and treacherous. I raced to her meet after having to return home to get the deeper spikes. Upon arrival, I see Rachel at the Starting Line hoping I got there on time. Finally reaching her in hideous weather with the cleats, she simply sits down in freezing, waist deep, muddy ice water that was the race Starting Line. As the muck and mire of dirt, grass and ice water engulf her lap to belly button level, she calmly puts on each spike, gets up and is at the line for the race. She just said "Thanks Dad." and took off into the woods full of muck, mire and Glory. One wet spike at a time. A Powell for sure.

MY DAUGHTER RACHEL SAVANNAH-ATHLETE, WARRIOR, SCHOLAR.
RACHEL LED HER CROSS COUNTRY TEAM TO ITS FIRST EVER STATE FINALS.

Same when Nico plays football. Whether he is standing on the side line awaiting his turn or smashing faces with bigger offensive linemen, his demeanor never changes. Head up, back straight, chest out, eyes focused on the action with "54 POWELL" proud across his jersey .

MY SON NICO ALEXANDER-ATHLETE, WARRIOR, SCHOLAR.

Incidentally, that is why the name of my dojo is "Powell's" Way of Kenpo Martial Arts School. Not because I think I invented anything new or great, though I did, but rather in honor of all the Powell's before me. The sign above our dojo has Powell's up top, Way of Kenpo in the middle and Martial Arts School on the bottom. Two solid lines separate the three sets of words to signify of who we are. 'Nuff said.

My wonderful Italian mother, Rosemarie Ann Powell, provided me with the balance of love and kindness that rounded me out enough to keep me out of Juvenile Detention Programs popular in the State of New Jersey with many wayward friends. In fact, we lived close to the Annandale Training School for Boys in Skilman, NJ and it took just a glance in its direction by either parent during a drive to remind me to be nice, respectful, mannerly and above all to stay out of trouble.

MY WONDERFUL MOTHER ROSEMARIE ANN POWELL WHO TAUGHT ME THE IMPORTANCE OF KINDNESS, CARING, TRUST, LOVE AND EATING ITALIAN FOOD.

MY FATHER ROBERT AND MOTHER ROSEMARIE AT "BUTCH" POWELL'S
INDUCTION INTO THE PENNSYLVANIA SPORTS BOXING HALL OF FAME.
DAD'S SISTERS, AUNTS JANE AND TRISHA, LOOK ON FROM TABLE BELOW.

My martial arts training began at birth. My father was a skilled fighter, educator and an expert wrestling coach and I spent the early formative years learning balance on the training center of his US Marine Corps-issued barrel chest. He would always work on my balance with drills unbeknownst to me other than as fun "Don't fall off the boat" games. I remember very young that he would unbalance a stability point like my arm and teach me to redistribute my weight elsewhere to maintain a stable position. He always expressed the Importance of Balance.

These training tools provided me with the balance necessary to succeed in sports such as wrestling, swimming and springboard diving at a young age. I also was able to pick up any sport relatively quickly and the ones I liked I excelled at. My Dad says it was from balance.
So it was. My formal training in wrestling started in a recreation program competing on the 7th grade team even though only in 4th. I found out that balance is only one part of training since my hairless 49 pound body was not as strong...nor as hairy as the junior high school boys that I competed against.

I was confident in my skills and balance but was just learning about the Importance of Strength to the martial arts/combat sports equation. My peewee wrestling coach, Paul Kolody, made sure my substantial weight disadvantage was hidden from the competition as best as possible. He did this by asking that I remember to disrobe to wrestling shorts BEFORE weighing in at the match. It seems that when I was running late for weigh-ins coming from another school across town as soon as school let out, they had to wait for me to start since I was the lightest. Stepping on the scale still in my full winter wardrobe, heavy coat, gloves, hat, boots, backpack, and gear bag still in hand, the 60 lbs weight class limit needle on the scale did not budge. Bet I only weighed around 49 lbs.

My much heavier opponents would just drool at the sight of my skinny, muscle-less frame and appeared ready to swallow me whole for an easy win. Only Coach Kolody and I knew that I was going to be as easy to handle as a sharp, oddly shaped chicken bone wedged mercilessly down my opponent's throat.

I had a successful wrestling career up through High School as the Team Captain under Coaches Otto Gsell (Vietnam Combat Veteran) and Rocco Forte. (Man of Integrity) Years later I had both of these great men, along with Coach Kolody and my Father, inducted into the United States Martial Arts International Hall of Fame for Lifetime Achievement in the Art of Combat Wrestling. Many memories flood my mind about these larger than life men and their legacy. I remember riding on the bus to an away wrestling meet when Coach Gsell boarded and sat next to me. Getting psyched for the upcoming match, I asked Coach when he knew he was a "man"? "Vietnam." he answered with a scary smile.

I loved that man. See you in Valhalla, Coach O.

HALL OF FAMERS: COACHES ROCCO FORTE, PAUL KOLODY, BOB POWELL, PHIL PORTER AND OTTO GSELL (POSTUMOUSLY) WERE INDUCTED INTO THE USMA INTERNATIONAL HALL OF FAME. I AM AT FAR RIGHT. ALL WERE RECOGNIZED FOR "LIFETIME ACHEIVEMENT IN THE ART OF COMBAT WRESTLING".

USMA HOF BLACK TIE AWARDS DINNER-FRONT ROW: PAUL KOLODY, DON PINKUS, RICH SEBEK AND PAT TODE. BACK ROW IS MOI, THREE OTHERS AND JACOB HONG.

COACH OTTO GSELL AND ME PRIOR TO THE FIRST OF TWO DISTRICT, TWO COUNTY CHAMPIONSHIPS AND TWIN REGIONAL BRONZE MEDALS. HE ALSO GUIDED ME TO ALL-DIVISION AND ALL-CONFERENCE RECOGNITION HONORS.

NEW JERSEY IS RECOGNIZED AS A WRESTLING POWERHOUSE THAT SENDS CHAMPIONS TO NATIONALLY RANKED TEAMS LIKE OKLAHOMA, OKLAHOMA STATE, IOWA, IOWA STATE, LEHIGH, PENN STATE AND OTHER TOP UNIVERSITIES IN THE UNITED STATES.

My wrestling career ended when no scholarship was available for my weight divisions at the University of Maryland in 1979 and the as yet untried activities of partying, beer and women outweighed the need for any further glory to be gained by losing 45 lbs as a walk on. My Senior year in HS, I lost those same 45 lbs to wrestle in the 115 weight class. Walking down the hall on my way to the locker room to sit and eat a stale Tiger Bar while staring at rolled up athletic tape and broken jock straps instead of enjoying the full hot lunches being served to my friends in the cafeteria, I must have looked intense and or insane. This was made evident in my sinewy, fatless, muscle shredded body and my distaste for anyone not up to the sacrifice required of Wrestling. In the walk to lunch or practice after school, huge football players would move out of my 115 pound way. Folks literally parted as I made my way through the hallways of Hillsborough High School in New Jersey in 1979. Scary is as scary does.

I did gain a measure of satisfaction by winning 3 of the 4 college intramural wrestling tournaments run by the U of M Wrestling team. The last year I lost for "unnecessary roughness" when I forgot that over the back Suplays were illegal in Maryland when an opponent stands up. It looks like a Pro Wrestling move where you grab your opponent from behind and throw him up and over your body as we both fly backwards with the opponent landing on his head. Up we went and down we went. As we were crashing to the mat, he went down hard, was knocked out cold and just like that my 4th Gold Turtle and amateur wrestling days were gone. Poof.

Needless to say that ground fighting skills, acquired at Butch Powell's Infant Chest Gym, augmented by my early start at competitive wrestling and tutelage from quality coaches, made WRESTLING the main source of SELF DEFENSE as well.

Wrestling, based on American Freestyle and Greco Roman technique, provided me with the same confidence-building character that the ancient Greek Warriors must have possessed.

I am thankful to participate in the sport at a time when competitors were clothed. I'd hate the early days of Greco Roman wrestling where there is a chance you could lose by way of "scrotal detachment" or some other hideous, appendage-altering technique. From childhood to the first formal Eastern Martial Arts training in 1976 in Okinawan ISSHIN RYU KARATE, wrestling was my thing. Many a disagreement was settled with me atop a much larger opponent whose face was planted, play dough-like on the pimpled gravel by way of a wrestling hold. Now, I must admit that even though I knew that Pro Wrestling was never to be part of my future, making a little money wrestling was not as far-fetched. I mean the difference between amateur and professional is the money, right? In fact, while attending the University of Maryland and with 3 Golden Turtles in my pocket for confidence, I started a quite profitable wrestling gig that turned into a business. Don't laugh. Here's what happened.

Baltimore is the home of Pimlico Raceway, which hosts the 2nd leg of the Triple Crown Series horserace known as the Preakness. In the center of the oval racetrack is perhaps one of the greatest annual parties in the country. While the Upper Class sit with binoculars, long cigarette holders and crystal champaign flutes, the hardcore 100,000+ folks on the infield enjoy a semi-controlled riot of partying intensity that is unmatched anywhere I have been. The temporary city-state created within covers every type of human being from college professors to baseball players, from accountants to soldiers, from life's rejects to scholars and religious folk. I mean young and old, black and white, strong and weak etc. AND EVERYONE IS DRINKING.

This setting was an excellent venue for my wrestling business. Every year for 14 consecutive years starting in 1980 I was there. Weather was no factor in attending. Rain and mud made for the most profitable (and fun) Preaknesses for my business. Set-up costs were minimal. I would warm up with a few Black Eyed Susans (Official Drink of the Preakness) draw a clearly visible sign on a post that said "WRESTLE YOU FOR $10.00." strip down to some baggy shorts, grab a beer, sit in my beach chair and wait. Me. My beer. My chair. My sign. My skills and of course, My cohunes. It was not long before I was open for business. It usually started innocently enough with a few passersby looking at my sign, seeing at my un-intimidating 5'7" 160-lb frame and wondering what the joke was. Then, inevitably a customer would come for business.. There were so many different challengers over 14 years that only the great ones do I remember.

Now, as a business, I had a successful business model that I followed every time. Throughout the 10-hour "workday" CaPoop Enterprises (our company name that consisted of a contraction of Powell and my partner K. Cooper) offered entertainment for a price with excitement and little REAL danger. In the 14 years I had over a hundred bouts. Actually, I am unsure of the actual total number but let's just settle on "plenty." I only lost once. We'll get to "The Loss" in a bit. There were rules. I had a significant group of large Terrapins to make sure things stayed cool and no one got killed. That would have led to a sharp decrease in profit and ruined everything. With horse-mounted Military Police and many undercover law enforcement personnel keeping order (as best as they could) in the Infield, it was important that no unauthorized brawling took place, no one ever felt cheated and all left knowing that got their ass kicked FAIRLY. And, most importantly customers were always welcomed back for another go at me. I have had many repeat customers that span over several Preakness' and some of the same folks 2 or 3 times in the same day. I made some good friends there as well.

CaPoop Enterprises also had additional revenue sources, like guest wrestling matches called "Pit that Grit" where our staff would pick two huge rednecks from the line to go at it. Winner got $15 and we netted a $5 promotion fee. We also sold beer bongs for a killing. On the way to Pimlico Raceway, we'd stop at a beer store to buy all we could carry in case it just happened to be Armageddon Day lest we be unprepared. Then off to the hardware store for 20 quart size oil change funnels, 40 feet of 1.5-to-2 inch thick hollow tubing, 20 clamps, and 30 feet of twine, rope or belts. We brought our own screw drivers to attach the hose to the funnel by way of banded clamps. Total CaPoop investment: maybe $45.

We left the beer bongs unassembled while going through security at the track and they were hidden or displayed out in the open as part of the legal items allowed in. Coolers, tents, chairs and the like made for easy hiding of our non lethal, and soon-to-be-profitable components. Once inside, and we were set up in our roped off piece of territory on the Preakness infield, we assembled the beer bongs. You can figure out the assembly system that ended up with 20 world class beer bongs with customized portable shoulder straps and a Preakness sticker (bought for a $1 in the Infield) slapped on the plastic side for "UnOfficial Authenticity." Cost investment for an unassembled CaPoop beer bong was $2.25 in materials. Actual cost to buy the assembled, quality control tested, CaPoop Unofficial Preakness Infield Beer Bong? $35.00 each. As they say..."Do the Math." We were poor college students, but very resourceful.

A few of us would wander the massive infield with 5 or 6 beer bongs on our backs and offer "Free demonstrations of CaPoop Quality Construction" by demonstrating each one we sold by slamming a few of the potential customers beers with it while they decided if it was worth the investment. Even when we not completing a successful sale, we were thankful as our commitment to quality control kept our college beer bellies filled. I know what you are thinking, Why would anyone pay $35 for a contraption they could have made for $2.25? You are not the only one with this question as we had our share of equally inquisitive mathematicians in the form of huge, belligerent, drunken rednecks with varying degrees of tooth retention. There were many different instances of inquiry and explanation but a memorable example comes to mind. I had sold 4 of the 6 beer bongs on my back and was doing a final arching sweep around the 3rd Turn

heading for home base when I heard a prospective customer yell "Hoy Midget, how muscsh for

deht bear bung?" I respond with the standard "$35!" He cursed an intense monologue of

unrecognizable redneck blabber laced with Southern-style hostile profanity. He approached in

what I'm sure HE THOUGHT was a menacing manner as I stood my ground prepared for a

tough sale. When he finished his harried and comical stumble walk, he stood over me at nearly

6'3" and was quite muscular in a Lynyrd Skynyrd kinda way. But what surprised me most was

that he had all his teeth...at least for now.

The man wanted to know why he should pay me "F'n $35" when he could have made one at

home for "F'n' $5." I responded that it actually could be done for "under F'n $3" and he didn't

like that at all. In classic Maryland grit style, he stood there wobbling to and fro and began the

traditional 8-Point Redneck Calculation on whether he should fight me or not:

1) Look at opponent's biceps.

2) Look down at own "bigger guns."

3) Use Grizzly Bear Technique of standing up straight to make self look bigger and more

threatening.

4) Stumble backwards uncontrollably while trying to stand up straight for Grizzly Bear

Technique.

5) Regain footing.

6) Look at biceps again for reassurance.

7) Make sure friends are numerous and paying attention.

8) Attack.

While watching him go methodically through the checklist, I thought of giving him a beer bong for making me laugh, but before I could, he moved forward with his decision based on his 8-Point Redneck Calculation with "How 'bout I just take it from you?" Taking a brief moment to look down at my own twin pipe cleaners, I led his gaze to the only tattoo that I have which is on my upper right arm from shoulder tip to elbow. It's a combination of Snarling Dragon facing Gnashing Tiger coming out of an American Eagle head and Yin/Yang symbol with Chinese lettering that read "Unity of Mind, Body and Spirit In Touch with The Way". Secondary script stating something along the lines of "Man of Infinite Stillness" translated roughly to "Man of Death." Then, through the whole inked battle scene, a big, thick samurai sword with a blood-red handle-wrap that skewers the art piece right through the middle, from top to bottom and from shoulder peak to elbow arm bend point.

As his eyes looked at the ink just described, I am sure that The Grit had no idea what the tattoo said because he was definitely not Chinese, but he was getting the idea what it meant. After a few more moments of him staring at my arm and me now staring menacingly at him, I felt the synapses in his booze-drenched brain fire off a few lucky neurons screaming "WARNING! WARNING! WARNING! DANGER! DANGER!" I think he started to "feel me."

I seized on the moment of indecision in a final confidence-crushing statement of my combat intention with "Do you want the beer bong or not?" "No" he said as he looked down and away for his beer as his buddies ran up to him to congratulate him on his victorious stare down over Midget Man. Wished I had a free pass on me to the "Wrestle You for $10" pit on the other side of the Infield, but didn't and just walked away instead.

After realizing at a later date that the redneck could not read the symbols and just figured that "I don't know what they mean, but it just ain't good." I had English words added to the tattoo so my meaning wouldn't ever be misconstrued. "KENPO JIU JITSU" and "THE ARTS" now adorn the ominous "Pin Arms of Death." My tattoo artist buddy respectfully recommended hitting the weight room if I want to add any more ink to my skinny arm canvass. But, short of an actual pop-up-and-out-on-a-retractor mechanism, shoulder-fired .44caliber Derringer pistol, I really don't know what else to include on the arm.

So I get back to the Wrestling Pit and am happy to see a line of business awaiting me. A huge Redneck with a Confederate Flag tattoo covering chest and swastikas on his forearms is up first. A former wrestler from nearby Owings Mills High School is on deck. They are followed by six or seven other miscreants patiently waiting in line to have the crap kicked out of them. Various tooth counts interestingly enough are seemingly relative to their apparent educational back-ground. They pay $10 to my best friend "Grit" (real name John Corlett.) a 6'2" Scary-Ass Hoss from nearby Severn, MD who explains the rules. 1) It's a wrestling match. No punching or kicking. No biting. No eye poking. No weapons. 2) No refunds.

But before the action, I want to tell you how I met my lifelong friend John C. Great story. In college, I stayed in a dormitory called "Allegheny E" with a campus wide reputation for serious partying. Having not even drank beer in HS as an athlete, I was ready to meet my new environs head on. Within the first week of staying there, we hosted a "50 keg Blow Out" that would serve as a "mixer" for new students to feel welcome. "E" was the only dormitory to be allowed to join in the campus fraternities' annual Greek Olympics where Beer Versus Man (BVM) was the point of The Games.

As such, we were invited to participate in the festivities and field a "team" to compete in all the craziness. I was tasked with putting together a Tug-o-War team that could compete against the seasoned veterans and skilled tuggers and chuggers of other Beer Olympians. I took the command seriously. Legend held that one frat won the tug every year and was basically unbeatable. Like a more fun version of the Battle of Thermopylae, we would put their legend to the test. I started to weed through the best, biggest and strongest talent available but had to settle with the folks who actually lived in Allegheny Hall. Beer slamming legends with names like "Hopper" "Naz" "Rio" "Ike" "Marine" "Coop" "Head" "Manson" "Piper" "FlyRon" "Billman" and me "Billy Jack". It was an assortment of big color personalities from all over the country, and with a little planning I thought we could win. That's when I saw him.

The huge, non-smiling behemoth redneck hailing from the battery-stealing capital of Severn, Maryland. Even the town's name wreaked of Bubba Central. I would come to know him as "Corlett" but thought of him fondly as "Grit". He often wore this Molly Hatchet heavy metal band shirt with Frank Frazetta fantasy art image on the front and long muscle stretched light blue ¾ sleeves. We caught eyes regularly, but didn't speak for fear he would eat my head in a single chomp like those Cinnamon Toast Crunch cereal commercials. As well, he was one room to far east and resided in Allegheny D, a distant step child of the legendary Allegheny E but only about six feet of hall separated famous from unknown. I could tell that Grit wanted to be part of the E Experience and so I tucked my head down between my shoulders like the "Fear The Turtle" Terrapin I was and walked over to Massive Molly Hatchet Man.

When I got close, he kept his head straight and his eyes rolled down to look at me like a Great White shark in preparation for dinner. Here is what basically transpired:

Me: "Hey man! I'm Billy Jack and we are forming a tug of war team to kick some Frat ass."
Grit: "Name's "Corlett".
With the ice broken, I say "Look man, I am putting together a team of f'd up dudes from E and I

was wondering if you wanted to join in the carnage. Plenty of beer and babes!"

Grit: "Whatta I have to do?"

Me: "Well, it's a 12 man team on each side with a thick gym class type of rope and a big pit of cold, wet, muddy foam in the center. Winner pulls loser into the foam."

Grit looks at me for a moment and then says "I ain't goin' in no foam."

And that is how I met one of my best friends over 30 years ago.

Allegheny E did win the 1980 U of M Greek Olympics going undefeated in TOW competition.

Martial Note: Know your enemy. Never go into battle blind. Study the opponent for strengths and weaknesses prior to conflict. And never assume away the skills and capabilities of your opponent.

As the great Chinese General Sun Tzu wrote in "The Art of War":

"Know your enemy and know yourself and you can fight a hundred battles without disaster."

We defeated the defending frat champions with espionage and counterintelligence rather than skill and power alone. The mind is the ultimate weapon and after all we were in college at the time. Here is a brief recap of the Championship match between the Defending Champs and the Hellbent Misfits of Allegheny E:

As we won the first three tugs with relative ease, we were never pulled forward one step. E just pulled and whole teams flew face first into the foamy muck. Sure looked cold. Brrrrr. As we watched the Champions do their preliminary victory march through their bracket, a buddy Billman (from DC purse snatcher fame-story to follow) tells me that they are cheating by adding additional tuggers once the whistle blew. Not cool.

So I grab a bunch of non-tugging, beer-swilling E members and form a secret spy network with clandestine, classified code names like "Arthur Algogne" "Semorous Payne" "Stanislov Felenki" "Thomuth Raye" and "McWillipur Steele". Whenever such a name was mentioned from that point on, it was met with a spy-like 'Shhhhhhhhsssshhhhhh". Covert for sure. Their job was to infiltrate the frat boy team under the guise of pledging their fraternity or just to slam a beer and make friends All the while, reports were coming back to Command (me) that they were cheating but have never been caught. Tell that to Stanislov Felenki and now we know and can adjust strategy. Martial Note: Gathering "Intel" BEFORE the battle gives you the best chance to win.

Now E being men of beer honor, we decided against adding our own cheaters to even the tug for the title. Instead, our Merry Band of Malt-Beverage Loving Mayhem Makers would wait on the enemy side until they tried to cheat and then intercede by tossing away the illegal tuggers. Here is a recapped "Live version" from my perspective of our Championship Tug-o-War victory over thirty years ago.

Allegheny E is first to the pit as we check in at the scorers table. I thought, what an easy job scoring a tug of war match. Anyway, I grab the rope 2nd in line from the foam with only Rio (of DC soccer kick to the chops of purse snatcher fame) in front. As he grabs the rope, we look across the neutral zone to The Champions as they enter the pit with matching shirts and shorts with all kinda Greek letters on them. They had names embroidered in gold thread across their heart. The approached in formation, each to his own position following commands from their captain. They did look impressive both organizationally and biologically. Big guys all.

Rio looks back at me and says "Those guys look tough. Not sure we can take 'em." and doubt begins its nasty creep into my mind. I start looking at their bulging biceps, matching team outfits and determined faces…eep. Just then, I look back over my left shoulder to see the hideous craze in the faces of the maniacs amassed. I see Ike, a huge dude that looks like Sam in the awesome "Supernatural" TV series, wrapping the rope around his rugby trained arm. It is looped so tight that it looked like it could be pulled right off at the elbow. Ike just smiles at my gaze. I take in the brazenness of all members in a single glance.

The last image I see before returning my head forward is the huge US Marine who is anchoring the team as the last man. He wraps the massive rope around his body several times. Marine screams "On the count of three-WE LOOK TO THE SKY!" I return my gaze to Rio who had followed my attention and his fear of defeat was now zero. Last thing I remember before the whistle and 3 second countdown was seeing the elite secret spy group that had taken up positions around the Champions to assure no extra tuggers jumped in.

On the count of three, we looked to the sky and tugged the entire opposing team so hard into the mud and foam that some enemy members were pulled over the pit completely to our side and barely got wet. The rest will have to get some extra strength detergent to clean up as they retire their Champion sweaters. From post battle reports from ""Arthur Algogne" they tried to cheat. But since the losers got yanked so far forward so fast off their feet, the four additional tuggers barely made it to the rope. If they did, they too became foam lickers as well.

Martial Note 2: Don't be deceived by looks. Don't sell yourself short. Gather intel. And don't tell your secret tug-o-war cheating strategy to an secretly embedded 'Stanislov Felenki".

IS THIS IN FACT THE SECRET COVERT GROUP OF "ARTHUR ALGOGNE" "SEMOROUS PAYNE" "THOMUTH RAYE" "MCWILLIPUR STEELE" AND "STANISLOV FELENKI" IN THE CAR'S DRIVERS SEAT? MAYBE IT IS. MAYBE NOT. CLASSIFIED INFORMATION.

Now back to the Preakness "Wrestle You for $10" action.

So it began. Most of the time I would shoot a hard DOUBLE LEG TAKEDOWN with a lift and slam or a trip straight back. Perhaps a DOUBLE to a SINGLE LEG TAKEDOWN with a groin and hamstring wrenching twist from moi. Then depending on where and how hard they hit the ground (sometimes they would get knocked out cold, throw up from being slammed with the wind knocked out or just quit after REALITY jolted their party buzz) I would follow along with MOUNT position on their chest and a DOUBLE LEG GRAPEVINE if they are on their back with a forearm bone blade across the throat or a double knees on the kidneys forearm shiv across back of the neck if they were stomach down. Possibly adding a spreader using a Double Leg Grapevine to pancake smash them hard to the ground if they were on hands and knees.

I was NEVER taken down as the result of an offensive technique executed on me at the start of an 'official match' but have ended up on the bottom of a battle by tripping in the mud or getting saloon-style chucked over a neighbor's cooler. Most times the takedown led to one of the three positions I mentioned and then the fun began. I was getting submissions before "tapping out" became popular. I accepted many different types of surrenders like a breathless "Dude that's enough!" by a 6' 4" rugby player whose face I held 5 inches under the mud until the terra firma milkshake in his sinus cavities fired the correct brain responses to quit. The only time I ever purposely hurt any client was when they were clearly trying to hurt me. I live by the old creed:

"I Have a High Art. I Hurt with Cruelty Those Who Would Damage Me." Archilocus 650 BC

It sounds cool too.

Usually, I would wield the "Ring of Retribution" to rule breakers by rotating my college ring so the stone was palm down and would go back and forth on his same head spot until a welt grew up and out. Kinda like a Flintstone cartoon where Fred gets hit in the head and a huge, tall lump grows a few inches in height. This was a rare occurrence and usually all it took to correct poor sportsmanship violations. If the offender was not of the understanding type, he was dragged away by several of my Behemoth Henchmen with "No Return" instructions. If he cooled off and apologized for his intent to hurt tactics, he would be allowed back in line for another crack at me. It's business. Nothing Personal. $10 Please.

The stories could fill another book titled "WRESTLE YOU FOR $10." I know. The one you are probably interested in is the one I lost. Ok. Here you go:

It was my 14th year of Preakness attendance, cemented forever in time, in what became known as "The Loss." The Loss recapped:

It had been quite a busy day and having just gotten back from a walk I noticed this muscular redneck lying down in the grass staring at me. I replied to the social interaction as it were with the traditional "I see you too" return glance shot back in lieu of a hello. I was sure of seeing him before but not sure if it was a different Preakness or just earlier that day. After slamming a beer it was time to get back to work. No time to stop and stare. During the next 4 consecutive victories, I had taken a moment from each match to glance at the guy lying on the ground. We will now call him "Watcher." He just continued to lay there observing while I am going through a fairly tough series of matches against former wrestlers that were a blast.

Fortunately, my knowledge of joint locks and pain submissions combined with good wrestling skills and height-deprived mental toughness proved too much for wrestler alone. Many times the match ended with an ankle crank, toe wrench or knee on facial nerve, as they were more focused on pinning me while all I had to do was get them to submit or pin them. Most realized that pride and/or $10 was not worth a dislocated shoulder blade as that would hinder subsequent proper beer slamming efforts.

In the match preceding The Loss, I was actually wrestling with three (3) skinny brothers (not slang for African American, but real family members) who were wasted. This was a rare instance since a MULTIPLE ATTACKER CONFRONTATION IS ONE OF WRESTLING'S ONLY WEAKNESSES. In those situations, the additional use of hands, feet, elbows, knees, teeth and weapons are required. But it was sunny and considering their heroin-sculpted body physiques and state of inebriation, I chose to go for it. The only additional rules were:

1) Once a member of the trio was submitted or quit verbally, he was out of the match for the rest of the challenge and 2) Their entry fee was $30 while the House was only responsible for $20.

It was 3 on 1 you know!

So here I am with one brother pinned facedown in the mud drowning from the pressure of my knee AND the weight of his two bros all applied to the back of his neck. My guys were yelling to me that he was trying to quit, but I was busy with the two other knuckleheads. With Bro #1 submerged under my right knee, Bro #2 is being strangled/choked by my left arm in what I would later learn to be called a "Rear Naked Choke" and Bro #3 is in front of me standing with my right arm holding his left leg behind the knee and then snaking back over to complete the choke on Bro # 2. It is only after Choking Bro quits do I realize that Drowning Bro is not moving. He was just floating there. With Bros #1 and #2 being fished out of Lake Muck, I quickly finish of Bro #3 without memorable incident.

As I stand up walking muddily and out of breath to the temporary sanctuary of the beer cooler, it happens. Apocalypse now. After bending over slightly to remove a cold one, Watcher leaps to action and unbeknownst to me, tossing $10 in the direction of the admission line. I learn later that that nearly started a riot as Watcher inadvertently became a line jumper. Anyway, Watcher rapidly approaches from behind and pulls my surf shorts to ankles and grabs me in a tight, sharp-boned, muscle-reinforced headlock as he chucks me to the ground with a Balls-a-Smack'n, Dick-a-Slapp'n, Crotch-a-Crack'n Fury! (BASDASCACF) And it's on!

After keeping Watcher from snapping my neck and repositioning my body to an angle that neutralized the choke-out attempt, I had a dilemma. The problem was that I am now keenly aware that my ass cheeks are spread wide with my a-hole catching an unprotected solar burn in the hot midday sun. And this exhibition of innermost personality was there for 100,000+ to see. It was a choice that had to be made. Either concentrate on total defeat of Watcher and his Pearl Harbor style attack or give in to man's most basic, primal instinct...COVER YOUR ASS!

So, in a decision that would haunt me for the better part of an hour, I chose to focus my skills on getting my shorts up to usual ass-covering position. The only way I could cover yon a-hole was to devote BOTH my arms AND the crucial body angle position that was keeping me conscious to this point to the cause. The end result was already written and it soon came to pass. While my lower eye was now at peace in the darkness of its surf shorts crypt, my consciousness was dimming and I tapped.

My first reaction when the snow cleared was to get up and make a fuss about rules infractions. At first, I thought that was a proper response. But as blood flow returned me to a semi-clear thinking state and as I watched all my buddies doing "You are God-like" bows and toasting beers to the New Champion, and Watcher became an instant legend, I thought better of it. It was never my intention to win all the matches and after this first loss the word RETIREMENT blazed in the neon sign of my mind. I sat down and drank a beer as the former CEO of CaPoop Enterprises

and pondered a dynasty and its inevitable end. At least I no longer had to wonder how to get

a walker or wheelchair through the Infield muck of Preakness' in years to come.

Sitting there, moments after defeat, I pondered the meaning of it all.

Kind of like Caesar, I thought for a moment. Hmmm...probably not.

But the 14-year experience was a great one with many memories that proved to me

ABSOLUTELY that WRESTLING and the GROUND FIGHTING ARTS are instrumental to

the success of a COMPLETE Martial Artist and Self Defense Expert.

RAMPONE "BIG GRAB" IN ITALIAN WAS THE NAME OF THE PRE-GRACIE SYSTEM OF GROUNDFIGHTING THAT I TAUGHT AS A COMBINATION OF WRESTLING AND JUDO. THAT'S ME IN THE BACKGROUND ATTEMPTING A DOUBLE LEG TAKEDOWN ON MY DAD AND HIM SAYING "I DON'T THINK SO" WITH A WICKED CROSS FACE TECHNIQUE.

WHILE WRESTLING HAS SETTLED HUMAN DISPUTES SINCE THE BEGINNING OF TIME, A WARRIOR NEEDS A COMPLETE ARSENAL OF TECHNIQUE AND WEAPONRY TO WIN.

CHAPTER TEN

The Importance of: KNOWING THAT WRESTLING ALONE IS NOT ENOUGH.

As we discovered in the last section, Wrestling is a powerful and effective form of Self Defense.

But just as it is very effective in a sport/SD situation where the conflict is limited to a One

on One contest, wrestling's limitation as a self-defense system is revealed in mass attack

scenarios. Don't get me wrong, a big, powerful wrestler can and has won a fight against several opponents at the same time, but victory is less likely as the number of encounters and assailants goes up and/or weaponry is employed. A great lesson was taught to me directly.

My favorite self-defense wrestling move for a one opponent fight is the standard "Double Leg Takedown Slam" with follow up Mount position either front or back and Spreader (Double Leg Grapevine) applied for total body control with neck/throat pressure applied by forearm bone-blade until submission is achieved. It works and has been responsible for many victories in sport and "on the street." We referred to success of this technique during the "WRESTLE YOU FOR $10" encounters at the Preakness.

This simple series of techniques combined together creates a battle plan that is quick, efficient and surprisingly easy to perform successfully time and again. It can be taught to a student in one class and be immediately ready for use thereafter. I'll bet that I have taught this technique to maybe a thousand students over 35 years.

The quickness, violence of action, and the simultaneous control of the opponent, preventing him/her from hurting you, is what shocks the offender. The attacker is usually much larger than the defender since not that many short, fat dudes attack larger humans on a regular basis. So when that attacker is unceremoniously picked up, slammed down and submitted so quickly, the surprise and embarrassment is substantial, immediate and leaves a lasting emotional imprint.

As a high-ranking martial arts instructor, I can confirm its effectiveness as a self-defense technique of the highest order. The technique has NEVER failed me and is #1 in my Personal Self Defense Technique Hall of Fame (PSDHOF). This next story, while again confirming its power, also shows most clearly its limitations.

So, to make a short story long...

I had returned home to New Jersey during a break in classes at the University of Maryland. Still in the youthful throes of college partying and the subsequent stupidity and lack of judgment that only Higher Education brings, my friends and I drank some beer and went out for more fun. We decided to go bowling at what could only be called the bad part of town. Actually it was another town completely called Manville. This place was headquarters of Johns Manville Corporation. Back then it was referred to as "The Asbestos Capital of The World." When I was a little boy growing up, I remember seeing all those workers at shift change scurrying around to and fro, from building to massive building. Only now do I wonder how many of them suffered firsthand from the dangers of that f'n asbestos. My dad was a school teacher and drove a forklift there as a second job to feed me. I worried about his exposure to asbestos my whole life.

In fact, asbestos exposure was to blame for death of my legendary High School Wrestling Coach, Rocco Forte, who was diagnosed with incurable Mesothelioma (lung cancer from contact with the substance) and died within a year of diagnosis. He was a Rock of a Man. There was no problem putting him in the VIP suite when he checked into Hotel Valhalla.
Anyway, back to the bad town.

The Manville Bowling Alley was perched at the far western corner of a shopping mall with the usual stores, eateries, and pizzerias of varying quality, lined in a row on the long north side of this rectangular tract of land. We (me and 4 buddies) were playing pinball in the front of the bowling alley, when one of the local vermin banged into the machine I was playing causing it to "Tilt."

When no apology was forthcoming, the usual social skills of young folk ensued as the curse-laden, free-flowing challenges were colorful and quite poignant. As such, I requested a

85

"further clarification" appointment with "The Tilter" outside. Since I happened to be closest to the door, I motioned the Tilter and my buddies outside and off I went...leading the way. After me and my opponent exited, we were followed immediately by the loads of patrons from the packed lobby and bowlers from the alley itself. It looked like a cut in a hose as the human water flowed endlessly out of the gash.

As I moved out and away from the door, I looked back through the human geyser for the familiar faces of my friends. Recognizing no faces to my liking, I remember at that very moment, how oddly appropriate the phrase "Uh-Oh" really is. By now, as the group continued to stream out endlessly like a river branch meeting the ocean, the lobby group surrounded me completely and the parking lot came alive. The scene resembled a bizarre zombie movie with visually accurate corpse-people emerging from dark nooks and crannies of cars, eateries and the like.

Seems everyone wanted to party hard...on my head.

Soooo...here I am totally surrounded by a mob of hostile degenerates and the crowd is growing fast. It was at that bleak moment that I finally saw a ray of hope; my friends, all four of them with their seemingly distorted faces not 40 feet from my Position Of Peril. (POP) It then occurred to me that the distortion was not the result of a blur of their faces in my racing mind, but rather the visual effect rendered when faces are pressed up against the INSIDE of a pane of glass. In this case it was the panes of the CLOSED bowling alley doors! It seems the owner of the bowling alley was preventing them and others from coming outside. Fortunately for the mob, plenty had already exited and enough were already out there in the parking lot.

Here I was surrounded by at least a hundred meanies (who knows how many exactly-let's just settle again on "plenty") and clearly the singular focus of their teen angst. Thinking quickly and with literally no other option, I scanned the crowd for a worthy opponent since I couldn't find "The Tilter" and had no time to go looking for him. Settling on the biggest, meanest looking SOB available, I engage him in a loud challenging way with "Hey Fat F**k, Why are you so F'n Stupid looking?" While this may appear suicidal, I HAD TO MAKE SURE that he and HE ALONE accepted the challenge and would "represent" the mob as their "Champion." THE ADDITION OF EVEN ONE OTHER OPPONENT WOULD SHIFT THE ODDS IN A DANGEROUS WAY AGAINST ME. Once I hooked the Giant Redneck's (GR) total attention, I kept at it, jibing him to make sure that he made this fight HIS FIGHT. This would assure that he would want to smash my face ALL BY HIMSELF. Wonderful way to meet someone, Uh.

It worked so well that he literally calmed the crowd down, like an old EF Hutton commercial where everyone gets totally quiet. They acknowledged his role as their Champion and his immortal battle cry "I'm gonna kill this lil f**ker!" (In case you are still wondering why I asterisk* or skip the full curse words is that I promised my parents that I would. No lie.)

So far so good.

As a battle circle formed around me and Giant Redneck, it quickly became thicker and thicker as more folks gathered in to try and see into the pit they created. I wasn't in a jellybean counting mood, but I'll bet "plenty" now meant hundreds of people providing human fence posts and wire mesh of the impenetrable parking lot that became a Flesh Octagon. Even if the cops arrived right then, they couldn't get through the ringed walls in time to save me. Assuming of course that that would be what the police intended to do. No sirens. No flashing lights. No friends. No hope?

In a timely karmic happening, the innermost wall of the pit was now bolstered by my four friends equidistantly spaced to provide a "got your back" vigilance. How they transported from doorstop to fence post wasn't but a fleeting thought since I wasn't looking for direct help. It would be dangerous for them to reveal their allegiance to me. I mean 5 versus 300 doesn't really strengthen the odds all that much no matter how many times I've seen Bruce Lee and John Saxon do it in "ENTER THE DRAGON." My main hope was that they could at least keep others from joining the fight once it started going badly for their champion, and it would.

Equally important was to make sure that my back remained a "Weapons Free Zone."

The stage was set. Surrounded by a group of blood-thirsty pond scum of humanity, I stood alone with only my skills, my luck, my brain and a condom-thin wall of protectors on the periphery of the inner circle. Oh yeah, I wasn't totally alone, lest we forget Giant Redneck who had by now stripped down to sleeveless tee and head bandana. His muscles were huge (not fat as I had earlier suggested) and his eyes had the sharpest color of red that I had even seen. It was like a bad photograph where his eyes glowed crimson red like those in a scene from "The Omen." Then, bathing my ears like a soft, beautiful yoga CD, I heard the Giant Redneck announce for all to hear, "The li'l f**k is all mine and mine alone!" along with the supporting, "No one else gets in...Until after he's dead!" Well, maybe not THAT soothing, but my plan was moving along.

Now it was just Him and Me. (The "TERMINATOR" movie reference is intentional.)
He approached with my favorite Grit Fighting System Technique (GFST) normally showcased in fights between Pro Basketball players, where they charge forward with their arms purposely pulled back way behind them. Yes, the solar plexus-leading, arm, fist and elbow self-neutralizing approach favored with chest bumpers everywhere. As he approached, I smashed him hard on his xyphoid process (that little nub of bone on the lower part of your rib cage where the two halves meet) with a punch that could have come out his back in an elastic, gummy kinda

way if it had been in a cartoon. Not waiting for his response to the hit, I shoot in with a Double Leg takedown that sawed a piece of my kneecap off as it scrapes the ground. Oops, forgot to remember that we were NOT on a wrestling mat.

Martial Note: Mind The Terrain. No matter. It's just skin and I continued on with a perfectly executed Double Leg that hit him sharply in the upper stomach with my right shoulder causing a puke jet to slosh all over my back and hair. We are in midair, its gross and now I am pissed.

We hit the ground hard and GR is trying to say something, but his internal bleeding and mouth full of vomit make communication iffy at best. I mumble something like "gross man" and quick elbow slam him on his left cheek and then move to Mount. But in a "surprise" move that would shock the Ancients, he rolled over onto his stomach to avoid a revisiting elbow that I had ordered up. He popped up to his knees and I threw on the Spreader and flattened him out hard. It would be like taking a person and suspending him three feet above the ground, then jumping on him from 10 feet above, slamming his body against the hard pavement, limbs splayed. He was out!

And that's what happened.

I can immediately feel the pressure being released from as the crowd as it started to shift from mob-mentality to crowd-awareness to a group-like function such as attending a kids baseball game. Maybe it was the severity of the champion's defeat or the grossness of my situation as I stood up covered in cheap bowling alley semi-digested pizza puke. Yet things were still at a point where the next few actions taken by anyone could direct the rest of the evening's action.

So, glancing toward the police station, which was only on the opposite side of the parking lot (didn't they look out a window and see the mob action 100 yards away?) it finally appeared to stir as red and blue flashing lights started glowing by the side of the station where they usually park the cruisers. Not sure how long I was really out there ("plenty") but real sure that this was some police activity that I actually WANTED to be a part of. Still unsure if they would get there in time when I heard the familiar puke-jawed Giant Redneck starting to stir. He must of figured out what happened, as a few people were explaining it to his contused head while pointing in my direction. Come on Cops!

As mentioned, with next few moments crucial I turn my attention away from the police activity in the too-far distance and toward the rising pile of puke formally known as Giant Redneck: The Mob's Champion. Seemed he understood what was going on and started accusing me of throwing up on him! A few guys nearby fanned the fire looking to reignite the crowd's blood thirst. Just as I was wondering what to do, one of my buddies raced over and kicked semi-standing GR right in the face! Down he went again. Before he hit the ground, either a dried piece of puke glimmering in the light of the moon, or dental enamel in the shape of a tooth was ejected from Giant Redneck's mouth. This happened as he did a sideways roll in midair before returning to basically the same spot that I had left him in a short while ago. All attention now turns to my kicking buddy as he morphs from soccer player to sprint runner, blazing through the crowd. Someone yells "Get Him!" and off the lynch mob goes running and screaming for a new person to beat up.

Actually, Rising Redneck did not have time to rally the troops before getting the face boot and the group never reached "fever pitch" again. In fact, I smelt weed being lit and different groups of people starting to mingle back into their own cliques, leaving only a handful to chase after my buddy. But he was long gone. Guessing the general feeling was "fight over and here come the cops so let's get out of here." Ok then.

90

As for moi, my three remaining buddies came over to grab me...well, with all the puke, let's say they "ushered" me hard between some pick-up trucks where we stayed for a few minutes as the cops arrived, then casually slipped outta Dodge. With our entire group reunited at my house, we slammed more beer and recapped the evening's events from all of our different perspectives.

"Did you believe what happened tonight? Good stuff for a book someday!" I remember saying.

How clairvoyant. As I reflected on the true seriousness of the situation, especially the other possible outcomes, the most important things I took from the intense experience were:

1) I was frig'n lucky.

2) Wrestling alone was not the best option when facing multiple attackers.

3) I needed more skills and I needed them ASAP.

So my vision of a Self-Defense System now meant looking beyond a single opponent.

As well should yours.

MORE THAN ONE ATTACKER CAN MEAN A TRIP TO THE HOSPITAL.

MY SON NICO ALEXANDER WAS ON THE MATS SINCE HE WAS BORN.

DOWNTOWN CHICAGO DOJO CIRCA 1997. A TRUE SCHOOL OF THE WAY.

KUNG FU SUBURBAN STYLE.

BROOKFIELD, IL KENPO SCHOOL CIRCA 2005-A 2ND WAY PLACE.

CHAPTER ELEVEN

The Importance of: UNDERSTANDING MARTIAL EDUCATION.

At this point, we concluded that WRESTLING alone is not enough to assure victory in all SELF-DEFENSE scenarios of multi-person attack. We have, however, deemed it excellent in one-on-one situations even against bigger, stronger opponents. In talking about learning Multiple Martial Arts (as opposed to Mixed Martial Arts training) MULTIPLE means learning a complete discipline from beginning to end. MIXED martial arts fighting, when taught as a singular system by many modern academies, practices bits and pieces of DIFFERENT martial arts at the SAME TIME. These select techniques are combined to provide a well-rounded curriculum suited to winning a competition IN THE RING as a SPORT. For sure, MMA easily transforms easily to effective SELF-DEFENSE without any alteration. But it is a different training method.

The Path that I had chosen was to study multiple martial arts in varying degrees of intensity during particular periods of time. The goal of what became an ongoing 35+ year journey started off simple enough; find and learn what works to prevent an Inadvertent Ass Kicking (IAK) and TEACH OTHERS to do the same. Wrestling. Check.

Learning the martial arts, whether singular, multiple or mixed is very different from a traditional Western-style education. Here in the US, as children we are taught material content aligned with a particular GRADE. In 1st grade we learn things that help our mind expand as our bodies are learning physical skills as well. After graduating 1st grade we move on to 2nd, learn the material, test, then onto 3rd and so on. We LEARN what the TEACHERS believe we NEED TO KNOW in order to be successful at the next level. We are expanding our intelligence mostly through information memorization and recital of this knowledge back to the teacher via oral and written examinations. We are required to remember ONLY certain information to ascend to the next level. Information that helps prepare us to understand the next grade's requirements. The rest is basically forgotten. In martial arts education, forgetting something can get you killed. This style of learning JUST WHAT WE NEED TO KNOW to advance continues up through Junior High School, HS, College and Graduate studies. So learning traditionally in the West means starting on one step then moving up to the next one, then the next one, and so on, upward in a STEP BY STEP manner.

Learning the martial arts is not a step by step proposition. Rather it is more like a SPIRAL STAIRCASE going upward. On the ground level you might have a beginning student working on a Reverse Punch. He/She is studying the new technique for the first time and works on its mechanics while trying to best emulate that which the teacher has shown. On the 2nd level of the spiral staircase, directly above the beginner, maybe a Yellow Belt is training on the exact same technique as the beginner below. Maybe they are even in the same class at the same time practicing Reverse Punch together. Then up on the 8th level, a Shodan (First Degree Black Belt) is ALSO in the SAME class practicing the SAME technique as the White and Yellow Belt, but is learning DIFFERENT things from his Reverse Punch. This upward spiral continues into infinity or until the Warrior stops training or dies.

At every level of training, the technique provides information unknown to the levels below. The SAME technique PRACTICED over and over again reveals NEW INFORMATION to the one training. The person who has done 10,000 Reverse Punches knows more about that technique (and the Art as a whole) than an individual that has done 1,000 repetitions, who is superior to one with only 500 punches under his belt. This differs from STEP BY STEP education in that REPETITION of the SAME material yields NEW UNDERSTANDING. By contrast, you could not learn new information from repeating 1st Grade material over and over again. New information MUST BE PROVIDED for you in the 2nd Grade to reach the 3rd. In Spiral Staircase, you need only practice that which you have learned in order to gain new insight to the same content and advance in rank/grade simultaneously.

As your success grows from extracting new information from repeating the same material, your ability to accept and process NEW information provided by your instructor increases as well. I often tell students that you could learn only the Yellow Belt technique sheet from KENPO KARATE, go to a deserted island, PRACTICE JUST THOSE TECHNIQUES for 30 years and return a Master. The information IS IN the techniques. REVEAL THAT WHICH IS HIDDEN through repetition, dissection and integration OF WHAT YOU HAVE LEARNED into that WHICH YOU DO NOT YET KNOW. A Great Master once said:

"From One Thing Know 10,000 Things!" That sounds about right.

Another way to look at martial education is what I call the BLEACHER WAY of instruction similar in some ways to Ninjitsu. This is where you are standing in front of a set of empty bleachers (in your mind of course) with lables every 20 ft or so with a martial arts style to be learned. Each level up the bleachers is an advancement in the knowledge and rank of the student. On the far left point maybe is marked Karate. The next one marked inward is Jiu Jitsu. Next is Judo. At the center point is Muay Thai. The marking to the right of center is Knife. This continues through the rest of the points to the right of center to the end of the first step on the bleachers. On the 1ST LEVEL, you learn the beginning techniques and philosophies of Karate, Jiu Jitsu, Judo, Muay Thai, Knife etc. After you have learned all this information and can automatically DEMONSTRATE PROFICIENCY, you move up to the 2ND LEVEL and learn all that that entails. You will NEED TO RETAIN what you have learned on each previous bleacher step to understand and execute the new information on the next. By the time you have reached a certain point on the NEVER ENDING rising bleachers (unless you quit or die) you will have acquired Black Belt knowledge in MULTIPLE martial arts at about the same time. So, you have been trained in MULTIPLE MARTIAL ARTS. As well, you could learn MULTIPLE Arts consecutively (one at a time to completion). After becoming a Black Belt in JUDO, you may begin training in KARATE. After getting a Black Belt in Karate, you might move onto Muay Thai, then Jiu Jitsu, and so on.

As you can see, the latter methods of martial arts instruction differ greatly from the way we are USED TO learning. It is also one of the great things about learning the great MARTIAL WAY. That reading books and learning the Arts in a STEP BY STEP manner is insufficient for proper study and understanding of the information. I am sure that some Book/Video taught "masters" would beg to differ, and that's fine. The TRUTH is apparent in the students they turn out. Books and videos are fine SUPPLEMENTS to learning but are no replacement for the DIRECT TRANSMISSION from Martial Arts Master to dedicated student.

Next up? KARATE.

VAMPIRE TRANSPORT SPEED...

…PWOK STYLE.

WHEN FIGHTING AN UNTRAINED OPPONENT, BOTH HE AND ANY OBSERVERS CAN NOT KEEP UP WITH THE SPEED OF YOUR MOVEMENT, IT LOOKS LIKE MAGIC BUT IS ACTUALLY THE TRAINED WARRIOR'S SKILL AT MOVING THROUGH TIME AND SPACE WITH DYNAMIC MOTION. WE CALL THIS APPARENT PHENOMENON OF MARTIAL ARTS "VAMPIRE TRANSPORT SPEED".

CHAPTER TWELVE

The Importance of: KARATE.

Wow! What is the Importance of Karate? That's like starting a conversation with: "Let me tell you about the Universe." It is a topic so immense that no one could completely explain Karate or its importance to man in any one manuscript. But I will humbly take a whack at it.

Since I was a 4 year old child, I prayed to be a Master of Karate.

Every night, for as long as I can remember, while kneeling at bedside and at the end of my prayers, I would add "Please God, let me learn to be a Master of Karate. Let me learn to defend myself and my family in any situation against any amount of attackers." Probably not the same type of Heavenly request common with my classmates in Sunday School or Catechism lessons. My Father came by my room to say goodnight as I was finishing prayers one evening and asked "What are you praying for Son?" "I want to be a Master of Karate!" I replied. He smiled, hugged me and mentioned that it would be difficult because we didn't live in Japan, but also said to keep dreaming and praying and "Anything can happen since you've got the world by the tail!" My Dad was very positive and I still hear his wisdom and pass it along verbatim to my children and students with "Everyday ABOVE Ground Is a GOOD Day!" and "NEVER Turn Down a Breath mint!" These were but a few of the many educational phrases that I grew up adhering to.

Remember that this was the mid 1960's and Karate was just beginning to become popular in the

United States. So to my Dad's way of thinking (which at the time was accurate) most of the Oriental Masters were indeed...in the Orient. So he was right. The fact that DESTINY would provide me with the opportunity to study DIRECTLY with the Great Martial Arts Masters in the years to come was nothing short of a Heaven-Sent Miracle. (HSM) This happening, while surely due to a combination of earthly factors, made me a strong believer in the POWER OF PRAYER. (POP) This differs from the earlier chapter where POP meant Position Of Peril.

As mentioned, my Father and Mother always found out what interested me and provided avenues of exploration to grow that interest. My parents would take me to many martial arts events and demonstrations that came to town. In fact, one of my early childhood girlfriends Michelle M. (we used to call her "Mike") was a high ranking student in her Father's "TIGER SOCIETY" Karate System. My Dad and I would go to the high school gymnasiums to watch the awesome demonstrations of Self-Defense, Board Breaking (Tameshiwara) and Kata (dance-like forms with martial applications). It was a strong influence on my growing LOVE of Karate and kept my interest prior to beginning formal Karate training in High School. It was also pretty cool that "Mike" M. was my girlfriend and everyone was afraid of her.

Very Important Stuff (VIS) in the "cool" department as a kid.

My Dad demonstrated not only his love, but his understanding of my interest by taking me to the many martial arts movies that were just starting to hit the Big Screen. After Bruce Lee rocked the world in "ENTER THE DRAGON" the flood gates opened. The success of this type of movie, in concert with emergence of Karate Point Fighting Competitions, proved America was

following MY LEAD and falling head over heels for Karate! Just kidding...sort of.

One night would stay forever in memory and represented the "PASSIVE TRAINING"

portion of my life. The local movie theatre was playing a TRIPLE FEATURE of Karate

blockbusters "FIVE FINGERS OF DEATH" "CHINESE CONNECTION" and "HAMMER

OF GOD". Now my Dad is great, but sitting for 6 Hours straight watching "Chopsocki" is a bit

much to ask of any man. Even a Leatherneck! He agreed to watch the first two movies and that

was OK with me. I just hadda be there. It was the only Karate "fix" that was available to me at

that age AND I NEEDED IT! I can remember to this very moment the growing tension feeling

when the final credits started rolling at the end of the 2nd Film. I was hoping that the 3rd movie

would start immediately after the 2nd, just as the 2nd did after the 1st. To my horror, the lights

came on and "INTERMISSION" appeared in big sad lettering on the screen. I turned to my Dad

to say something persuasive and he said "Relax, we can stay for the last one." It was one of

THOSE MOMENTS like Christmas morning when the biggest package is for you. I had the

Best Dad in the World and was pumped for "HAMMER OF GOD!" It didn't disappoint.

Just as memorable, BEFORE the Triple Feature, Mike M, her Father and The TIGER SOCIETY

were doing a demonstration in the lobby of the theatre. I remember, leaning on those fuzzy

purple/maroon velvet stanchions that roped off the demo area as Mike and her SENSEI Dad

amazed the crowd with fierce, power-filled Karate techniques and piercing spirit yells. While

leaning on the ropes with arms folded and my chin resting on overlapped hands, I locked eyes with the Sensei as he whirled through a Kata. It felt like a jolt going through me, kinda like a lightening bolt! I remember thinking that some day it would be me on the INSIDE of the stanchions doing a demonstration for a crowd of my own.

It was twenty years later that I would be doing a Kenpo Karate demonstration at a Jackie Chan movie premiere of "RUMBLE IN THE BRONX" in a downtown Downers Grove, Illinois theatre. I was executing a spinning, slashing version of Kenpo Karate's "Whirling Blades" defense against two attackers, when my eyes caught the gaze of a little boy leaning on the velvet stanchions watching the demo. It was an immediate and explosive revelation that I had come full circle and had actually become an Expert, and wondered if that boy would someday become one as well. So this period in the life of a child with a wild fascination for the martial arts, would have to settle for movies and demonstrations, prayers and dreaming until I could find the real thing.

I would just have to wait until the Masters got here.

CHAPTER THIRTEEN

The Importance of: KARATE...CONTINUED.

Now I probably should have mentioned that the many "WRESTLE YOU FOR $10"

victories...and defeat, as well as, the harrowing escape from Bowling Alley Death were not

without SOME knowledge of KARATE. Probably only enough information to be a danger to

myself rather than an attacker, I had started Karate training in High School which preceded those

storied events. But looking back at how much I thought I knew versus the reality of what I was

really capable of doing makes that training almost insignificant. It was better that I thought

myself a Wrestler rather than a Karate Man because that is really what it boiled down to.

But to get caught up, I continued passive training in the martial arts via demonstrations, hanging

out with and kissing Mike, books, movies and dreams through Elementary School while telling people that I was "into" Karate. Not quite lying, but maybe stretching the truth a might. These claims ended when two instances of "To Tell the Truth" stopped a young man from telling people that he was "doing Karate." The first instance happened while bragging of martial prowess to a few friends regarding the "secret" training facility in the basement of my parents' home. So deadly was the training I went on, that "even my parents were afraid to go down there." In defense, it was more of a lively imagination than ill-willed intention to fib.

Anyway, my friend Peter A. had had enough ear work when he said, "OK Billy, let's go see your secret dojo right after school." After many lame excuse-laden attempts to avoid it, I said ok, but that I had to go home first to tell my parents of the arriving guests. As soon as the bell rang, I sprinted home and down to the basement I flew. First up, several Bruce Lee posters on the basement wall torn from my bedroom, draw a quick rendering of a dragon and tiger on some construction paper, and nail up a hastily made "Powell's Karate" sign. As well, swinging to and fro, was a bunch of half moon shelf braces hung from a cut extension cord acting as some type of spiked training mechanism. That's all I had time for when my Mom yelled down, "Billy, your friends are here!"

As they came down, I pretended to awaken from meditation and greeted them in some type of half Chinese, half English blat of "Oahhchi Ha My Friends!" After painfully hitting the impromptu shelf brace spiked device a few times (man that hurt), I launched heavily into the story of secret training methods when all of a sudden my Mom came down the steps like a Doomsday Messenger. She says in what is forever burned into my Top Embarrassment Memory Parchment (TEMP) "What the heck is all this stuff?" My friends looked at me snidely.

Tunnel...vision...pressure on my skin...gonna puke...images fading to black. Repressed memory mercifully blocks the rest. End of Story #1.

Story #2 of why you do not tell people that you know Karate when you don't, occurred while saying it to someone who actually did. It was 6th grade, during daily conversation with my buddy Joe R. about the martial arts when he said, "I just got my Orange Belt in Judo!" Instead of congratulating him, the Idiot Puppet Master (IPM) that takes control of the brain and mouth in such situations blurted out "I've got Purple in Karate!" (which was a lie.) The only purple belt I owned was on the shorts of last year's Hulk Halloween costume.

But that didn't matter so on it went. Joe R. handed me a rank card that had his certification for Orange Belt and asked to see mine. I replied nonchalantly that our organization was so secret that they didn't issue ID cards... (Nice return Billy.) But Joe had had enough and asked me to demonstrate a Purple Belt technique. When I resisted, he asked me to punch at him. As I punched, he grabbed my arm at the wrist and shoulder and launched me up and over with a perfect Judo hip throw. He controlled my landing so that my story and self-image were the only things that came crashing to the ground that day. To make matters worse, Peter A. from Story #1 was coming out of the bathroom as I was flying through the air, orange Converse sneakers scraping the hall ceiling while in mid-tossage. End of Story #2 and the end of tales of martial arts expertise during the remainder of the passive training portion of my life. Embarrassing.

Moral of these Stories: If you are going to talk the talk, you'd better really be walking the walk.

Or better yet, Just Shut Up and Train!

My first real exposure to formal Karate training began in 1976 as a freshman in high school. It was the first day of the first year of HS wrestling and I was on the practice mat with members of the team, many of which I didn't know personally. While scanning the group and sizing up anyone that could be in my weight class... something caught my eye. It was a muscular farmer-looking kind of guy named Spencer who was down in a FULL SPLIT! I'm talking balls flat tire to the mat split here. He popped up and dropped down over and over again like a banana peel on ice. It was absolutely amazing.

It looked so wild that I think my mouth dropped open. This must have caught Spencer's eye since he nodded hello and I smiled, pulling my jaws closer together and then looked away. Well, as practice went on that week, I realized that Spencer was a beginner at the sport of wrestling. I planned on going over to help him with some moves, but just never pulled the trigger and probably would have focused on my practice if an intense event didn't occur right in front of me that changed all that.

I was coming out of gym class a few weeks later and heard a confrontation brewing in the hallway right outside the boys' locker room door. It seems this guy Jay M. was threatening Spencer with a whupping for some reason or another. Now Jay M. is a big dude and supposedly was into Boxing or some other street fighting stuff. He was towering over Spencer, who was calmly leaning against the wall, arms crossed at chest level with one foot on the ground and the other bent at the knee behind him placed flat heeled against the supporting wall. A crowd was forming and Jay M. wanted to get on with it so he put his hand on Spencer's upper chest... and then it happened.

It was a move that was so fast, so quick, so sharp, it scared me. In one motion Spencer unfolded both arms and using the palms of both his hands simultaneously, he smashed Jay M. at the wrist snapping the offending arm like a twig. I almost threw up when the sick sound of the break met the visual grossness of a hand free floating in its wrist skin. Spencer returned to the exact same leaning against the wall position he was in just prior, looking down as Jay M. turned ghost white, threw up and collapsed in agony on the floor at his feet.

No expression.

No change of demeanor.

No effort at all.

God HAD HEARD MY PRAYERS and responded with a glorious miracle just for me!

Finding a Karate Expert in a High School Hallway… WOW!

Welcome to KARATE.

More on Sensei Spencer later in TEACHERS.

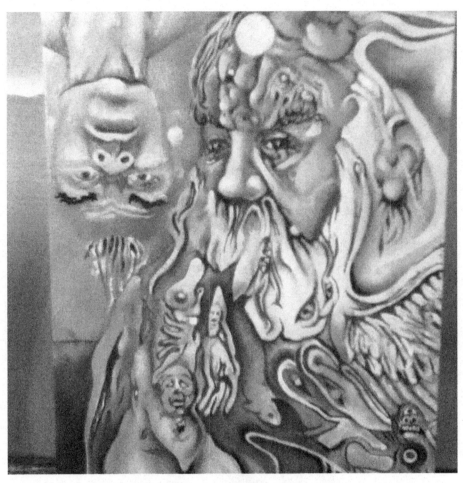

KARATE, AS WE ALL KNOW, CAN MEAN MANY THINGS: EMPTY HAND, HAND OF CHINA, ART OF FIGHTING WITHOUT WEAPONS ETC. AT ITS VERY CORE, KARATE MEANS "ONE WHO CAN SHEATH THE SWORD". THIS IS BEST AS HISTORY HAS SHOWN THAT "HE WHO LIVES BY THE SWORD SHALL DIE BY THE SWORD."

"HAMMERS OF THOR" SIFU JASON SCOTT AND "HANNIBAL" SKOIRCHET DURING A STREET DEMONSTRATION IN BROOKFIELD. THE BRICKS ARE READY AS WELL.

NO RISK.

NO GLORY.

MASTER VIC MEZERA AND SENSEI BARB MILLER DURING PWOK STREET DEMO AT 4TH OF JULY PARADE ON SIZZLING HOT ASPHALT IN BROOKFIELD 2006.

IN THE BACK OF THE "WAR TROLLEY" WE HAD TWO BLACK BELTS CONSTANTLY HARD SPARRING THE ENTIRE LENGTH OF THE PARADE ROUTE. SOME WERE TOSSED FROM THE WAGON BY JUDO THROWS ONTO THE HOT STREET. PWOK WON 1ST PLACE FOR "BEST IN PARADE" DEMONSTRATION. MY SON NICO HAS THE ESCRIMA STICKS WALKING TO THE PICTURE'S LEFT.

CHAPTER FOURTEEN

The Importance of: DEMONSTRATIONS.

Martial Arts demonstrations are an excellent way to show skill, inspire others and have some fun. If you are doing demonstrations as a way to build your student enrollment, you might as well spend the time at a local carnival, pitching undersized rings at oil-laden, angle-altered bottles. Don't get me wrong, I mean come on, with all the martial skills and mystical ties to The Ancients, of course I can "chi" a ring onto a bottle neck. But then again, who hasn't spent $30 in singles to try and win that small, 75 cent, stuffed tiger?

The first demonstrations that I remember was as a child in movie theaters and various gymnasiums as part of that venue's promotion or a school sponsored event. I mentioned these life altering experiences, courtesy of a Marine father, who knew of my heavy interest in the martial arts. But even after witnessing these tremendous displays of focus and power that resonate with me to this day, I did not leave those demonstrations and immediately ask to join a local Karate School. Now, if someone who has a childhood dream of becoming a Karate Master doesn't join a martial arts school after a demonstration, most likely neither will you.

I didn't always know this. I was a huge proponent of demonstrations throughout my 35+ years in the Arts from Beginner (Kyu Ranks) to Serious Student (Black Belt) to Advanced Master Instructor (Shihan). SHOWING and SHARING was what it was all about. When you witness the speed, power and grace of a skilled martial artist, it seemed logical that others would want to do the same. WRONG. Most folks either are afraid of the martial arts or think they are a joke. This is due in part, to what I like to call the "Partial Arts" schools interested only in profit that turn out pathetic, ill-trained charlatans as Black Belts. You would probably recognize them by the huge, out of shape bar room show offs with overly aggressive tee-shirts or some skinny ass 20 year old 'master" with the gold Karate jewelry. There are other irritating indicators that they are partial artists… like everything they say or do.

Usually it's the guy with the biggest mouth whose bragging of his martial exploits, shortly before he shuts up via a Bubba-delivered beer bottle to the head. Thank you Bubba. These basically unskilled asses are the ones who got their Black Belt from an online video exchange or the local Black Belt Mill (BBM) sandwiched between the Kinko's and KFC in the strip mall. Now there's nothing wrong with having a dojo in a strip mall, but avoid the ones with the GUARANTEED A BLACK BELT sign in window. Life has no guarantees and neither do the martial arts. There are no short cuts to mastery. Especially if promised so for a hefty price. It is ok to wear martial arts shirts as long as you are friendly, approachable and of course, capable of backing up in a variety of ways whatever your shirt says. In other words, don't wear a shirt that says something stupid or challenging that you can't back up.

Ok. Now that I got that off my chest…hmmm, not yet. Do you know how many times that I have been at a gym working out only to hear some weightlifters or body builders say that they kicked some Black Belt's ass in this situation or that? It makes my neck hair stand on end as thoughts of Mexican cantina vampire slaughter in "Dusk til Dawn" race through my mind. I wanted to put down the measly 175 lbs weight I had been working with, pick up the short bar of an unadorned dumbbell and "explain" Reality to them. Then again, the thoughts of jail and the near daily use of the Arts for sphincter protection intrude. I think its probably better relax before Big Otis says it to me in prison. Ouch.

For those that fear the martial arts its that they mostly don't understand what's going on. The Arts are not about intimidation. Their focus is respect, discipline, self discipline and unity of a clear, calm mind with a strong, healthy body. By and large, real practitioners of the Arts do not act like jerks. Let me restate that. They do not act like jerks in relation to anything to do with their skills or ability to rearrange your body parts in non-functioning ways. I mean, many a Karate Master who had a bit to much bubbly might act like a goofball, but rarely if ever does the subject of martial prowess surface or any threat thereof. Real martial artists are a blast to be around. Being relaxed, friendly and quite deadly allows for genuine conversation and sociability with all types of people. Below is a gathering of Grandmasters, Masters and Black Belts having fun.

TALK ABOUT A BAD ASS TABLE. MOVING BACK: WORLD CHAMPION MASTER BOB SCHIRMER, CHICAGO CHALLENGE MMA CHAMPION AND CARLSON GRACIE BLACK BELT JEFF NEAL, MASTER SEAN BAKER. HANSHI SHORTY MILLS AND ME IN THE VERY BACK. ALL THE OTHERS ARE AT LEAST BLACK BELT LEVEL WITH MOST BEING MUCH HIGHER RANK THAN THAT.

Now, I know what you are thinking. From all you've read and seen and heard about Karate masters is that they don't drink. Some do. Some don't. It's their choice. But be wary of attending a dojo where the instructor regularly wreaks of booze. I really haven't noticed an epidemic of "Johnny Walker Black Label" Black Belts to think it an issue. For all we know, the teacher could have just won a huge money sweepstakes and was showered with champagne before he raced to teach class.

I, like many people, enjoy and celebrate Life and the occasional drinking conversation of other Warriors. But as far as a personal preference toward anyone who wants me to stand still while they demo a technique like "Monkey Steals Peach" where he kicks the crap out of the front of your body and then spins you around to start on backside strikes ending with a full on, grasp and twist, tendon and muscle ripping groin detachment...I prefer he or she be sober.

A new student who had joined the Kenpo School a few months earlier once said to me "Sensei...my friend says Karate masters don't drink and if you do then you can't really be a master!" My first reaction was to come back sharply with "First of all, I don't trust people who don't drink!" But after looking at the genuine concern on his face, it irked me that all the new Death & Destruction, Ability, Confidence and Power he gained over the last few months could so easily be unraveled by a buddy's comment and the idea that he was somehow being misled.

Was it true that he was the victim of Kung Fu shenanigans perpetrated while at the same time he learned to throw a 220 lbs wrestler through the dojo wall and into the adjoining office? Is it not possible that one could learn to fight under the supposedly drunken tutelage of Rum Barrel Billy? Anyway, after the question visited various compartments of my mind, I rejected the idea to rip his ear off as a gift to his friend while explaining in non-slurred English that that is the result of a Southern Style Eagle Claw strike and not the wistful musings of a Drunken Master.

"No David, that is not true. Do you know how many kung fu styles got from China to Japan? Some drunken Japanese Karate masters/fishermen got so wasted on sake that they would pass out off Okinawa and wake up off the coast of China. Going ashore they might stay months maybe years learning local styles and testing their fighting skills against the local Chinese methods. If they survived, sobered up, and made enough money, they eventually made their way back to Japan to head shaking but relieved family members. These masters also brought new styles of Kung Fu to Japan. Kenpo is the Japanese word for the Chinese art called Chuan Fa created at the Shaolin Temple. In fact, our dojo patch symbol is based on two crossed swords, one Chinese and one Japanese paying tribute to the combined cultures that created the powerful Art of Kenpo."

"Or if that doesn't convince your friend of what is taught here, just invite him to one free PRIVATE lesson with me or any of the Black Belts of his choosing for a first hand, yet mild ass beating. And to assure that he doesn't feel he is becoming an "enabler" to drinking masters, we won't even charge him for the introductory lesson!" David smiled and said thanks for taking the time to explain. He was now hoping his buddy would request further clarification, but never heard about that subject from him again.

Back to demonstrations. They can be great, average, awful or insignificant. And while increasing student enrollment is minimal, they have provided for some interesting experiences. They can definitely provide lessons that every martial artist should know. I'll share a few of the more memorable with you.

Back on the East Coast in the early 1980's I trained at Martial Posture Studio of Kenpo Karate/Modern Arnis in downtown Philadelphia near the Liberty Bell. My Teacher, Tom Updegrove THEN a SIXTH DAN in Kenpo was One Deadly Dude. (ODD) He was amazing in both teaching and demonstrating techniques of Ed Parker's American Kenpo, but also added Remi Presas' Philippine Stick Fighting (Modern Arnis) into one bad ass martial posture. Simply put he was awesome. Tom (he did not believe in titles and everyone addressed each other by first name) also taught me the importance of SHARING Kenpo knowledge properly in a Teacher-Student setting. We all feared being his "attacker" (Uki) as he rained laser fast, controlled but painful strikes so perfect to varied body targets, that you felt like you had been tossed through a bee farm and were tumbling across various sized hives. With each ensuing sting depending on the size of each hive. In other words, you "attacked" Tom and in less than a second had been hit so many times, in so many places, that you didn't know whether to grab the most painful or cry for Mommy. I often did both.

In fact, to this day while SHARING Kenpo knowledge in class, I pick the biggest, strongest and toughest of the attending students of higher rank (Brown/Green Belts) and do the same. It is essential that the students watching see in real time the power and speed of Kenpo and its devastating effect on another human. They can tell by the grotesque winces and fearful facial expressions of the Uki. (training partner/attacker) Only in this way, can students truly begin to understand the nasty nature of fighting and even more so, the harsh reality of attacking a well trained fighter. It can be the equivalent of walking face first into a spinning helicopter rotor or jumping headlong in front of a farming thrasher. Got the visual?

So back in the day, Martial Posture Studio was to perform a demonstration at SUPER SUNDAY, a huge city wide celebration in the middle of Philly. I remember walking toward this HUGE raised stage in the very center of the event. No hiding here. Like they say, you can see if someone can dance when they get out on the floor.

SUPER SUNDAY IN CENTRE CITY PHILADELPHIA. THIS IS AN EARLY PICTURE TAKEN FROM THE STEPS OF THE ART MUSEUM. LATER THE STREETS WERE JAM PACKED.

My pubescent Kenpo was not good enough to make the first team so that part I got to watch. But I was a real Black Belt in Karate Do and was tasked with a solo demonstration of the Okinawan farm implement turned weapon-the nunchuku.

Since most readers are familiar with" nunchucks" I will only recommend that as you learn the hard way from training with this painful, self abusive weapon, please make sure that the whirling, high velocity striking pieces are secured with chain not rope. I mention this because during our Studio's last minute demo practice, Tom sees my routine and walks over. "Not bad" he said and asked if they were old nunchucks and I said they were my first pair and yes very used. He mentioned that there were several sets of new ones on the wall and I was welcome to use them for the demo. I said thanks, but I was "used to" the ones I had and didn't want to change them at the last minute. He nodded slightly and as he walked away, I heard him clearly say to "watch the frayed rope".

SHOWTIME.

Super Sunday. The party of the year in Philly and we are at the epicenter.

After watching Tom and his demo team blow away the crowd with a blistering display of the power, beauty and grace of Kenpo Karate, it was my turn. Still being a Kenpo toddler, I knew what The Who must have felt like as they took the stage following a new warm up band called "The Jimi Hendrix Experience". There is no way to eclipse "perfection" but I was game. "GO AHEAD, COMPETE WITH THE IMMORTALS!" was my mantra. Still is. The solo routine started off well enough. I was well-trained and knew exactly the movements that I was about to perform. Even standing alone on a huge, raised stage in front of way to many people, I was a Warrior and had a job to do.

My mind cleared as I entered a state of Mushin (Focus the Mind) and Kime (Let the Mind Flow) and probably a few other intense Eastern philosophical concepts learned about in all the martial arts books that I was reading at the time. Reality and Illusion took control at the same time. I was not yet a Kenpo Black Belt but I was a Martial Artist. My body exploded into action with unconscious yet precise firing of the correct synapses in my brain sent to waiting, well trained limbs via a adrenaline charged body and a maelstrom of pent up fury. Not anger, but a feeling that The Ancients had done this type of activity in the mountains of China or India 2,000 years ago and their power reigned through me across time. ELECTRIFYING!

I was an Armed Warrior with his weapon in full function and unstoppable! No one was going to take MY MOMENT of Martial Glory. Not now. Moving across the stage with precision and internal tempest, it was near the middle of the stage with about 30 seconds left to enjoy, when it happened... SNAP!

CRACK!

SWOOOOOOOSH!

Zzzzzzzzzzzzzzzzzzzzzzzzzzzzzzzzzzzz...

PHOTO WAS SNAPPED JUST BEFORE THE NUNCHUCKU ROPE BROKE ALMOST HITTING A WATCHING NUN IN THE FACE. NEBRASKA FAN ON LEFT WITH BIG "N" TEE SHIRT.

As I brought the speeding nunchuku down from my right shoulder to right thigh, I bent over at the waist in simulation of avoiding a sword decapitation strike. It was then, as I was already looking through my outstretched legs, that a different impulse was sent back to my flowing brain through the same neural pathways that so far had been sending signals of proper movement. As the weapon hit the exact spot on my thigh that it had hit 10,000 times before, I noticed that there was a weight shift. Not in my body posture, but in the fact that the rope had broken, sending a speeding piece of solid oak directly targeting the awaiting face of an unsuspecting nun. Nun-chuku? I'm talking a fully adorned "Flying Nun" 70's TV version with glasses on and my tickets to Hell in her purse. While standing there bent over like a prison inmate at Attica, Alcatraz or any proper US "Penal" institution, time just froze. What a moment earlier was an unending tie to The Ancients, was now a nightmare as they probably saw what was happening and pulled that 2000 year old time chord attached to my soul. No use dragging them down with me as I was about to FUBAR. (F'd Up Beyond All Repair)

The projectile was speeding directly toward her face and all I could do is watch. Never mind think about the conversation with Tom about the frayed rope an hour earlier. I might become his permanent Uki back at Martial Posture. Awaiting impact, I watched the nun stand unflinchingly as the wood approached. In one of the greatest acts of defying the laws of physics that I had ever seen or maybe was just witnessing the true power of God, the 12" missile simply changed direction a foot from her face and sailed by to land some 40 feet away harmlessly on the ground. To this day, the other lasting memory of that day was this huge guy with a Nebraska Football tee shirt on who made eye contact with me, looked at the still unfazed nun and at the half of my deadly weapon that exited stage right. The look said that was close. The feeling was man I screwed up and someone almost got hurt. Eehhhhhh.

So, martial arts demonstrations can be DANGEROUS TO OTHERS.

Heritage Fest. Downers Grove, IL sometime in the 80's and I was training in a new Kenpo

School under the expert instruction of Master Bob Wainwright, one of the strictest instructors

that I had ever trained with.. I'm talking old school demands for technical perfection. I owe so

much to this man for his friendship and patience over the years that the debt is unpayable.

The Japanese use the terms "On" and "Giri" which translates roughly to an unpayable debt (On)

and the impossible attempts to repay that debt. (Giri) As I ask my students "How much is your

life worth to you? How can you calculate the price of what I teach you?"

YOU CAN NOT PAY ME ENOUGH for what I will show you. You CAN honor your Giri by

coming to class regularly, being a good student and practicing in a way that brings Honor to

You, Your Art and Your School." Master Wainwright allowed me to learn his High Art while

letting me teach my barbaric brand of Karate Do//Wrestling/ Kenpo mixture to his students,

which helped me grow. We became great friends and started the "Way of Kenpo" Martial Arts

System as a way to avoid the politics and bad blood between Kenpo Schools. Everyone was

"The Best" or "The Most Pure" we couldn't stand it and so broke away. After many years

together, while thanking Master Wainwright for teaching me his awesome Tracy System-based

Kenpo, he said "I taught you Kenpo. You showed me its color." Cool stuff.

More about Master Bob Wainwright later in the Chapter on TEACHERS.

At the Heritage Fest, they block off the "small" (compared to Philly) area and have the

usual fanfare of food, entertainment and beer. We were asked to do demonstrations on

the main stage and those went off without incident. Nice to know that I could do my Art

on stage and not endanger clergy or any onlookers. While handing out Downers Grove

Karate and Fitness Center brochures over walks a good looking, in shape African-American gentleman up to our booth. Being from the East Coast, I did not recognize him as World Karate Champion, Larry Tankson. (Now a Grandmaster of the 9th Dan) We became good friends and are still in touch today. As Master Tankson arrives at the counter of our covered booth, I start into a salesman's pitch about the martial arts, Kenpo and the need for self defense "especially in the 'ghetto' were everyone attacks you".

He listened patiently with a smile that was so large that he looked like a "Pac Man" figure with perfect teeth. He didn't interrupt me while going down the list on the brochure as he nodded and smiled. It was then that Master Wainwright noticed my flapping gums trying to sell "Karate lessons" to a World Champion Fighter. He rushed over, pulled the paper from my hand, and apologized to the visiting Master. He then formally introduced us and I was so shocked at my ghetto comments. He just kept smiling that unforgettable smile and said "Nice to meet you Sensei Bill." I replied "It's my pleasure Sir." HE TOOK THE FLYER ANYWAY and walked away. Class act.

So, martial arts demonstrations can be EMBARRASSING.

The Heritage Fest is a weekend affair and the second day was unusually hot and humid. The main stage demo went off without a hitch again. Not surprising. Like I said Master Bob ran a tight ship and flawed technique was not accepted. Probably why our Way of Kenpo Schools take a dedicated, regular class-attending student between 7-10 years to achieve a Black Belt. NO Guarantees here. NO 1 year Black Belts for $2500 up front. Not here. Master Bob had many years of low school income, his only job, by making sure we were damn good by Black Belt. Many students just couldn't hack the demands.

MASTER BOB WAINWRIGHT CENTER LEFT AND TAKING A SHOT TO THE RIGHT AT HERITAGE FEST DURING A HOT SUMMER BACK IN THE DAY. GREAT MEMORIES.

So being hot that day, we did smaller, shorter demonstrations in front of our booth in a roped off 7x7 square from our booth to the curb. Since we were in the middle of a street, it didn't take long to notice that asphalt in deep summer is not conducive to barefooted activities at all. Being a Warrior and the vocal proponent of hourly demos and the tender of the little placard with the moveable plastic time hands that say "Next Demo at 2:00." I was out there every hour, feet a blaz'n for a quick, visually powerful routine with my partner Sensei Mike Olish. Sensei was about my size 5'7" but thinner and way faster. We regularly rendezvoused at the booth on the hour to do our well rehearsed demonstration.

SIGNING SOME BROKEN BOARDS FOR A FEW KIDS AFTER THE DEMO. IF THEY HAD WAITED UNTIL THE 7 PM SHOW I COULD HAVE SIGNED MY BROKEN TEETH.

SENSEI MIKE OLISH TO THE LEFT DURNG OUR HOURLY DEMOS AT HERITAGE FEST IN DOWNERS GROVE, IL. THIS WAS BEFORE A POORLY TIMED BEER GARDEN VISIT, A POWERFUL KICK TO MY TEETH AND SUBSEQUENT TRIP TO THE DENTIST.

The show consisted of a variety of attack-defense scenarios where one of us was the bad guy. Same attacks. Same defenses. Same moves. Same polite applause. Pass out flyers before the crowd dissipated. Yep. We did maybe 6 straight hourly demos. I also did one of my first public displays of concrete patio block breaking (Tameshiwari) Currently with chipped, floating bone fragments from smashing hard things with my elbows, I have long since retired from the Art of Tameshiwari, but will touch on a few entertaining stories accrued along The Way in a bit.

Best advice from a friend who can't lean his elbows on a bar or kitchen table "Don't hit anything that doesn't say ouch." That is my common response to questions about breaking inanimate objects with flesh and bone alone. A reminder…your hands are not swords or clubs. They are hands that hold your child or a glass of wine. Your legs are not 2x4s. They are legs connected to feet that take you around. I guess the damage to my busted up body was the martial way to mind

128

my manners and keep elbows off the table while eating. Once asked Master Tom Updegrove of Martial Posture (Sorry Tom, It's still hard to call you by your first name to this day) what he thought about "Iron Palm Training" where you toughen your hands through pounding and spading them into increasingly dense materials to callous the skin, deaden the nerves, strengthen the bones and harden the mind. He looked at me in the same way years earlier regarding the frayed nunchucku rope and said plainly "It's fine. As long as you don't care that you won't be able tell the difference between the feel of velvet and concrete when you are older."

No large, hot sand urns for me.

After the 6 straight hourly demos at our booth with Sensei Mike, I was thirsty and asked if he wanted to go to the beer garden for a much needed respite. He mentioned that we have another demo to do at 7 pm, the last of the day. Something about the way he said it made me pause, but the flurry of thirst-quenching beer commercials danced in my brain. "I'm heading over for a beer and I'll be back by the 7 pm final demo." Ok he said.

So, like a college student onward to "The Source of All Truth" the beer tap. I kept track of time as beer after freezing cold beer tossed merrily down a parched gullet. I never count beers just time. So by 6:50 pm I had had my fill and moved with buzzed purpose to the final demo. Maybe I'll try to break 2 or 3 slabs of concrete to finish the festival. For some reason it took me 10 minutes to find the booth when the trek over took about 3 minutes. WARNING! DANGER! CAUTION! flashed neon in my mind. Ah…just fleeting thoughts as its 7 pm sharp when I finally get to the roped off demo area at the booth. Sensei Mike is just finishing a wicked cool staff set just like we had rehearsed. NO PROBLEM. Self defense techniques next. I'd light them up, break a couple of bricks and go home.

In the middle of the demo we used a portion of the Kenpo technique CRANE LEAP, where you are shaking hands with a dickhead that is squeezing your hand hard and won't let go. Pretty cool. You grab the NATURAL HANDLE of his elbow so he can't retract the hand. Still holding the tough guy hand shake, you step off and forward to his side, pulling both arm and wrist back behind you as you deliver a "Nice to meet you too!" roundhouse knee to his unprotected core. Then, we apply a plethora of strikes that makes overkill like saying a Navy SEAL "is in shape".

So the Crane Leap was fine and the crowd in the packed area let out an "OOOOOOOO!" as his controlled knee hits me midsection. I fake damage and am leaning over holding my stomach in imaginary pain as he finishes with a short, tight OUTSIDE CRESCENT KICK that nips me in the back of the head and he finishes with a perfectly controlled shin to my face where I fall down "unconscious".

Oops forgot something.

After the Crescent Kick to the head I am to lean over and then wait for his controlled kick to stop millimeters from my face. Well, courtesy of beer brain, I am moving down fast as his shin is coming up hard. He would have stopped exactly where he always had, but I insisted in over dramatizing the effect of the stomach-head combo by crashing through "Zero Barrier" at terminal speed, leading with my once-pretty face. As his very sharp and angular shin played kick the can in my puss, I felt various facial features becoming distorted. Probably the result of being hit in the chops with what felt like a full uppercut swing of a sharpened baseball bat. It turns out that my face is not as well trained as the rest of me.

In reality, perhaps moving my head backwards once contact was made, then maybe the face wouldn't have exploded. But being a disciplined demo team member, and an idiot, I stayed put. If I had followed the kick and went the same energy direction as it did, it might have been better. But pretty sure that the ensuing rooster tail of blood spraying the crowd might negatively affect any potential students. After all, who wants to take a blood-stained flyer home anyway?

So I stay bent over and take the full force feeling both lips split from side to side as my exposed teeth took the energy wave. As Sensei Mike felt the unexpected contact, he instinctively turned off the juice. A bit late since my beer influenced distance judgment was indeed impaired. When you are talking martial arts CONTROL, you are talking in terms of millimeters and tens of thousands of a second. Not any place to screw up. By the time he lowered the kick back to the ground the damage was done. Now comes Damage Control. If I stood up and all my teeth fell out, it would definitely impact the student recruitment effort. We still had to bow to each other and then to the audience followed with flyer pass out. That was of course if I didn't pass out first.

The biggest problem was being in a mild state of shock while still bent over. My mind raced as the pain interrupted any sense of "unconscious effort" and regular human thoughts of ambulances, surgery and possible acting roles in Scar Face 3 returned. Slowly rising up as streams of deep red blood flowed to a growing pool below. Now it's well known that the head bleeds easily due to capillaries close to the surface, but my blood-letting looked more like I was shot. Rising, I felt three of my front teeth moving to and fro as I tried to breathe through my mouth since nostril function was nil. It didn't help that my tongue was cut and swollen delaying much needed air by partially obstructing my windpipe. Finally standing up straight and wiping bits of enamel, skin and blood from the remnants of face, I smiled (hoping no teeth would fall out) and said "Welcome to Kenpo Karate!" I had hoped that my cool demeanor might make them think it was theatrical exploding ketchup packets or something. Wide-eyed people quickly gathered their young and moved away. Some rapidly. Some slowly. No one took a flyer. I healed. Although the eventual loss of those same three front teeth is associated with that demonstration. Beer garden. Stupid me. It was a painful combination.

So, martial arts demonstrations can be DANGEROUS TO YOU.

The world renowned FERMILAB is a major research center in pursuit of the unseen. Atom smashing, quarks, super colliders and the search for the "God Particle" whose discovery would unlock the mysteries of the Universe, and we were asked to do a demo. Now why some of the most brilliant men and women on the planet wanted to see a barbaric demonstration was the question I had when saying "Of course" to their request. The answer was simple. They didn't.

In what can only be described as a "clash of cultures" our second public demo of the newly formed POWELL'S WAY OF KENPO (PWOK) Martial Arts School in Old Town Chicago was a disaster from the get go. Turns out that we were called up because FERMILAB wanted to celebrate the Chinese New Year during four consecutive half hour lunch periods. Barely time to eat. Never mind watch a demonstration of "physical brutality" by black pajama-ed goofballs. If you sense any hostility on my part, it's because we practiced very hard to do a nice thing FOR FREE and the 500 folks in each lunch period couldn't care less.

In addition, while getting dressed in the cafeteria kitchen, I was hopping on one leg to put my bottoms on. In a masterful attempt to avoid a threatening piece of uncooked mostaccioli on the floor, I backed into a hot stove with my ass flesh and burned my buttocks pretty good. Ouch that hurt. With the movements of my part in the demo which no one was watching, the rubbing of the hard cotton material on the now blistered, half dollar sized burn on my backside was starting to irritate me. We finished to polite applause from maybe 15 people at the tables nearest us. They probably applauded that we were done. We were. We got dressed ASAP and got out of there. I had to sit on my right butt check the whole ride home.

So, martial arts demonstrations can be A PAIN IN THE ASS.

Just about everyone enjoys roller coasters, so we jumped at the chance to perform a demonstration at Six Flags Great America in Gurnee, Illinois. It was "Martial Arts Day" at the park and tickets were discounted for card carrying martial artists. I always wondered how many Oriental folks got the discount without having to show any martial ID. Anyway, it was a beautiful sunny day and very, very hot. PWOK's Demo Team, now experienced after several successful post-FERMILAB demonstrations, was ready.

Our slot in the program was sandwiched between a Christian Tae Kwon Do Club that moved well enough, but when they were emphasizing their powerful technique with a "Spirit Yell" they screamed "Christ!" or "Jesus!" instead of the usual "KiYa!" and an odd demo of some Combatives Dojo where a Brown Belt smashed his Teacher in the face with a sledge hammer after missing the huge cinderblock placed of his chest while lying prone. Nothing wrong with either I guess.

Both demos just caught me by surprise.

PWOK then rocked the crowd with fast paced, heavy drums and shredding guitars rock music blaring LOUD as we ripped through vicious sets of attack-defense Kenpo Karate. But as one of my great Tai Chi Chuan teachers, Master Kimball Paul would say after executing a crippling technique "But we do it how?" And the students would reply "In a Loving and Caring Way!" The crowd was into it. The music, the fury, the speed, the skill were all in harmony. That energy feeds off its sources and comes back tenfold. I still get goose bumps when thinking of the members of that demo team that day.

THIS AMAZING GROUP OF WARRIORS GAVE ALL...OF THEIR FOOTSKIN TO THE BURNING ASPHALT SCALDING KENPO DEMONSTRATION AT SIX FLAGS, GREAT AMERICA. SEMPAI NICK, WHO ACTUALLY SHOULD HAVE BEEN TAKEN TO A BURN UNIT, IS FAR RIGHT WITH SIFU DOUG E. DOUG JUST BELOW NICK'S SCALDED AND SCRAPED HEAD.

As mentioned, the day was very hot and we usually do demonstrations barefoot. Even adding a light sneaker dulls the sharpness of movement, Ok for street defense where firm footing neutralizes lost quickness of mobility. And once a Kenpo Warrior goes into Self Defense Auto Mode (SDAM) we don't go anywhere as WE TAKE THE FIGHT TO THE ENEMY. No need for sneakers to run way.

As my Grandmaster, Hanshi Shorty Mills says "I don't teach track!"

So, after seeing the Tae Kwon Do Club and their cute little 3 stripe "Combat slippers" I rejected the idea to put on any footwear.

I like analogies since they paint a picture in the mind that strengthens the point. If you have read this far, you already know this, When it was our turn to go, I stepped onto the unshaded asphalt of our demo area for the first time and heard the bottom of my foot skin sizzle off before the pain registered. It sounded like bacon when first laid into a hot skillet. After tightening the mind and ignoring the pain, my well trained students followed. I hoped they used my tracks of foot skin as a way to gain relief, but they moved in formation to their respective positions. A few of the newer students winced a bit, but after looking at the dead, wooden doll-like faces of the higher ranked Kenpo Warriors, they did the same.

At PWOK, as in the military "You Don't Have To Like It. You Just Have To Do It." and "Its Only Pain. Ignore It!" PWOK can be described as a military organization in civilian clothing. Now there is a BIG difference between "simple pain" where you know the cause and can ignore it and "unknown pain" where you don't know the cause. If you awaken in the middle of the night to chest pains, that pain you do not ignore.

Look, martial arts hurt to learn. You will get punched, kicked, bruised, bashed, banged, jolted, slammed and bloodied if you train long enough to get any good. Eventually, you'll find that "pain don't hurt." Now injury is different from being hurt. You can still train if you are hurt. Being hurt is temporary like a bruised rib or a twisted ankle. Injury is excessive damage to a body system that needs repair or time to heal. Injuries like torn ACL knee ligaments or a broken arm need medical attention. At PWOK, you train when hurt, you watch when injured. Regardless of hurt or injured you are still expected to attend class.

The crowd was stunned as several front row members put their hands down to feel the temperature of the tar. No one was unimpressed with our self discipline as we stood there waiting for the song that would trigger our action. With heat vapors rising in between each PWOK member, it seemed an eternity until the sound man got with the program. Not sure if the movement from standing still to action did anything for the foot skin burns, but at least our minds were now in FULL FOCUS to share our Art with the

BURNT OFF FOOTSKIN IN THE CAUSE OF KENPO GLORY MEANS NOTHING.

crowd. As different segments were performed by several different groups of students, the ones that were done or awaiting their turn looked at me with eyes that said "Sir, May we please move into the shade?" With a nod that said yes, THEY WALKED slowly and deliberately onto the cooler asphalt of the shade. They were DISCIPLINED folks for sure.

Toward the end of the demo, we were showing the importance of falling to the ground properly. We had brought with us a standard blue gym mat for this purpose. At the right time, my Uki, Sempai (Senior Student) Nick Black, dragged the mat over and wanted to say something, but I was not receptive since the segment music was just starting. Did figure out what he wanted after he launches a pre-rehearsed right stepping right punch. I execute a simple over the shoulder Judo throw with him going heels over head and onto the mat. Now Sempai is a big guy and crowds love to see the lil guy throw a bigger guy. So I did. As Sempai Nick hit the mat, his eyes widened so far that I thought they might really pop out. Of course only I could see his face, as the rest of his massive body continued to cook on the superheated mat that I found to be much hotter than the asphalt! In a return to attack position as rapid a recovery to standing as I have ever seen, like flipping a waffle on a griddle he seemed to defy physics as he went from prone to upright in one movement bereft of hands or feet.

As I watched has FBI-like forensic chalk outline on the mat evaporate in the heat, crispy Sempai immediately moves close and finally got his message across. The mat was twice as hot as the asphalt. After a slight, unnoticeable pause, we simply moved the last part of our throwing demo back to the skin-stained tar area. Sempai Nick was tossed repeatedly using a variety of throws until he was well done. And so were we. Very proud of our effort we spent rest of the day on rides and watching shows.

A great time was had by all.

While walking through the theme park, we notice Sempai Nick Black sitting in a beer garden taking in the sights. I asked him if he wanted to go on some roller coasters with us. He looked at me with a stone face, adorned with burns, cuts, scrapes and abrasions on his head, face, elbows, arms and body which he carried as Badges of Honor. He was bruised, baked and burned from many hard slams to the scalding hot ground during the demo. After a moment, he simply said "No thank you Sir. Roller coasters scare me." Chuckling while walking away the irony made me laugh. The students laughed too.

So, martial arts demonstrations can BE FUN.

The final account on demonstrations was perhaps the most gripping. Being from the East Coast, I was unaware that in the late 60's and early '70's Chicago was in the throes of real life "Dojo Wars". We're talking right out of the movies, warning scroll messages left on doors "Close Your School Now or Die" type stuff. Student "poaching" was a hot issue.

In fact, people were killed, hurt and others went to prison. Not sure if threatened "regulation" by authorities ensued or not, but something ended the conflicts and each school, system and style retreated to their own places to train in their particular Art. Interaction between the martial arts systems ended. Not knowing what I had walked into when I got to Chicago, I soon learned that I was "targeted" for promoting the concept of sharing the Arts with everyone and learning the different styles from other schools. We called them "Shiai". (Warrior Gatherings) Apparently this was unacceptable to studios that had come out of the dojo wars with a "never the twain shall meet" isolationist philosophy. The tension caused by my involvement in reintegrating many of the various martial arts schools in was heightened when I hosted the SHAOLIN MONKS OF CHINA at my tiny School in downtown Chicago.

It basically ended when many, many area Grandmasters, Masters and School Heads saw

POWELL'S WAY OF KENPO MARTIAL ARTS SCHOOL for the first time in a public

demonstration at Master Joe Gangi's KICKBOXING EXTRAVAGANZA 2.

POSSIBLE BROTHERS FROM DIFFERENT COUNTRIES, CULTURES AND PARENTS?

THE SHAOLIN MONKS VISITED MY TINY DOJO IN OLD TOWN CHICAGO IN 1998.

CHAPTER FIFTEEN

The Importance of: THE SHAOLIN MONKS OF CHINA.

In 1998, Powell's Way of Kenpo was contacted to be the training site of the legendary

Shaolin Monks of China as they prepared for a full US Tour that would start at the Arie

Crowne Theater, near O'Hare Airport. Their whereabouts were to be kept secret. Not really

sure why as I don't see them getting mugged even if they walked downtown in their orange

robes. Considered not only a National Treasure of the Peoples Republic of China, but the model

for every true martial artist as they are the epitome of discipline, self discipline and martial

prowess.

These are the guys who spend most of their lives in a monastery at the base of the mountains in Hunan province, China and tear bark off trees with Tiger Claws and do superhuman feats like hanging a huge heavy rock from their scrotum to increase internal power.

At PWOK, we have pictures of these Warrior-Priests doing the impossible with a wooden sign next to them that says "You Train How Hard?" I mean if an old monk can plow his field by pulling a thick rotating log with spikes and a rope tethered to His Tool, we certainly could knock out some more push ups.

The following chapter on the Shaolin Monks is taken in its entirety (with permission) from a manuscript by one of my students, Jennifer Harris, excerpted from her published work "HOW TO KILL IN A LOVING AND CARING WAY-Chronicles of the Happenings at Kenpo School and Crossroads Academy in Chicago, Circa 1997"
Jen wrote:

"Hold fast to the way of antiquity, In order to keep control the realms of today."
–Lao Tzu, Tao Te Ching

"I hate Valentine's Day, because usually I'm either seeing someone I don't like or no one at all and either way I end up feeling like I must be doing something wrong. This Valentine's Day, the Shaolin Monks came to our dojo. A day celebrating the heart and there were the monks, in their blood-orange robes, bowing to Sensei Billy. The greeting card guilt didn't have a chance.

I was so excited I woke up at six that morning and got ready for the day. Everyone was supposed to be at the Dojo by nine but I got there at eight. We wanted the Dojo to sparkle, so I started working. I put on my favorite CDs and sang along while I worked until everyone else started showing up. Then we all cleaned the place until it could have passed for a hospital.

Sensei invited 31 instructors from the area to come and watch the demonstration. It all came about because the monks were scheduled to perform in Chicago later that spring, and Sensei figured to help spread the word, he could invite area masters to a small scale demonstration and learning session. In turn, each master could promote the forthcoming event at their schools. It was a logical grassroots marketing plan, but shocking when we sat down and thought about it. I mean for me, it'd be like William Blake showing up at my door and saying, hey, let me teach you a little about poetry; just you and me.

Sensei and Kimball (Tai Chi Chuan Master) transformed into eleven year olds on their birthdays, staring at an enormous chocolate cake; big, wide eyes, gleaming. Actually, it was everyone. Even me. After all, the Monks are considered one of the Seven Treasures of China, and they were visiting our tiny dojo! Odd wasn't really the word. Neither was fate or bizarre or cataclysmic. And luck didn't seem right either, so maybe I'd have to call it fortune.

Whatever the word was, they arrive at quarter to eleven-fifteen minutes early. The Monks ranged from 78 years old to eight and a half. They had two teachers with them plus a translator. Their master, the 78 year old, walked in first, hands chest level palms together in prayer. He nodded and bowed to us as we bowed to him and the others. Earlier, Sensei had lined the chairs up in an L-shaped form around the dojo, all the masters from other schools seated around the room, and students from our school, my peers, sat cross-legged or hovered near the walls.

The place was packed.

The Monks came and sat down with their weapons. Since they were a little early, Sensei Billy wanted to wait to make sure everyone who was coming was there before they started, so he asked Kimball to demonstrate a sword form. Kimball is not what I-or probably anyone else-would call a shy person. But when Sensei asked him to perform in front of the Monks, Kimball was visibly taken aback. Billy grabbed his sword off the wall and handed it to Kimball. Kimball turned to the old master, who was seated in Sensei Billy's chair, and then bowed. Then he started his Tai Chi form. The sword moved like a part of him, cutting through the air. When Kimball plunged and transferred, you could see the sword vibrate with his chi. The older monk sat perfectly still, smiling the whole time. I thought the old man looked enchanted. Actually, what I thought was that he would start levitating at any moment, he looked so other worldly.

I ASKED MASTER KIMBALL TO DEMONSTRATE CHINESE SWORD FORM TO THE SHAOLIN MONKS OF CHINA. DO YOU KNOW THE STONES IT TOOK TO DO SO?

When Kimball finished, the Monks bowed to him and then clapped like we did. Then Sensei Billy started welcoming all the masters to the dojo. I realized it must have been a pretty strange experience for the monks. I mean, to them, they saw Billy speaking and heard; blah blah blah, clap clap clap, blah blah blah, clap clap clap. It was sort of funny.

When it was eleven o'clock the Monks took over. And do I mean took over; they mesmerized us. The first monk got up an fixed his robes, then he was quiet for a moment, focusing. Next thing I knew, he was throwing himself around the room like a human bouncing ball. It was unbelievable. He jumped three or four feet off the ground in a side kick and landed flat on his back, bounced back up in one swift movement, circling around, then another leap and fall. All the while, he was perfectly composed; his movements sharp and dagger-like.

He barely broke a sweat.

The next monk got up and walked to the center of the room. He took off his robe and started a meditation that looked like he was directing energy to specific parts of his body. When he finished that, he got up and tightened the belt around his waist, cinching it. A different monk got up holding a staff and walked over to the monk who had been meditating. The first monk extended his arms outward, parallel to the ground, and the second monk, who was holding the staff, took it and hit the first monk's upper left arm as hard as he could. The staff broke in two as if it were straw and all the monk did was blink. Then the second monk grabbed another staff and broke it over his right arm.

Again, the monk hardly flinched.

*INCREDIBLE FEATS OF SKILL, FOCUS, GRACE AND POWER ARE STANDARD FARE
WHEN WITNESSING THE NEAR SUPERNATURAL KUNG FU OF THE SHAOLIN MONKS.*

Another of the monks got up and held up a foot-long piece of two inch thick metal, taking

it around the room so the Black Belts could feel it. Once it was established that this was

a real piece of steel, the monk went over to the guy who had just been flogged and bowed

toward him, facing him straight on, the other monk bowed and left his head down.

The monk with the piece of steel brought it up over his head, and whacked the other

monk hard, right on his head. The piece of steel snapped right in two like a candy cane.

It gave me a headache just watching.

They took their seats and another monk came forward carrying one bundled up Chinese

Chain and Blade weapon in each hand. When he got to the center of the room, he bowed to us

and his master (the old man) and began. He threw the chains out into the air, holding tight to the

handles. The chains extended about 5 feet in length, but you hardly saw them at all. Instead

what you heard was the sound of them whirling around the room, a metallic swooshing. The

monk was circling around us, swirling them in high and low circles. Everyone in the front rows,

including me, crept backwards, concerned with being decapitated. Even the old monk leaned

way back in his seat, still grinning. The young monk was austere. As the chains whipped

around the humming tickled my ears. The monk flipped up and over himself, landing on his

back, letting the chains circle him, one up and one under his body. The motion never ceased. I

have never seen anything like it.

I was at once horrified and delighted.

Then the youngest of them came forward. He was shiney, like a new bright dime you'd

find somewhere unexpected. His kata, or form, was full of splits, falls, and high kicks.

At age eight, this small man was already more focused than most every adult I knew. As

he performed, he looked nothing like the child he was, but as soon as he stopped, his

toothy grin revealed his age.

THE YOUNGEST MONK WAS SO CUTE... IN A BABY BLACK MOMBA KINDA WAY.

Then the old monk came forward ad performed stretches. The interpreter told us he was 78, but he was able to stretch farther than me, and I'm fairly limber. The old monk had a sweet demeanor, well, they all did but I was quite taken with the old man. Every time I glanced at him, I found myself drifting.

As if I was looking at an ocean, not a man.

TAI CHI CHAUN MASTER KIMBALL PAUL AND THE ABBOTT OF SHAOLIN TEMPLE.
GRANDMASTER FRED DEGERBERG OF DEGERBERG ACADEMY IS TO THE LEFT.

What came next was fantastic but true. Had I not seen it with sixty other people to back

me up, I'm not sure I would have believed it. The same monk who had the staffs broken

over his arms, hopped up again and did the same meditation form he had done earlier,

once again tightened his belt at the end in some ceremonial gesture. While he was doing

this, a couple of other monks got up carrying long, dagger-headed spears. They stuck the

tips into wood, showing us that the metal tips were quite sharp. When the meditating

monk was finished his preparations, the dagger end of the spears were placed tip first

against his neck, right near his jugular, with the long, wooden bodies angling from the

ground. Then, in a flash, he moved forward, leaning way into the daggers up against the

monk's throat, balancing on the two bent poles, as another monk brought out a concrete

slab which he placed on the back of the leaning monk's head. Now I was thinking that

this guy is totally insane, but there in front of me was the most bizarre feat I'd ever

encountered. The monk who put the concrete slab on the other one's head, grabbed a

sledgehammer and proceeded to smack the concrete block that was on the monk's head, whose neck was being stabbed by very sharp daggers. A second later, he leapt backwards, letting the spears fall to the ground.

His neck was not even scratched.

While that was going on, I imagined an announcer saying, Please kids, don't try this at home. When they finished, Sensei Billy asked the translator if one of the monks would be willing to teach the Black Belts some sort of technique. One of the monks came forward and taught a series of offensive Kung Fu movements. All of the Black Belts lined up behind him as the monk went through the techniques several times.

THE SHAOLIN MONK THAT TAUGHT US TECHNIQUE GAVE ME A YELLOW BEADED BRACELET AS A GIFT. I SEPARATED THE BEADS AND MY BLACK BELTS WEAR THEM ON A LANYARD AS A NECKLACE- A SYMBOL OF THEIR CONNECTION TO SHAOLIN.

AMERICAN MASTERS LEARNING FROM THE SHAOLIN MONKS.

GTIAT Author's Note: The monk leading members of Powell's Way of Kenpo and other invited guests was photographed in two different pictures that ended up appearing ON THE FRONT PAGE of the CHICAGO SUN TIMES and the FRONT PAGE of the "Tempo Section" of the CHICAGO TRIBUNE newspapers. PWOK's "Street Cred' may have been rising, but so was the temperature of the "isolationist" masters that for one reason or another did not attend the event

Back to the last bit of Jen's well documented experience of the Shaolin Monks:

After the teaching was finished, there was a brief question and answer period. At one point, Kimball raised his hand and asked any of them if they had ever seen "Fa Ging" used. There's a legend that some masters are able, by the pure perfection of their chi gong, to send their chi out and hit an opponent without ever having to actually touch someone. When it was translated, the old man giggled. He nodded while he was chatting, as if he had indeed seen this, but the translator only said he had been thinking about it. But from his body movements, it seemed clear he'd seen such a thing. After the monks left everyone was dazed.

It's easy to write what I saw in specific terms, but there was something far more subtle to it. The undercurrent of the day was really what it was all about. And that is difficult to connote. At one point, a classmate of mine, smiled over at me and we nodded to each other in silent recognition. And that's what it was: a shared silence. Past the obvious language barriers, everyone in the room was working toward the same goal. The monks who demonstrated their skills train at least 5 hours per day, every day of the week. For years they've kept this schedule, and it was more than apparent. When they were still, they were perfectly still. Calm minds. Calm bodies. Everything sharp and focused. For me, they represented the living goal of a warrior." Thanks Jen for the clear writing that captures perfectly that amazing day in 1998. So, martial arts demonstrations can be MINDBLOWING.

SEARCH OUT TOPICS AND EXPERIENCES THAT YOU FIND MINDBLOWING. DIG 'EM. THEN LEARN WHY THEY FACINATE YOU AND MOVE ON TO THE NEXT ONE.

*AN OPEN DOOR POLICY ASSURES QUALITY CONTROL OF WHAT YOU CLAIM TO BE
TEACHING. THE DOWNTOWN CHICAGO SCHOOL HAD PLENTY OF VISITORS.*

CHAPTER SIXTEEN

The Importance of: AN OPEN DOOR POLICY. (ODP)

After the Shaolin Monks demonstration at PWOK, I received many calls of thanks and letters of appreciation for the invitation to witness the epitome of what we do from those that attended. Funny though, there was a spike in "wrong numbers" crank calls and unrecognizable messages left on my cell, which also served as The School's business line. Not thinking much of it at the time since I also had an" Open Door Policy" (ODP) where if you had something to say, I was available to have you say it to my face.

Looking back, it seems silly that anyone would try to scare or intimidate a KENPO WARRIOR with prank calls, but I guarantee you, and it probably occurred to them, it was a lot safer.

The mumblings and grumblings of the "univited" were starting to reach my ears more often and with increased intensity after the Shaolin demonstration. The final straw came from a conversation with Kimball after an intense training session in his powerful Occidental Tai Chi Chuan at his Crossroads Academy, then in Bridgeport near White Sox Park. We had finished working out, I hugged him and was about to leave, when he said "Billy, Be Careful. People are watching." It was in the clear, non-joking way he said it that struck me. Kimball doesn't say things that aren't funny. Even when serious, he makes it seem funny.

So I inquired further.

In a look that said he was betraying a confidence, he told me that one of the "univited" local experts had complained to him about the gathering of masters at my dojo for the Monks and that others felt the same. Sad Man continues to bend Kimball's ear with my lack of knowledge of the history of the Chicago martial arts scene and how things are done. I think my "East Coast training" was brought up negatively as well. I guess he didn't know that Kimball and I were very close friends when he said to Kimball that he was going to go up to Old Town and "teach me a lesson". Kimball responded, "If you ever say that to me again. I will bring you to him." Kimball knows me and my ODP.

That was it. I was starting to lose the "calm mind" as thoughts of reignited dojo wars and what was the need for all the hassle raced through my mind. I did not invite only 31 masters to the Shaolin Monks by picking the best, it's because they were the only ones I knew. If I had known any of the "univited", they would have, well, been invited. We needed a way to show Chicago what Powell's Way of Kenpo Martial Arts School was all about. Then I got THE CALL from Master Joe Gangi, of GANGI's KUNG FU SYSTEMS, regarding his upcoming KickBoxing Extravaganza 2 event.

I had met Master Gangi when I first opened PWOK on the third floor of a building at 1610 N. LaSalle in Old Town, Chicago. He was a well known, highly respected and highly ranked in Kung Fu. Master Gangi blew us away with his ferocious skills. Back to Master Gangi in a bit.

Let me tell you, having a martial arts school in the city is WAY different from owning and operating in the suburbs. I had all kinds of off the street "masters" of this Art or that, that would either want to "teach" their Art at my dojo for payment, or as a barter system so I could learn of their secret, deadly Art.

Yes, occasionally there were challenges. Therefore there was the need for an Open Door Policy.

Let's see.

There was the guy who appeared mysteriously at my door with such an offer. He came in quietly, paused and then sat down. I said hello and asked if I could help him. He responded curtly that it was he who could help me. Curious, I asked how so? He will teach me the real secret of fighting. I asked who he had trained under and he replied "God". After I realized he wasn't kidding, I asked if he could show me some of it without killing me. That's all I'd need is to mock a true Warrior of God and end up sitting there as a burnt crisp, the result of a lightening strike or something. So we walked from my office to the main dojo floor. He started to hum and twitch as he barked something from the Bible then leapt toward me in a both arms over head, grizzly bear like attack. I waited to see if he was really coming full on and he was. Amused, I cave in his sternum the result of a straightforward, simple, but well-delivered, earth-emanating, FRONT THRUST KICK from moi. He spit up some bile, spittle and maybe a bit of puke as he crumpled like a buck on one of those shotgun hunting arcade games.

After a few awkward moments of indecision on whether to be The Good Samaritan by helping him up and remembering that he did not make a direct challenge, he simply wanted to share his art with me. I shared mine with him. Finally, he arose and simply left. It's nice to share.

Then there was also a huge college wrestler that grappled for the NCAA Champion Iowa Hawkeyes, who hadn't yet been introduced to the benefits of adding Carlson Gracie Jiu Jitsu to his formidable mat skills. Being a wrestler myself, I was more than patient while showing him the dangers presented by some wrestling moves in facing arm-locking, heel hooking, strangling/choking techniques of Jiu Jitsu-trained fighter. After showing the techniques slowly and explaining them, I could tell that this was going to end in a challenge. He just didn't think that any of that stuff would work. And that was ok. So with little fanfare, I pulled him close from my GUARD and whispered into his ear "Wanna try it for real?" Felt kinda bad as his outstretched arm prepared to snap at the elbow as I locked it hard and painfully while he was working to "pin" me. The attack on his elbow not only caught him by surprise but the pain and the ensuing thought of a broken arm, had him yelling "OK! OK! OK!" Don't think he had heard of tapping out. The hardest thing for a wrestler to do is be on his back since that means defeat in the sport. If you fight off your back and GIVE it to me, I will SHOW YOU THE SNOW, the buzzing feeling and visual effect as you are about to go unconscious via a rear naked choke or MATA LEON. ("Lion killer" in Brazilian)

As they say in Brazil "Rank does not matter when the choke is set deep." The wrestler did join the dojo for awhile and I still believe that it is easier to teach Jiu Jitsu to a wrestler than teaching a Jiu Jitsu man the ancient art of Wrestling. He just didn't stick around long enough to see that.

Oh yeah, one of my favs, was "The Boxer". Now I am a huge proponent of the "Sweet Science" of Boxing. My Dad was a Champion and his 1950's Boxing portrait hangs proudly at Kenpo School, along with his Olympic Trials Finals gloves. Learning to hit hard with your hands while moving skillfully through different angles is VERY IMPORTANT in learning to fight. My second teacher, Sensei Dickie "The Hammer" Hone, a KICKBOXING CHAMPION and World Contender, taught me the lessons of Boxing during late night training sessions in Central Park in New York City. One time, he clarified a point I couldn't get with a sharp left hook to my head that sent my contact lens to the top of a wall. I got it down, but my eye was swollen shut and it wouldn't go back in. Martial Note: NEVER blow your nose after getting socked in the eye or it'll slam shut and you'll look like Popeye. More on The Hammer later in TEACHERS.

One of my top female students at the time, Heidi, was a skilled Black Belt in Jiu Jitsu, Tae Kwon Do and a Brown Belt in Kenpo. The reason I mentioned gender at all is something fairly unique to training at PWOK. Women train with the men 100% in EVERYTHING we do. That means, it is not uncommon to see a petite 140 lbs woman appear squished under a sweaty 200 lbs man, shortly before she does LEG SWEEP #1 and ends up on top punching and razor-elbowing Big Man's face to a simulated pulp.

WOMEN AND MEN TRAIN IN THE SAME CLASSES WITH THE SAME INTENSITY.

A great story associated with this type of training revolves around a mask that adorns the southern wall of Kenpo School. It is a wood and straw head of a female lion with shells and beads making the facial features of eyes, nostrils etc. It was given to me many years ago by a female student who traveled to Central Africa with her Marine husband who was a "Defense Attache" probably a spy but I don't know that. Anyway, she travels into The Bush to seek out a legendary tribe of Warrior Women whom even the local tribesmen respected. She is introduced to the Queen who is interested why this American would venture alone (with interpreter) to meet them. My student responds that in the middle of America (Chicago) there is a place that trains BOTH men and women EQUALLY to become Warriors. The Queen pauses as she is listening to the translator. She then reaches up to the left of her "throne" and takes the mask off the wall and gives it to her saying "Please bring this to your Teacher as a gift from the Women of Africa."

 Now that is cool.

Back to "Boxer". So Heidi also had a personal trainer aka Boxer, whom she trains under at her gym when not doing martial arts. To make a short story long, he is not a fan of Karate and thinks she should spend more time at HIS gym working out and learning Boxing. He keeps "threatening" to come with her to class to prove his point. Heidi smiled and relayed our ODP. On many occasions, she said he was coming to class and never showed. Then one night, I had run across the street to my home in Old Town to grab my gi top and was a bit late getting back for the start of class. While walking through the cinderblock walled alley that leads to the lone black steel door of Kenpo School, an odd feeling came over me. Not sure what it was, but something was wrong.

Entering the dojo, class had started on time, as usual, at 7 pm sharp. Moving toward my office to change, I see a huge, African American gentleman, teaching his partner the superiority of Boxing and what he would do in a particular attack situation. Now, don't get me wrong, being the learn-from-anyone-who-knows-something kinda guy that I am, we often have visiting teachers from other martial disciplines come to PWOK to share their knowledge. But this is not what was happening here. As one of my Black Belts is trying to run class, Boxer is talking while Sifu is giving instructions to the students and disrupting what is normally a highly disciplined class environment. Catching my Black Belt's eyes with a glance and getting a return eye text that said basically, "I am awaiting your orders, but request permission to end the Boxer chatter."

Being Zen-like, I shake my head "No" imperceptible to anyone else. It would handled as soon as I got changed in a calm, masterly way. It was then that I saw Boxer's shirt that had two boxing gloves on the front that said "I WILL KNOCK YOU OUT". Well, that was enough. When you visit any place that has a certain environment and associated values and beliefs, you SHOW RESPECT. Period. His shirt was equivalent to walking into a church meeting with a shirt that says "I Love the Devil". Any way, when I saw his shirt, I was about to walk over and kick the s**t out of him as a lesson for him, Heidi and the assembled students regarding the dangers of disrespecting KENPO and PWOK. Instead, I continued to my office to cool down, gather my thoughts and decide what to do with Boxer. The thoughts of a violent demonstration continued in my mind, as finally, training took over and I chilled out substantially.

As the first UFC Champion, Royce Gracie, once said about belligerent people "If I beat them up, they won't become my students." And "If he knew who I was, he wouldn't act like that." More great sayings later.

As I walk out, catching Heidi's eye about the lack of notice of the class attendance of Boxer, her eyes apologize, and her look said please don't hurt him. Going to Boxer, he continues to talk to his student partner as I am standing there awaiting an introduction. He knows I am there because the front of the whole dojo is lined with mirrors. I wait patiently for a break in his teaching. I say hi and welcome him to Kenpo School. I tell him I am a huge fan of Boxing and maybe toward the end of class, he could teach us some of his skills. This caught him by surprise as he thinks about it and says sure. I asked him to save "the good stuff" for later and to please work out in sync with what we are doing. Feeling empowered, he agrees and now I start TEACHING him.

I ask one of my other Black Belts to partner with Boxer for the next drill. The series is an elbow break snap responding to a jab from let's say a Boxer. I don't say that, but watch as Boxer's jabs are being regularly caught and "snapped" at the elbow. The fact that Boxer was also a personal trainer and weightlifter, his body was muscular and not very flexible. After having his "fast" jabs caught painfully, but not "injuringly" with a technique called SNAPPING TWIG, his demeanor via body language is starting to change. He recomposes himself.

160

Now I switch the attack to a boxing body hook punch which will be met with a CRANE STYLE rising knee, descending elbow block strike/defense. If done right, and my Black Belt did it right, the opponent, in this case Boxer, would smash his hellfire body hook fist into rock hard bone of defending elbow and knee. As anticipated, after Boxer's "stumble" with the elbow snapping jab defense, he came HARD with a right body hook that would have destroyed ribs.

Unfortunately, it was his bones, cartilage, tendons and nerves that were pulverized as he hit full force into Black Belt's pointed kneecap. I chuckled slightly under my breath with the sound of bone on bone contact (like cracking an egg) that made others stop and look. There is Boxer, wide-eyed and in pain with either a broken or badly damaged fist. He was falling and I wanted to keep it going, but not so much that he would be broken. If I break him, he won't come back. After the fist smash, we go into rear naked chokes and he is tapping, coughing and gagging all at once. REALITY TAUGHT HERE was now becoming apparent to Boxer.

After the blood-deprived brain of Boxer starts to clear from the mata leon drills, I can see he is drowning. His eyes are glazed over, shoulders slumping forward, and previously impressive vascularity is retreating deep inside his rudderless shell, as I call off the dogs. In a glance to Boxer's partner, my Black Belt that said "Point made. Let him work. He's done." The amazing non-verbal communication between Master and Black Belt is fascinating.

So there stands Boxer, dazed, as I walk over, look into his martial soul through his foggy eyes and jump in to save him like a pool lifeguard. I say to the School "OK let's get the hand mitts for punching work. "We work the next 15 minutes on basic Boxing technique as Boxer's punches are in a familiar training method and he begins to arrive back to himself as he is now working out WITH US not FOR US. We continue his revival as I ask him to show us how to work the heavy bag. With six of them hanging by chains from the ceiling, we already know what he is showing us. But that was fine. In 90 minutes, he had been transformed from a belligerent jerk, to a nice guy who was welcome to come back anytime.

All this was done without one single strike fired in anger.

As class finished and he was about to leave, the Boxer stood at the door, bowed a real bow said "Thank you Sensei." With a look that said he really meant it.

I replied "You are welcome back any time, Boxer." Heidi smiled.

He never came back.

The next to last example of my ODP, but by no means the only ones left to tell, regarded a NINJA. I was standing on the main floor of the downtown PWOK dojo when I guy walks in says he wants to teach NINJITSU at my School. I ask "Are you a Ninja?"

He replied "Yes I am."

I then said "Well you are not very good."

Looking confused, I elaborated. "NINJITSU is the Art of Invisibility, right? Well I SEE you." I continued "If you had, maybe, just appeared at my desk, or came up out of the mat to take me down, then I might be interested. Sorry man."

He did use some of his ninja skills as he disappeared out the door. Besides, I don't think I could wear those toe splitting, Mr. Spock Vulcan Prosperity Sign-like tabi socks they wear. I can barely stand my big toe separated from my others by a summer sandal.

The last ODP tale occurred after moving Kenpo School to a southwestern suburb of Chicago. The village of Brookfield is an old community that is quite hard on new businesses and the failure rate is very high. It just seems that Brookfielders want to wait until they think you are viable enough to support. As of 2013, we will be in business 14 years, the 2nd oldest business in downtown Brookfield. Its true Brookfield is like Mayberry from the "Andy Griffith Show" a beautiful place to raise kids with some of the top educational institutions in the state. So we love it here, but equate it to a "Copper Village" where everything is made of copper. If someone finds a gold mine and everyone else says "look at this strange new copper. Its shiny and soft, but we already have copper!" In other words, Kenpo School was not anything new to them, just another of those local Karate Schools like at the YMCA. WRONG!

THE BEST OF ANYTHING HAS TO BE SOMEWHERE.

Some of the best martial arts training happens right here in little Brookfield, Illinois. There are many great schools across the country and we just happen to be one of them.

Warrior Copper for sure.

The thing that Brookfield does have is bars. There are two on either side of PWOK, with twin dental offices sandwiched in between. The irony is not lost on me and think, get drunk, come in and wise off, lose some teeth and the dentists are right next door. It seems ideal. Anyway, besides those two bars, there are two more at the south end of the small block and two more across the railroad tracks 200ft from the corner bars. There are others, but the ones by my Kenpo School and adjacent dental offices lead me to this story of Open Door Policy.

Being half Irish-Welch thanks to Butch Powell's fighting DNA, I am not unaware of the stereotypes associated with Irish drinking and fighting. Is it really a stereotype when it's accurate? I don't know a single Irishman that does not drink. I am sure there are, but in 50+ years on this Earth, I haven't met any. As with all drinkers, the urge to fight seems inevitable to some. Thus, the last ODP story.

I was on the mat at PWOK when a group of fresh-in-country Irishmen must have just left the local Irish Pub across the tracks and I could here them approaching loud. The dojo door was open trying to remove the stench of last night's class and the needed to be cleaned cages of "Odin" my pet Anaconda, "Thor" a Boa Constrictor, and "Serena" a Python. We keep snakes as PWOK mascots because they represent the changing skins of The Warrior. They molt into new, bigger, badder snakes and as we train to evolve in a similar fashion as Warriors.

In fact, the name of this book is related to the GROWTH and change occurring in the snake TERRARIUMS at PWOK. Rather than snakes, I use TIGERS to represent the aggressive determination to GROW in humans rather than snakes. It makes for a cooler book title too.

So, as the smell of crushed rat bone feces in need of a White Belt to clean, wafts with the accompanying music of Blue Oyster Cult's "Don't Fear the Reaper" out into the summer Brookfield air, in pokes the heads of the drunken Irishmen. I say hello as they start to laugh and their beer brains are on full sharpness as they say in an annoying, overdone, drunken Irish brogue "Look Peter, it's a Karate School...ahahaaa!" I glanced at the Anaconda with his eyes and darting tongue shifting from me to them in a "Dinner?" kinda way.

Peter says in slurred speech ringing the ears of his potential murderer "Hey, do you teach Irish Boxing here?" I respond with a slightly uncharacteristic "Why the F**K would I do that?" Taken aback, they enter the School AND STEP ON THE MAT WITH THEIR DIRTY BOOTS! The look on my face now of a dead, wooden doll, augmented with the physical oddity that happens when involved in serious ODP, foes have said my dark brown eyes turn jet black. Sort of like a Great White Shark, or more accurately a Man of Death.

Whether it's theirs or mine is yet to be determined.

As Carlson Gracie Jr. says "Your Momma Gonna Cry Before My Momma Gonna Cry!"

As I approach, Peter stands his ground as the others back off the mat to near the door. I am offended now, as I see the dirt foot steps on the mat. Moving to Peter and ask him if he wants to test his Irish Boxing against American Kenpo. As he opened his mouth in what I assumed was the word "Yes" I grabbed him by the shirt and threw him face first into the heavily weighted lat pull down machine that was closest. As his face, head and upper body hit the heavy iron dead on, I grab his foot and pull him back to mat center and gave him a few "baby" shin kicks to his exposed ribs. Pretty sure that he was jolted by the reality that his well financed beer buzz was just cancelled via a mild ass beating. I looked to see if his buddies were interested in joining the lesson, but they remained frozen at the door. As he attempted to rise, I continued "shin-pushing" Peter, still on all fours "gently" to the door. His friends grabbed him and they raced off. I yelled "Hey Peter, you owe me $10 for the private lesson!"

He never came back to pay.

THE GREAT AMERICAN KENPO GRANDMASTER EDMUND PARKER ONCE TOLD ME THAT THE DIFFERENCE BETWEEN AN INTRUCTOR AND A TEACHER IS THAT THE INSTRUCTOR <u>SHOWS</u> YOU THE ART WHEREAS A TEACHER <u>SHARES</u> THE ART WITH YOU.

IT WAS TIME TO SHARE POWELL'S WAY OF KENPO MARTIAL ARTS SCHOOL WITH CHICAGO IN A BIG WAY.

CHAPTER SEVENTEEN

The Importance of: MASTER JOE GANGI'S KICKBOXING EXTRAVAGANZA 2.

As mentioned, before sandwiching the "Open Door Policy" Chapter in between, I got a call from Master Gangi about doing a demonstration during Intermission of his upcoming Kickboxing event to be held at the Park West in Chicago. Something about the way he asked made me realize that there was MUCH MORE to the request than the need to find a demo team to fill the spot. Master Gangi is a famous martial artist and knew EVERYONE in the martial arts community and they knew him. He could have filled the demo spot with any number of top notch competition demonstration teams that specialize in that stuff. I got the call. It seemed as if we were speaking in a dual meaning language, like a Chopsoki movie with English subtitles. He asked. I replied. With the simultaneous ghost words of "Sensei Bill, this is your chance to shut up all the talk." and my intention was clear.

"Then Powell's Way of Kenpo will be there." in acknowledgement of the favor he was doing me and Kenpo School. It was the way to demonstrate the blistering power of Kenpo and a call for unity amongst those that had ill will toward a bridge-building martial arts philosophy. That's exactly what I had been looking for. Since Master Gangi had accepted an invitation to come and teach a class at PWOK after it first opened, I knew what view he held. I am so thankful that Master Joe Gangi knew me and what we were all about after coming to our miniscule dojo to share his Kung Fu Systems in a most intense, mind blowing way. I needed to return the gesture.

My mind immediately started forming ways to get everything we wanted everyone watching to know about PWOK and why promote the importance of cross training in the martial arts. All

167

this had to be done in our 7 minute time allotment. So here is what we did.

First, speak to Kenpo School and lay it on the line. This is our chance to show who we are, our vision of friendship and the strength of our meaning. After explaining the history of martial arts in Chicago and the importance of this one chance presented to us. To the person, my now Black Eyes pierced theirs as if to say "This is ODP, a CHALLENGE to us and what we do here. Failure is not an option" After the fiery monologue that had me whipped into a lather, the talk ended with "AM I CLEAR?" "YES SIR!" came in unison.

This would be no ordinary demo. I had been to many Kickboxing events where the intermission was the time for the audience to use the bathroom, get another beer or something to eat. Mostly no one paid attention to cute kids doing kata, folks breaking bats with their shins or even the Competition Demo Teams (CDT) that did music choreographed movements like synchronized swimmers. I normally went the way of the audience to grab a beer. That COULD NOT happen if we were to achieve our goals. Everyone needed to be watching. But then how to assure that?

Our training for the demonstration took on war-like preparations. Our motto was amended from "No One Left Standing" to "No One Leaves Their Seat". We became quite intense in focus. As we trained in the various segments that would flow in concert to hard rock music from Led Zeppelin, Pink Floyd and Black Sabbath we liked it LOUD! At the same time we were training, Video Editing Master, John LeSanche. was busy filming our practices, digging through archived footage of past events like the Shaolin Monks and other special segments that we created for the accompanying video. So, when were introduced and were going to enter the darkened stage, the video would begin to play on the three HUGE Megatron-type monitors on three sides of the ring and all the various TVs and monitors at the bar and near the bathrooms. I'm talking slightly smaller than movie theatre size displays on the big ones that would be clearly visible for anyone who could tear their eyes away from the Mayhemic Rockfest Action (MRA) going on in the actual ring at the same time. The idea was to have so much multi-media, music-laced martial arts action going on that the audience didn't know where to look. But look they would.

That was the plan. It worked exactly as PLANNED, TRAINED and EXECUTED.

The night of the event, we met at Kenpo School (PWOK) at 7:00 sharp. No one was late. There was a tension in the air that was a bit unsettling. All our preparations were done. Now it was time to Stand and Deliver. Looking into their eyes, the steeled determination was evident, but the deep down feelings were less unified. As if any one person was "afraid to mess up" and ruin our important night. The pressure on these students was immense.

I explained to them that they were well-trained and simply had to recreate the same movements that they had been practicing for weeks. The IMPORTANCE OF TRAINING, I went on, is that if you have trained properly, your mind will be calm and you will effortlessly do that which you have been trained to do. No need for thought. No need for worry. And certainly no need for fear! Adding that the whole demonstration was designed to overwhelm the senses with the audience looking at one thing and realizing they were missing fifteen other things. Just like Kenpo, where the strikes come from every angle so fast that you don't know which body part hurts more and where to grab to ease the pain. So, they shouldn't worry about people watching.

We walked the short distance from the School to Park West and dressed there in our traditional black gis. Kenpo was the first martial art to wear black uniforms. When Grandmaster James Mitose (23rd Generation GM) brought his Kenpo to Japan from China, he wanted to separate it from all other styles training in Japan, which wore only white gis. When asked why he would dare desecrate the long Japanese Karate tradition of only wearing white uniforms he replied.

"Kenpo is for Death and Bruising" And that is why we wear black. You gotta love that.

The venue is packed as we arrive and change then security ushers us to our staging area, a long unlit corridor of tall poles and velvet colored drapes that hung from ceiling to floor. We put our bags and gear down, and I peaked through the curtain to see every seat filled and the balcony overflowing with standing room only spectators. I resisted the urge to have everyone take a peek and decided that ignorance was really bliss. So we sat there focused, quiet except for the occasional joke or funny statement to lighten the air. We got the signal from the event volunteer that the last fight before Intermission was in the final minute. With Shifu John LeSanche at the video helm and my friend, and Park West Event Planner, Bonnie at the lights and controls, it was time.

Like magic, before the last fighter left the ring, down go the lights and on comes the soundtrack that would start it all. "Ladies and Gentlemen, The Teachers and Students of Powell's Way of Kenpo, just down the street in Old Town are honored to participate in Master Joe Gangi's Kickboxing Extravaganza 2…Please enjoy!"

The audience lights rise slightly for those who really had to pee, but the stage was still dark and as "Please enjoy!" drifts into the smashing, rip-roaring drumbeat of Led Zeppelin's "Rock & Roll" the ring lights rise up to full max as my black clad Warriors break into eight sets of two, executing near perfect Kenpo (for their rank) as the tunes are blaring. Simultaneously, John L.'s synchronized video is reeling out sharp, professional studio produced cuts and fades. What was happening on the videos screens and monitors throughout Park West was related to that which was going on in the ring.

Not a duplicate, just related.

As the Zep tune continues, I yell break and all students sit down in an L-shape along the ropes. They were sitting back straight, legs crossed and eyes focused on the action in the ring. There was no gazing about the audience, the monitors or joking to each other. While the majority were finished with their only part, they sat stone-faced and focused like the Warriors they were. You can tell a lot about a Teacher and a School by the students they produce. From a few new White Belts working the only three techniques they knew to the Black Belts flowing through intermediate and advanced technique like WHIRLING BLADES, HANDS OF JADE or SHOOTING STAR, everyone had rocked the house and now sat down as it was my turn.

You'll remember my favorite Uki of the time, Sempai Nick Black of sizzling asphalt at Great America demo fame, and the look in his eyes matched the fury in mine. As we met alone at center ring, I smashed, thrashed, mashed and trashed my attacking partner in a brutal display of "Now That's What I'm Talk'n About."

I could hear the crowd's "oooohhhhhh! aaaahhhhh!" over the pounding music as I blistered Sempai's body in a way that SHARED THE POWER OF KENPO with the audience and the attending Masters. Sempai Nick's pained facial expressions were priceless I was told. By the time my short segment was finished, Sempai Nick looked like he preferred the waffle iron throws into hot tar at Six Flags to this routine.As we were going through our part, speeded up video clips of the two of us doing a street clothes version of the same techniques going on in the ring appeared on the huge monitors above. Very cool I thought.

As we caught everyone's attention with the Kenpo opening, it was point-making time. Master Kimball broke out his "Tai Chi Sword" and cut the air in the ring to shreds. It was the same form that he had demonstrated at the Shaolin Monks event. As he finishes and is moving to

171

rings edge, Jiu Jitsu Black Belt Laurie M. begins an amazing Falling, Rolling and Flipping form that showed how experts fall to the ground when thrown. After she finished her solo kata, I arose as the attacker and conducted a series of throws that corresponded to the falling techniques she had just demonstrated alone. It was a very effective way to show the importance

of making the ground your friend. If not your friend then its your enemy.

As she rolls back to her previous sitting position, her face returns to stone as she watches Tai Chi Master Kelly Carter rise and move to center as Pink Floyd's "Breathe" begins its slow blare out of the Park West speakers. His Tai Chi form slows the pace but not the intensity. As he moves beautifully in his Art, panoramic landscapes of downtown Chicago splay across the humongous displays above. Just as the song is ending, more Floyd in the form of the screaming "Ahhhhhhh-Dun. Dun...Thought you'd like to know." comes crashing out of the state of the art audio system. In sync, the massive monitors above have me smashing 5 slabs of concrete to the sound.

The rock tunes continue as I now attack Master Kelly, fresh from Tai Chi utopia with a double leg takedown and off we go with a demonstration of groundfighting and Carlson Gracie Jiu Jitsu. Sweeps, Mounts, Arm locks, Leg Triangles, Chokes and other Submissions are shown in a quick rapidly moving 6 technique set each. As we hear the music change in concert with our ending technique set, the end is near as Knife Master Ron Scaggs, slices and dices the ring from corner

to corner with a live blade and Black Sabbath's "Paranoid" to accompany. Of course, his knife

form is showing above from a practice session at our dojo that he wasn't making moves up.

Scary stuff. Both beautiful and deadly. Just like the Teachers and Students at PWOK.

As the music is ending, we all rise and bow to the audience in appreciation of their appreciation.

No, there were not many empty seats when we started and there were no empty seats 7 minutes

later.

So, martial arts demonstrations can be IMPORTANT.

JUST A FEW OF THE WARRIOR SCHOLARS AT POWELL'S WAY OF KENPO SCHOOL.

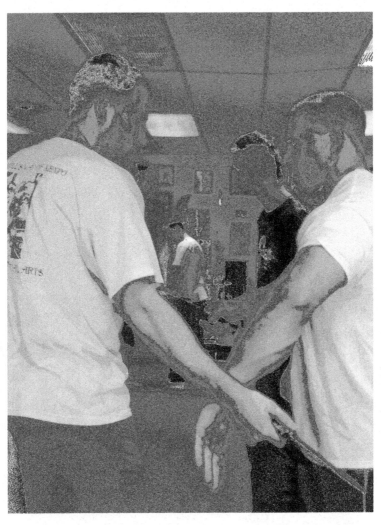

"ROAR" MORRISSEY AND "IRONMAN" PLIGGE WORKING KNIFE TECHNIQUE.

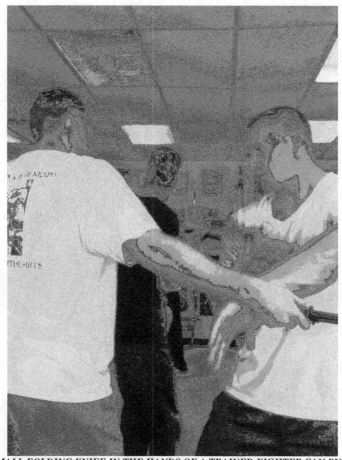

EVEN A SMALL FOLDING KNIFE IN THE HANDS OF A TRAINED FIGHTER CAN PUT FOUR OR MORE ATTACKERS IN LETHAL DANGER. AND THAT'S EXACTLY HOW IT SHOULD BE.

"ROAR" CHOKING OUT "SLIM" JANETOPOULOS WITH A REAR NAKED CHOKE.

CHAPTER EIGHTEEN

The Importance of: FINDING A REALITY-BASED SCHOOL

It is extremely important to the purpose of this book that you find a true WARRIOR HOUSE. This is a type of training that approaches within a hair thickness of REALITY. Why only a hair thickness? Because people would be injured, hurt, crippled or die during training and that wouldn't do anyone any good. MMA tag line "As Real As It Gets!" is accurate. When they get in the ring they are equipped only with their fingerless gloves, fight shorts, athletic supporter, their mind, heart and skills. Because that is SHOWTIME and all their training is revealed. In truth, there ARE RULES and no matter how brutal the match, it is still a sporting event. In practice training they come close too, but do not exceed fight time intensity for fear of a fight-postponing injury. Though they try to get as real as possible, it's also a financial consideration. Get hurt training and you could possibly lose out on a piece of the multi-billion dollar MMA business.

For full time professional fighters, that is not good business.

As far as the Martial Arts for Self Defense goes, SHOWTIME is when attacked on the street. Then it is a matter of not just victory and defeat but LIFE or DEATH. So we too train to be as close to real as possible in the dojo without maiming each other. But just as in MMA training, injuries do occur. If you are injured (not hurt) you simply cannot train and that leaves you vulnerable.

If you can't fight, you can't defeat an attack and therefore Your Momma Gonna Cry.

In Japanese, the word for martial arts school is "dojo". Do-jo means "Way-Place" or a "Place to Learn The Way". You will see the suffix "do" meaning "Way" in the names of many martial arts styles and systems; KARATE-DO, JUDO, HAPKIDO, COMBAT-DO and TAE KWON DO to name a few. As well, the suffix "Ryu" is associated with different schools in Japan, Okinawa and countries as in: ISSHIN-RYU, WASHIN-RYU, GOJO-RYU, SHOREI RYU etc.

In China, The Way is taught in a "kwoon" or a "daochang". In Korea it is a "dojang". No matter where in the world you study, the names of places, arts and language may be different, but they all try to "Teach The Way." The Way can be "The Way of Life" "The Way to Enlightenment and Self Realization" or in our case "The Way of The Warrior." It is "A Way Place: A Place to Train As Warriors and Live The Way".

The IDEA behind the creation of POWELL'S WAY OF KENPO MARTIAL ARTS SCHOOL was simple enough. Open a REAL martial arts school that trained people in REALITY-BASED techniques and movements that were PROVEN in personal combat and COULD REALLY save their lives. Sounds easy enough, have a vision, create a plan and execute it. Hey, people create things all the time. My creation however, if wrong or unneeded could get me killed. Literally. By the time that I open KENPO SCHOOL in downtown Chicago in 1988, I had studied The Arts That I Thought Necessary (TAITNA) for many years to achieve this goal. At the time that was serious, near everyday training in one or more of the following:

ISSHIN RYU OKINAWAN KARATE under Sensei Spencer DeVito in New Jersey, where I learned the importance of Hardcore Training by doing THOUSANDS of Jumping Jacks in his muddy backyard where we sunk knee deep in the muck and pulled up and out with each and every rep. Mental toughness, endurance and powerful strikes were "The One Heart Way". Isshin Ryu taught me the importance of straight linear power and breath control.

JAPANESE KARATE-DO, AMERICAN FULL CONTACT KARATE, BOXING and KICK BOXING under the painful "Reality is Everything" tutelage of Sensei Dickie "The Hammer" Hone. I basically spent most of this training GETTING MY ASS KICKED as I was taught that traditional Karate alone was not enough. I got my worst beating after telling Sensei that "I could take World Boxing Champion, Marvelous Marvin Hagler, in a fight outside the ring" The loving whipping offered up in response made me regret the former statement. I also learned the importance of footwork, angles of attack, as well as, learning to take hard shots to the body, legs and head.

CHINESE KUNG FU from several different Teachers over a few years on the East Coast that taught me the speed, flow and power of circular movements in attack and defense. I was to train much deeper in this discipline after getting to Chicago, courtesy of Master Kimball Paul's deadly SHAOLIN KUNG FU and OCCIDENTAL (anything but Chinese) TAI CHI CHUAN which means "GRAND ULTIMATE FIST." In China, you don't say anything is "Grand Ultimate" without being able to prove it. Master Kimball also taught me the fighting styles of Tai Chi Chuan, BAGWA, and the traditional Chinese Weapons of Kwan Dau, Tiger Fork, Broad Sword, Tai Chi Sword and Staff.

I also learned Internal Power Transfer of "Chi" (energy) into an opponent at close range with a strike or tip of a sword. He transmitted many long held secrets through the FOUR PERFECT FORMS of WARD OFF, PUSH, ROLLBACK and PRESS.

Also, I learned the ability to know what my opponent was going to do before he did by way of many, many hours of PUSH HANDS training with Kimball so intense it made me cry on occasion. Umm...actually it was probably some dust blowing around or maybe dried contact lens. Yah, that's it.

JAPANESE TOBU AIKIDO under Sensei Rich Sebek of the Brookfield Police Department.

HALL OF FAME AIKIDO INSTRUCTOR AND CAREER POLICE OFFICER RICH SEBEK.
OFFICER SEBEK WAS SHOT IN THE LINE OF DUTY AND RECEIVED HIGH
COMMENDATIONS FOR VALOR.

AIKIDO is "The Way of Harmony" and in Flow with the Universe. It is often viewed as a Defensive Art in the same way that as a snarling badger is seen as a kinda weasel. It is a beautiful, powerful Art and the favorite of my Grandmaster Shorty Mills of the TENTH DAN.

PAGODA RYU under the 25+ YEARS of TRAINING with the LEGENDARY Hanshi Shorty Mills, who taught me the true importance of BUSHIDO; THE WAY OF THE WARRIOR.

WRESTLING and JUDO was my base of Self Defense, which we covered previously, then combined them (pre Gracie Jiu Jitsu) as our groundfighting system with the name RAMPONE. That was Italian for "To Punch in The Dirt" or "The Big Grab" depending on which translation you like. Training in these Arts began in earnest as a toddler, starting with my Dad and followed throughout High School with other great coaches, teachers and mentors providing the passion, knowledge and training. From these I learned balance, quickness and violence of action in takedowns, ground control, holding techniques, arm locks and chokes.

MUAY THAI learned from Master Benny Ghofrani, who was The World Cage Fighting Champion at the time, when I got here to Chicago. He taught me the power of the Muay Thai neck clinch, knee strikes and elbow-launched knockouts. My favorite thing was the single shin leg kicks to the opponent's outer or inner thighs that would drop them or at least cause a crippling wince. Hitting that spot repeatedly would cause many an opponent to quit. It hurts that bad.

KENPO KARATE/MODERN ARNIS: I studied both Ed Parker's AMERICAN KENPO in Philadelphia under Tom Updegrove and The TRACY SYSTEM of KENPO when I got to Chicago from Master Bob Wainwright. I learned the true lethality and subsequent consequences if you let the Power of Kenpo take you over. It's intoxicating. Also, the fast, violent combination of multiple circular and linear strikes in less than a second to muscular, skeletal and nervous systems, that literally shut the body down as it is overwhelmed with negative stimuli.

KNIFE FIGHTING under Master Ron Scaggs. 'Nuff said.

BRAZILIAN JIU JITSU under Carlson Gracie, Carlson Gracie Jr. and Coach Jeff Neal.

Also, HANDGUN and SHOTGUN training which is SLIGHTLY outside the scope of this book.

FIND THE MASTERS IN WHATEVER ENDEAVOR YOU WISH TO EXCEL. IT IS NOT ALWAYS EASY, BUT AS I HAVE CLEARLY SHOWN IN THIS BOOK, IT CAN BE DONE.

So, with top notch training in MULTIPLE martial arts and an IDEA, I needed to find a location

for the soon to be "REALITY TAUGHT HERE WAY PLACE". Living in a high-rise condo in

Old Town, Chicago, had to look no further than one street over. It turns out there was martial

activity in the form of Gold Coast Martial Arts on 1600 Block of LaSalle Street. As I walked

through the alley between Wells Street and LaSalle by way of a cinderblock tunnel that would

eventually lead to the steel black door entrance of the future PWOK, I met the owner of

GCMA, Sensei Kris H. Sensei was a fast talking, nice and smiley former NFL player who took

his retirement money to open a martial arts school. How fortunate for me.

We discussed the availability of space for me to teach during his non-class time. When he

asked how many students I had, smiling said none. He looked at me strangely, but then

gave me a great opportunity. How about a set three day a week schedule, Tuesdays, Thursdays

and Saturdays, 2 hour classes and would pay him ¼ of each student's tuition. That meant for

every $80 per month per student, I would pay Sensei Kris $20. That was awesome, as it

allowed me TO START A NEW BUSINESS WITH NO OVERHEAD FROM THE BEGIN-

NING. Without the pressure of debt to start, I could pick and choose my students without

needing to take just anybody to generate the revenue to pay the rent. Black Belts thinking of

opening their own school would be wise to use this successful dojo business model.

MY FIRST SCHOOL ON THE 3RD FLOOR OF GOLD COAST MARTIAL ARTS IN CHICAGO.
THAT'S WIFE BONNIE AND FIRST WARRIOR RACHEL ON THE MAT. MAN THAT DOJO WAS COOL.

It would be just like those Kung Fu movies, where you see the Teacher and one student, then

three, then six, then ten etc. And that is kinda what happened. I say kinda, because our

BRUTAL training made student cultivation difficult, attrition regular and my income low. But

that DID NOT MATTER since in the type of School I was trying to build, students could not be

found through a Yellow Pages ad (no websites then) or from demonstrations at the Old Town Art

Fair.

No they would have to be found.

They needed to be tough, yet have jobs to pay for class.

Rush and Division Streets in Chicago IS THE party center of the City. Don't get me wrong,

there are plenty of cool places to eat, drink and get wasted if that's your thing. All cab-ready to dart you to and fro the best of everything that makes Chicago a World Class City. But if you ask most anyone who lives here where the tourists, suburban visitors and the girls are its Rush and Division. Rush and Division is home to some great bars like "Mothers" "The Lodge" and "Whiskey Bar & Grill" among the many others that transforms the several city blocks into an environment reminiscent of the great French Quarter in New Orleans. Being there during the Chicago Bulls Six NBA titles (would have been 8 with MJ) and you would grasp my meaning.

But alas, I was not there for the tourists, the beer or the frivolity.

I was there to find students.

So, I went bar to bar to visit with the Bouncers, Coolers, and any Security Personnel tasked with keeping the business moving as the booze were flowing. Not always an easy proposition. Their job was basically to keep order by keeping drunken idiots out and plastered morons within from killing each other while doing "The Macarena". Hard job. Hard folks. Tough sell. I went door

to door of these places mostly in the early evening, before the crowds came, and as the bar

employees readied for the nightly onslaught.

Handed out my very first business cards there.

They said simply:

<u>**P O W E L L ' S**</u>
WAY OF KENPO
MARTIAL ARTS SCHOOL
312-951-0771
Karate.   Kung Fu.   Self Defense.
1636 North Wells Street, Chicago, IL
William Powell- Black Belt

The School was literally walking distance from these bars. The looks,

reactions and comments from the Curious Bar Security Personnel (CBSP) were varied. One could

tell by looking that most were hired for size and strength, not necessarily for skill and sharpness

or intelligence. But hey, I'm not in the Bouncer Hiring Business (BHB) so what did I know. At

first, many looked at me as if I was a paid "flyer passer-outer" hired by PWOK to hand out

cards and solicit business.

Most were polite.

Some were rude.

Others were apathetic.

None said anything that caused them to limp around for life.

BAR TO BAR TO BAR I TRUDGED THROUGH THE HEART OF RUSH AND DIVISION STREETS IN THE PARTY CENTRAL OF DOWNTOWN CHICAGO...IN SEARCH OF STUDENTS. NO REALLY... I WAS THERE TO FIND STUDENTS.

But the vast majority were curious. Can you imagine how funny it must have looked to anyone present, when this little guy who looks like a shoe salesman walks up to a huge bouncer and basically asks him if he wants TO LEARN TO FIGHT? These guys are in violent encounters nightly, but they are not necessarily IN A FIGHT. With communications and swift assistance from other huge dudes, Bouncing is an art form within a system. One time, while looking up the flared nostrils of this huge bouncer with his non-tilting head and Great White Shark eyes rolling down in their sockets, he looks at me and growls "OK, I'll bite. What's the joke?"

I guess my return upward glance backed with a heart-driven mission made it clear I was neither a comedian nor was I kidding. "I run a REALITY-BASED martial arts School down the street in Old Town. Please pass this card along if you are already too skilled to fight multiple attackers with weapons who are awaiting you after work for tossing them out." All it takes is one drunk punk with a knife to slash your femoral artery and you bleed out in front of your parked car or right here at the door." "No one can save you...even if you attacker was a doctor." Point made. Leaving him with "Thank you and have a great day. Remember to keep your blood inside you."

Off to the next bar.

A few of the guys that I talked to asked when classes were and when they could stop by. Others just thanked me, took the card and never showed. But some did show up at my Kenpo School door. Either way, I never had a problem getting into a packed, line-waiting watering hole there whenever any of those gentlemen were working the door.

Like a scene from "Dragon: The Bruce Lee Story" a lone bouncer from "Mothers" appears at the School, then on the 3rd floor of GCMA on LaSalle. He pokes his large, bearded head in and with my business card in hand says "Hello...here for the class." I smile and say "You ARE the class." We both laughed since I did make it clear when passing out the cards that this was a brand new project. He said his name was Mikey and that he wanted to "LEARN REALITY". Wasn't sure if he was being sarcastic but then he asked how much this now private lesson would cost him. I told him that it was FREE UNLESS HE LEARNED SOMETHING of value, then its $5 and he'd pass the word to his colleagues on Rush and Division. PWOK needed real students not a big class there for Karate lessons.

Once we worked out the financial details, TEACHING and PWOK officially began.

I asked him to attack me-without use of weapons for now. He looked at me, face in a scrunched series of ripples and creases then threw a ¾ speed punch at my face. I used both hands snapping sharply at his elbow to hyperextension, kicked him square in the jewels, and dropped him with a "soft elbow" (using my tricep instead of a sharp elbow tip) He went down hard. Hurt but not injured. "F**k man, what the hell? He muttered. I said to ATTACK ME! He got to his feet and charged me Redneck style. Gee, where have I seen THAT attack before? Side-stepping, I revisited his clams with a hard RIDGEHAND that screamed "Hello. This is KENPO!" As he re-crumbled to the mat, I said "Mikey. Now I want you to STOP attacking me. Do you understand?"

If his pain and anger had gotten to him and he rose to strike, he would have been knocked out cold. Hey any message back to the bouncer community is better than nothing. Mikey gathered himself and asked why I did that to him. I responded that while a bit painful, it took a lot less time and convincing BY SHARING what I offer rather than explaining to him why it works. He just looked at me. Wish that I had a picture of his expression for a flyer "Got Kenpo?"

After that, we spent the remaining time talking about life at the bars, other martial arts then some Kenpo teaching him some of the basic technique. As he left, I said "Mikey, you coming back?" "No" he said as he handed me a $10 bill and said "Sir, please keep the change." He finished our class with a statement that this was just not for him, but said "some of my friends will be very interested". Cool.

So, Day One of PWOK's financial ledger read: 1 new student. $10 in tuition. 1 quitting student.

Pondering the thought that maybe I should soften the "Introductory Lesson" approach, I just refused to alter my vision of a TRUE WARRIOR HOUSE. So I went to the bar next door called "The Last Act" across from the famous Second City comedy club for a beer. After two beers, I left a tip and walked back to GCMA and handed Sensei Kris his PWOK cut of 25% or $2 net.

This slow moving, labor intensive building of a HARDCORE DOJO took at least a year to take off. Bouncers, Coolers and their friends would come, stay awhile and go. But some stayed long enough to actually LEARN SOMETHING and our reputation as "The Real Deal" spread among those that were "touched" by the vision. I guess that I had 4 or 5 hard students at the time when I received a call from a non-bouncer who had heard of us from a bouncer. Networking works. He said his name was Nick and he was looking for a REAL martial arts school since he spends time going from dojo to dojo beating up the instructors. I asked what time could he come by? He said that he also had some weights for sale and he'd bring them by to see if I was interested.

Nick arrived the next day promptly and was polite but stone-faced. When he got there, he was sizeable; well over 6 feet and probably 240 lbs of muscle. He wore a sleeveless black tee and had cool, piercing eyes. Thought that I might have something here. He entered and said "Weights are in the car, I wanna see if it's worth the time to bring them in." Fair enough.

"Let's spar! He said.

"Sparring is in Karate. We don't spar in Kenpo...too dangerous." I replied.

"Let's fight then." as he threw a boxing combination of jab, right hand and left hook; all of which missed by inches. Then a strong front thrust kick that would have sent me out 3RD story window had it landed. Slightly impressed with his moxie, I wanted to keep him as a student. After his thrust kick failed to land, he put his leg down and I executed a near perfect SPINNING OUTSIDE CRESCENT KICK that normally would wipe that smug look off anyone's face. But instead of the usual full contact, side blade of foot to face move, I pull off millimeters to the strike in an attempt to just brush his nose. In all the excitement that didn't happen.

As the fast, circular kick just brushes the facial nerves on the very bottom of his chinny-chin-chin it knocks him out cold while still standing. I mean, he stood there unconscious for a second or so then sat down straight to his butt with legs still fully extended like the letter "L". Still out, he starts to fall backward until the wall catches him and he is in a safe lean against it. He awakens shortly and says "I want to join NOW!"

I ask "Can we still keep the weights?" We laugh as he agrees.

That student was Nick Black, eventual Sempai (Senior Student) of Powell's Way of Kenpo Martial Arts School and became a long time friend and a dedicated martial artist. Funny as hell.

With Nick a keeper, he recruited other like minded friends and together we basically created a platform for those who really wanted to learn to fight. The stories and escapades of Sempai Nick and me could fill another couple of Chapters. Suffice it to say, he was instrumental in the successful forming of PWOK. We now had a steady stream of PEOPLE WHO HAD HEARD FROM PEOPLE about our WAY PLACE. By the time a new student came through the door, he/she already knew what we did, the intensity of training by way of those that told them about us. Many came. Some stayed. Most didn't. Those that did stay got what they came for. More on our unique somewhat unorthodox drills and training techniques later in this book. If you want to realistically have the skills to protect yourself, your family or others, YOU MUST FIND AND TRAIN AT A TRUE WARRIOR SCHOOL, or you might as well just BUY A GUN AND CARRY IT WHEREVER YOU GO or JUST STAY HOME. Those are your CHOICES.

So, finding a proper dojo is essential to YOUR TRAINING and SURVIVAL.

AFTER A YEAR OR SO ON THE 3RD FLOOR OF GOLD COAST MARTIAL ARTS WE MOVED DOWN TO THE BOTTOM FLOOR WITH A COOL ALLEY ENTRANCE TO THE DOJO.

A WARRIOR STRIVES TO FACE HIMSELF IN BATTLE AND THE CONFLICT IS EPIC.

WARSHIPS ARE LARGER THAN HUMANS AND A SKILLED WARRIOR SHOULD BE AWARE OF EITHER THREAT WHEN SITTING IN PLAIN SIGHT. PRACTICE THIS REGULARY.

CHAPTER NINETEEN

The Importance of: DIPLOMACY.

Her Majesty's Ship (HMS) HERMES, the spear head of the powerful British Armada that retook the Falkland Islands back from Argentina, made a Port of Call in Philadelphia in the 1980s. Martial Posture Studio was on 2nd Street in Philly very close to the docks. Leaving Kenpo School, I turn right and up a few blocks and would catch a fast train across the Ben Franklin Bridge, to my apartment in southern, NJ. Had my Warrior Skills (WS) been more acute, I might have looked left to see a MASSIVE AIRCRAFT CARRIER that is NOT NORMALLY THERE.

Martial Note: LOOK ALL AROUND when leaving a building lest you get run over by a speeding tank or out of control rickshaw.

Anyway, proceeding north up Chestnut Street, away from the carrier, I do my usual peek into a favorite bar of mine then called "Seconds". Cool concept; Buy a beer, get the second one free! So, after Kenpo I would usually stop in for a few beers before walking to the train. This was a rare occasion where I was simply walking past and glanced through the window to see a guy dancing on the bar wearing only UNION JACK flagged underwear. Around him were wall to wall sailors in dress uniforms as they cheer on the Wild Brit (WB). Noting that they are not AMERICAN clad naval personnel, I am puzzled. Not looking over my shoulder to see the huge warship hovering in the distance, curiosity leads me in to find out who they are how they got there. Come to find that this REALLY IS the British Royal Navy and that they came in a BIG warship.

So I peek my head out of the bar and look to the left for the first time and see the ship.

Being from a maritime military family, and a close follower of the reporting of the Falklands Campaign, I feel right at home with these WARRIORS. Making my way to the bar through the load of seamen, I pull out my Amex Gold Card and ask the bartender how much a shot of Jack Daniels was. She said all shots were $2 but there were no seconds for free. Scanning the crowd, I guesstimate and order 72 SHOTS of JD for our cross-pond allies.

It takes a good ten minutes to fill and distribute the gesture to the happy Royal Navy. They hold their shots until every one has one. Now at the center of the room surrounded by the crew of the Hermes and raising my glass, I scream out in what I thought was a rallying cry "TO THE FALKLANDS!" About to drink, I notice NO ONE has raised their glass or responded to my toast in any way.

You literally could hear a pin drop. Finally, I feel my stomach sink as the first guy says "I lost my brother at Goose Green." Another, almost in tears "My cousin's body is still underwater at Port Stanley." At least three or four others chime in a "let's beat the ignorant American" way.

As I am standing there about to take a ROYAL ass beating, a lone British Sailor standing next to me says "Now wait a minute mates. This here bloke just bough us 100 shots of whiskey! He wasn't there, he doesn't know." The HMS Hermes crew listens to their shipmate and stand down. I yell "Let's try this again! To the Great British and American Navies, Allies til The End!" Or something like that. We ALL raise our shot glasses to their "Here! Here!" reply. They said thanks, I paid the bill and got the hell out of there. They went back to partying. There could be no repeat of the luck I had with the enraged mob at the Manville Bowling Alley years earlier. No "pick the biggest guy and defeat him to escape" This was the time to remain calm while scared to death, use my brain, my smile and the CORRECT WORDS to defend myself. So, martial arts training teaches the importance of DIPLOMACY.

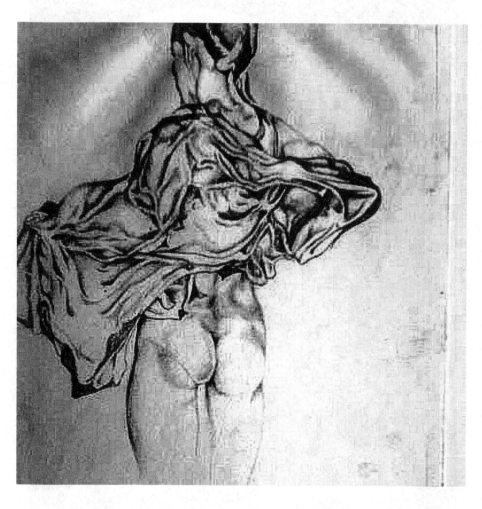

SOMETIMES WORDS AND ACTIONS, NO MATTER HOW APPRORIATE THEY SEEM AT THE TIME, NEED TO BE CONTROLLED TO GIVE DIPLOMACY A CHANCE TO WORK.

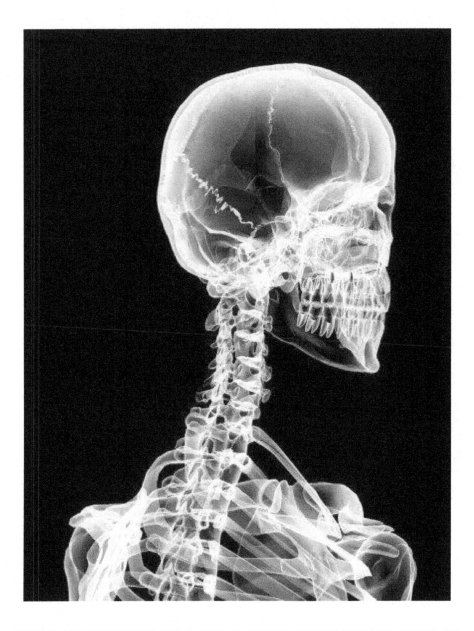

SOMETIMES BEING NICE AND COURTEOUS SIMPLY DOES NOT COMMUNICATE.

CHAPTER TWENTY

The Importance of: BACKING DIPLOMACY WITH THE THREAT OF FORCE.

This concept is nothing new and is the basis for REALPOLIK Look at the world today and you see the value to and limitation of diplomacy. That topic is for scholars, think tanks, governments and diplomats to write about and beyond the focus of this book. But in reality, WE ARE ALL DIPLOMATS, as we move through life trying to make friends, keep enemies at bay, foresee trouble, protect our interests and create smooth relations in whatever we do. We want things others have and we do not. Others want things we have and they do not. How we maneuver these situations in a "civilized" society, is by using DIALOGUE TO SETTLE DIFFERENCES, and WORK to attain things that we desire to own. If you use force to take something that is not yours its robbery. Forcing yourself on another against their will is assault, battery and rape.

But if these things are ILLEGAL IN A CIVILIZED SOCIETY, then why are people still being raped, beaten, robbed and murdered?

The answer is that SOCIETY IS UNRAVELING AT THE SEAMS OF CIVILITY.

There have always been criminals, bandits, thieves and lawbreakers. But as a nation of laws, we are supposed to be FREE and able to walk to the corner store without being attacked. The trouble is that the POLICE ARE NOT THERE TO PROTECT US, they are there to enforce the law. Not UNTIL A CRIME HAS ALREADY OCCURRED is it police time. Who then is going to protect you as you are leaving a Four Star restaurant downtown and there are two big, 5th grade educated thugs sitting on your BMW waiting to rob you? Will you ask them nicely to stop beating you to death and raping your wife?

NO, YOU ARE ALONE IN SELF-PRESERVATION AND PROTECTING LOVED ONES.

History is packed with violent stories of bystanders WATCHING someone get stabbed to death, or beaten in the middle of the street AND DOING NOTHING! There are also examples of HEROES with the courage and skill TO TAKE ACTION in that same moment that others are frozen in panic or afraid to get involved.

WHO ARE YOU?

That is why I am writing this book. Sure the stories have some humor, but they ARE NOT FUNNY. Any number of those stories, or the ones to come, could have gone down wrong. I use humor to soothe the fearful, as I tell them matter of fact, you are in constant danger of attack as we devolve to a less civilized society as a whole. As those that have not, want to take from those that do. Taking of course, even the most valuable things in creation, like your life or your family's freedom by threatening their safety and security. Doubt me? Read the papers, watch the news or listen to the radio. Hell, watch "Cape Fear" with Robert DeNiro or any episode of TV's "Criminal Minds".

Evil is everywhere and THE DANGER IS REAL. It's enough to make you sick. I used to cut out these type of random, savage, inhuman criminal attack stories from newspapers and put them upon a huge wall in Kenpo School as a reminder of why we train as intensely as we do. I ran out of adhesive tape and wall space.

WE ARE GOING BACKWARDS in Ethics, Morality, Responsibility, Civility and Manners.

Now back to the importance of the Threat of Force: Post-Diplomacy. (TOFPD) Diplomacy in both international affairs and personal combat, must be BACKED WITH A CREDIBLE

THREAT OF FORCE. The type we are addressing here is personal combat. There is diplomacy of varying types even before a fight or attack. A predator sizes you up by the way you move, carry yourself and are aware of your surroundings. Are you a lone fawn aimlessly walking the streets with your headphones on, hoody up, head down as you text on your expensive cell phone with $160 Air Jordans on? Or are you a smooth moving, always-aware prowling and growling Tiger Way Man, walking the street at ease but prepared to kill any attacker you meet?

Only **YOUR THREAT OF FORCE** in response to his stalking calculations will keep an awaiting attacker at bay. Numerous documentaries have been done on rapists, robbers, murders and serial killers. Nearly all say, they chose a victim by an apparent weakness or they were simply caught off guard with the violence of action. Most muggers say they look for the easiest target that will be least likely to resist. If **THEY THINK** you will fight back, most likely they will await another prey. And you say; What if they attack me anyway? What if the serial killer who chops people to pieces and eats them chooses me at random?

THEN IT'S ON. SHOWTIME.

And you had better be **TRAINED AND READY** to use that training if you don't want to be butchered alive and become Jeffrey Dahmer Soup.

Now a humorous story of a Diplomacy with the Threat of Force that was successful. This will be followed by a more dangerous, less comical example when **DIPLOMACY WAS NOT ENOUGH** and the **NEED** for Force was required.

One of my favorite friends and Teachers is Master Ron. I mentioned earlier that he is a Knife Fighting Expert and Kung Fu Master. He has so many knives for different purposes on his body, within reach in his car, home or bathroom at any given time, he throws a cutlery beatdown to

Edward Scissorhands. Master Ron, two other skilled Kenpo students and I decided after having some beer at a few local bars that we would "go check out" the Doll House Gentlemens Club on a cross street off North Avenue in Chicago. Our state of inebriation was irrelevant in the fact that we were cabbing to and fro. DUI IS A NO! NO! Its $10 grand minimum these days. If you drink, then walk or cab. Anyway, we arrive at the Club and when scurrying to pay the cab fare, we realize that, except for Master Ron, we were out of money. Not a good thing when going into a place that expects you to tip everyone including of course the dancers.

Now I'm no angel and have found myself, through no fault of my own, in "gentlemens" clubs across the country. I say this only because it is pertinent to the rest of the story and when you've been traveling for 20+ years for business, you've got to be selective in your wind down spots, so I knew how things WERE SUPPOSED TO WORK in these places.

Master Ron, just looks at us with a "Are you kidding?" kinda look as I say something like "It's OK Master Ron has money!"

He just shook his Marine Corp hardened head as I'd seen him do a hundred times before.

Master Ron can get testy for a variety of reasons but not money. We all like to have fun and give everything we have for a great time. We would have made it up to him next time. But the night would get worse for Master Ron and by close extension, us.

Fortunately there was no cover charge at the door or Master Ron may have cut his way in. As we enter, the three of us are standing in front of one of those long steel beer tubs filled with ice and beer. They are situated throughout bigger bars to ease the traffic at the main bar and keep the booze flowing. The young lady tending the tub is looking at us awaiting our order as we are looking for Master Ron awaiting money. We don't see him anywhere. Finally I hear him before I see him with "Son of a B*tch, This f'n Miller Lite cost $10 God D*mn dollars!"

Actually, I don't have enough asterisks to type what he really said. The three of us just looked at him and I said "What?" He shows me the now vintage beer and says "$10!" I said "My buddy here was just charged ten dollars for a bottle of Lite" "She says "Oh! He must have been frequenting The Champagne Bar Section" as she points to a pink velvet roped off stanchion surrounding the exact same beer tub that we stood before. It even had a similar looking girl selling $10 bottles of beer to be part of the "in crowd". I looked at Master Ron and thought he was going to literally explode! Ever see a "Popeye" cartoon where he is in hot water and his temperature rises as a red line moves up his body and his pipe starts spinning? That was what MR looked like. Being a compassionate friend and realizing that this was the 2nd bad mojo to hit him in the last 20 minutes, I soothe him with "It might be a vintage year or something" and "Can we have some money the beer is cheaper down here with regular folks?" He hands me a hateful ten dollar bill and I turn to BeerTubGirl (BTG) and say "$3 Miller Lites please." "That's $9 please" I gave her the $10, said keep the change…hmm 3 beers not 1 for $10. Better deal I said to Master Ron. He glared at me as usual.

So making our way to the table that was open, we sit down. All the way, we are shielding MR's precious vintage triple priced liquid to avoid accidental breakage. He must have sipped at that one bottle for an hour. It's good to be able to enjoy the finer things in life. Master Ron is starting to relax and says something funny for the first time since we got out of the cab. All is well as we have beer, a table and beautiful semi-clad women dancing all around us. Strike Three is coming on fast. In my past experiences, a Club will turn up the lights a bit to have all the dancers come out to shake their stuff to get you interested in purchasing a "lap dance"…whatever that is. So, it came as no surprise when a young lady hopped up on our table and began to dance. It was happening at every table throughout the Doll House. She was cute enough but not my type so I clapped politely when she was done with the song. As I helped her down she just stands there looking at me. Being as sharp as I am, I realize that she is awaiting a tip.

I look at the two students who give me a buck or two each and I added a dollar. I then looked at Master Ron and decided not to ask. The surprise came when the girl says to us "Table Dances are FIFTY DOLLARS!" I look at her waiting for the punch line but none was forthcoming. I explain the misunderstanding to her in my smiley way and she's not budging. Hand out, she says "$50" I say "Master Ron, Do you have $50?" The "F**k No! reply was not unexpected. Saying sorry didn't matter as she says something to someone and we are shortly visited by a huge bouncer in a tuxedo that asks if there is a problem. I tell him the same story that I relayed to you a moment ago about how these clubs ARE SUPPOSED TO WORK. You do not have any woman just jump on your table without the customer knowing the terms of the transaction.

After patiently listening with the ear that also had the microphone in it, he says, "I understand, Sir, just pay the girl and that'll be the end of it." I glance at Master Ron and he shakes his head no as usual. I answer that we don't have the money and wouldn't pay if we did."
DIPLOMATIC FAILURE #1

The bouncer now has been playing Radio Shack with his team mates and I think I am at a wedding, as more tuxedoed men gather and are chatting about how to beat the money out of us. Master Ron has to use the potty and gets up moving toward the bathroom situated by the front door. As he is walking there I see five TuxDudes (TDS) following him. Now as stated, Master Ron is a KNIFE MASTER and armed to the teeth with cutlery. Its not that I was saving him from them, if they tried something in the bathroom, but protect them from him lest the once clean toilet room takes on the trappings of Texas Chainsaw Massacre.

As he enters the bathroom, two TDS follow him in and three stand by the door as I brush past them to enter. I take up a urinal next to MR as the TDS just stand there. Made it a bit difficult to get the pee flow going, but I did. MR glances over his shoulder at the TDS in the way Sean Penn, in has early role in "Bad Boys" glanced over his just before he bashes his attacker in the face with a pillow full of unopened soda cans. As he is finishing his business, he says "This place sucks! Let's get out of here." totally ignoring the two TDS in the can and the now 8 or more TDS between us and the front door exit. All four of us are now back together and ready for diplomacy to work.

I say" seems we are at loggerheads." As I look at the perplexed looks of the TDS who think I said we in a gang "The Loggerheads" or something. Seems silly now, but this all was over one dance, one girl and $50. Was it worth the carnage that was creeping closer? I'm aware that Master Ron is deciding which blade to start with as I unleash DIPLOMATIC EFFORT #2. "We'll fight you for your jobs!" I say in a quite serious matter of fact offer. I suggested they pick four guys against us four and we would settle the $50 question.

As they looked at each other in confusion on whether this is really worth it and Master Ron just looking at the ground brushing a boot from side to side awaiting the word. The ear pieces must have been screaming "Where are all the bouncers?" as the bar is now totally unprotected and they begin to realize they are not getting the "$50.

We exit. They follow. We cross the street. There is now 15 (we counted) TDS on one side of the street in front of the club and the 4 of us on the opposite side of the street just staring back. If they crossed the "demilitarized zone" represented by the street, they would be in the wrong legally. If we breached the line, then we would be legally liable for whatever happened. With the fight being four against fifteen, someone was going to die, go to the hospital and or jail.

Finally, after looking at Master Ron, he wanted to split. We caught a cab back to Old Town.

So, DIPLOMACY BACKED WITH THE THREAT OF FORCE can be effective without having to resort to VIOLENCE.

In the second instance, DIPLOMACY WAS NOT ENOUGH TO PREVENT CONFLICT and if there was no other option, I probably would not be here to write this book. It all started simply enough. My wife had invited her best friend and her new boyfriend over for dinner. When they arrived, we talked a bit and then the women were drinking wine in the kitchen and I took Brian to the second bedroom where, in fact, PWOK really started, as I had been teaching one student private lessons to in the 2nd room turned dojo. My erstwhile dojo's days were numbered as soon as my daughter Rachel was born. In with the crib and rocking chair; out with the swords and pictures of ODEN and other famous Warriors. Anyway, as we enter the room with our beers, Brian is taken aback by all the wall-hung weaponry, books on war, history of conflict and martial arts books numbering in the hundreds.

In taking in the images, he says something along the lines of "Man, You are obsessed with violence." Feeling my initial desire to smash him through the wall into the master bedroom while barking "Yes I am!" under control, say "Just an area of study". Thought that was the end of it, but he continued the conversation in bits and pieces over dinner. My wife was amazed at my socially acceptable responses since the four of us were to go to a Pink Floyd concert, at what was then the Rosemont Horizon, later that week and she wanted us to get along. So I listened patiently to his commentary about violence and the fact that he has never been in a fight or attacked. "You will." As my reply raised an eyebrow or two while mentioning the scenario of 5th grade educated thugs on his BMW and him getting beaten to death…ending with AND THERE'S NOT A D**NED THING YOU ARE GOING TO BE ABLE TO DO ABOUT IT!" That ended that topic for the night as we retreated to small talk about the Bears, Cubs and Sox.

Concert night, we go, we park, we enter, we are blown away by PF and we return to the car. Rosemont Horizon parking is the worse and leaving a show is like racing out to get to your car and sit while thousands of others do the same. Brian's red Camaro was parked on the farthest edge of the lot nearest a guard rail that would normally have left room for a single lane of traffic toward the exit in the direction we were facing. However, with Floyd in town, that lane was blocked with cars facing the opposite direction and we were going no where.

As people are returning to their cars, the vehicle parked parallel to the guard rail, facing in the opposite direction, but even with us has their driver's side window facing Brian's driver side window. Glancing over, I see the big face of some Ethnic Dude (ED) screaming something that we thought to be "Great Show!" as give him the thumbs up and say in my best hippie voice "Yeah man!". As Brian rolls down the power window a bit, I hear the ED scream "You guys are f**k'n gay!" Brian ups the window and is now looking straight ahead in a bit of confusion as to why someone would say such a thing FOR NO APPARENT REASON. I knew we were not gay and that is probably where the story should have ended, but that wouldn't have made the very selective cut of the myriad of stories and experiences I have had and chosen to share with you.

Now, I see that maybe ED had the right idea parking that way, since a few smaller cars in front of him manage to squeeze out and make their way to the exit line. Now with about 15 feet to maneuver, ED starts moving forward, then cuts hard left in an attempt to "K-turn" and join the non-moving line in our direction and T-bones our rear end. His vehicle's wheel well gets stuck on top of the Camaro's rear bumper and they are stuck. Assessing the situation by glancing at Brian, who has not moved from the "gay" comment steering wheel death grip and saying "Man they just hit your car!" Luckily Brian drove. Had it been my cherry 1989 Firebird Formula, I would be writing this from prison in what would have been known as the "Rosemont Massacre".

Brian in a breaking voice says "its ok, let's just get out of here." "Where are we going to go?" I ask. Realizing that Brian was locked in fear and would be of no use at all, I glance back at my wife and say "Stay Here". That's code for "This could get serious and I don't need to be worrying about you at the same time." Do you know how many husbands or boyfriends lost their teeth as they are defending their spouse only to have said lover hold their arms down to prevent a fight and you take a full shot to the chops? The answer is PLENTY.

So with the women safely in the back seat and Brian safely at the wheel, I exit in an attempt at DIPLOMACY. Upon reaching the back of the Camaro, I see the metal on bumper connection and more importantly looked through the windshield at the two men sitting in the front with maybe three or four other darkened heads in the back seat. Looking at the driver who was the expert on spotting sexual orientation, is in a rage. He is deciding whether to get out and kick my ass, floor the car or just simultaneously implode. Noting that his passenger seated friend is calmer and trying to keep his buddy in the car. Good friend. Raising a finger in a "Wait a minute" diplomatic gesture offering assistance while putting both hands under the stuck wheel well of his car as I am telling him "Slowly go in Reverse".

Of course, his pent up fury has him floor the gas and smash his once nice ride rear-end first into the solid steel guard rail. The accordion effect smashed his long back end a good foot and a half inward. My attempt at diplomacy now was a secret plan to have him smash his car for calling me gay.

SHOWTIME.

Driving ED finally breaks the dual grasp of this passenger and seat belt as he swings the car door open and races towards me. Martial Note: WHEN YOU ARE WELL TRAINED, ATTACKS COME AT YOU IN SLOW MOTION. It's as if the opponent is moving through thick jelly.

Warriors train for real and regularly see every kind of hard-hitting, laser fast attacks and defenses that there are FOR THOUSANDS OF YEARS. So that "haymaker" that ED was thinking of throwing didn't have a chance. This time-space phenomenon can be explained simply with; you train against fast attacks of a skilled fighter, and the untrained attack looks like it is moving through jelly. That is also why one trained fighter can defeat several attackers in what looks like "Vampire Transport Speed". (VTS) As ED driver approaches in slow mo, ED passenger begins getting out as well. The folks in the back seat either couldn't find the seat latches or just wanted to watch the fight from their spots. But I was aware of them and their head bobbing for best view positional movements which meant, for the time being, they stayed put.

By the time ED driver finally gets to me, I try once last time for a DIPLOMATIC SOLUTION with "Your glasses…" Too late. My LEFT HAND JAB removes them in halves as my OVERHAND RIGHT CROSS smashes his teeth all the way in like those puck-slid, pin-sprung bowling games in some bars. They do return back, but continue to leave his mouth in unison. They do disperse into several different directions as they hit the ground with the sick sound of "Chicklets" hard gum. As he drops to the ground to be closer to his teeth, I do not strike a third time. Martial note: FIGHTING COMBINATIONS SHOULD BE EXECUTED IN THREES.

Whether, the 3rd strike omission was mercy or flaw, it didn't matter since ED passenger is now rounding the front of their car and opens his mouth to say something that I ASSUMED would be War-like, so I bury a RIGHT UPPER CUT into his stomach and smash him hard face-first onto the hood of their car. He is not fighting back. I recall the pre-conflict mental file in video replay that reminds me that he was trying to control his friend in the car and maybe that could be used to stop further carnage. Oh yeah, a reminder why you should ALWAYS use a 3 Strike Combination is that as I am trying DIPLOMACY with ED passenger, ED driver regains his focus a bit and sees all his teeth and blood courtesy of That Gay Guy. Not wanting to disrupt the diplomatic efforts underway, I do the right thing martially with the delayed 3rd strike by way of a rising right knee square to his face that knocks him out cold. All this diplomacy/violence is occurring simultaneously as I still have ED passenger, now The Diplomat (TD) pinned doggy-style on the hood. I say "Look man. I am a trained fighter and will butcher all of you if this goes on." Never mind the fact of being outnumbered or that they may have had weapons, then I MIGHT BE DEAD. But as Kimball often says "He who lives by the sword, shall die by the sword." Ok then. WE ARE ALL GOING TO DIE! The Way of The Warrior IS DEATH! TD says "Look what you did to my friend!" And I swear that I borrow a line verbatim from a Chuck Norris flick, and say "That's pain friend. But it could hurt a lot worse." Man that's cool.

By now, as in Manville, we are surrounded by all the bystanders that got out of their non-moving cars to see what they could. It again occurred to me that there would be no police, event security or heroes to help me. After glancing at their car to see an empty back seat it means all of head bobbers are now around me. If taken to the ground I could be stomped to death or stabbed in the back. So time to lay it on the line for all to hear. "I am a KILLER and ready to die! Let's get on with it! Here and Now! Live or Die! Let's Go!" And I am serious as a heart attack.

The only "taker" is the toothless ED driver who stumbles to his feet, trips and falls, hitting his forehead on the parking lot. He had balls, as he got up again and took a step before The Diplomat intercepted him AND THEY BEGAN TO FIGHT. As attention turns to them and the head bobbers are trying to separate them, they finally ALL get back into their smashed car. We are still stuck in the same gridlock as before and I simply lean on the back right corner panel of the Camaro and watch them menacingly. Finally, the cars start moving a bit and they get to complete their K-turn and pull in behind us. They kept a safe distance until the exit, then they raced past and probably to a hospital. They will probably get pulled over since both taillights were smashed to bits from the guardrail and inoperative. The cop would probably say to driver "What the Hell happened to you?" Wonder what he'll say?

Oh, and getting back into the Camaro, I say nothing as Brian was still in the same spot that I had left him. He just mumbles a barely audible "Billy, you were right. We didn't do anything and then you just kicked their asses." I replied "Lucky that time. It could have gone down differently." He asked if he could come for lessons. I say "no." and we drove home in relative silence with Pink Floyd playing "One of These Days" on the radio.

Remember that FIGHTING IS DANGEROUS TO YOUR HEALTH.

The more often you fight, the greater the odds of getting hurt or killed. So, if at all possible, AVOID FIGHTING, but be PREPARED TO USE FORCE or the THREAT OF FORCE when DIPLOMACY FAILS and THE NEED TO DEFEND YOURSELF OR ANOTHER arises.

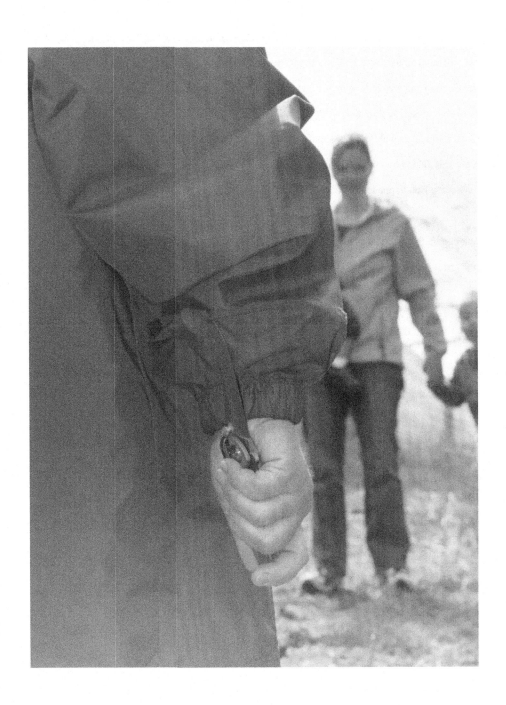

CHAPTER TWENTY ONE

The Importance of: COMING TO THE DEFENSE OF OTHERS.

I am not a vigilante. Nor propose taking the law into our own hands as that just helps erode the fabric of society. There are capable men and women in uniform paid with our tax dollars to uphold the law. It's the Criminal Justice System and it is one of the three main pillars of our American Government. You remember, checks and balances: Executive, Legislative and Judicial. It's the last one that I have the most problem with. Who is going to accurately JUDGE the loss of my kidnapped, raped and murdered child in terms of years in prison or what if they go free on a technicality? That is where the system fails and that's when I become a murderer.

You can study this stuff on your own, but looking at FBI crime statistics, criminals released due to over crowding and the sometimes poor case presentation of the prosecution leading to a mistrial, its troubling. So in my view, TAKING ACTION TO SAVE MYSELF OR OTHERS COMES FIRST and the legal consequences a distant second. As American Kenpo Karate Grandmaster, Ed Parker once said "It's better to be tried by twelve than carried by six."

Again, fighting is dangerous and illegal unless for a sanctioned sporting event or as provable self defense. So when to fight? When to run? When to act? What action to take? When not to take action? Several of the previous chapters have given some answers to the questions THAT I FACED and the RESPONSES THAT I TOOK. Your circumstances will definitely be different, and the answers to the above questions will be answered by you alone. Those answers must occur in less time than you might think. It's nice to think that everyone KNOWS THAT IT IS WRONG to do something illegal. But guess what? It doesn't matter what your view is.

The attackers don't give a "Flying F**k" that you are a non-violent, law-abiding citizen with the flu, who had a tough day at the office and just wants to go home to your family for dinner!

SO WHAT TO DO AND WHEN?

At Kenpo School, I tell the students that "We will not preach to you were to DRAW THE LINE. That is your decision. Is it when someone insults your wife or mother? Spills beer on you without apology? Or is it when someone bumps your car after tailgating you in traffic? What if someone challenges you to fight? We will not tell you when, where or why to fight. THAT IS YOUR DECISION ALONE. But when you do make the decision to step across that line, THAT IS WHEN WHAT YOU'VE BEEN TAUGHT AND YOUR TRAINING COMES IN!"

TRAIN. TRAIN, TRAIN UNTIL YOU DIE. IT WILL PREPARE YOU TO MEET YOUR DEATH WITHOUT FEAR KNOWING ALL THE ANSWERS ARE TO COME AND YOU ARE READY.

In other words, it's SHOWTIME.

SHOWTIME #1: Washington DC. 1982

A junior in college at the University of Maryland, I was with three other friends and my new puppy "Opie' as we are walking along the National Mall between the Capitol and the Washington Monument. We were there quite a bit since the District of Columbia is only 9 miles from our University. It was a beautiful with The Mall full of tourists and local businessmen and women having their lunch. We had just gotten hot dogs from one of the many vendors that line Pennsylvania Avenue. Walking toward The Monument, we were commenting on the two different shades of stone that make up the huge structure. Bringing up the idea that the Civil War had stopped work on the project and that by the time work resumed, the new stone didn't match the original. There were other theories as well.

My close friend, Billman (he ended every sentence with "man") floated the concept that "Maybe aliens had dipped it partly in bleach when no one was looking, man!" It was about that time that Billman points to The Monument and says "look at that, man!" As we focus where he is pointing, there is a man running with a purse carried like a football being chased by about 25 Boy Scouts 20 yards back and followed by a game old woman a distant third but running like hell. Must have been her purse. It was surreal, like the scene in "E.T." of the boys pedaling their bikes through the sky with the moon in the background.

Anyway, the lead between front running purse snatcher and his boy-muscled leg-shortened pursuers was widening. As granny crossed The Monument marker, the kids and crook where outta sight. As we are following the distant action, Billman yells, 'There he goes Man!" while pointing at this Sleek, Slender and Tall Man (SSTM) streaking toward PA Avenue, but also toward us in an angular sort of way. As Billman begins running down The Mall toward SSTM, another buddy Rio, a Brazilian soccer player, races down the sidewalk parallel to The Mall on the left and PA Avenue to his right to assist Billman's Geometric Containment Attempt. (BGCA) Still standing there with my friend Bonnie, I take Opie from around my neck and toss him in a short paws up arc to her awaiting arms and off I go. Now my two friends' excellent angle of attack have SSTM moving his escape route ever closer to me. If SSTM is successful in crossing heavily trafficked Pennsylvania Avenue, he will be gone and with it the old lady's purse.

With Opie safely in Bonnie's arms, I make the short twenty yard sprint on a 45 degree angle toward PA Ave and SSTM. In a move that would impress even "Starsky & Hutch" with SSTM one lane deep into Penn Ave traffic, I step my left foot on the front bumper of a classic VW Beetle and use the recoil to launch myself vertically and horizontally onto the back of startled SSTM. He must have thought that he had been hit by a vehicle from behind as WE DO SMASH forcefully into a maroon van trying not to run us over. As we hit the unmoving mass, my hero leap ends hard as we hit the ground. At first contact, it was like tackling a smelly garbage bag full of rotten meat as we did a "Pepe Le Pew" roll over unwelcoming hot asphalt on PA Ave. I grab and drag him to the side of the road just so we don't get hit. Billman, Bonnie and Opie race over, followed by Rio who arrives with a soccer style kick into SSTM's face. It seemed a bit unnecessary since he was not resisting, but couldn't fault Rio who was fresh back from an exhausting 150 yard round trip sprint chasing this guy.

Looking at Rio with a "he's not a soccer ball" glance, we stand him up and lean him against a parked car. While awaiting the police, a VERY LARLE MUSCULAR MAN ON A BLACK HARLEY PULLS UP. What does he see? Three white men holding a bleeding from face black man. Ut oh…this about to turn into a RACIAL THING, which it was not. He gets off his bike quickly, takes off his helmet and grabs it by the mouth protection piece and is about to go "Thor's Hammer" on our college heads. When he removed the helmet, I was hoping to have time to explain, but his face had a hostile look similar to "Predator" when he removes his face plate in the swamp before kicking Arnold's ass. There would be no reasoning with him.

As I leave the side of SSTM to confront threatening BIGGER and MEANER MAN, two cab drivers, who had witnessed the whole thing, get in front of him and explain the truth. They point to the lady's purse and explain that the blood is from our van collision. Not exactly true, but I was in no hurry to clarify the details. Satisfied with their story, the biker re-helmets, re-mounts and removes himself from the scene. For once I was thankful for cab drivers.

Our attention is now focused on the departing motorcycle avenger, I hear "swiiishhhhhh" as SSTM bolts from the weak grasp of my two friends and makes a dash for freedom. We might have let him go had he not still had the purse that he picked up off the ground. Revisiting "Next What To Do Mental Manual" (NWTDMM) I race after him AGAIN and tackle him from behind by wrapping around his fast moving, high stepping, smelly ass legs. We fall facedown IN THE MIDDLE OF PENNSYLVANIA AVENUE IN DOWNTOWN WASHINGTON DC WITHIN VIEW OF SEVERAL WHITE HOUSE WINDOWS! Where are the Secret Service, DC Police or for that matter a frig'n PARK RANGER? Now with me atop the back of prone SSTM, I put him in a hard CHICKEN WING and lock his shoulder up tight. Awaiting any sign of authority care of The Most Powerful City on Earth, finally two DC motorcycle cops race up and do a very cool brake slide that surrounds us. They ask me to release the lock and I mention he is fast and stinky. They reply "Roger that".

I rise and am walking toward my friends, when a Tour Bus driver beeps his horn, as all his passengers' faces are squished up against the huge front windshield. They are trying to say something as they point to the front of the bus. Thought that perhaps I'd left some face skin or an ear in the grill, but that wasn't it. Under the front right tire of the huge bus were my sunglasses that must have flew off during APPREHESION LEAP #2. The driver held up traffic on the busiest street in DC so as not to run over my shades. I like bus drivers now too.

Rejoining the group of four, Bonnie hands me Opie and we continue our walk down The Mall towards The Monument. While walking, I mention that we should not make a statement lest we have just had a gang member or some assassin's cousin incarcerated. In what today remains a great mystery, as we are walking farther and farther away from the scene of the crime, more and more tourists are congratulating us and thanking us. How did word spread so fast in a forward direction? Very bizarre indeed. As we decide that we should get lost in the crowd by cutting across the grass of The Mall, a slow moving DC police cruiser gives us a polite "woot-woot" of his siren and pulls to the curb. In the back of the car, we see the old lady with her purse and a loving, thankful look on her face. The officer exits and pulls out a note pad. "Gentlemen, Miss" he starts "There was quite a commotion down street and we are going to need a statement from each of you." With looks that said "you have plenty of witnesses and we have done enough" he starts anyway with Billman, "Name? he asks. Looking down at his sneakers and with a very respectful tone, Billman says "Brian Piccolo". The cop, amused says "Brian Piccolo? from the 'Brian's Song' movie?" "Yeah. I get that all the time, man. Uh Sir." says Billman. The officer could have asked for Billman's ID but did not. "And you Sir?" directed at me. "Gale Sayers" I reply stone faced "and the dog is Opie." "OK he says, we have some heroes here, two of which are Brian Piccolo and Gale Sayers who chased down and captured a purse snatcher in the middle of Pennsylvania Avenue? Is that what you are telling me?"

"That wasn't us Sir." Rio chimes in. Bonnie smiles and we are allowed to go on our way.

"God Bless You!" the lady from the back of the cruiser says as it pulls away.

SHOWTIME #2: Chicago, IL Mid 1990s

There was a cool bar in Chicago that had a bodacious reputation for partying hard. It was a place to really cut loose, pushed the alcohol filled jelly shots and looked more like a fraternity house than a bar. A fun thing they did was provide all patrons with a complementary can of silly string to which everyone got wasted then pasted. I had been there several times without incident but the last time there was quite different. In a group of folks talking, doing relentless waitress-urged gelatinous shots and string shooting anyone that got to close, everyone is having a blast. As I am standing about 7 ft in front of a beautiful girl with gorgeous curly hair and she is lighting a cigarette.

Just then a jet of silly string hits the flame and the propellant ignites setting her on fire. The flame is so intense that I can no longer see her.

In what I attribute to TRAINING and ABILITY TO TAKE ACTION (ATTA), I cover the distance in less than a second. While tackling her to the ground, I am aware that she is burning and her hair and clothing are on fire. The smell of burning hair and skin is unforgettable. I cover her with my body in an attempt to fire blanket her out. Onlookers said the flames were coming around my armpits and upward into the air. I wanted to protect her face, so that is where I concentrated. By then, assistance arrived in the forms of water and ice from glasses and pitchers of those around. I stood up, saw her scorched hair, but her face was unburned. I was a bit singed but no hospital visit. She was in shock and as the paramedics left with her, so did we. Party buzz zero. Not knowing her name or what hospital she was at, I never heard about her recovery.

I was sitting with my wife at a café-style restaurant having lunch some 5 years later when a silver stand with a bottle of chilled champagne reached our table. Confused, I looked at the waitress, and she pointed to several women sitting at the bar. Not recognizing any of them as my wife's face looked a bit more intense than mine. Finally, this beautiful woman in a black turtleneck and slacks comes over to our table. Her short hair and cute face had fooled me. She simply said "Hi. I want to show you something." She took her right hand and pulled down her turtleneck about 3 inches to reveal a small, crescent shape scar that rose up from her skin. She still didn't mention her name and again neither did I. She just said "You saved me. You saved my face and my life." I smiled and thanked her for the champagne.

So, martial arts training and ATTA can SAVE A LIFE WITH NO FIGHTING AT ALL.

TAKE ACTION OR GET OUT OF THE WAY SO SOMEONE ELSE CAN.

WE ARE ALL PART OF LIFE AND NOT APART FROM LIFE. YOU HAVE A DUTY TO PROTECT THE WEAK, DEFEND THE INNOCENT AND TAKE ACTION WHERE POSSIBLE.

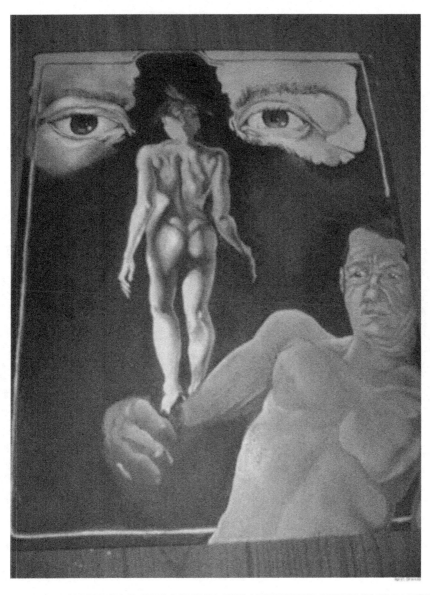

BE PREPARED TO IMMEDIATELY COME TO THE ASSISTANCE OF THOSE IN DANGER.

SHOWTIME #3: Brookfield IL 2012

My Beautiful and Intelligent Fiancé (BIF) and I were enjoying a great conversation at a local Beer House and the place was humming with its usual collection of misfits, losers, pity-party pros and a general lowering of the human condition. It's also one of our favorite hang outs, because the beer is cheap, ice cold and the place is within walking distance of our home. Remember: DUIs ARE A NO-NO! Now, its not uncommon for "gentlemen" to talk with her since she can be quite a debater, an engaging conversationalist and is smokin' hot. She has a huge heart and listens deeply to the problems of others. In this instance, she brought a wasted dirt bag with women-issues to sit with us for company while his girlfriend is out having a cigarette. This guy was a real winner and stood the whole time to the right of BIF while I was seated to her left. For some reason, he takes out a box cutter and is fidgeting with it for a while as I ask him to "Please put the blade away" but instead seems to be getting more agitated with the ongoing absence of his "Natural Born Killers"-type companion.

I buy him a beer, and he starts staring at me while extending the blade and retracting it. He is no longer fidgeting with it as before. He says something challenging, so I calmly reach over and take back the untouched beer just bought for him. I SEE that his right hand held the blade and it was literally a swipe way from BIF's throat. We're talking maybe 16 inches from delinquent's razor and the love of my life's jugular vain. I realize that even with all my skills and training, it would be impossible to stop an unexpected attack before the blade sliced her face, neck or throat.

Why?

1) I WAS OUT OF POSITION WITH THE GUY ON THE OPPOSITE SIDE OF BIF.
2) ACTION IS ALWAYS FASTER THAN REACTION.

So, making a distraction, I SAY SOMETHING AGGRESSIVE TO BRING HIS ATTENTION TO ME and do a quick semi-circle around BIF and slap the blade from his hand which falls to the ground. He also crumples to the floor via a short 1-2 combination to his face with a trachea grab that guides him down to the copper foot rest bar below and sufficiently makes my point.

Martial Note: A major point when involved in conflict resolution in a place where you are known is to remember that "friends" can get you hurt. Just as a loving spouse can get your teeth broken holding your arms while you are in a fight, some regular bar patrons may want to keep you from further hurting the bad guy by grabbing you as well. THIS CAN BE VERY, VERY BAD WHEN THE BAD GUY PICKS UP HIS BLADE AS YOU ARE HINDERED BY "FRIENDS".

BE AWARE OF "FRIENDLY" BAR REGULARS TRYING TO "HELP" YOU BY HOLDING YOUR ARMS AS YOUR ASSAILANT SLASHES YOUR FEMORAL ARTERY AND YOU DIE.

And that's what happened here. During the dispatch of would be Slicer, I see the box cutter and reach to pick it up to hand to the bartender, three or four Male Barflies TACKLE ME to the ground. Through the pile, I glance to see BIF safely near the front door with a huge guy that she knew. At that point Slicer picks up his blade and is slashing it in my direction. I had to get up quick, but with 800 lbs of beer-bellied man meat atop me, that was easier said than done. While on the ground, one of the tacklers says "Stop! You are on the ground and now you're blind!" I assumed he meant that my Karate was useless while I was down there. Ok I thought, maybe he is right, so slam him HARD in the temple with a very poignant and sharp EMPI UCHI ELBOW TIP STRIKE. He rolls off me holding his contused head with both hands and the others follow suit as I am barking "Knife! He has a Knife!" When Moronville relocates off me to controlling him, Slicer is dragged from the bar with No Return Allowed. (NRA) instructions.

I immediately move to BIF and make sure that this guy was an ally. He was, so I returned to my beer. My long sleeve Harley Davidson shirt, ripped bad, was the only casualty and thankfully so.

Martial Note 2: If it had been a strange environment and not knowing anyone else, it would be hard to determine who the bad guy's friends were, if they were armed and how many would try to back him up. In that case Kenpo would have been brought to bear in a more intense way. KENPO KARATE IS VERY EFFECTIVE IN MULTIPLE ATTACK SCENARIOS.

In this case, a disarm with a few punches to the puss and a throw down was all that was needed. A timely EMPI UCHI to the temple of a "friend" and a new Harley shirt was required as well. So, martial arts teach you to BE AWARE YOUR SURROUNDINGS even in a "friendly" place.

SHOWTIME #4: Indianapolis, IN 1999

While on a business trip to Indy, I was having dinner with a customer winding down a long day

DO NOT LET PEOPLE CHOKE TO DEATH BECAUSE YOU DIDN'T TRAIN ENOUGH TO ACT.

of travel, sales calls, meetings and was enjoying a peaceful dinner at a very nice restaurant when guess what? Yep…SHOWTIME. I am watching a thirty-something, well-dressed couple eating about four tables away. She is talking and he is not listening. He appears to be scanning the crowd in a "see and be seen" manner. While looking at her reaction to his inattentiveness, her face changes from irritation to what I thought was anger, but it wasn't, it was fear, as she is choking on something. She is holding her throat A SURE SIGN THAT SOMONE IS CHOKING. She is looking toward her companion who doesn't even notice. INSTINCTIVELY A CHOKING VICTIM WILL MOVE TO THE BATHROOM FOR PRIVACY, WATER OR TO AVOID FEAR OF EMBARRASSMENT.

She is now in the ladies room as I excuse myself and move quickly to the bathroom door which is locked. Knocking several times knowing she can not answer, and in a move that must have shaken a few wine glasses, I FRONT THRUST KICK the door open and enter. The door slams shut behind me and she is starting to turn blue. THAT IS BAD. IF SHE WAS COUGHING AND TRYING TO REMOVE THE OBSTRUCTION, YOU DO NOTHING! IF SHE IS NOT COUGHING OR TURNING BLUE, YOU ASK "ARE YOU CHOKING?" A NO ANSWER OR A HEAD NOD MEANS YES I AM CHOKING! TIME TO TAKE ACTION.

So, I spin her around and perform the Heimlich Maneuver by putting my overlapping hand over fist two inches above the belly button. If the person is obese, you can locate the Xyphoid Process (the bone bump that protrudes from the bottom of the chest where the two cages meet) Be well BELOW the Xyphoid and ABOVE the belly button and sharply pop your fist toward you until the choking matter is expelled. This amazing technique alone has saved more choking victims' lives than any other. EVERYONE should know how to do it and have the guts to apply it. Funny, the hand position of the Heimlich Maneuver is about the same as the Kenpo Karate salutation; a closed fist with overlapping hand over top.

TAKE ACTION.

As she regains oxygen, and with my arms still around her lower chest, Her Champion enters and attempts to pull me off her TO SAVE his woman from attack. As he spins me around, I let go of the girl, follow the circular movement of the pull, and slam him hard head and upper back into the paper towel dispenser. "She was choking to death F**khead!" or something like that and left the ladies room. Diners heard her yelling and slapping/punching her boyfriend/husband as the door closes more naturally this time.

Rejoining my table to a curious look on my client's face "She was choking." I said. "Good thing you were here." he said. The couple eventually returned to their table, got the check and left. She mouthed "thank you" and then shot a nasty glance at her cowering companion. He wanted to "see and be seen". And so he was. Dick.

By the way, it was an improperly chewed piece of blackened prawn that caused all the drama.

So, martial arts training and ATTA can be valuable EVEN AT DINNER.

ATTA- Ability To Take Action or to not do so is up to you. The ability to come to the aid of and successfully help someone in need is (should be) among the most basic human instincts. Whether that "hero factor' is slowly eroding away with our DNA or some other societal reason has yet to be seen. I hope the writing of this book and any knowledge gleaned may save your life, the life of another or just keeping someone from getting hurt. In taking action to save folks from drowning, burning, choking, being mugged, getting beaten up, helping in car wreck, YOU ARE STANDING UP FOR WHAT IS RIGHT MAKING YOUR ACTIONS IMPECCABLE- THE RIGHT ACTION.

Martial arts' training imbues you with ATTA and that allows you to stand up for what you believe in and who you are. When your cause is right and in harmony with the flow of the Universe, your actions will be true and beyond defeat. Unless, of course, you die in your Attempt At Noble Action. (AANA) In that case, "WE WILL WARN THE DEAD IN THE HALLS OF VALHALLA* THAT A (KENPO) WARRIOR IS COMING!" *For those that have a religious upbringing, or are not descendants of Vikings, think of Valhalla as a part of Heaven.

It's a special place where Warriors go AND THE BRAVE WILL LIVE FOREVER! JUMBO!

LOOKING FOR, DESCERNING AND UNDERSTANDING PATTERNS CAN GIVE YOU A BETTER VIEW OF THE WHOLE PICTURE. THERE ARE PATTERNS EVERYWHERE YOU NOTICE.

CHAPTER TWENTY TWO

The Importance of: UNDERSTANDING PATTERNS.

Patterns, as you know, are a sequence of events that repeat enough for you to notice.

If I go to "Jack's Beer and Brawl" and have confrontations there regularly, that's a pattern. Pretty easy to see a pattern with its information and EITHER USE IT TO ADVANTAGE or AVOID THE PATTERN altogether. A nice place with fun, pretty women might cause you to EMBRACE THE PATTERN. The difficulty comes when the patterns are less clearly defined and interspersed with moments of non-pattern appearance. But if you are aware and clearly SEE what is REALLY HAPPENING in any given situation, YOU WILL SEE PATTERNS that you've either noted before in past experience or are related to a specific kind of venue or event. It's like "déjà vu all over again" to quote Baseball Legend, Yogi Berra.

One of my most curious, ongoing patterns is the fact that there is always have some kind of anomaly when going to see my favorite band PINK FLOYD. The years are different, the circumstances vary, but I must always be especially aware when attending. And it's Pink Floyd; mind-blowing, other-dimensional, cerebral-engaging stuff, not slam-dancing at a Black Flag punk rock show or the tougher elements that make up say an audience for Judas Priest. No, after having been to enough concerts, I KNOW HOW THINGS ARE SUPPOSED TO WORK. Find out about the event. See who is interested in going. Buy tickets. Arrange a ride. Get dressed in concert-appropriate clothing. Go to show. Enjoy. Leave and go out or go home thrilled. It's a simple pattern that we have all repeated to the chagrin of millions of brain cells.

Not sure why, but attending a Pink Floyd concert ALWAYS leaves me with a story to tell. The first one is when I purchased eight (8) front row, dead center seats to see the ORIGINAL, brand new show "THE WALL" in the early 80's at Nassau Coliseum in NY. This was the first performance of The Wall when all Pink Floyd original members were still together. (Except of course, the great Syd Barrett) The original The Wall Tour only played at three venues IN THE WORLD; NY, LA and London. Talk about exclusive. Anyway, with the millions of Pink Floyd fans worldwide, you may wonder how I got those front row seats?

There was a time when concert tickets were purchased at Ticketron (not even in this laptop's vocabulary anymore) outlets inside department stores. You actually WAITED IN LINE like today's over-the-top Techies do to get the latest version of iPhone. Anyway, a few friends and I camped out in a van near the store that housed our tickets. Like idiots, we fall asleep in the van and awake at dawn to see about fifteen people ALREADY IN LINE! "$&*(^$#@!" we say scrambling out of the van to beat the throngs of people approaching the line from all directions. One half hour later, there are well over 100 people waiting in line the length of the strip mall.

I am steamed because we were the only vehicle in the parking lot at 3 am when our SENTRY SKILLS FAILED, we fell asleep and were now line members 16 through 19. This fact precluded us from being first in line. Duh. Any martial application lesson-appropriate here would be "ON A MISSION? STAY THE HELL AWAKE!" As we are standing in line, we are bitching up a storm at each other placing blame, when the Store Manager arrives looking quite perplexed. He wants to know why we are all here. We yell "Pink Floyd-THE WALL, Man!" as he pulls out a small blue book and says "Sorry folks, you've been misled. I have the events schedule and their on sale dates right here." He goes through a series of concerts, baseball games and other sporting events that Ticketron would be selling tickets for. No mention of Pink Floyd. We are trying to remember who told us about the shows and the ticket sales date as doubt starts creeping in. As the news travels backwards through the line, chunks of people leave the line and the size reduces by a third.

The first 19 of us in front don't budge as we repeatedly ask the Store Manager to go check inside with Ticketron, but says they don't open sales their sales window until 9 am along with the store itself. It's now 8 am and we are deciding what to do as more people join the line and it again extends well over the original 100. Then, six people in front of us, tired of waiting for a measly three hours, leave the line. We now move up six spots in a line that is probably useless.
With nine folks still in front of us, we are waiting when, at 8:50 am, the Store Manager, unlocks the door and pokes his head out. We're pretty sure he was going to say "Go Away! I told you no Pink Floyd concert on the docket!" Instead he says "You guys were right. Since the venues are limited to only 2 US cities, it didn't appear on the schedule. Wall tics on sale at 9 am!"
HOLY %&*$! AWESOME!

Martial Note: WAIT. BE PATIENT. GATHER AND TRUST YOUR INTEL...TO A POINT AND BE PREPARED TO IMPROVISE.

So, as the eternal last five minutes tick down through molasses, we discuss our purchasing strategy. There was an 8 ticket limit per person and figured that we had a good chance of being ON THE FLOOR! But while listening to the chatter in front of us by Seasoned Big Concert Ticket Getters (SBCTG) They were in line in front of us, right? I pick up some possibly important intel as the nine frontal interlopers are all together. They are saying that since Ticketron opens at the same time WORLDWIDE, everyone is going to be trying to purchase the best floor seats possible. The problem is that could land you in the very back of the floor in unfavorable seats. We didn't know that at THE WALL, it didn't matter where you sat, PF would be coming for your mind. Leaning so far forward to hear, I almost plane-out and fall into

233

the girl in front of me. Moving back to vertical, I hear their strategic decision. When the 9 am PF Stock Market Bell rings to open buying, each member would ask for THE BEST SEATS IN THE MEZZANINE. It made perfect sense, let the worldwide masses fight over the floor seating and we (now included us within the SBCTG group who knew best.) VICTORY and seats WOULD BE OURS!

9 am. SHOWTIME. (The non-violent kind)

SBCTG members 1 through 9 move with swift determination toward the uprising window of our PF salvation Ticketron. One by one, they execute their plan as I can only await my turn to join their brilliance. There are two people before me, then one. It's my turn. "May I have the eight best seats you have in the Mezzanine?" The lady behind the counter, with a look of mild disgust on her face, says "DOES ANYONE WANT THE FRONT ROW ON THE FLOOR?" What? Flabbergasted and unable to speak, as I open my mouth, my wrestling buddy Gary, slaps me hard in the middle of my shoulder blades and with mouth still open I spit out something like "GHAAA!" which thankfully the lady took for 'yes'.

As my eyes pop out in a cartoon way, the automated machine is spitting out EIGHT (8) FRONT ROW DEAD CENTER SEATS TO PINK FLOYD THE WALL at Nassau Coliseum. Turning to see the line I yell "Front Row! The Floor! F**k the Mezzanine!" I was offered up to $300 a ticket for them. That's was a lot of money in the early 1980s. I had only 3 people in mind for the show including me and could have sold 5 and pocketed $1500 for beer money. Instead, gave them away as Christmas presents that provided a memory of a lifetime.

Make it a PATTERN to SHARE GOOD FORTUNE with FAMILY and FRIENDS.

While the Epic Glory Of THE WALL (EGOTW) concert is forever locked in my mind and those present, KARMA plays a big part in the YIN/YANG balancing of all things. The second Floyd story was not as cool. I was in Philadelphia at a company sales meeting that was scheduled after having purchased, much less dramatically, six tickets to the Chicago Soldier Field show of Pink Floyd's new tour "MOMENTARY LAPSE OF REASON". As the meeting drags on, realizing that I may be late for the show and tell my boss that "I have to be in Chicago for a Baby-naming!" He let's me out early and I race to Philadelphia International Airport under sunny, blue skies. Awaiting departure to Chicago, O'Hare, also under perfect weather, we now have plane trouble. That problem lasts several hours and it becomes clear that I will not see the show. After calling my wife and friends who are already at the show as it starts, I wanted to cry. That wasn't the worst of it. Being stuck in Philly overnight, I called a friend and colleague to come pick me up, we spent the night drinking, talking and mourning the injustice. Forgetting to tell my buddy what I told my boss (that I was leaving early for a baby-naming when in reality, was going to a rock concert) he inadvertently almost gets me fired for lying to my employer, by saying "Yeah Billy had to spend the night and missed the Pink Floyd show."

Martial Note: If you need to keep your job to feed your family and pay for classes, don't lie to your boss and get caught. It may ruin your employment PATTERN.

The third and final Pink Floyd story does have a martial arts part that was quite interesting. I asked another Kenpo Master, Jason Gose if he would like to go see Roger Water's presentation of THE WALL 2011, nearly THIRTY YEARS since seeing it done at Nassau Coliseum. Now I have seen the truly Genius/Madman Roger Waters, in concert before quite a few times. With Pink Floyd now Waterless, they just are not as engaging as before. They were still cranking out mind-altering music, but without the voice and lyrical mastery of Roger Waters, it just was not the same. Any Pink Floyd aficionado would tell you as much. Master Jason Gose (MJG) and I arrive at the United Center, home of the Chicago Bulls and Blackhawks, and our seats are so-so. Upper balcony, second row from the top with an empty row of seats separating us from a guard rail. Why does the word guard rail conjure up a past bad PF concert experience?

Anyway, Master Jason had broken his nose in a quite serious way while teaching Kenpo "Sparring" (not the same as padded point sparring) and was in a lot of pain awaiting some reconstructive surgery. That is why Black Belts say not to worry about the middle and high ranks, it's the beginners that will hurt you doing stupid things like kicking you full force in the knee. A reminder to Teachers that White, Yellow and Orange Belts mean "DANGER! CARE! WARNING!"

"OF COURSE I'M GOING TO THE CONCERT TONIGHT SHIHAN. WHY DO YOU ASK?"

Back at the concert joking that "We better not get in a fight tonight" or if we do I asked MJG not get involved. To bad that I didn't hear the "Karma Train Rolling In" over the buzz of the crowd. So as we are sitting there having a few beers, enjoying the show in a very mature adult manner, we glance at the "cool dad" that brought his two young 9 or 10 year old kids to see the music he loved. Roger is belting out a wicked intense "Hey You" when this "Indiana Hick Moron" (IHM) stands up and is screaming the lyrics of the song as he pumps his fist and spills some beer on the guy next to him. As they say…not cool.

Now, don't get me wrong, at GRATEFUL DEAD shows across the country I have been known to do the Dancing Bear Shuffle (DBS) peacefully across much of any given stadium. BUT THAT'S WHAT WAS EXPECTED TO HAPPEN AND OK WITH EVERONE PRESENT. That's what you do during "Space" at a GD Show. It is NOT what you do at a Pink Floyd Show, especially when it's a relatively soft, vocals dominant piece. People may mouth the words, but do not ruin the song or the experience for others. If a song is SO MOVING that you NEED TO STAND, always look behind you to see if you are blocking anyone's view. To not do so is a breach of common courtesy, civility and manners. If the folks in front of you are standing, turn to the seated folks behind and say "Everyone is standing up in front and I can't see." And Smile.

Martial Note: MAKE A HABIT OF SMILING. ITS HARD TO BE ANGRY AT SOMEONE WHO IS SMILING. What they don't know is that YOU ARE SMILING BECAUSE OF WHAT YOU KNOW. Most likely they will stand as well, or if they were dragged to a concert they didn't want to come to, they will sit there and relax. Either way, you did the right thing. Its simple courtesy and manners. Make them a part of your demeanor and in your combat arsenal.

But IHM IS NOT DOING THE RIGHT THING. I look at MJG and we can't believe it, in the whole section we are sitting in, from bottom row to top, no one is standing up but him. At first, I

237

figured that it was a love song thing for Indianans like "Jack and Diane" or "Last Dance with Mary Jane" and he would sit down after "Hey You". But no he continued to stand and annoy the whole section AND NO ONE SAID A WORD in protest. After "Hey You" Roger continues into the next song and now IHM is spilling his beer, yelling for everybody to stand and ruining the experience.

It was too far away to use DIPLOMACY, so I yell "Dude, sit down! Folks can't see!" He turns around, not able to discern the source of the non-Pink Floyd words and flips the whole section the "double birds" while screaming "F**k Y'all!" Now the words made the two little kids in front of me, put down their GameBoys and look to their Dad. The father had a look similar to Brian during the Rosemont Horizon PF concert.

That was enough for me.

Standing with Master Jason (again the row behind us is empty) I do something keenly aware its uncharacteristic of me; I chuck an ice cube from my soda cup that travels in a perfect arc at least ten rows and strikes IHM corner first on the top of his head. As he turns, the whole section seems to look away and I do not. Our eye sockets meet over 40 or so feet since eye to eye contact was not possible Had it been, perhaps Indiana Hick Moron might have seen my now Black Eyes and sat down. But he did not and he makes his way aggressively toward the isle that was at least 8 seats away to his right. In a scene right out of a "Bugs Bunny" cartoon, where Bugs is moving through a crowded movie theatre of seated patrons saying "Excuse me. Pardon me. Terribly sorry. Excuse me. Pardon me..." but IHM has no such manners or any common courtesy as he rudely plows through the legs of seated patrons since he KNOWS who threw the ice.

Perhaps it would have been better for everyone if he didn't.

As he reaches the isle, I am growing a beard awaiting his arrival up the steps to our nosebleed seats. Ha ha...nose bleed...how apropos. Scanning the area and seeing one loan security guard within earshot I bark directly AT HIM "That drunk guy is coming to ATTACK ME!" pointing to the Ascending A-hole (AA) coming up strong. Not that I thought this rent-a-cop was going to do anything in time but WANTED THE AUTHORITIES AND THE WITNESSES TO HEAR MY CALL FOR HELP AS I WAS "ABOUT TO BE ATTACKED!"

Use your brain as it can be the ultimate weapon. While drawing the attention of the whole section from IHM's row on up to us, and watching the "security" guard frantically interacting with his colleagues, IHM turns sharply into our row and the unprotected me. I was also aware that the kids in front of us were in danger if we exchanged strikes or fell on them. As they are huddled with their father, I get a bit overly dramatic with "Stop! No! The Children!" or something goofy like that.

NOW I AM NOT ONLY DEFENDING MYSELF, BUT PROTECTING OTHERS AND CHILDREN. With this purposely arranged pre-fight landscape-laying, I was NOW IN THE MORAL RIGHT and ACTION IN DEFENSE OF SELF OR OTHERS IS PERFECTLY LEGAL! In the State of Illinois, THERE IS NO DUTY TO RETREAT. Besides, where was there to go? I had Master Jason's broken nose to protect by not banging into it. With children in the row right below, MJG's itching-to-hit-someone, nose ache or not, next to me and everyone watching, sorry Mr. Waters, but THE SHOW was in Section 223 of the United Center.

Indiana Hick Moron finally arrives in anger.

THIS IS a book on the martial arts and am aware my stories can take a bit to get to the point.

Martial Note: The body of an attacker can be defeated by ANY TECHNIQUE that CREATES A CREASE or ATTACKS A CREASE. If you bend your elbow, or it is bent it for you, that Creates A Crease. (CAC) If I straighten your arm out and attack the elbow hard in a direction that it does not bend, that is Attacking A Crease. (AAC) THE WHOLE BODY WORKS THAT WAY. Take a good uppercut to the gut and you will lean forward at the waist creating a crease. Stand erect and have someone attack that same crease point, in this case your waist, by driving the head back with a PALM HEEL strike under the chin and basing a POST HAND at the base of your spine...well that is a nasty version of AAC. Also remember that any technique whether offensive or defensive MUST CONTROL THE HEIGHT, DEPTH AND WIDTH OF THE ATTACKER. With Height, it means controlling the UP AND DOWN MOVEMENT of his body. With Depth, you stay agile and mobile enough moving either forward, backward or to either side of him to control the DISTANCE BETWEEN YOU. While controlling Width is stopping or LIMITING YOUR FOE'S ABILITY TO PIVOT ON HIS CENTER, which is how powerful strikes are generated.

Ok, back to the concert and the just-arrived Indiana Hick Moron. (IHM)

He gets to me and is greeted by a short hidden VERTICAL FIST to his beer-filled gut and... wait for it... creating a crease. As he rises, surprised at the sudden discomfort, I use a short, quick AIKIDO throw as IHM flies safely over the children, that sends him pin-wheeling about 15 rows back down the middle of the section. The throw definitely controlled Height as his hands and feet were stretched out in an "X" shape as he cart-wheeled off the tops of heads and seatbacks all the way down. Finally coming to rest some 5 rows past his seat he disappears between them for a while.

Hoping that I didn't kill him, I eagerly await his awakening. It took a few minutes and the whole crowd is clapping and saying thank you for dealing with show-ruining IHM. I respond "Please stay after the show to be my witnesses or I may go to jail".

Martial Note: No matter who is right, IN A FIGHT, MOST TIMES ALL INVOLVED GO WITH THE POLICE until things are sorted out. Thus the need for WITNESSES TO BACK UP YOUR SIDE OF THE STORY. Master Jason just leans over to me as we are again watching the concert as if nothing has happened and says "Shihan, Please remind me later to tell you how cool that looked."

Finally, IHM's head pops up between the seats as he tries to get to his feet. The total lack of blood made me happy and I hoped that that was the end of it and he'd just return to his seat and sit down. Nope, in the same beer and drug soaked mind that brought us together in the first place, here he comes again. Still no security? His inner ear balance from all the cartwheels and the occasional head-to-seatback meetings during the pinwheel down must have affected his stability and thus his mobility. Between the side to side stumbles and the extra 5 rows to traverse, it took longer for Arrival #2. Now its getting a bit irksome since I paid to see The Wall, not Indianan Hick Moron acrobatics.

By the time he gets to me again, there are now three security guards that are trying to get a grip on what's going on. Didn't the first report to security say that a drunk guy was moving upward in this section to fight ten minutes ago? They must have thought they were in a time warp, since they are standing there as the IHM begins his staggering walk up the stairs "to the fight". With no blood, it must have seemed odd that they got there just in time. But time warps, especially at a PF/Roger Waters Show are common place and hard to manage on occasion. So AS THREE SECURITY GUARDS watch, IHM walks right past them into my row just like before. Really?

As we "scuffle" so I don't look too skilled, more security arrives. While waiting for them to "Get this guy off me!" He tries to push me over into the kids row. In order not to hit them with my body, I redirect the weight and smack my lower back hard on a now kid-cleared seatback. Realizing that this is ridiculous, I put my foot via a bent knee, in IHM's gut and do a picture perfect JUDO throw. You know the kind that you've seen a million times. The one where you pull him in with your arms, foot in stomach, then straighten the coiled leg out hard while pulling his upper body toward you. It's sends him flying over head at various heights and distances depending on how hard you push and pull.

Even though Judo is the "Gentle Way" there was nothing gentle when IHM landed face first, after doing a 1½ midair flip that looked like a springboard dive. Section 223 now familiar with IHM flight patterns just moved out of their seats when he came by so as not to be pin wheeled in the head again. No worries. The Judo throw provided him air passage in a high apex upside down "V" flight vector. This combined with his 1.5 dive mug-first waterless entry into an empty seatback trashed his face.

This time as he rose, blood was pouring out of his face. Now, he is psychotic as re-races back up and NOW THE SECURITY GUARDS GRAB HIM and drag him up the stairs, down the concourse and outta sight. The remaining security guards are looking at me, as is the whole section, and as I sit down with MJG, so does everyone else. The apparent calm, and the absence of IHM, seemed to cool the situation. Still arriving security elements, that were not there for either attack, are gathering info from the guards present and they are pointing at me. The new guards come over and ask me to "please come with us".

"No I am watching the rest of The Wall but I'll be right here after the Show." I say to their confused faces. They talk on their ear pieces and say authoritatively "OK, but don't try to leave!" I reply, "I paid for the seat and I'll be here when its over." Perhaps the look in my eye and the comments about what the other security guards witnessed made their decision not to press me a good one. Knowing what I was going to say in my statement and if only one other witness in addition to Master Jason would come forward, things would most likely work out.

Just then, I hear a screaming, cursing, wasted IHM, being carried this time in a horizontal "X" position, by FOUR CHICAGO POLICE OFFICERS! I wondered what he did when security had taken him away to piss off THE POLICE.

Martial Note: Make it a habit to be respectful to the police. They have a rough job and don't need any wiseass comments from you. More often than not, that respect will yield the best outcome. My case was getting more clear-cut with this IHM additional outburst.
The two posted security guards follow the cops to assist and I am again alone with MJG watching Roger Waters. When the two knucklehead security guys realize they left their post, they race back to find an seat empty and Master Jason gone as well, They immediately call for back up and 15 or so personnel arrive as they are pointing at the empty seats.

I wait a few moments, then say "Over here." As they were looking for me in the wrong adjacent section, same row about ten feet from me to the right. Now they are all wired with my apparent escape attempt and buzzing to and fro. Talking on their "Flashpoint" style headphones and mouthpieces the newly arrived reinforcements, probably sent by Roger himself so as to quell further distraction, have "stern and menacing" faces on as they tell me to come with them now.

Rather than weaken my case by sealing a few of their smug faces, since they were just doing their job, I acquiesced. Rising like a death row inmate on the way to some unforeseen termination chamber and reminding folks around me that my Show is ruined because I was busy protecting theirs and to please stop by the Security Center to help me out. Being led away, we (me and maybe TWENTY SECURITY GUARDS) are walking behind the screen of The Wall itself as the Goose Stepping Crossed Hammers (Nazi Reference) are scissor-walking across the length of the front of The Wall and reflecting off me and the guards in a surreal SS STORM TROOPERS TAKING A PRISONER OFF TO THE GALLOWS scenario from the back of it.

I stop to tie my shoe as all but three guards just keep walking. One of the three remaining guards barks "Let's go keep moving!" and as our eyes meet, the two other guards say something simultaneously (maybe they say he's the good guy or maybe they saw me and IHM) and the Hitler Youth says "Please." Chuckling while rising we finally catch up to the group at the elevator. Now all big event venues have a Security/Detention Center staffed with real police and security heads. They question you, interview witnesses and decide whether you can go back to your seat, go home or go to jail.

After entering calmly, the staff looks up and then stands me 10 feet from the handcuffed to the wall Indiana Hick Moron and he looks bad. Not sure if the damage was from the "inadvertent falls he suffered" or a chill out message from the Chicago PD for kicking and struggling during his transportation to holding. Just standing there, he looks at me as I look at him as he screams "There he is! That's the guy who nearly beat me to death!" and "Don't you ever kick my ass again!" I remain silent. There was a drastic difference between my clean, pressed, non-coagulating collared shirt and jeans and his blood drenched, in need of medical attention, crimson soaked clothing.

Not sure if he was trying to yell something, or spit blood at me via his ever filling oral cavity, but asked politely to be moved away from my attacker. The staff says "of course" and provides a seat out of blood spewing range. IHM is screaming that he wants to press charges, and this is where it gets tricky. If MJG is my only witness and since he is my friend that really doesn't help that much. Friends stick up for friends. Sitting there for over an hour with no one coming to get a statement and seeing no fellow audience members being interviewed the words "2nd Degree Battery. He's going to jail!" reach my ears." Now I did not look battered. But IHM did and he was the first one to say he was pressing charges. Man, I thought, this could go down the wrong way and wishing he would stop bleeding already.

CLEARLY UNDERSTAND THAT ANY PARTICULAR MOMENT COULD BE THE MOST SIGNIFICANT ONE OF YOUR LIFE. DO EVERY SINGLE ONE 100% JUST TO BE SURE.

By this time, the concert is clearly over and I am still sitting there going on 2 hours when the VERY FIRST security guard is now in his Chicago Police Department uniform. He is the one that heard my calls for help, saw the attacker come at me and simply told his Superior seated in a Judge-like way on a little riser, that the offender repeated to "Fall due to intoxication and a purely self defense reaction from Mr. Powell. In addition, there were children present and their father has stated on record that Mr. Powell was protecting them from injury. We have ten other witnesses that tell the exact same story. All said that they would be willing to testify." Whew!

I'm thankful that this cop was moonlighting as a security guard and became the KEY WITNESS. When my statement was required, I made it and was free to go. Leaving the office, I finally notice all the people, including the dad and kids, that stayed after the concert to come to my defense. They were interviewed in outer offices to keep them from being viewed by the people involved in the situation. Thank you all so much. I met up with Master Jason and we went home. Good thing I was familiar with the last part of THE WALL, or I would have asked for a refund.

This chapter was about recognizing PATTERNS, SNRETTAP, PaTtErNs, P#T#E#N#, PTEN.

In the martial arts, as in life, recognizing Hidden Patterns can be like a Self Defense Word Jumble:

LEERVA AHTT CWIHH SI NHDEDI.

REVEAL THAT WHICH IS HIDDEN.

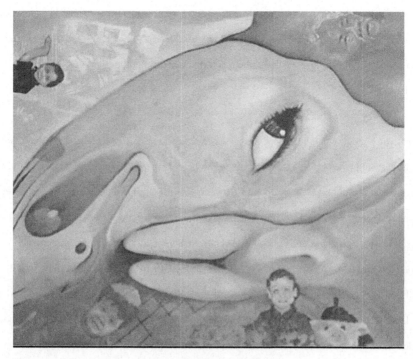

TO REVEAL THAT WHICH IS HIDDEN, YOU MUST FIRST UNDERSTAND WHAT YOU ARE LOOKING AT.

CHAPTER TWENTY THREE

The Importance of: REVEALING THAT WHICH IS HIDDEN.

It is very important to REVEAL THAT WHICH IS HIDDEN. Your training should be dedicated to and focus on smashing through any façade, illusion or puzzle that attempts to keep you from getting to the heart of matter BY UNCOVERING THE TRUTH. The very first chapter of this book regarded "Plateaus" faced by the martial artist throughout a lifetime of training. To compound the Warrior's already difficult traverse in pursuit of The Way, there are puzzles to be solved, choices to be made and trust to be garnered between you and anyone that claims they have something to "teach" you. I always think of Jethro Tull's song "The Teacher" when pondering this topic. Check out the lyrics if you are unfamiliar with this brilliant classic rock band's song.

Is what you are being taught real? Does it work? Can you understand and execute that which you are learning when outside the view of the teacher? Is there a better way? Is there another way that is easier to grasp? Why spend 7-10 years learning Kenpo when you can get a Black Belt in another art in 1.5 years? If you achieve a Black Belt by completing a set of standards by that school or this teacher, aren't you a REAL BLACK BELT? Who's to say you are not? No one can tell you that you are not a Black Belt if you BELIEVE you are and CAN BACK IT UP. The only Teacher that can alter your truth is Reality. And The World and its REALITY WILL BE THE TEACHER THAT MATTERS. (RWBTTTM) Tom at Martial Posture Studio handed me a pink phone message note when I was leaving Philadelphia for Chicago that said:

"The more you practice, the less accepting you are of 'accepted practices'. The more you see and hear, the less likely you are to believe what 'experts' write and say." I never forgot that.

As well, Gichin Funokoshi, The Father of Karate Do and author of many books including the great "Karate Do: My Way of Life" said:

"You may train for a long time. But if you simply move your hands and feet and jump up and down like a puppet, learning Karate is not very different from learning a dance. You will never have reached the heart of the matter. You will have failed to grasp the quintessence of Karate Do."

In 1981, as a sophomore at the University of Maryland, I had gone over to Washington DC to join the rally welcoming home the American Hostages from Iran after 444 days of captivity. They rode by in a big yellow bus with their arms hanging out the window waving American flags as we cheered and clapped like crazy. The thing remembered most that day was a little white sign that a freed hostage stuck out the window that read "BUY IRAQI WAR BONDS!" The Iran-Iraq War was in its beginning and everyone just loved Iraq. Kind of ironic that sign. The reason for bringing up that story, is that sometime afterward, I got into the usual intense yet peaceful debate with Nic, a Persian friend of mine about the Hostages, the deposed Shaw, the Desert One failed rescue attempt and the ongoing fiercely contested Iran-Iraq War. Since he was manager of the local beer mart and owner of second bar, I was honest yet diplomatic, lest my brew costs go up. We talked often about world affairs, American politics and the poor state of US-Iran relations and the unusual fact that we became good friends.

"Coming from Iran, I have seen the truth about this country and why we have problems with the US so much. You have never been out of this country, so what do you know, Billy?" he said. " Nic of Persia, I hail from The Great State of New Jersey, Where the Weak are Killed and Eaten!" responding laughing. He smiled as the intensity drained from his face saying "You are a good person, my friend." About to leave and as Nic is placing the Jack Daniels bag atop the case of Budweiser cans I say "At least we are free!" He shoots back "You only think you are free!" while handing me the change. After that, we Bro-hugged goodbye and I took my package goods and left the store. Wish the beer was free. Well, no lunch or dinner tomorrow.

But what he said had stuck with me while about learning of the world at the University of MD. I asked one of my favorite teachers, Professor L. from the Humanities Department "How can anyone really know THE TRUTH on world affairs if we have never left the country? Aren't we just swallowing whatever we are told by our teachers, friends, government and media?"

"Yep." he replied. Knowing there was more of an answer than that, I probed until he finally said "The truth? You can never KNOW the truth unless you are there. And even being there you assess the event only from your perspective giving you only partial truth. However, even if you are not there, you can still SEARCH and FIND PIECES of TRUTH if you try." He continued:

"Read the three major news magazines Time, Newsweek and US and World Report. Then read some more points of view from agenda style publications like the New Republic, the New Yorker, etc. Then watch all three major television network newscasts (no CNN at the time) and read the NY Times, Philadelphia Inquirer, Washington Post, Chicago Tribune/ Chicago Sun Times and the LA Times plus any other regional papers you can get your hands on or access from the library. After all that, sit down some place quiet and make a decision on what you believe to be true. And that is as close to the truth as you will ever get." He left the room.

In the martial arts, it's a bit easier, because we ACTUALLY ARE THERE and EXPERIENCE PIECES of the TRUTH every time we TRAIN, just as the above sources provided glimmers of truth from their given perspectives. Hypothetically, you go to the local martial arts school that teaches "Arachno-Do" or "Way of the Spider". (No such art. If there is, apologies with no disrespect intended) and you learn to move your hands, feet and body like a spider. You study hard and can crawl across the mat like a spider, kicking in 8 directions all the way, and earn a Black Belt there. Finally, you need to test your skills in self-defense and like a spider, you get squished. Did the teacher mislead you? Was it the wrong art for you since you only have 2 legs? Or maybe The Way of the Spider is designed to increase internal power but only after many years of practice crawling around? The point being, keep your mind open, learn many things from many sources to find YOUR TRUTH. Then Train. Train. Train Until You Die.

In the martial arts, as in life, the Truth may be hidden and you must move through the diversions and subterfuge to REVEAL THAT WHICH IS HIDDEN.

The dojo is a microcosm for what happens in the real world. We face our fears and insecurities in the school so that we can apply what we have learned outside its walls. It's not just the self-defense element that we train in to face a confrontation out there, but the mental and spiritual components like self confidence, self discipline, focus and mental toughness. These are just as important in a job interview as in a fight. Let's say that you, like most people, are afraid of public speaking. It is one of the most common fears. In reality, if you can speak clearly and effectively to one person, you SHOULD BE ABLE TO speak to any number of people. But it takes training to speak to a large audience effectively. That's why there are organizations like "Toastmasters" and "Dale Carnegie Institute" to teach these skills. How well you are trained in anything will determine how well you perform at that task UNDER PRESSURE.

Imagine that you are at a company event sitting around one of the many dinner tables with family, friends and colleagues, when unexpectedly, the owner takes the microphone and says "Tonight we would like to recognize the loyalty and dedication of one of our top workers. Let's give a round of applause to 'Tom Schmeck' as he is The Employee of The Year! Tom, come on up here and say few words!"

SHOWTIME.

Scenario #1: You panic. Your world closes in on you. Tunnel vision. You walk up there, go to say thank you, but instead utter "I'm not feeling well" and pass out. Folks rush up to assist and you are taken back to your seat. As you calm down, you see the shocked faces of your family as your son asks you "What happened Dad?" Your night of glory just became a nightmare.

Scenario #2: You don't panic. You are a Warrior. You are trained to "Expect the Unexpected. Improvise and Adapt. Failure is Not an Option". Sure you get that rush of adrenaline from our millions of years old "Fight or Flight" mechanism. But do you channel it to fear or excitement? What makes a roller-coaster more fun than running around in a tornado? The difference is that on a coaster, you will be ok and you know it. A tornado, not so much. So, you stand up at the announcement and ENJOY EVERY MOMENT OF IT. The surprise on your families faces and the applause of your colleagues as you walk up to the stage. The pride in your accomplishment as you shake hands with the boss. You face the microphone and say "Thank you." or whatever you want to say. No passing out. No need for others to come to your aid. No need for false explanations later to worried family members.

Which scenario would you prefer?

REVEAL THAT WHICH IS HIDDEN OR THE WORLD WILL REVEAL IT FOR YOU.

If you noticed a lack of humor this chapter, it's due to the seriousness of the subject. At Kenpo School, the highest placement of any wall adorned object is a 6 foot long black wooden sign with big white 6 inch oriental style lettering that says "REVEAL THAT WHICH IS HIDDEN" with a piece of bamboo hanging just below it.

If you pull at the ends of the bamboo a hidden razor sharp samurai sword is revealed.

Probably better if YOU REVEAL the sword rather than someone else REVEALING IT TO YOU.

WITHOUT TEACHERS WE WOULD ALL BE IGNORANT... LIKE A WORM TRYING TO UNDERSTAND ASTRONOMY BY STARING INTENTLY AT THE NIGHT SKY.

MASTER VIC MEZERA, MASTER JASON GOSE, SHIHAN WILLIAM POWELL, GRANDMASTER HANSHI SHORTY MILLS AND MASTER SEAN BAKER OF PWOK.

MASTER DON PINKUS WITH SENSEI AL FISH JUST BACK FROM INVADING IRAQ.

CHAPTER TWENTY FOUR

The Importance of: TEACHERS.

Without teachers, we would be uneducated. Unless we self study the vast information on the infinite subjects there is to know. But someone or something had to create the idea, test its merit and prove its value in order to relay information that we could actually use to generate our own ideas and inventions. And that would make them/it teachers. Let's say the very first person on earth sees water, he understands drinking it, but doesn't understand swimming or its relationship to drowning. So, as he ventures in over his head and unable to swim, drowns. Second person on earth walks to waters edge and sees face-down floating First person and retrieves his body by long stick. He learns that First person is dead. So who is the teacher? The dead man? The water? The interaction between the two? Myriad of other unseen factors?

Does it matter who or what TAUGHT Second person the danger of water? What will Second person learn and what will be done with that information? Will Second person just see the drowned person and learn nothing? Or will he learn to respect water, discover how to float or what floats to allow him to cross water? Will that information be of value to the Tenth person on earth as they see rafts and discover they can make the body buoyant like a raft, the precursor to swimming? Will he TEACH others what he has learned or keep that information to himself?

If you learn something, you have been taught by a teacher whether living or inanimate.
In the martial arts, the term is SENSEI in Japanese or SIFU in Chinese. There are many other titles that refer to teachers, but these two are the most commonly heard. The word SENSEI translates roughly to "Before-Born" or someone that is born before you. But since

255

many of my students are older than me, this can't be a chronological term. It's not. Sensci refers to one who has "been down the road" before you. Someone who can show you things that they learned along The Way as they traversed it. An Unknown Master once said:

"Follow not in the footsteps of the masters; but rather seek what they sought."

As discussed earlier, learning the martial arts does not fall into the standard idea of self study or formal Western education. YOU CAN NOT become skilled in the martial arts by reading books, watching videos or by mail exchange courses alone. The Martial Arts Must Be TRANSMITTED DIRECTLY FROM TEACHER to STUDENT or MASTER to DISCIPLE. The other sources of information may help but there is NO SUBSTITUTE for DIRECT TRANSFER OF MARTIAL ARTS KNOWLEDGE. A book can not physically correct you when you have a foot out of place, when your breath is not in control or when you truly understand the material, can properly execute it and when you are ready for advancement. Only a highly knowledgeable, passionate and communicative TEACHER can do this. Look at the best schools and they have some of the best teachers. Those same places also consistently produce the best students.

Another barrier to learning Eastern Arts here in the West is that we are not accustomed to the Master-Disciple relationship. We cringe at the idea of being told what to do, especially in front of others. Heck, we fought the Civil War in part to Abolish Slavery. Americans can be hostile to the very term Master. So what to do? How can we take a cultural teaching method that is foreign to us and still get that direct transmission. It's called trust and respect. Do your research, check out different schools and the Arts they teach, but MOST IMPORTANTLY, find a Teacher that you trust and TRUST HIM/HER. Call it a Leap of Faith. If you do your homework then it will be more like putting your toe in to test the water. Once you are ready JUMP IN!

That is how I learned which Arts to study and what Teachers to learn from.

So let's talk about some of the greatest Teachers and what they taught me. When discussing them, the focus will be more on who they were, and what they taught me rather than their many accomplishments. Otherwise, the book would be massive with all their titles, championships and accolades. To learn more about them use a search engine and have at it. To keep with the flow of the book, I will use anecdotes, analogies and short stories with the martial lesson within. Also, since I trained with multiple Teachers at the same time, the order of introduction is tied to a particular timeline and not to their rank, current or past friendships or the value placed on what they taught me. These are my Teachers of The Animate Kind. (TOTAK)

WEAPONS MASTER KIMBALL PAUL TAUGHT ME TAI CHI SWORD, CHINESE BROAD SWORD, TIGER FORK, KWAN DAU AND STAFF. ALL WERE FULLY WEIGHTED HEAVY WEAPONS. NO BENDING, FLASHING, NOISEY ALUMINUM FOIL BLADES FOR US.

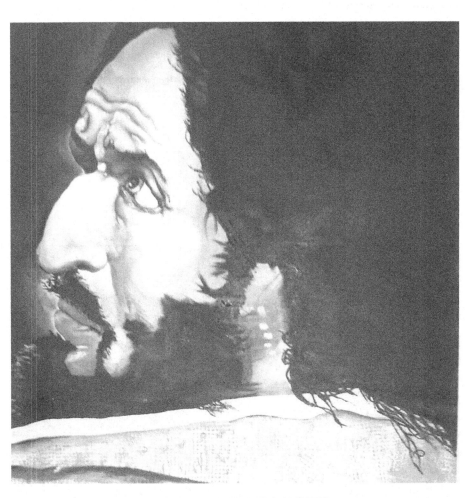

TEACH AND BE TAUGHT.

SENSEI SPENCER DEVITO, MY FIRST FORMAL KARATE INSTRUCTOR AND HIS LANCE MISSILE BATTERY TEAM GUARDING THE FULDA GAP WITH THE US ARMY IN GERMANY CIRCA 1980. SENSEI IS 2ND FROM LEFT WITH THE JOHN DEERE HAT.

SENSEI SPENCER DEVITO of Isshin Ryu Karate taught physical and mental toughness and its importance to the martial arts. After watching him do full splits at wrestling practice and snapping Jay M.'s wrist at school, I asked him to teach me . Now talk about all around toughness, Sensei would awake every morning at 4 am to work at a local dairy farm where he would do hard labor that would make other High Schoolers cry. Few hours later, he would go home, clean up catch the bus to school. At 3:05 pm everyday of the school week, he would go directly back to work at the farm until 7 o'clock. Our Karate School met at 7:30 sharp. We would work out until near 10 pm. He was so badass, that after a full day of hard farm work and a full day of school, Sensei would come directly down to his basement dojo where we were assembled, grab his gi from the wall, brush any remaining straw from his shirt and suit up.

SHOWTIME.

THOUSANDS of "Samurai Jumping Jacks" on the balls of your feet with heels forbidden to touch the ground. We did 6,000 on one occasion. It took over 3 hours straight. My calves burned for a week. Sensei said that forearms and calves were the most important muscles for delivery of martial arts power. To this day, weightlifters comment on my shredded calves. Usually 1K to 2K JJs to warm up, then Push Ups. Push Ups. Push Ups. Sit Ups. Sit Ups. Sit Ups, followed by Instruction then Sparring. Sensei led from the front and did every rep with us. We learned the importance of "Spirit Yells" when striking or taking a hit. And WE WERE struck and hit. HARDCORE TRAINING with a stick to the thighs for a poor HORSE STANCE and bare-knuckle, pad-less sparring in every class that would have The Humane Society in an uproar. We learned the need for a power word to use instead of the unacceptable "Ouch" when hit or the usual "KiYa" when attacking. Sensei's chosen word was "Joy!" Scary stuff when he hit you and just said joyfully "JOYyyyy…" as the pain set in.

We all used JOY until we found our own power word. Being loyal, I borrowed from Sensei with my "Oy!" I still use it after 35 years in The Arts, mostly after making a powerful point while teaching. "Then twist the head sharply, snapping the neck and hold the limp head in your hands as you lower the body silently to the ground! Joy!" (or Oy!) You get the idea.

There was this beast guy, Glenn P. who was a man with full beard in 7th Grade and he was the dojo's biggest, baddest, meanest student. He had "man-strength" and could toss us around or beat us to a pulp in every sparring session. And he did. I wanted to quit several times from the painful, embarrassing ASS KICKING IN EVERY CLASS. In talking to Sensei after a harsh sparring session where Glenn's SIDEKICK slid up my chest and into my throat,

I thought that I was really going to die.

As he already knew what I was going to say, Sensei started the conversation with "He knows that you are afraid of him." Agreeing that was true but what could I do to lessen the beating? He told me to MAKE A DECISION TO STAND MY GROUND AND THEN JUST DO IT. There were further beatings to come before taking Sensei's lesson to heart. It already hurt to get pummeled, but the fear of it getting it even worse was an even harsher possibility to consider.

We were all training in the backyard of Sensei's house which we would do when the weather was nice…or when it was extremely nasty. In the pouring, freezing rain, we would be out back doing a couple thousand jumping jacks in the knee deep mud. The suction of the earth juice made pulling your legs up and out extremely hard. The energy to do 1 JJ must have equated to 5 more. Push ups sunk you in elbow deep with face in mud. This type of hardcore, all weather training continues as part of what we teach today. Kenpo School has run miles barefoot in knee deep snow, driving rain or intense heat. At the downtown School, when hundreds of people died from the heat well over 100 degrees, and the Heat Advisory told everyone to stay indoors, we were out running in full black gis over 3 miles through Lincoln Park in Chicago. It was nice since there wasn't anyone else out and we had the Park and our heat exhaustion to ourselves. Many other stories to relive over beers with those that were there.

That backyard was also were I BECAME A MAN. It was a nice day and we were just beginning to spar. I was paired with Glenn and readied myself for the standard beating. As Sensei yelled "Hajime" (begin in English) I began the usual step back to avoid the customary lead side kick that normally started the punishment. Following the step back were more and more retreating steps as the animal named Glenn was craving some contact. So I gave it to him.

After about ten steps back that had me facing away from Glenn (some would say running away) I was stopped by a thorn bush that blocked my tactical retreat. With Glenn's eyes wide with anticipation of the kill, things temporarily SLOWED DOWN. At the same time I saw the thorn bush and thought of the damage it was going to do with Glenn ready to pounce, Sensei's words come racing back to my mind. STAND YOUR GROUND. So I did.

With my face an inch from the bush and by body scrunched over in a standing fetal position, Glenn launches a big OVERHAND RIGHT to my leaning away head bone. As it is coming in slow motion, I chamber a RIGHT REAR KICK (toes down) and launch it FULL FORCE, HEEL FIRST into Glenn's totally exposed solar plexus and he drops like a stone. Retracting my face from the threatening shrubbery and my heel from his lung place, I looked at the carnage that I had wrought. And loved it. Glenn didn't get up for quite a while and sat out the next two or three matches. It felt awesome. Sensei looked at me and simply said "Joy." And I responded "Oy" with a sh*t-eating grin. Now Glenn would continue to pound on me in future sparring sessions, but his attacks now had a bit of control to them. His merciless onslaught slowed a bit and my sparring improved.

Let's call it RESPECT. Thank you Sensei Spencer for that and many other lessons. OY.

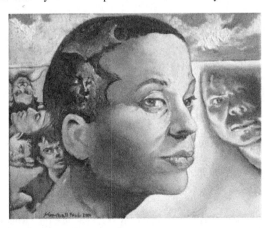

THE REALIZATION OF THE WARRIOR BEGINS IN THE MIND.

THE JOURNEY IS ALL YOU REALLY HAVE. RELAX. ALL THE ANSWERS WILL COME.

SENSEI DICKIE "THE HAMMER" HONE of Wrestling, Jiu Jitsu, Isshin Ryu, Karate-Do, Boxing, Full Contact Karate and Professional Kick Boxing taught me that traditional Karate alone was not enough. Sensei Spencer had left to join the Army and was stationed in Germany. There he led a Lance Missile Battery Unit at the Fulda Gap where NATO expected any Soviet Union/Warsaw Pact tank attack to start. I have a picture of Sensei Spencer leaning on his missile launcher smiling with a "Come on Rooskies, let me rain a little "JOY" on you." I needed more training but couldn't really commute to Germany. Sensei Dickie was more than happy to train me and we knew each other since we were little kids wrestling on opposing recreation teams.

He always had this HUGE SMILE. Always. Perhaps that is why I am constantly smiling. Sensei was not that tall, but man could he HIT HARD. Seeing him in a professional kickboxing fight punch the opponent's hips, with boxing gloves on, so hard that the other fighter couldn't move or kick. After just a few more to the same spot KNOCKED THE GUY OUT with BODY SHOTS TO THE HIP! Are you kidding me or what? I wanted to know how to do that!

Not only watching him do it to others in the ring, but learning firsthand the importance of hitting hard during private lessons with him. He not only taught me the limits of traditional Karate alone, but the importance of MOBILITY and ANGLES of ATTACK from Boxing. It was a humbling, painful experience, but put me on the right track immediately as far as my martial education and future direction would go. Sensei was the very first person to say to me "Wait until World Class Wrestlers start getting into the UFC. Then you will see the power of Wrestling." Man was he on the mark. This was immediately after the second UFC.

During "sparring" which basically entailed him "hammering" me at will, with unexpected strikes from perfectly achieved angles, only hard enough to rattle my cage instead of knocking me out. Guess it was easier for him to explain these fighting principles when I was conscious. The thing remembered most when sparring with Sensei is that after he would teach me something and we put our hands up, his face would change. It would go from a smiling "do you understand what I am saying?" and drop like a swipe on the inside of a foggy windshield, to an emotionless, dead, wooden doll face. It was f'n scary as all get out! The first few times, it looked like he was going to kill me. No anger. No life emotion at all. It freaked me out so much that I would step back and ask him a question. Like a window shade being drawn up, life and emotion would immediately return to his face as he answered me. Then hands up, DEATH FACE ON and the lesson continued. Sensei taught me to be not only a martial artist but to be A FIGHTER.

Thanks Hammer. I am forever indebted to You and Your Brutal Teachings. (YAYBT)

Isshin Ryu Karate Club of Maryland (Univ of MD) where as President in 1982. I trained under several distinguished Masters as they rotated instructors during my time there. Most memorable was learning the power of Isshin Ryu's signature strike, the VERTICAL PUNCH by literally being blasted with it repeatedly the length of a gym floor and through two closed push doors into the hall by Master Mike Wells. I learned the effectiveness of many similarly devastating techniques of traditional Isshin Ryu Karate during that time and also how to count to twenty in Japanese.

TOM UPDEGROVE. (DOESN'T LIKE TITLES) JUST BEFORE THE SUPER SUNDAY DEMO.

TOM UPDEGROVE of Martial Posture Studio and American Kenpo/Modern Arnis taught me Power, Speed and Effectiveness of Kenpo Karate. Besides the SUPER SUNDAY Nun-chucku near disaster, he taught me the philosophy of developing a MARTIAL POSTURE in everything I do. That didn't mean walking around scowling like a tough guy, but to be focused and aware. Teaching me that Kenpo is a lot like playing billiards where everything you do in attack or defense was key in setting up the attacker for the next technique. Every next move is a logical extension on that which just preceded it. This was a concept that he drilled into his students and showed that it could be done over and over results would be the same.

A Nasty, Devastating and Painful case in point:

Sparring with Tom was like poking at a cobra with a REACH toothbrush going "Na-na-na-na na!" Anyway, he had this technique to demonstrate the above principle at will. He would defend your attack, or if you were too chicken to get close, he would attack you. Then, NO MATTER WHAT YOU DID, he would use some hand strikes to your body front rendering your attacks/defenses useless, and spin you around in a way that had you leaning over at the waist EVERYTIME. Then he would use a downward moving, scraping BALL OF FOOT RAKE from PRANCE OF THE TIGER to your lower back which when completed had pulled down your protective groin cup a few inches. As his foot quickly tapped the floor and with your nuts hanging unprotected in limbo, the cup would snap back from the elastic and ALWAYS catch any out of position testicle between the returning cup edge and your pelvic bone. He only put his raking foot to the ground to give the jock strap time to return to position for the final clam slam. Only after the cup-snapping ball smash, did the first offending, groin-exposing, raking foot quickly rise from the floor to seal the deal with a TOP OF ARCH FOOT KICK to the just traumatized jewels. It was an example of RETURNING THUNDER in the extreme. If your scrotum wasn't quick enough to retreat after the jock snap assault, the rising kick to the cup finished the lesson. Tom could do this EXACT technique over and over again from most any situation. I am thankful to all you taught me Tom, and since I have two children, the technique did not affect virility and was a great lesson that is still told to students even 30+ years later. I still watch for any frayed rope as well.

EMPTY SHOTOKAN SCHOOL entered when I moved to downtown Chicago and couldn't find a Kenpo Studio in the City. So walking around one day after work in The Loop, I saw a sign on Wabash Street, under the elevated train tracks (The EL) in Japanese that I was able to actually translate. Not that big an accomplishment since the words "SHOTOKAN KARATE" were in English below it. Anyway, I walk up these long stairs to the second floor and peek my head into the dojo. It smelled like death and was immediately interested. A rolled up carpet with the rough backside showing was wrapped tightly with chords and hung from the ceiling as a heavy bag. There was no one there to answer my calls, but the bloody carpet bag and crimson stained gis that were hanging on hooks on the back walls, made me smile. If someone was there, would probably have joined on the spot. Since not, I walked back down the steps thrilled that some dojos still train the right way-by spilling blood. If I hadn't located a Kenpo School in the South Western suburbs, there would be more of a Shotokan story than this.

MASTER BOB WAINWRIGHT OF DOWNERS GROVE KARATE AND FITNESS CENTER TAUGHT ME KENPO AND THE IMPORTANCE OF PERFECTION OF TECHNIQUE.

MASTER BOB WAINWRIGHT of Downers Grove Karate and Kenpo Karate taught me the techniques and forms of the Tracy System of Kenpo. We were great friends and started the Way of Kenpo system together. Master Bob taught me the many things too numerous to cover here. But among the most important, he taught me that perfection of technique is essential and that the search for perfection is what its all about. We would spend many hours before and after class just talking about philosophy, the martial arts and life. I learned as much at these sessions as I did on the dojo floor.

Master Bob's wisdom and Kenpo knowledge is brilliant. His requirements for technical excellence unsurpassed and his stone faced humor unmatched. He not only taught me Kenpo, but how to teach it and also how to look cool wearing Kenpo School shirts without any aggressive attitude. That way they become advertisements and sources of inquiry as opposed to challenges. I wear a Kenpo shirt or jacket nearly everywhere I go and it has generated students.

A funny story with Master Bob is the time that we got into the War-like game of paintball which was in its infancy. We bought a new PB gun called a "Splatmaster" that was a single shot at a time pistol. So here are two Warriors studying it and what do you think we cared most about? Yep, what it felt like to be shot with it. So here we are agreeing on each of us taking a shot to the body to judge if the game was worth our Warrior Ethos. So, after taking turns proving our fearlessness by volunteering to go first, I defer to his higher rank and let him get shot first. He strips his shirt off and is walking to the firing line, when at the last second, he grabs a gi top and puts it on "just in case". He turns around, and I proceed to shoot him between the shoulder blades that hit so hard and fast that his elbows met behind his back before any pain curse came out of his mouth. After he catches his breath, he removes the gi top to reveal a bleeding circle on his skin, encompassed by varying degrees of blue bruising expanding outward from the center like an archer's target. And he had only just been shot a few seconds ago.

Now it's my turn. Using Training and Warrior Courage, I throw him the gun and run for the door. He uses his Kenpo Focus to chase and load at the same time and spikes me in the lower, fatty, ass-part of my hip with a hellfire shot. I drop and am rolling around pleading with him not to shoot me again. Not sure if it was his self-discipline or my pathetic wailing wafting out the front door of the dojo that held that second shot. Maybe it's when I showed him the same PB markings of blood and bruise. I thought he might shoot me in the exact same spot anyway for running and say it was a Kenpo lesson on RETURNING THUNDER. RT is when you hit the same spot on the body with repeated strikes from the same or different hand or foot techniques.

Not a great martial arts tale that I would tell to say…Thor, but worth sharing with you.

Thanks Master Bob for all the Teachings, Workouts and Great Times.

OUR PAINTBALL EXPERIMENT EVENTUALLY FIELDED A FULL WARRIOR TEAM.

HE WHO COMETH TO KICKETH YOUR ASS.

MASTER KIMBALL WAS SO POWERFUL THAT EVEN HIS HUMOR HURT. NOT JOKING.

MASTER KIMBALL PAUL of Crossroads Academy and Tai Chi Chuan, Shaolin Kung Fu, Bagwa, Tai Chi Sword, Kwan Dau, Tiger Fork, Broad Sword, Spear, Staff and QiGong Internal Arts. This one is hard to even start. To explain Kimball is like describing the length and depth of an enigma. No that would be easier. Here we go.

While Kenpo training and teaching continued unabated at Downer Grove Karate, I began to hear whisperings of what can only be called a "Magic Man of Martial Arts". I heard his singular name over and over again in different social circles. There was this huge bouncer at a hard core punk rock club called "Exit" on Wells Street in Chicago that would sit at the door checking IDs with a large, burning candle atop his head. He would say nothing as the hot wax dripped down his face and he looked at each identification card to see if it matched the owners face. It probably didn't as people's faces where either contorted by fear or crunched up with confusion.

I am sure some folks even left their licenses in Kimball's hand and just split.

Hearing that Kimball could "kill you with his touch" while thinking "Oh Baby Yes" lets add Dim Mak (Death Touch) to my training. Imagine misunderstanding a technique and then you accidentally off your dog. Then there were further tales of people "who actually saw" or "their friend saw" Kimball disarm knife and gun attacks or defeat multiple attackers at "Exit" or later at the nightclub "Neo". It was some juicy stuff for sure. Was he the Real Deal or an Urban Legend? The answer is yes to both. So off I go "In Search of Kimball". At a reported 300 pounds and standing over 6 ft tall with a massive shaved head, I figured he'd be easy to find.

It might have been easier to find a Yeti

The reason he was a bit hard to locate, was the nature of his School, THE CROSSROADS ACADEMY. His calling at the time was to take in recovering heroin addicts and give them a place to stay, train, get clean and sober then move on. No money required. Donations accepted.

He only had The Three Rules:

1) No Drugs or Alcohol.

2) Get your own food.

3) You must attend ALL THREE DAILY TAI CHI CLASSES.

There was a class first thing in the morning, one at midday and one at night.

Break a rule and you were out. Don't want to leave? Kimball removes you HARD.

A friend of mine was working at a bar called "At The Tracks" aptly named since it sat alone in a desolate area of Chicago near a length of railroad tracks that crisscross the City. My buddy tells me that while bartending she hears something about "Kimball is teaching a class across the street!" She goes out front to see a huge bald man in flowing black robes leading three others in a slow-moving, incredibly graceful Tai Chi form. I'm stoked at the news.

Many consecutive days of drinking beers after work At The Tracks in hopes of catching him teaching class again. Nothing. Like I said...searching for a Yeti. We figured he must live around there somewhere. But where can a huge 300 lbs myth live in secret? It was like a ghost movie. Hear of a sighting, go to the spot, search for evidence and find no Kimball. Grrrrrrr.

Chicago's Chinatown is one of the largest, most beautiful in the country and the food is fantastic. It's a great place to spend the day walking with friends and buying jade Buddhas and porcelain dragon figurines; At night, not so much. Chinatown can be dangerous after dark even to the Chinese that live there. But hey, ANYWHERE CAN BE DANGEROUS AT ANYTIME. It was the Chinese New Year and there with a few students to celebrate the very colorful block-long dragons with 30 little feet scurrying below as it snakes its way in coils and leaps down the main street with firecrackers booming and people cheering. If you haven't been to a Chinese New Year celebration in a major city put it on your to-do list. It's that cool.

CHICAGO'S CHINATOWN NEW YEAR'S PARADE THE DAY I MET KIMBALL.

So while standing in the center of Chinatown at the corner of Cermak Road and Wentworth Avenue, my view of the Sun is being blocked by a colossal man with flowing multi-color robes and a matching "African-style" cylindrical 6 inch high head dress. I look up. He looks down. It's him and I know it.

"Are you Master Kimball?"

"No" he says. "My name is Kimball."

"Do you teach the martial arts?" I inquire.

"Yes. Do you?" staring into my soul.

"Yes. I teach Karate." I answer.

"Don't think much of it." He retorts.

"Most of the Tai Chi I've seen is Bullshit!" I shoot back.

A HUGE SMILE crosses his face and he says "I know, right!"

That was a much better response than the death touch expected.

"Actually, teach KENPO." I add. To which Kimball barks:

"I love Kenpo! Killing people the old fashioned way, by quickly beating them to death!"

I was enthralled with his Way from that moment on and spanning over 25 years to this day.

After asking him to train me, he smiles in a way that makes me think of the candle burning down his head and says "Are you sure?" Creepy, scary, unnerving answer, but I say "Yes!" anyway.

He gives me the address of his CROSSROADS ACADEMY which is on the 5th floor of a huge multistory "abandoned factory turned loft apartments" building caddy corner from At The Tracks. That explained why his classes were held in the huge, unused parking lot of the defunct factory. It was so exciting to go to his class that I could barely sleep the night before. After work, grab my gi and hurry to the address he had provided. It was right out of an old kung fu movie. The front of the dilapidated building had one oddly placed entrance with a single steel door elevator. I press "5" and the interior elevator gate closes first then the outer door. It must have been a Tai Chi elevator since it moved slow as molasses upward to Floor 5.

After a short nap the door opens to reveal…a broken wall. The hallway was scary, dark and foreboding. With the scurry of vermin, poor lighting and thoughts that this could be a Yeti plan to trap, kill and eat me still on my mind, down the hall I go. Eventually seeing a little bitty sign of writing on a huge wooden door that said "Crossroads Academy". I open the door and enter a room so massive that it took up about half of the entire 5th floor. There were swords and other weapons hanging from these huge 4 x 4 ft square floor to ceiling 30 ft tall wooden pillars that kept the high ceiling and the 6th floor where it was. There was magnificent artwork all around and a large easel with an unfinished piece of Kimball's amazing paintings on it. Walking in deeper toward the center of the old school, the wooden plank floor creaks announcing a visitor. The brick walls, wood floor and very high ceiling is what a real dojo should look like.

Three things stand out crystal clear in my mind from that Tai Chi sojourn over 25 years ago.

The first was the overwhelming smell of chocolate. It was so intense it couldn't be real. Have you ever walked down a street and smelled a delicious hamburger that made your mouth water, only to look down and see a decaying animal or something that smells like a delicious burger but was not? Well that was my thought about the chocolate smell. It turns out that there actually was a NESTLES candy factory just down the street. Oddity answered. The second thing that I remember was the incredible panoramic view of Chicago that was visible from the huge 20 ft windows that lined the farthest wall of the School. Not only did the windows offer the view, but added the natural light that made early evening classes quite surreal.

And finally, the third thing noticed just inside the entrance door, was by far the most bizarre. Attached vertically to the wall was a queen size box spring that just hung there. The only thing anywhere near it was a large black "X" about twenty feet away in front of the wall bed. Did Kimball sleep standing up? What the hell was a bed doing on a wall? Maybe an art piece? Yes it was an art piece; a martial art piece of training equipment that I would learn of soon.

Future occasions found me "flying up" to the high part of the box spring with my little Tai Chi shoes a good 3 feet off the floor and the energy of my end flight absorbed by the box spring instead of my body. These scheduled flights came courtesy of Kimball's demonstration of TRANSFER POWER via Tai Chi Chuan's FOUR PERFECT FORMS of PUSH, WARD OFF, ROLLBACK and PRESS. To have a 300 lbs man throw you 10 feet is one thing. To have that same person barely touch you and send you FLYING OFF GROUND 20 feet is an experience. Looking for Kimball in his own home/school was a bit easier than finding him secretly cloaked somewhere in the City of Chicago, but not by much.

Hearing a television in a distant room, I follow the sounds to a curtain covered doorway. After knocking, I hear Kimball's now familiar voice say to come in. There is Kimball sitting in a chair, watching an old episode of Star Trek and eating a bowl of white rice with chop sticks. He says "Rice over there in the cooker if you want. This is the episode where Kirk fights The Gorn! Hurry up!" Doing as instructed and after the Star Trek episode, we spent the next 3 hours talking. Kimball is one of the funniest people that I have ever met. He is also a brilliant martial artist and an incredible Teacher.

Our journeys over the past 25 years together would fill another book. A last story on Kimball will give you the clearest example of his teaching skill and a time that I remember oh so well. I was having some financial issues after buying a high rise condo on the 17th floor of Americana Towers in Old Town Chicago. The building was right next door to The Second City Comedy Club and across the street from Kenpo School. PWOK's Hardcore Training regiment kept student turnover high, but the School was still growing and making some money. Students came from all over, traveling some serious distances to train at the "Reality Taught Here Way Place". One student drove 2.5 hours each way from Sterling, IL to Chicago for Tuesday and Thursday classes. Others didn't come that far, but still impressive the effort. But as I like to say, repeating whomever initially said it:

"If you want a haircut, you go to the Barber. The Barber doesn't come to you."

Want Hellfire KENPO? Then I was the Barber in downtown Chicago.

So at a training session with Kimball, many years after we met, he was teaching me Chinese Broadsword. It must have weighed twenty pounds. You didn't wield that sword, you rode it like a wild mustang in whatever direction you had directed it to go. Once the slash or stab was initiated you went with it to completion, then redirected the Broadsword in a new vector lest you rip you arm out of the socket or cut your own leg off. No lie. Since Kimball taught martial arts for a living and had a son, I had no problem paying my $100 per month train all you want fee.

I had told Kimball my financial history of not being that great with money. I made it, but just couldn't hold onto it as well. It is said that the Samurai were not good with coin, since not knowing if they would be dead in the next second they spent freely. I lived the same, but the bill collectors didn't grasp my Warrior thinking. I knew it was a character flaw that bothered me deeply and found it quite embarrassing. Anyone who knows me will tell you that I am not easily embarrassed. So, I pay Kimball with a $100 bill upon arriving at his house and we commence the Broadsword training. ¾ of the way through the 2 hour brutal heavy weapon swinging, I am getting tired and was about to stop as Kimball is explaining an important part of what I was doing wrong with the sword. As it must have appeared that I was not getting his point on the need to thrust then twist a 20 lbs Broadsword that I could barely hold up anymore, Kimball says:

"Ok Billy, we are done for today. And its alright, I know you need the money."

Confused, I said "What do you mean?"

"The hundred dollars. I know you took it off the table as we were coming out here. It's OK."

My blood went from 98.6 to 106 degrees in a microsecond. My head filled with explanations to police of why I beheaded my Master. Or, the thoughts of Kimball dismembering me in a "Monty Python" kinda way. I was FURIOUS! My eyes go Black and I am ready to strike!

Just then, Kimball says, matter of fact "Yes! That's the feeling, energy and focus you need when you thrust and twist a Chinese Broadsword! Otherwise your strike will fail!"

Kimball smiles and says "Now please put the sword down."

I am blown away at the power of what had just happened.

"So you know I didn't take the money?" I inquire.

"Of course not. You gave it to me. Why would you take it back? You could have just not given it to me in the first place, right?"

I felt like a puppet at the Feet of The Master. And I was.

THE GREAT TAI CHI SWORD MASTER KIMBALL PAUL.

PICTURED WITH CARLSON GRACIE JR. JUST AFTER WINNING THE CHAMPIONSHIP AT THE PAN AMERICAN GAMES IN ORLANDO, FLORIDA IN 2001.

BRONZE MEDAL FINISH THE YEAR BEFORE AT THE PAN AMS IN 2000.

CHAPTER TWENTY FIVE

The Importance of: TEACHERS...CONTINUED

CARLSON GRACIE JR, CARLSON GRACIE and JEFF NEAL of Carlson Gracie Jiu Jitsu Academy taught me The Most Feared Art at a time when it was Most Feared. After the first Ultimate Fighting Championship in which a tall, thin Brazilian in a traditional white martial arts uniform and Black Belt defeated all comers of any size or martial arts style. Royce Gracie won several UFC titles at a time when THERE WERE NO TIME LIMITS, VERY FEW RULES, NO WEIGHT CLASSES AND YOU DID ALL YOUR FIGHTING IN ONE DAY REGARD-LESS OF INJURY! Now that is as about a as real as it gets in terms of fighting. In the street, you do not get to pick the size of your opponent, what he weighs, what experience he has, or how long the fight lasts.

The advent of time limits, rules and weight classes, may have made the UFC a spectacular, multi-billion dollar business with the top athletes in the world, but these changes ended the "No Holds Barred" total domination of Gracie Jiu Jitsu that spanned more than half a century. The original UFC created by Royce's brother, Rorion, was true extension of the famous GRACIE CHALLENGE, whereas the new-ruled UFC was a different animal altogether. Had the rules of the first UFC continued, the sport would not have grown, maybe outlawed completely, but it is quite possible that the Gracie's may never have lost.

Brazilian Jiu Jitsu is in no hurry to get your submission and can wait HOURS in a match until you make a mistake that seals your fate. In addition, BJJ spends most of its time on the ground and that can be viewed by the untrained as boring. People want to see spectacular KNOCKOUTS, not the 20 minutes you spent expertly defeating an ARMBAR. This truth did not mesh well with schedule-sensitive media like cable, TV or Pay Per View that needed to know the maximum time length of an event to avoid going off the air in the middle of a fight. This happened and it was a financial disaster to those entities involved.

As POWELL'S WAY OF KENPO (PWOK) was up and running with a certain Mayhemic Warrior Consistency (MWC) that was producing quality students who, check this out, COULD REALLY FIGHT. We actually had our own MMA Team called "THE HAMMERS OF THOR"

THE IMPORTANCE OF THE HAMMERS OF THOR.

HAMMER OF THOR JOHN "GRAPPLER" PASSARELLA TO THE RIGHT IS ABOUT TO KNOCK OUT HIS OPPONENT IN A FIRST ROUND VICTORY.

The original purpose in the creation of PWOK's HAMMERS OF THOR MIXED MARTIAL ARTS TEAM was to test in the cage that which was being taught on the dojo mat. You do not claim that to teach REALITY if you don't know what that means. In self defense and in martial arts contest, the goal is total victory. Just as the Samurai and Gladiators knew long ago that 2nd place was not good enough and meant Death. As this book attests, I could do most of the fighting challenges quite well. But could I teach others to do the same. That was the question.

The answer is Yes.

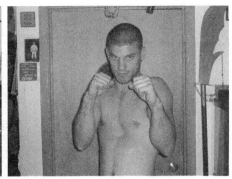

JASON "SUPERMAN"SCOTT   *ANDREW "HANNIBAL" SKOIRCHET*

SEAN "3RD SEAN" GOES   *BEN "NATURAL" MCCLAIN*

JOHN "GRAPPLER" PASSARELLA   *COACH BAKER*   *COACH MEZERA*

We were VERY successful in the cage. In our very first competition in the cage in Plainfield, IL we WON ALL FIVE of our fights. Funny one was when our guy, who we call "Hannibal" gets in the ring in our red and black team shorts. His opponent, with green hair must have heard us calling to Hannibal and the guy wears one of those Hannibal Lector cage-type catchers mask into the ring. He was mocking Hannibal. As he removes the mask and drops it to the top step leading to the cage, he crushes it with his foot. Watching this, its clear that this guy is tough, muscular and moves smoothly. A glimmer of doubt crosses my mind, until I look at the REAL HANNIBAL and he is just grinning in a happy, murderously psychotic kinda way. I scream "Hannibal! Leave No Doubt!" And he didn't.

The bell rings and Hannibal leads off with a monsterous REAR LEG WHEEL KICK that crashes into the side of fake Hannibal's face and head. The crunch sound was mildly sickening yet beautifully glorious as he goes down unconscious and doesn't move for several minutes. I thought he might be dead. He wasn't. There was no more mocking of our fighters as Team Captain Jason "Superman" Scott flew into the ring and threw a merciless beating on his opponent that should have been stopped sooner.

You could only become a "HAMMER" by training at Kenpo School for a 6 month minimum and then try out for the team. Since we devoted only a few hours a week to MMA training, we felt it was not fair to put our part time MMA fighters in the ring with opponents that trained in that discipline full time. There were other top quality MMA Gyms that we would send any inquiring fighters to. When our Team Captain Sifu Jason Scott moved out West, we ceased competing in cage matches. Judging from how good we were in the cage and in Jiu Jitsu competitions, a few fulltime trained HAMMERS OF THOR fighters could have risen to professional level. But alas, there is only so much time to train in one day and our focus was on Self Defense not sport.

Outside the ring, the quality, quantity and intensity of our training was clearly evident when we would host "SHIAI" or "Warrior Gathering" by inviting different Schools over to train with us. Or we would go mobile and visit any dojo that would have us. We wanted the students to see other Arts and how they compare to what we do. We were always, friendly, respectful, skilled, courteous and deadly. Our conditioning drills were often too intense for most others. And with fast and powerful Kenpo leading to our aggressive Rampone ground fighting, our training results were quite convincing. My Grandmaster, Hanshi Shorty Mills commented over the years on the incredible focus, loyalty, desire to learn and CONSISTENCY of the students that PWOK produced on a regular basis. I dubbed this system "THE MACHINE". And it was driven. Hard.

The reason for the above paragraphs, is with the UFC in full swing, I was eager to learn the TRUTH about the fearsome Gracie Jiu Jitsu. Wrestling and Judo, got it. But if you are a martial artist and don't always search for the best, eventually it will find you. Hard. After all the years in Wrestling and successes against all comers in impromptu brawls and grappling matches at the Preakness, I was very confident in the Rampone groundfighting system that I developed. But I needed to test it. Off to the Ultimate Fighting Championship.

So I went to **watch** UFC 5 in Raleigh, NC and the "SuperFight" rematch between the two top UFC 1 fighters, Ken Shamrock and Royce Gracie. The fight ended in a draw I believe, but in contrast to their first meetings, Royce took a nasty beating and went post fight to the hospital. In that same event, Dan "The Beast" Severn, a GRECO ROMAN WRESTLER had pounded a tough RUSSIAN SAMBO fighter into a bloody pulp. When the fight was stopped, Severn raised his hands and the opponents blood POURED down his arms and off his elbows to the wet red-saturated mat below. As he is bellowing some primordial Gladiator scream, the crowd is crazed with bloodlust and cheering wildly. It was reminiscent of the death matches in the Roman Coliseum. I wasn't at those, but am sure that it was similarly intense but with death at the end.

At the after-fight party that I was invited to, folks got the chance to meet their favorite fighters and get autographs, take pictures and talk with them. All were incredibly nice and approachable. They were skilled people who simply enjoyed fighting. What struck me most was when Dan "The Beast" Severn, fresh from a blood-cleansing shower, was dressed in a dark blue business suit with a PENN STATE ALUMNI pin on his tie. We spoke and I found his transformation from clean cut Nittany Lion to Blood Craving Beast quite fascinating.

Seeing the UFC matches up close (3rd row from the Octagon) I realized that without the magic of TV broadcasts and commentator analysis, these two men were JUST FIGHTING. Now sure every knucklehead whose had a few beers thinks they can jump in the ring and do that. Point being, that after all the analysis of the experience when leaving Raleigh, that these men were not Invincible Reincarnations of Ancient Death. (IROAD) But rather they were brave gentlemen Warriors who loved the martial arts and just enjoyed fighting.

After hearing that UFC Champion Royce Gracie was coming to Chicago for the first time to do a GRACIE JIU JITSU seminar, I was psyched. While many other martial artists still dismissed the importance of the ground fighting arts, even slammed in the face of the UFC evidence, they just refused to go. In the martial arts, ignorance is not bliss, it can get you killed.

So I went.

The huge multiplex-type gym that hosted the seminar was on Fullerton Avenue in Chicago. I got there and followed the signs to the tennis area. There were mats that covered at least 8 full size tennis courts (nets taken down) with well over a hundred martial artists of varying rank milling about. Yummy! An early taste of Valhalla? When Royce and his beautiful wife entered, followed by several assistant instructors, we all cheered. We were there to meet the Legend, see

289

what it was all about and to learn the Truth.

After reading that Royce's brother Rickson used to grapple with every seminar member in a row and submit them all, I was psyched. Hell, let's get in there and FIND REALITY. Get submitted in the process in front of a hundred local martial artists? So what? To quote Moi:

"Never fight. If you fight, never lose. If you lose, be unconcerned"

Well, with more and more people coming in as the seminar started, the submit everyone thing wasn't going to happen. I did hear that after the 2 hour seminar, there would be a special advance training session for an additional $100. Rolling with the legendary Royce Gracie would be an honor that couldn't be passed up for a hundred bucks. But I wanted to see what the story was first before committing to the extra training session.

During the 2 hours of training, we learned some basic Brazilian Jiu Jitsu techniques that we drilled hard. When saying we, I mean Kenpo Master Terry O'Shea of the Sixth Dan, who met me there. Master T had a great interest in ground fighting as well. Everything that we were expertly taught by Royce, Master Terry and I would go to our spot and DRILL, DRILL and DRILL. We're talking as many reps as each of us could get in before Royce called us back to group. NO ONE anywhere on the mats was working as hard as we were. To make it even more comical, Masters with their Red and White or Red and Black high ranking belts DIDN'T EVEN TRY THE MOVES! They walked around "helping" others as if they had any idea what the hell they were doing. What a joke! Well, at least these Masters showed up, so that says something.

The last 45 minutes, we were grappling each other trying to use the techniques we were just taught. I kicked the sh*t out of everyone including wrestling coaches, wrestlers, judo guys and anyone else that I was paired with. Hoping to catch Royce's attention in the event he wanted to find the best of the group to "make an example of". It didn't work. The first session was now ending and hearing that Royce would not be rolling today. Damn. No truth. Now what?

As we are helping to roll up the mats that would not be used for the smaller "Advanced Training" I walk up to Royce Gracie, UFC Champion and say "Sir, really enjoyed your seminar, but haven't learned what I came here to know. May I roll with one of you instructors?" He asks my name and calls over a Purple Belt (PB is expert in BJJ) and instructs everyone to leave the last 1/3rd strip of the three part HS wrestling mat in place. So I step on the mat with this tall, lanky Gracie Jiu Jitsu Purple Belt and we THROW DOWN. I shoot a hard double and drive him into the mat. Hard. Falling right into his GUARD we spend the next ten minutes with me trying to choke him out and him playing puppet master with his long legs to prevent it. I think that one could be raining down an unacceptable level of punches and elbows to his face through his guard, but that was not the point. So, as we continue rolling, after PASSING THE GUARD, he simply RECOMPOSES THE GUARD. I am getting exhausted since in WRESTLING, it is 100% action for six minutes in a match and Purple Belt is hardly breathing at all. Great Lesson.

Martial Note: Only use the muscles and energy needed to execute a specific technique or you will fatigue, become exhausted, quit and lose. They say "Fatigue makes cowards of all men!" Well I'm no coward, but was definitely outta gas and that meant defeat. I am not used to losing a ground fight but was enjoying myself anyway. I mean "Test the Best, Leave Fear for the Rest".

Now, the whole crowd is into it as is Royce and his wife. I hear yelling and coaching but am just about out of fuel. One more burst left, let's go for it with a STACKING HIS GUARD attack used to defeat an ARMBAR, neutralize a TRIANGLE CHOKE or PASS THE GUARD but with his flexibility, knowledge and conditioning superior it was TITANIC time. As the last ditch effort fails to work, he calmly, expertly slips inch by inch taking my back like a python as I submit to a mata leon. Tap, jump up, hug the Purple Belt and thank Royce for the seminar and the special session.

KENPO MASTER TERRY O'SHEA, UFC CHAMPION ROYCE GRACIE & MOI.

UFC Champion Royce Gracie says "Billy, You are an Animal! Keep up your Jiu Jitsu."

"Thank you Sir"

The walk home was euphoric.

After spending many hours thinking about the experience at the Royce Gracie Seminar, I came to the decision that while very potent stuff, the need for me to go to a far off Gracie School to train from the beginning was not going to happen. The fact that I could whip most folks on the ground, as experienced at the seminar, and could at least hold my own (for a while) against a Gracie Jiu Jitsu instructor, influenced the decision. But the Search for Truth will on occasion give you a mulligan…another chance to rethink a decision or path. Thanks Truth.

At Kenpo School we believe in the Yin/Yang dynamic as it relates to everything. In this case, we teach both the martial arts and the equally important healing arts. In fact, we used the term "Daifu" to designate those School members that were doctors, nurses, surgeons, chiropractors, acupuncturists, massage therapists or Yoga, Reiki and Rolfing teachers. Pretty simple concept: Get hurt while training, go upstairs to the Daifu Room and get treatment. Then back to training. We took HEALTH and THE HEALING ARTS as seriously as we took KENPO and THE WARTIME ARTS. Imagine putting down a plastic cover on the dojo mat with each student and teacher having half a raw chicken (resembles human flesh) to slice and stitch under the instruction of Kenpo Warrior and skilled surgeon Dr. Riz. "Rambo" stuff- sewing bloody meat.

KNIFE AND CHI DAO GUNG FU MASTER RON SCAGGS AND TAI CHI CHUAN MASTER KELLY CARTER WHO IS ALSO A HIGHLY SKILLED IN THE HEALING ARTS.

One of the top Daifus, and martial arts Master, Kelly Carter had been treating a patient for several months, when he lets the cat out of the bag and tells me that he has been bartering acupuncture treatments with Jeff Neal, a teacher at the Carlson Gracie Jr. Team and current CHICAGO CHALLENGE MMA CHAMPION. I say "What"? Turns out Master Kelly was training with the Gracies at one of those huge fitness gyms down in midtown Chicago. He asked me to stop by the gym sometime to see what he's been up to. I agree to visit his secret temple.

When I first met Jeff Neal as he came by Kenpo School to get his weekly treatments from Master Kelly, I found him to be big, powerful looking and QUIET nearly to the point of stand offish. As we became great friends, I realized that he was just a Soft Spoken Killer (SSK) weary of most people, all of which wanted to learn the secrets of the feared Gracie Brazilian Jiu Jitsu.

BLACK BELT IN BJJ AND COACH OF CHAMPIONS, JEFF NEAL & ME AT PAN AMS.

I eventually joined the Carlson Gracie Jr. Team and started learning what really had once been a SECRET ART. I had to PROMISE to teach the techniques only my students. Powell's Way of Kenpo was one of, if not THE FIRST Stand Up (Striking Arts) School in the country to be taught Carlson Gracie Jiu Jitsu! There is also a secret handshake to recognize members. Can't tell you what it is or I'd have to kill you. Just kidding. Sort of.

But let's not get ahead of the story. Finally getting over to the huge fitness center that was home of the Carlson Gracie Jr. Team (CGJT) it was a double bonus. I also got to meet Muay Thai Master and World Cage Fighting Champion, Benny Ghofrani, who had his own school there as well. Kinda like a martial arts Christmas! Anyway, noting that the CGJT workout area is nothing more than a few removable wrestling mats that made up the training ground for what was at then THE TOP COMPETITION SCHOOL teaching the Gracie System. This was a time when Carlson Gracie Jiu Jitsu dominated competitions in Brazil. Now the quality of competitors from different branches of the extended Gracie Family Brazilian Jiu Jitsu is much more equal.

Watching them workout, it looks so cool and now with the gym just a cab ride away from my Kenpo School, I am thinking of getting the BJJ training that would augment the Rampone. At the same time I continued to see Jeff Neal getting his acupuncture treatments from Master Kelly at PWOK. Then, one day, The Great Thunder of Thor (GTOT) rumbles into my dojo as Jeff tells me that their gym is under new ownership and that they do not want the Gracies there. Without hesitation and with no ulterior motive, I tell Jeff that they are welcome to use Kenpo School for classes any time that we are not training. He smiles at me for the first time.

"How much to rent the space?" Jeff, also the financial mind for CGJT, asks in a business way.

"Nothing." I reply.

He just looked at me as I say "Look, you need a place to train your students while you are looking for a new location. You are friends with Master Kelly and therefore a friend of mine. We would do this for any Warrior House that was in a similar situation." Jeff said he would relay the amazing offer to Carlson Gracie Jr. (CGJ) later that day.

When I met CGJ the following day, he was another Smiling Killer that had a cool Portuguese-Brazilian-American accent. He bowed at Kenpo School door and introduced himself in a self-effacing way. He looked around at the very intense environment that was our downtown School. Skulls, weapons, paintings, books, scrolls etc on the brick walls, a blood-stained canvas mat over thick tatami and mirrors the length of the front wall with 5 (at the time) heavy bags dangling by large, long chains from the high 20 ft ceilings. Definitely NOT A HEALTH CLUB scene. You can see pictures of this energy-spewing Way Place throughout this book.

"This is perfect, eh Jeffone! We got to pay something to train here." CGJ said to Jeff Neal "How about you just do a short seminar for me and the students and we'll call it even?" I say.

"Ok. Done." was his reply and the "official" beginning of our friendship that continues to this day and the formal instruction of CARLSON GRACIE JIU JITSU to the Warriors of POWELL'S WAY OF KENPO MARTIAL ARTS SCHOOL had started and continues now.

Not only was the Barber coming to me, but he was bringing over the whole damn Barbershop!

Another great CGJT Champion named Daniel was an instructor for The Team and also began getting acupuncture treatments from Daifu Kelly at the recommendation of Jeff Neal. Meeting Daniel, he was pleasant, smiling and humorous. We spoke for awhile about the Arts and told him of my experience at the Royce Gracie seminar and the match with the lanky Purple Belt. Then I asked him if he would roll with me before Sifu Kelly arrived. He obliged.

I will never forget shooting in for the double leg, getting pulled into Daniel's guard and after a bit of ineffective movement on my part, picking him up high and slamming him hard into the mat. He looked at me as his smile faded. The Chill of Death (TCOD) ran through me as Daniel calmly looked into my eyes and said "Don't do that again." He said it in a way that taught me that that is not an acceptable way of training to Pass The Guard in Jiu Jitsu without breaking my arm, leg or neck. Message received. Daniel then lets me onto the mount where I have been pummeling rednecks for years and proceeds to sweep me at will and always ends up on top. His technique was so effortless that I was in shock. No one has ever tossed me around like a rag doll with such ease. I was blown away...and grinning ear to ear.

I DEFINITELY WANTED TO LEARN THIS. HELL YEAH!

And so I did.

After working out a deal with Jeff Neal, the CGJT would continue to use PWOK as its training facility and IN EXCHANGE, I could train with the Gracies for free. To explain what this meant at the time is like trying to relate finding a treasure chest in your back yard to a squirrel. I would train hard, make every class and learn the secrets of the feared BJJ dominance at the UFC and beyond. Then I would teach my Kenpo School "SUPER RAMPONE" imbued with Carlson Gracie Jiu Jitsu. It would be years until I had permission to say that we teach CGJJ at PWOK.

As previously mentioned, I got my ass kicked in every class, as it should be. A bit humbling that a high ranking Black Belt could be easily submitted by a Gracie student with 6 months of training. But I kept going back. Most Black Belts would have quit or not go anywhere near the Gracies for fear of embarrassment. After awhile, I didn't tap out as much. With more training and instruction, I rarely tapped out to my opponent. Soon after that, I did not tap and began submitting those that had once submitted me. Loved every minute of it.

The Team finally found a new location for their training at another multiplex-type gym on LaSalle Street about 6 blocks from Kenpo School. We were Brothers, became "Sister Schools" and trained as such.I continued to train at their new location and achieved the lofty rank of Blue Belt. With a similar philosophy on rank advancement, Jr. and Jeff made sure that we were darn good to get a Blue Belt. In most martial arts, Blue is an intermediate belt rank. In BJJ, it means "I'll Choke You Out!" Jr. used to talk about the long time between rank promotions with memorable comments:

"It's not your Birthday! It's not Christmas! I am not the Santa Claus!"

He also gave us an idea of the importance of the Blue Belt in Brazilian Jiu Jitsu by telling us:

"You know the top fighters that you see in the Octagon at the UFC...the Stars? When they come to Brazil to train they get choked out regularly by Blue Belts."

So Blue is Cool. I eventually received my Purple Belt (Expert level) after a few more years.

Like I said, fell in love with The Art, The Teachers and The Folks that I trained with. You might even have heard of one of my training buddies. We used to call him "RoboCop" for his freakish strength, hand size. physique and power. You would know him as Stephan Bonnar, who along with his costar Forrest Griffin on the hit reality television series "The Ultimate Fighter" battled in one of the greatest fights in UFC history. Only the winner was to receive the prize money and a contract for the Ultimate Fighting Championship. The fight was so amazing, that mainstream America was now hooked and many consider it the one that legitimized MMA as a real sport. They BOTH received huge checks and BOTH have become UFC legends.

While not as history changing as RoboCop, my time with the Gracies' garnered honor as I became the East-West Submission Wrestling Champion in 1999, the Pan American Games International Jiu Jitsu Bronze Medalist in 2000, and the Pan American Champion in 2001. Being the first American to win the "Pan Ams" for the Carlson Gracie Jr. Team helped my Giri.

MASTER BENNY GHOFRANI of Muay Thai, Thai Boxing,Vale Tudo and Cage Fighting taught me how to knock folks out in more different ways than almost any other person. After seeing Dickie "The Hammer" Hone knockout a fighter with punches to the hip, I was into that concept. Master Benny taught me the most brutal shin-led leg kicks that I have ever felt and then SHOWED me HOW to deliver them as well. It was so cool the way he would deliver a kick and as he returned to a fighting stance he would *vibrate*. His whole body was just screaming "JOY!

My students have dropped folk with a single Muay Thai leg kick. Just one! If the guy was tough, it might take several, but his leg was telling his brain to "get me out of the way or shut it all down!" The pain is unbelievable like a super-sized "Charlie Horse" same spot over and over. It's funny how we met the same day while going to see the Carlson Gracie Jr. Team for the first time at their former gym. When the place changed ownership, they not only asked the Gracies to leave but Master Benny's Muay Thai classes as well. Must have needed the extra room for step classes or Boxercise. After the Carlson Gracie Jr. Team left PWOK for their new home on LaSalle, guess who called to set up an amazing lunch meeting at the awesome Reza Middle-Eastern restaurant on Ontario Street and left with the same dojo rent deal as the Gracies? Yep, Muay Thai Master Benny Ghofrani! PWOK would now be further educated in the devastatingly brutal and scarily powerful Arts of Thai Boxing and Vale Tudo. Yee hah!

Eventually, I received a VERY HIGH MUAY THAI HONOR by receiving the "Monkol". This is the Thai Warrior headdress worn in the ring before ancient death matches or modern Muay Thai fights. Master Benny went directly to and received permission from the authority of the International Muay Thai Association to bestow this Honor. I was told that I was the FIRST American to receive this High Honor without being of Thai dissent or formally ranked in the Muay Thai fighting hierarchy. Master Ghofrani surprised me and Kenpo School by bringing his students out to Brookfield from Chicago one evening and performing a ritual Thai dance unseen to anyone below my new Muay Thai rank. Master Benny told me that if I were to wear that particular monkol ANYWHERE in Thailand, the level of respect that I would receive would make me uncomfortable.

Is cool even the right word here?

POP. (Power of Prayer) and the Masters just kept coming into my life and that of my students.

USE YOUR ABILITIES AND TALENTS TO THEIR FULLEST WHILE HURLING HEADLONG TO YOUR DESTINY. IT IS THE WAY OF THE WARRIOR TO MOLD YOUR REALITY IN THE FIRE OF YOUR WILL AND AT THE LIMITS OF YOUR COURAGE.

USMA HALL OF FAMERS: WILLIAM POWELL, MASTER BOB SCHIRMER & MY DAD.

MASTER BOB SCHIRMER of the All American Academy of Combat-Do taught me how to be tough, funny, cool and deadly all at the same time. As a former Marine Recon Combat Veteran, Master Bob Schirmer (MBS) and I became great friends and had sister schools. PWOK would compete in his Grappling/Jiu Jitsu/Submission Wrestling Gi/No-Gi Tournaments and Kickboxing/MMA events. He is a class act, a great fighter and a Legendary Teacher.

What stands out among the things he taught me was the concept of not DEFEATING THE WHOLE OPPONENT, but rather to FOCUS ON ATTACKING THE NON-EXPENDABLE Parts of him. MBS would say that if a 250 lbs huge fighter came into his Academy for a challenge match (knowing MBS, I personally would laugh) he wouldn't concentrate on using his size, strength and skill DIRECTLY AGAINST a bigger, stronger opponent. Instead, he would USE HIS COMBINED MIGHT to defeat an integral part of the man, like breaking his arm, tear his Achilles heel or taking his neck and consciousness via a rear naked choke. Nite Bro.

Another funny story was the time that Master Bob came to Kenpo School to teach a class and stayed to assist me in testing a small group of students for rank promotion. At one point, we were in my Jeep Wrangler and Master Bob is in the passenger seat, two of my Black Belts in the back and the heater was on. Seems that it was near freezing out, and the testing students were to PUSH THE JEEP AROUND THE BLOCK. The vehicle was on, since we needed heat, but in neutral. At one point, looking in the rear view mirror, the students are dogging it a bit since we were on a slight downward hill. Asking Master Bob to look back as I slam on the brakes and all their faces do the squished mug-against-glass face plant into the rear window. Then removing my foot from the brake, we tell them to pick it up and they spirit us back to Kenpo School.

Sound sadistic? It may be. But if any of those students' car broke down in a snowstorm and they had to walk 5 miles in ONLY their business shoes, skinny black socks and suit jacket while trudging through mile after mile of deep, wet, near-freezing slush in the dark, know what?

<u>EVERY SINGLE ONE OF THEM WOULD MAKE IT THROUGH AND SURVIVE.</u>

It's called MENTAL DISCIPLINE and it's MOST IMPORTANT to YOUR SURVIVAL. Anyway, as we exit the Jeep, one of Master Bob's instructors from Combat-Do was waiting there to pick him up. He watched the whole thing. Master Bob explains that this is ONLY A PART of an ongoing 4 hour BLUE BELT rank test that included his class that night and a series of brutal, pre-Jeep Muay Thai leg kicks. (to emotionless, wooden doll-faced Kenpo Warriors) The Instructor says "Master Bob, don't bring that back with you, or we are going to have no students." That made me smile inside a bit. Par for the course in building Warrior Discipline.

Truth is Master Bob's students are tough as nails, but I liked hearing the Instructor's comment.

Thanks Master Bob for sharing your Combat-Do with your Friend and Student.

MASTER BOB SCHIRMER-USMC RECON, WORLD CHAMPION AND AN AMAZING MAN.

HERE HE APPEARS TO BE MAKING A STATEMENT TO THE MEDIA WITH HIS TYPICALLY INTENSE LOOK OF "GET MY POINT OR I'LL RIP YOUR FACE OFF?"

IN MEMORY OF THE GREAT O-SENSEI PHIL PORTER.

O-SENSEI TEACHING HIS VERY LAST SEMINAR ON EARTH. IT WAS WITH THE WARRIORS AT PWOK JUST PRIOR TO HIS DEATH. WE MISS HIM DEARLY. JUMBO!

O-SENSEI PHIL PORTER *of the Tenth Dan* in Judo

With the death of the Great Teacher in August of 2011, it is appropriate to recognize his lifelong love of the martial arts. O-Sensei's last seminar before his death was at Powell's Way of Kenpo. This is taken directly from his Biography using an Internet search engine (Wikipedia):

"Porter began his Martial Arts career as a boxer in 1943 at age 18. He was later a member of West Point Boxing Team and, in 1950, Light Heavyweight Boxing Champion of the Western Area of the Air Training Command, USAF. He graduated from the United States Military Academy at West Point in 1948, and served in the U.S. Army and Air Force for 25 years, retiring as a major in 1967. Porter started training in Judo, JuJitsu, and Karate in 1951 while serving on a Strategic Air Command (SAC) combat crew at Travis Air Force Base, California. His first teacher

was Walter Todd, 2nd Degree in Judo and the first American to be awarded a black belt in Shotokan Karate. Todd was later promoted to 8th Degree Black Belt in Shudokan Karate. Porter started competing in Judo in 1951 and had a competitive career spanning over 50 years. He was US Air Force USAFE champion in 1957, won a Bronze Medal in the US Senior Nationals in 1963, won the US National Masters Championship four times (1975,1977, 1980 and 1981) and won two gold and a silver medal in the 1998 World Master Athlete Games in Ottawa, Canada in 1998.

Porter was active as a national and international referee in Judo for many years. He rewrote the IJF contest rules in 1967. He refereed the finals in the 1965 World Judo Championships in Brazil between Geesink and Matsunaga. He served on the six-member Consultative Committee of Referees for the first Judo Olympics in Tokyo in 1964, and was the referee for the team finals in the World CISM Games of 1971 in Vienna, Austria.

He was one of the founders of the USJA (United States Judo Association) formed in 1954, He also served three years as National Chairman of the AAU Judo Committee (1961–1964), Chairman of the U.S. Olympic Judo Committee (1964–1968), Secretary General of the Pan American Judo Union (1964–1967), Technical Director of the Pan American Judo Union (1967–1969), President, U. S. Judo Association

(1980–1995); Editor, "American Judo" (1960–1995), President and Head Coach, National Judo Institute and National Judo Team, (1980–1995).

In 1995, Porter founded the United States Martial Arts Association (USMA) and remained President until his death in August 2011."

JUDO COMPETITION RECORD

- 1951: started competing in Judo
- 1957: US Air Force USAFE Champion
- 1963: Placed in the US Senior Nationals
- 1975, 1977, 1980, 1981: Won the US National Masters (over 30) Championship
- 1998: Two Gold and a Silver Medal in the 1998 World Master Athlete Games in Canada.

MARTIAL ARTS RANKS

- Budo Taijutsu - 10th Dan, Masaaki Hatsumi 1998.
- Judo - 10th Dan, from USMA. 2004.
- Judo - 9th Dan, from USJA. 1994
- Jujutsu - 10th Dan, from USMA and Beikoku Mizu Ryu JuJutsu. 1997.
- Jun Kin Shin - 10th Dan (Soke). (Porter founded Jun Kin Shin)
- Taiho Jitsu - 10th Dan, from Mid-Atlantic Self Defense Association. 1997
- Karate - 8th Dan (Honorary), from American Shotokan Karate Alliance. 1996.

O-Sensei was one of the most incredible historians that I have ever met and would use that knowledge in his martial arts teachings. I learned BASIC Judo from others, but learned The Way of Judo from the Great O-Sensei. He taught me proper Judo technique and understanding of the difficulty of teaching it. On that subject, he once said:

"Now imagine this…I have a picture in my mind of a technique that I want to teach you. This picture is made up of my own thoughts as to what I am about to show you. The thoughts fire brain synapses that move my mouth, push air through my vocal chords- my lips to form words that I speak. Then this visual "mind picture" is transformed to sound which travels through space to your ear drums. The vibrations of the sound transmitted reaches your brain which then recreates the visual mind picture that was once in my brain and now in yours. The key is to make our mental pictures the same. Do you know how hard that is? It's amazing actually. This communication is augmented by other means like physical demonstration and repetition. At

least 5,000 reps of the same technique and our mind pictures will be alike and the technique is now yours"

NICO ALEXANDER & RACHEL SAVANNAH WITH THE "COMMADANTE" MOMMY ROSE AT THE UNITED STATES MARTIAL ARTS INTERNATIONAL HALL OF FAME BANQUET.

THE WORLD FAMOUS KARATE LEGEND AND MY GRANDMASTER SHORTY MILLS.

CHAPTER TWENTY SIX

The Importance of: THE GRANDMASTER.

At the beginning of the Chapters on TEACHERS, I said that we would not be focusing on my

Teachers' accomplishments, but rather on what they taught me. Grandmaster Phil Porter

was an exception. With his recent death, there is need for any martial artist to recognize what a

Warrior can accomplish in a single lifetime. The commitment to the thousands of people he

Influenced and taught to live to their fullest potential. Now its time to return to stated format.

But not before telling tales of MY GRANDMASTER, the legendary HANSHI SHORTY

MILLS *of the Tenth Dan*. Let's start with an article off the internet that sums up Hanshi pretty

well. Then I will share you just a few martial arts lessons that this Great Man has taught me the

last 25+ years as his loyal student. Martial Note: Even the Masters have Masters.

Hazel Crest, IL-(ENEWSPF)-"World-renown martial arts guru Vincent "Shorty" Mills recently

received a resolution from the Illinois House of Representatives honoring his many

accomplishments and thanking him for his service to the community. The honor was presented

by State Representative Al Riley, D-Olympia Fields. "Shorty Mills is one of the most respected

living martial arts instructors in the world," Riley said. Mills is a 10th Degree Black Belt in

Pagoda Ryu, in Shuri Ryu and in Moo Do Kwon Tae Kwon Do. He was the founder of the

Pagoda Ryu Martial Arts System, which was tested and certified as a viable system of martial

arts in 1996 by the World Martial Arts Federation and the Midwest United Martial Arts

Association. Mills is also 6th Degree Black Belt in Aikido from the Yoshinakai System of Aikido

and a 5th Degree Black Belt in Kendo.

"You have helped thousands of children learn self-esteem," Riley told him. Riley is no stranger to the martial arts. A Black Belt himself, Riley and Mills have friendships with many other martial arts practitioners going back to the '60s and '70s. They nostalgically call that period "The Golden Age of Chicago Karate."

A longtime south suburban resident, Mills began his martial arts career in 1956, at age 14. His devotion to martial arts has extended into volunteering for various community events and programs. He designed self-defense training programs for the Cook County Sheriff's Court Services Department. He developed and taught rape prevention seminars for the Chicago Police Department and the Cook County Sheriff's Department. He also teaches underprivileged children martial arts through his non-profit organization, Pagoda Ryu System.

"What I try to get across is that martial arts is only 10 percent physical," said Mills, who currently has a studio in Beverly. "It teaches character development and life skills. We as teachers want to see students become good persons and successful citizens. That's what it's all about."

But martial arts isn't Mills' only area of expertise. He's also a licensed pilot, a certified diver, a licensed electrical engineer and electrical contractor, and a member of the Rotary Club and Kappa Alpha Psi Fraternity, Inc. Mills played professional basketball in Italy in 1969 until an injury forced him to leave the game. He earned his Bachelors Degree in electrical engineering from the Illinois Institute of Technology in 1964, his Masters Degree in operations research from Roosevelt University, and another Master's Degree in urban development/city planning from Northwestern University. He earned his Ph.D. in martial science from the University of Connecticut in 1995.

Mills joined the United States Navy in 1964 and was admitted into the Navy's Officers Candidate School the next year. In 1968, he served in Vietnam for a total of 26 months. After completing two 13-month tours in Vietnam, he was stationed aboard the USS Sylvania for a year, and was honorably discharged in 1969.

Mills and his wife Pamela have two daughters and live in Hazel Crest."

When I first met Hanshi Shorty Mills after moving into the then new Presidential Towers on Madison Street in Chicago, it was a process. One day, after teaching Kenpo at Downers Grove Karate and riding up the escalator toward my high rise apartment I saw a gathering of people all standing around one seated man. Everyone was laughing and the source seemed to be the seated man. I didn't dwell on it for long and continued on the way to my place. This started to be a near daily occurrence with the same social activity going on at the same place at about the same time. Finally, I walk over, wade through the crowd and see this huge man sitting on a marble rectangular indoor tree square. Our eyes meet and I smile as usual and he was already smiling. He notices the workout bag slung over my back with the ends of two bamboo rattan fighting sticks poking out.

The Big Man says "Do you train in the martial arts?"

I reply yes and return the query with the very quick witted "Do you?"

He says "Oh a little bit a long time ago."

"My name is Billy."

"My name is Shorty."

"Oh" I utter, seeing for sure that he is not short.

I close with "Well, gotta go. Nice meeting you. Maybe YOU can workout with ME sometime."

He just smiled with the most pleasant of faces and said "Yeah, Maybe."

It must have been a few months of this type of social greetings and small talk between "Shorty" and me, when one day I sat down with Master Bob Wainwright (MBW) of Downers Grove Karate (DGK) for our daily otherworldly chats. I tell him that "I met this HUGE Black Guy where I live and he must know something about something by the way he interacts with others. He has a huge social following (way before FaceBook) and seems to be the nicest guy."

"What's his name?" MBW of DGK asks.

"Shorty Mills." I say.

"YOU KNOW SHORTY MILLS? HE IS ONE OF THE GREATEST MARTIAL ARTS MASTERS IN THE WORLD!" Master Bob is not one that gets overly dramatic about things.

I say "WHAT?"

MBW goes on to tell me of Shorty's 5 World Championships and his reputation as "The Best" and that he really is "World Famous".

"And I TOLD HIM that HE could workout with ME sometime." I stammer.

MBW continues my descent into the mental grave with "You are kidding right?
One time Shorty was at a Karate School that I was training at. When my HORSE STANCE
wasn't low enough, he smashed both my upper thighs hard with a rattan stick! I think I was only
a Purple Belt (Intermediate in Kenpo) at the time." Master Bob explains to my glazed over eyes.

I felt sick the rest of the evening.

It was later than usual when I returned home after class that night and hoping that Hanshi Shorty
Mills (HSM) would not be holding court at elevator apex. No such luck. As I escalate to the top
of the landing, Hanshi Shorty is laughing with a larger than normal group when he says "Hey
Billy!" as our eyes meet. The ocular communication transferred through space a message from
me that said "I Know Who You Are." Without a word back, Hanshi eyes send me a smiling
reply with a "Good. Then we'll talk later" non verbal transmission.

Working out in the Presidential Towers weight room, I see Hanshi lifting with just some workout
shorts, a tee shirt and sneakers on and realize that at 6'6" he must weigh near 285 lbs of pure
muscle. We shake hands and think that there are grizzly bears with smaller paws that he has.
After chatting a bit, we workout with the weights separately, and I then enter the sauna and see
Hanshi sitting there wrapped in what looked like a white table cloth that he must use on such
occasions instead of a standard towel. I sit down and burn my ass on the hot nail heads keeping
the sauna wood planks in place. Not wanting to embarrass myself in front a World Famous
Karate Master by yelling "Ouch!" or "Sh*t that's hot!" I just take the pain and use the adrenaline
dump to start the heated sauna conversation.

"How come you didn't tell me that you were a World Famous Karate Master?" I say.

"You didn't ask." he replies.

"True" I admit.

We talked and sweated for about a half hour while learning of his achievements, accolades and famous fights that would be just as thrilling as sitting around a campfire telling tales of glory, with say, Thor! At no time was Hanshi ever bragging and I had to eek out every morsel of information that the above article refers to… and then some. I also learned that he was brilliant, a member of Mensa Society, a Cook County Sheriff and a former NAVY SEAL WITH TWO COMBAT TOURS IN VIETNAM. Over the years to come, I would learn much more about this real SUPERMAN. But training directly under a Legend, well that would have to wait awhile.

Before we left the sauna and as I was about to pass out, the big question:

"Sir, would you take me on as a student and teach me?"

"No" he said smiling. "I am retired."

And now I am depressed.

GRANDMASTER SHORTY MILLS OF THE TENTH DAN PROMOTING ME TO MASTER LEVEL-
FOURTH DEGREE BLACK BELT. HANSHI GAVE ME THE TITLE "SHIHAN" FIVE YEARS
LATER WHEN PROMOTING ME TO FIFTH DAN. THE SHIHAN TITLE MUST BE BESTOWED
UPON YOU AND IS NOT AUTOMATIC ONCE YOU ADVANCE TO THE SIXTH DAN. THAT NIGHT
I HAD ATTAINED MY CHILDHOOD DREAM OF BECOMING A KARATE MASTER.

But being persistent when it comes to finding the best martial arts Teachers and Schools, there

WAS NO WAY that I would let Hanshi slip through my fingers, not without a fight. Well

um…maybe not a fight, but rather a badgering effort that became borderline obsessive. We

continued to talk regularly about the Arts, his history and why he retired. It turns out that Hanshi

turned His Schools over to his top Black Belts. It seems some of them forgot where they learned

the stuff they were teaching and were not giving HSM the respect he deserved. So rather than

return and beat them all to death in front of their students, Hanshi simply retired from teaching.

"I would never do that!" I proclaimed. "If you train me, I will be loyal to the death."

That sentiment uttered over 25 years ago is as true to this day as it was back then.

Most people have seen the very first episode of "Kung Fu" starring David Carradine as Kwai

Chang Caine. The one when the little orphan boy is standing outside the Shaolin Temple for over a week in all kinds of inclement weather and resisting all distractions as the Masters watch from secret openings in the wall. Well, my formal acceptance as a student of Professor Shorty Mills began in a modern version of the same story.

My wife at the time and her girlfriend would go dancing with Hanshi and me at a downtown Chicago nightclub then called "Ditka's City Lights." Believe me, I am no dancer and basically sat and watched the crazy folks boogie to unrecognizable music. Now, if the DJ had played Led Zeppelin, The Who, Jimi Hendrix, Yes, The Grateful Dead or Pink Floyd, the house would have rocked with my moves. That never happened however.

We always had fun and since Hanshi didn't really drink, I made sure he had plenty of water or the occasional beer. While this Dance Night going out stuff was cool, I wanted to be training in martial arts under the great Shorty Mills. He had politely refused me at least ten times. So we are at Ditka's, like any other time, when I become Kwai Chang. My wife has brought a few additional friends to share the fun and they were all dressed up accordingly.

The women are sitting at a table taking a break and having a drink, when Hanshi appears out of the darkness like a 6'6" ninja and says "Billy, can you do me a favor?"

"Of course. Do you need a drink?" I reply.

"No. See that empty stool next to our table? Go save it for me. I have to do something."

"Sure." while walking over to the stool near our female dance partners and sit down in the seat next to them.

Within a few minutes, this huge Drunken Tennessee Redneck (DTR) stumbles up to the girls' table and asks each of them, one by one, to dance in a slurred, Southern drawl. Of course they say no and are laughing at him as he is getting angrier with each rejection. He finally calls them all "The 'C' Word" and moves past them in my direction. Watching him the whole time, it reminded me of similar experiences with these kinda folk at the Preakness.

He walks up and says "Hey Lil Sh*t. You are in my seat!"

I smile and say "Where you from, man?"

"Tennessee. What the f**k about it?" he speaks in mouth ejecting spittles as his bad breath hits my face like a two day old skunk carcass.

"Oh, I love Tennessee! The Volunteer State right? (he did seem to be volunteering for a beating)

Also a Tennessee Squire and own 1 inch of land near the Jack Daniels Distillery in Lynchburg."
I say smiling at the true statement.

"I don't give a sh*t what the f**k you are. Are you with these "C words" here?" he spews out.

"Why yes I am." and feel the darkness in my eyes descending to black and begin to rise to his demise.

Just as I am about to smash his face hard, I feel a buzzing as the music seems to be skipping between notes, lyrics with Hendrix-like microphone feedback. Time slows "Matrix"-style with the crowd noise blurring and think it's maybe a stroke or something. As the DTR is still screaming for his stool in slow motion words, the strobe light is flashing wildly as I glance across the packed, over-crowded dance floor for no apparent reason. In the darkness of a far distant corner, I can see only one face illuminating with each pulse of the strobe.

It was the watching, unusually emotionless, face of Shorty Mills.

Upon seeing his face, I ease back down in my seat. DTR had not noticed the small couple of inches that my butt had risen, or perhaps he thought that I was giving up my seat to his Dixieland charm. As my ass reintegrates with the uncomfortable grain of the wooden stool, time speeds up and the music, strobe lights and crowd sounds all return to normal.

After wiping the Confederate saliva off my face say to the man "I didn't know that this was your stool. Can I rent it from you?"

"What the f**k are you talk'n about?" he inquires with a confused look on his face.

"Well, up here in these parts (trying to match his accent), if someone takes your seat by accident, it's customary to buy the person drinks to rent the space. How about…for every ½ hour that YOU LET ME sit here, I'll buy you a beer?"

"Really?" saying his first word without spitting.

"Yep" I reply, as I glance at my watch "Starting now, ok?"

He turns and walks right into Dr. Mills in a Drunken Tennessee Redneck Face to Large Black Man Northern Nipple. (DTRF) to (LBMNN)

As DTR looks up at Shorty, Hanshi smiles and says "Oh. Please excuse me."

Drunken Tennessee Redneck disappears into the crowd.

Hanshi walks over to me.

"I was about to beat him badly." I say a bit dramatically.

"I know." he replies…knowingly.

"Why did you make me sit here and take that jerk's jawing?" I query.

"I have watched him all night, knew he was trouble, would be rude to the ladies and was drunk. He was going to start trouble and I wanted to see your reaction." says Hanshi matter of fact.

"I was about a second away from sealing his face." I say honestly.

Hanshi says "I know. But if you had, I WOULD NOT AGREE TO TEACH YOU."

Sorry Kwai Chang Caine, your story has nothing on mine.

So that moment, forever imprinted in my mind, was when I became a student of the Legendary, World Famous Karate Grandmaster, Hanshi Shorty Mills, 10th Degree Black Belt. (Red actually)

The first time remembered training under Hanshi was in a wooden-floored dance/aerobic class studio in our building at Presidential Towers in downtown Chicago near Greektown. Hanshi had asked many of his Black Belts to come train at what became his "Coming Out of Retirement Party." I remember being so excited and honored that perhaps my badgering had in some way caused his change of heart and that the whole martial arts community was better for it.

Anyway, I met Hanshi at the entrance to the workout area where he is standing with this big, muscular kickboxer from a well known local gym. Hanshi introduces us and tells the guy that I teach Kenpo. Well the kickboxer looks at Hanshi and laughingly says "It's that Slap Art right?" (He was referring to the fact that Kenpo Warriors use OPPOSITE FORCE by striking ourselves with one hand in the chest, arm, oblique or thigh to balance out the striking hand that is busting you up) When asked why we use Opposite Force to hit ourselves, I usually say laughingly "We hit ourselves because no one else can!". Kenpo Humor. (KH)

Martial Note: Opposite Force is a fascinating technique. If you were to stand in a SQUARE HORSE STANCE and just send out a right chop to an imaginary opponent to the side, you would feel it to be awkward and with limited power. Now, in the same Horse Stance, as the right hand goes out to strike, take your left hand and simultaneously hit your right upper pectoral muscle with your palm. Keep both movements in sync so that the throat chop of the right hand hits its target at the EXACT SAME TIME as the left hand hits your chest. The result is mind blowing. Whether it's a right brain/left brain unison since each lobe controls the OPPOSITE side of the body, or increased power developed by symmetrical body part movements, the result is the same. The strike hits with substantially more power, focus and damage.

As well, when bouncing a hand off our body, as in the Opposite Force rebound of the downward HAMMERFIST to oblique side muscle with return upward CHOP to throat in Kenpo's EAGLES BEAK, the force is accelerated. Think of it as throwing a "superball" against a wall. As the force of your throw and the inherent potential energy in the ball hits the wall, the energy of the hard surface and its impact sends the ball rocketing back toward you much faster.

Another way to look at it using Eagles Beak, is to picture your right fist over your head and bring it down quickly to your right oblique just above the hip as if you were stabbing yourself with an imaginary knife. JUST BEFORE you make contact, stop the movement and return the right fist back over head in the same path it came from. You will find that the acceleration down, the energy needed to slow and stop the movement and then the effort needed to return it in reverse track motion is SLOW and STRIKE ENERGY DRAINING. By comparison, bring the right descending Hammerfist down to your oblique, like the ball to the wall, and use that CONTINUOUS MOTION to ROCKET the STRIKE BACK TOWARDS THE TARGET with INCREASED SPEED and POWER.. Do be careful when practicing Eagles Beak that you hit your oblique and not your floating rib. I nearly threw up dropping myself WITH MY OWN Hammerfist making that error.

Now with the kickboxer basically laughing at me and my Art, I thought of taking the time to explain the above information to him. Instead, I cut to the chase with a short, quick SPINNING SIDE KICK during sparring that night that inadvertently broke a few ribs, dropping him courtesy of my Slap Art. He would wear a "Hogu" which is a full chest protector used in Olympic Tae Kwon Do matches any time I saw him spar over the next several years.

HANSHI SHORTY MILLS, MASTER BENNY "THE JET" URQUIDEZ, ANOTHER DIGNITARY AND MASTER JIMMY JONES AFTER A SEMINAR IN STAMFORD, CT. IN 1996. LATER THAT NIGHT, HANSHI WOULD SURPRISE ME WITH INDUCTION INTO THE WORLD MARTIAL ARTS HALL OF FAME AS "KARATE INSTRUCTOR OF THE YEAR".

NICE 'STACHE FOR A WORLD MARTIAL ARTS HALL OF FAMER, EH?

I also remember the time that Hanshi took me to a Karate School on the South Side of Chicago. It was in a part of town that was not usually visited by people of my... size. When we enter the gymnasium that served as the dojo, there were many cultural affirmations in poster form on the walls like "BLACK POWER" and "I AM BEAUTIFUL AND BLACK". As Hanshi enters, he yells the customary Warrior Greeting "JUMBO!" a Swahili word saying hello. The teachers and students yell back "Jumbo!" in unison. As I enter barking "JUMBO! and bowing in respect to the School, there is absolutely no reply. Either didn't like me, didn't respect me or thought that Hanshi had brought me there to be a short, thick punching bag.

Anyway, after the "Daffy Duck Hear Only A Cricket" welcome, Hanshi tells me to go to the locker room an suit up. Well, as I mentioned, in Kenpo, we wear Black Gis. As an instructor, I am permitted to wear either a Black or White uniform or a mixture of the two along with a Black Belt. I usually just grab a top and a pair of bottoms from the several gis that I own. As I look into my workout bag, much to my chagrin, I see a COMPLETELY ALL WHITE GI. After suiting up and entering the gym, I \bow and Hanshi starts laughing as I look like something out of a "Mr. Clean" bleach commercial. My white ass couldn't have been in any more contrast to the surroundings. As Hanshi is cackling, the Teachers and other students are not as amused.

Now, you'd figure that being a guest of Hanshi's that they would make me feel more welcome. At first, I was nervous during the two mile walk of the forty feet necessary to join the class. It turns out that Hanshi had brought me there just in time for sparring. Yeah. I mean no time for martial arts bonding. No time to get to know each other. Just time for them to learn about me in the second most intimate way, by fighting. The looks in their eyes flashed me back to the early recreation wrestling days, when the big-n-hairy Junior High boys were drooling to smash my 49 lbs of existence. I also remember kicking most of their asses. With that little bit of confidence, I join the group, say hello and sit down. Hanshi introduces me and its then that I notice the non verbal communication between the hosts as to who was going to spar with me first. Looking at

Hanshi, realizing it was an intentional part of my training and a certain kind of test, I get ready.

The first "gentleman" that I am called to fight, I think his name was Sammy, hops up and faces the man in bleached white gi (me) and gets into a fighting stance after reluctantly bowing before our match. Not sure of school sparring protocol, I let him make the first move versus my usual predilection to attack and smash. The Teacher says "Hajime!" (Japanese for Begin) and my opponent launches a brutal front thrust kick that, if it landed, would have broken my ribs. Fortunately, I sidestepped it and used an INWARD MOVING DOWNWARD BLOCK to keep from dying. Feeling the power of the kick, and his desire to hurt me from the deflected strike we move backwards out of the ring. NOW, I know the rules of engagement.

I smile and say "nice kick" to his unresponsive face. SHOWTIME.

ME ABOUT TO SLAM "SAMMY" BUT GOOD AT A SOUTHSIDE OF CHICAGO DOJO TO SHOW THAT AS A STUDENT OF HANSHI SHORTY MILLS I HIT VERY HARD.

After looking at Hanshi for either permission or reassurance and getting neither, it's back to the center of gym floor for another go at it. This time, he throws another knock-out-blow-heavy-force REAR LEG WHEELKICK to my head. I step forward and off to the right and deliver a perfectly timed short SPINNING SIDEKICK (yes the same as Rib Breaker) to his floating rib. As he drops like a ton of bricks hard to the floor, he is face down on the nicely waxed wood, drooling out an air-spit mixture as his body assesses the damage. As he is face down, his fellow fighters are seated cross legged and leaning forward. They are saying stuff like "Wow Sammy! That looked like it hurt Sammy! Sammy, white boy got game, Sammy?" and the like. I looked at Hanshi who, along with the Head Instructor of the School we're visiting, are smiling and laughing to each other. I guess things were learned by all involved.

After a bit, Sammy rose and reentered the ring. This time when we bowed, our eyes met and Warriors exchanged respectful salutations. We began sparring again and both of us used the customary control of true martial artists. Don't get me wrong, we still went at it 100% but turned off the juice the moment the strike landed. After that match, I sat among the others with the camaraderie that Warriors are accustomed to.

The funny part of the story was after the workout concluded. We were all in the locker room changing, talking and laughing. Being the new white sheep of the family, I kept quiet as the others were commenting to each other about the class and what they were going to do afterward. While listening to the banter in s secondhand kinda way, as I reach for my underwear and put them on the room goes silent. I mean from Volume 7 to absolute quiet in less than a second. Seems that in my hurry to meet Hanshi to get to the South Side, I accidentally grabbed my wife's black panties, instead of my underwear. Pulling them up without noticing, and looking around to source the silence, I see their eyes glancing back and forth from my underwear to my eyes. When I finally looked down and saw the lace fringes, now I get it. As they were awaiting some type of explanation, I simply grab my jeans and put them on. After a few moments, it was clear that something needed to be said, so I did. "See man, deep down I'm really Black!"

Sammy simply said "Hey Bill…That's some sh*t." as he shakes his head and others burst out laughing. During the ride home, Hanshi called me the "Intrepid Enigma" for the first time. Martial Note: Warriors of different cultures around the world often have more in common with each other than with their own people.

There are so many stories of training and learning Bushido under the Great Hanshi Shorty Mills' that I could write a book on his teachings and experiences that would dwarf this one. I'll leave the history of this EXTRAORDINARY HUMAN for you to research and let it be known, that in fact, The Man Is Even Greater Than The Legend. JUMBO! HANSHI, MY KING!

DR. SHORTY MILLS, 10TH DAN

328

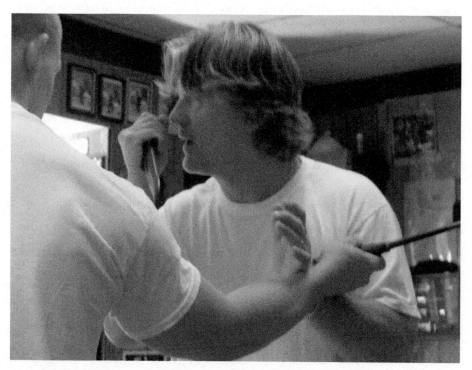

KNIFE MASTER AND FORMER US MARINE RON SCAGGS TEACHING AT PWOK.

CHAPTER TWENTY SEVEN

The Importance of: CARRYING A KNIFE.

Any thing can be a weapon for Self Defense. Be it a lamp, a hammer, a stick, coffee cup, dirt or

even a rolled up magazine. Some are better than others depending on capability and use. A

rolled up magazine is better than a hammer, if say, you need something to read after you've

thwarted a would be assailant while waiting for a bus.. However it's not as effective at smashing

the car window of a submerged vehicle's pressurized cabin to rescue the occupants. The examples here could go on and on as we try to balance what tools we will need for when we need them and the reality that we can't always be a human multi-tool like a Swiss Army Knife.

Besides, most regular folk and law enforcement are wary of a citizen walking down the street carrying a sword with an axe or sledgehammer slung from his/her back. So what to do?

CARRY A KNIFE.

A sharp folding knife can assist you in many ways that have nothing to do with Self Defense by cutting a stuck seatbelt in a car accident, slicing through rope, duct tape or twine that binds you or another, or just to poke a hole in something that needs poking. From scratch food preparation either at home or out in the wild, including survival hunting, nearly always requires the use of a knife. As well, the obvious capability of a knife to cut, slice and puncture also makes it an excellent Tool Of Self Defense. (TOSF) The knife also offers intimidation factors that increase your chances of fending off an armed assault or to be to able to survive a multi-assailant attack.

Before going into self defense aspects of a knife, let's look at the value of it, in a nonviolent way to save a life. One of my favorite Black Belts and great friends, Sifu Tony Krivak of the 2nd Dan, was working in South America when he came upon a village where the children were playing on a rope swing and some other vines hovering over the water that served as a true water Jungle Gym. Sifu was watching the fun, when one of the boys became entangled in the spider web of vines and rope. As the boy twisted and struggled, the vines encircled his neck and he started to literally hang himself.

With only a few other people present, Sifu Tony had ATTA. (Ability to Take Action) and he did. Using the blade from his own knife, he climbed the distance necessary to cut the ties and saved the child's life. By the time the boy reached waters edge, his father arrived, and rather than embrace him or appear elated, he began yelling and scolding the child in their native language. Sifu Tony asked a translator what the older man was saying. The father was furious that his son DID NOT HAVE HIS OWN KNIFE, was unable to free himself and almost died. Had the boy carried his knife as usual, he could've freed himself.

Martial Note: A knife is of no use to you if you don't have it when you need it. It may stay new, sharp and shiney in your top dresser drawer. And will look pristine when laid in the casket with you for otherworldly battles. Carry a knife everywhere you can. Courts and Schools are the ONLY EXCEPTIONS to this rule. Also, have different knives for varied occasions. From a gentelmens thin sleek folder for a night out to a full tang, fixed blade Bowie knife slung from your hip in the jungle or woods. There are all shapes, sizes, blade lengths and materials. Find a few of the ones you like and carry one wherever you go and TELL NO ONE that you do. The salutation for Kenpo Karate is a closed right fist with the left hand covering over the top of it. Essentially it means that "Kenpo Knowledge is Covered and Only for Use in Self Defense."

It can also mean that you "Have a Treasure in your pocket, but it is kept Secret." Having a knife can be a very important secret when you "Reveal that Which is Hidden" to a gang of attackers intent on hurting, maiming or killing you. Put it this way. If a well trained fighter can and has successfully defeated multiple attackers using Unarmed Self Defense Techniques (USDT) the addition of even a small knife blade protruding from the bottom fist of an ARMED Warrior puts ANY NUMBER OF ASSAILANTS in lethal danger. As well it should.

This is only important if you want to live.

As well, carrying a knife does not make you weak, paranoid or a bad person. So remove those thoughts and refrain from trying to explain your reasoning for knife possession to others. It will only create unease in the unfamiliar and disclose the tactical security you possess to a potential adversary. It is therefore best to keep your treasure hidden in your pocket.

Another reason to carry a knife is dog attacks. We're not talking decapitating any annoying dog that races over and nips at you heels. We are talking about <u>TRAINED FIGHTING DOGS</u> that escape confinement and CAN KILL YOU! Dogs like Pit Bulls and Rottweilers. Now before all you Pit/Rot owners, including my friend and Kenpo Master Harry Wheeler who rescues Pit Bulls and has had a few as pets, go ape sh*t on choosing these breeds as an example, let's face facts. THE MAJORITY OF ALL LETHAL DOG MAULINGS involve those breeds <u>WHEN TRAINED TO BE HOSTILE</u>. I own a large Doberman Pinscher named Zeus that is more than capable of defending the house and defacing an intruder, but he was also well trained and raised in a kind and loving environment from a puppy. Besides, the pure aggression of Dobermans as enemy-feared War Dogs in WW II has been bred out for the American market for generations. When was the last time, except in the movies, that a pack of Dobermans have purposely attacked, mauled or killed a human including children? Probably never.

MY DOBERMAN PINSCHER "ZEUS" AT LEFT. HE WILL NOT ATTACK WITHOUT CAUSE. JUST DON'T GIVE HIM ANY LIKE BREAKING INTO MY HOUSE AT NIGHT.

AT RIGHT IS FORMER MARINE RECON, 8TH DEGREE KENPO MASTER, PIT BULL ADVOCATE AND MY FRIEND HARRY WHEELER WITH HIS WIFE. MASTER H WOULD LOVE TO "EDUCATE' THOSE RESPONSIBLE FOR PROPOGATING THE BAD VIEW OF HIS BELOVED BREED CAUSED BY ABUSE, VIOLENCE AND NEGLECT.

Powerful dogs like Pit Bulls and Rottweilers <u>THAT ARE TRAINED AS FIGHTING DOGS</u> and escape confinement can cause some of the most gruesome, life changing damage and permanent disfigurement known to humans. A key reason is their biting technique and the incredible power of the jaws. Once a dog of this type clamps down on say your arm, no human can open their clenched jaws as it is crushing muscle, tendons, nerves and bones. When the dog removes the bite, it is not by opening its mouth to release, but rather by pulling away in chunks whatever it has clamped down on. This leads to excessive blood and muscle loss to the extent that the wound trauma makes surgical repair of the injury difficult. There simply is no tissue to suture with just a huge gaping hole where human flesh and bone once were. Rarely does the attack consist of only one such bite. The mauling comes from multiple chunk-taking bites to many different parts of the body often resulting in permanent disfigurement or death. To make matters worse is the situation of multiple attacking dogs and the people's lack of ability to defend themselves. Defense against a dog attack is not the same as repelling a human attack. A special skill set is needed to survive and that success is increased substantially if you have a knife.

Like any self defense scenario, and this surely falls in that category, there are ways to minimize damage and survive. Once again, YOU HAVE TO FIGHT BACK. Now we all have heard the stories of the strength and savagery of these animals. Police HAVE SHOT THEM several times before they ceased the attack. Huge grown men with baseball bats have smashed the dogs in the head with no release. I personally saw a High School friend's huge wolf-like German Shepard whimper, submit and start to die as a neighbors pit bull got free and attacked it with a powerful clamping bite to the dog's throat. My buddy Pat smashed a thick metal crutch full force onto it head and back without success. Only the neighbor's call to the dog caused him to release the death grip on the Shepard and return home. After witnessing first hand the power and fury of ONE ATTACKING ANIMAL and thinking of the horror that a MULTI-DOG ATTACK of this type could wreak, it was important to find a self defense answer to it.

333

To quote Arnold Schwarzenegger's character "Dutch" who says in the great movie "Predator"

"If it bleeds then we can kill it."

In the past it would be necessary to write here about specific ways to defend against vicious dog attacks. But again this not a book about technique but rather concepts and ideas to keep you as safe as possible while moving around in daily life. Besides, with the internet, you can search "Dog Attack Defense" and get all the technical information required to repel such an attack. BUT YOU MUST TRAIN in these techniques with the same intensity and commitment as your regular martial arts practice. Deterring a killer dog will be more successful if you have a knife.

The Knife expert that trained me was Master Ron Scaggs and he LOVES knives both in an artistic and realistic way. He taught me how to pick out, care for and use a knife as a martial Tool Of Self Defense. (TOSD) Here is his base philosophy on the subject of Knife Fighting:

"The reasons for carrying a knife in today's world should be more than the just the obvious one; self-defense. If you are carrying around and edged weapon it should have other implications that would then categorize it as a tool. When you carry a tool with you it seems the mind-set is different. When carrying a tool, it then has other uses than just one.

I'm not going to try and convince anyone that a knife when carried can, and if needed, will be used as weapon. But let's look at this from the simpler point of view; a knife is a cutting TOOL. It can be used to cut rope, materials, wood, and others. A blade is useful in mail rooms, garages, in the field, boats, and several other settings, as a tool. This is the frame of mind one must have to carry a knife without having some sort of bad karma to befall the person carrying.

The self-defense implications are as endless as the ones that were being described above as a tool. I myself personally can tell you of many times when the knife I carry has been used as a tool and there have been sometimes that it had to be used as a weapon. I do have to say that it has been used as a tool far more times than it has ever been used as a weapon.

There will be times that it will have to be used in a self-defense setting, and what I have to say, is make sure you have some sort of training in handling a knife just for these purposes. While you are training don't get caught up in treating your training as if it were a game. There is a demanding bit of attention that is needed. I like to explain to everyone how real that it is.

I'm going to end with two things. Your knife is as much of tool as it is a weapon, just like all the other tools in the tool box. If you are planning to use your knife as a weapon you must get some serious training.

Here's a small piece of thought from a from Hock Hocheim, a well-established martial artist and knife aficionado below the picture." –Master Ron Scaggs

KNIFE MASTER RON AND CHI JEN JOHN LESANCHE DURING KNIFE TRAINING AT PWOK.

Failing to See the Seriousness of Knife Fighting

"When you fight with a knife, you're trying to survive. This only takes place when all other events and karma have orchestrated such a bizarre set of circumstances that you must stab and slash another human. If you train with a knife and you don't truly grasp this vile and disgusting reality, you will forever be some immature pretender, playing "pass and tag" with a rubber toy. Knife fighting is a very serious business." -Hock Hocheim

KENPO IS NOT A SPORT. BUT WE ALSO BELIEVE THAT SOME COMPETITION IS QUITE BENEFICIAL. THIS WAS PWOK'S FIRST TRY AT SPORT MARTIAL ARTS AT MASTER BOB SCHIRMER'S MIDWEST JIU JITSU AND GRAPPLING CHAMPIONSHIPS. NICE HARDWARE FOR A NON- COMPETITION SCHOOL. MY SON NICO IS FAR LEFT WITH HIS CHAMPIONSHIP TROPHY AND DAUGHTER RACHEL IS IN THE CENTER JUST ABOVE THE GIRL WITH THE WHITE SHIRT. RACHEL'S 1ST PLACE TROPHY IS BURIED IN THE PILE OF KIDS.

INCIDENTALLY, THE WHITE-SHIRTED GIRL IS ANNELIS BAKER, MASTER SEAN'S DAUGHTER WHO WOULD EVENTUALLY BECOME A STATE WRESTLING CHAMPION.

So, as we say at Powell's Way of Kenpo "Get in over your head. Then swim!"

And Swim We Do.

A WARRIOR HAS A PRESENCE CALLED "SAI" AND IT IS APPARENT IN EVERYTHING.

PRACTICING FOR THE STATE DIVING CHAMPIONSHIPS IN MY YOUTH. AFTER GETTING OUT OF THE WATER, TWO SWIMMERS WERE SITTING WITHIN EARSHOT WHEN ONE SAID "BILLY IS SUCH A SHOWOFF." AND MY FRIEND "BEECHY" REPLIED "IF YOU DON'T BELIEVE IN YOURSELF, WHO IS GOING TO BELIEVE IN YOU?" SAGE WISDOM FROM A TWELVE YEAR OLD GIRL. THANKS BEECHY.

CHAPTER TWENTY EIGHT

The Importance of: OTHER INTERESTING STORIES.

Story #1: GET IN OVER YOUR HEAD. THEN SWIM.

In Chicago, the "MANCOW'S MORNING MADHOUSE" radio show was the highest rated broadcast to males in the 18-54 year old demographic. His "shock jock" type style was rude, crude and very successful. He may have had trouble with the FCC and station management, but had no problem with skyrocketing Arbitron ratings (#1 Share of Market) or his MILLIONS of loyal local and nationally syndicated listeners. He could be very funny if that's your thing.

So it was quite a surprise when I got the call from Mancow's staff to see if we were interested in hosting a "celebrity" fight between two on air personalities, "Turd" and "Pumpkin" at the Dojo. As usual, I say "Of course!" without really thinking it through. At PWOK, we have many mottos and one is "GET IN OVER YOUR HEAD. THEN SWIM!" So we did.

Knowing the type of humor and the "call-in" conversations between the audience "Hey Mancow! Love you. Love your show…blah blah" and Mancow's rapier retort wit, I was taking a chance that it could go badly for PWOK, Kenpo, the Martial Arts and my reputation. With millions of listeners and live conversation between host and caller, anything could be said including derogatory remarks about any of the above. That would not do. No it would not.

So I called the show and asked to speak with Mancow. His assistant said he was busy and to leave a number. This is standard policy for celebrities as they simply can not take the call of every nut bag that wants to talk with their hero. Leaving the message that the show had contacted me about hosting a live broadcast from PWOK must have gotten us an asterisk by our phone number. Milling about Kenpo School, thinking of new ways to ignite Warrior Discipline for that night's class, the phone rings and here is basically what transpired:

"Powell's Way of Kenpo Martial Arts School, May I help you?"

"Hi. This is Erich Muller…ahh Mancow."

"Wait a minute. Now I say 'Love You. Love Your Show, right?" pops out of my mouth.

339

"Ahaaaa…Good one!" Mancow replies.

"I understand that you would like to host a fight between two of your folks from the show right?"

"Yes. We would handle all the details and you would have your school name mentioned several times to all my listeners! It could be great for your business." says The Cow.

"Look Mancow, I have no problem helping you have a blast while doing this publicity stunt, but WE ARE OF DEATH here and have a REPUTATION that took years to earn. One comment like "Karate is crap!" or "Did you say "Bowell's Ken-Poo?' and that wouldn't sit well at all.

"Sensei, That will not happen. You have my word." states Mancow emphatically.

"Ok then. What do you need us to do in preparation?" I inquire.

"My staff will be in touch with the details and thanks." says he.

"We're looking forward to it. Bye" and I hang up.

The day of the event, the crew of "Mancow's Morning Madhouse" arrives at Kenpo School in Old Town in very cool Q-101 FM painted cars and vans as they pile out gear and personnel. I first notice the dwarf "Pumpkin" followed by "Turd" the huge guy. They are smiling as we meet and are extremely polite and personable. My surprised look must have shown as Pumpkin says "Yeah, I know. You thought we would be jerks! That's just our on air personality." This made me a bit more at ease when Turd confirmed it with "Yeah we're cool."

Ok then. I quietly put the samurai sword away.

As the crew explains to me the scenario, Mancow has been on the air all morning promoting the Full Contact Karate Fight between Pumpkin and Turd AT POWELL'S WAY OF KENPO MARTIAL ARTS SCHOOL 1610 NORTH LASALLE IN CHICAGO. It turns out PWOK was mentioned ON AIR to millions of listeners FOURTEEN TIMES over the course of the show! Pretty sure that we could not afford that type of radio spot advertising on our meager ad budget.

PWOK was built on smash of mouth advertising. All we had to provide was the real thing-LEARN HOW TO DEFEND YOURSELF-REALITY TAUGHT HERE. Our best advertising came in the forms of the bumps, bruises, black eyes, missing teeth and crutches that are part of the very nature of what we do. We do it to ourselves so that no bad guys can do it to us. Do you know how many students joined by way of asking a colleague or friend that was a current or past student where they got all "those cool bruises"? Kenpo Warriors wear them as Badges of Honor, the result of hardcore, reality-based martial arts training. There is no crying in Kenpo!

As a general rule, students were instructed to keep the bruises low key and wait until a prospective student asked about Kenpo School AT LEAST 3X before inviting them to class. PWOK Master, Dave Saboe of the Fifth Dan, used to roll up his business shirt sleeves at the office just enough to reveal the tips of bruises from IRON ARMS and BONE CONDENSATION strength training. He was asked about them regularly and merely replied "Kenpo Karate" to their confused, amused and inquiring looks. More about the amazing Master Dave in a bit.

At one point, while the class was showing off their Badges of Honor, all individual and unique, someone suggested a "Bruise of the Month Calendar" to exhibit either our toughness or our propensity to bust each others blood vessels and think its cool. After much laughter and consideration it was not to be. I could just see it…a new student gets hurt and sues me and PWOK for negligence or something. All the prosecutor would have to show the judge was "Exhibit A-The Powell's Way of Kenpo Bruise of the Month Club Calendar" and away I go.

So back to Mancow…

As the Morning Mad House team arrives and begins setting up, I am actually impressed with their professional precision. Cords, microphones, sound equipment were set up so fast that it's like we were part of a traveling circus and said as much. One of the tech guys replied…"The Morning Madhouse IS a traveling circus. The part of the whole escapade that I hadn't thought of was the Mancow Show's partnership with its listeners. As Mancow is doing his thing on the air promoting the "Big Fight" he is INVITING HIS LISTENERS to come by Kenpo School to see the fun. I had envisioned herds of Mancowians flooding the dojo and total chaos. Deciding to practice what I preach by relaxing and going with the flow. And that's what I did by welcoming almost 100 listeners that were in the area, work boots, overalls and tools attached, onto the mat of our hallowed Temple. No way of having them take off their boots was even workable. Besides not having either the area or the inclination to have a boot check room, and the fact that nearly every pair looked the same, how would they know whose boots were whose? The thought of the roaring variety of foot rot that awaited the faces of my students and I as we are ground-fighting was much nastier than the idea of just sweeping out dried mud and dirt after.

SHOWTIME.

The School stereo was temporarily hooked up in the weight room adjacent to the dojo floor. Its necessary due to the unusual sounding time delay between what is happening during the event, transmitted live to Mancow's studio, then resent out to the listening audience. If you are in the same room as the radio and are speaking with the radio station, they will ask you to turn down your volume for this reason. Otherwise this bizarre echo affects your brain and can cause confusion in speaking with the person on the phone. So here's what went down that strange day.

With a packed audience sitting or standing on near or against all four walls of the Dojo, and others peering in from the doorway, out of the weight room comes the battle ready likes of Turd and Pumpkin. A few of my students had prepared them with some advice and a full complement of martial arts sparring gear. Turd was so big that the protective gear made him look the a comical version of "Jason" from the "Friday the 13th" movies and Pumpkin's diminutive size had him looking like a bloated "Tasmanian Devil" from "Bugs Bunny" cartoons. It was a surreal setting that might have had two bloodied Roman Gladiators in mid contest take a break from their death match to sit and watch.

Mancow is on the other end of a portable phone as the from memory gist of our conversation is:

Mancow (MC) on the radio: "Ok. We are about ready to go live to POWELLS WAY OF KENPO KARATE SCHOOL in downtown Chicago for the much anticipated fight between Turd and Pumpkin...Sensei...Hello! Can you set the stage for us? What is happening there and what's the mood?"

Me Playing Along (MPA): "It's incredible Mancow! You can feel the tension in the air. The crowd is ready. The combatants are ready. What do you want me to do as far as refereeing?"

MC: "Well, just don't let anyone die and give us a color commentary...a play by play."

343

MPA: "Ok. Here we go. Pumpkin here!" (as I point to the line on the mat for KUMITE (sparring) "Turd you here!" pointing to the second black line facing Pumpkin. I have the phone on my right shoulder pressed to my ear with the then state of the art 12" metal antenna sticking out of the top making my bow difficult. The visual was from the 1970's TV hit "My Favorite Martian" where the antenna rises from his head. I had to be careful during the match not to lose communication with The Cow by forgetting about the antenna and breaking transmission with the station by snapping it off in Pumpkin's eye socket by getting to close to the action.

"Mancow. We are ready. Turd, Are you ready?" He nods. "Pumpkin, Are you ready?" He bows. The epic clash begins when I yell "HAJIME!' (Begin!). Well, actually, neither knew the Japanese word and just stood there until I adjusted the phone again and yelled "FIGHT!"

"Mancow, the action is furious! Pumpkin is racing in with a head long frontal assault that has Turd turning away in fear! No wait! Turd's protective headgear has turned around backwards as he was adjusting the strap! OOOOOOOhhhhh Pumpkin takes tactical advantage and socks Turd right in the groin! Clear shot in the clams! Can I say that?"

MC: "You just did Sensei."

MPA: "Oh…now Pumpkin is continuing a relentless assault that has Turd totally off guard. I don't know how long this will last as Gladiator Pumpkin is unleashing a barrage of tiny kicks to Turd's shins and knees while raining heavy hand strikes to Turds hips and boobs…ahhh chest! Wait. Mancow…Turd has finally got his headgear on the right way. He can now see the attack. Oh!…Turd is now picking up Pumpkin by the groin and face! He is…is lifting him over his head like a log! He is holding him there just showing his power!" The crowd is going nuts…it's a bloodlust here Mancow! He's going to throw Pumpkin down. I hope they practiced this!"

344

Authors Note: I don't think they did. Turd slams Pumpkin FULL FORCE on his side. Now I respect all people, but unless you have heard the sound of a 6'2' man throw a thick, well-muscled prone dwarf hard to the ground from overhead 8 ft in the air, you haven't really understood the word "IMPACT".

MPA: "Oh Noooooo!....BOOM! Cow, I can't be sure, but I think Pumpkin may be dead!" (I know he's not and so does the screaming crowd, but the SLAM was momentarily alarming.) He's not moving! Wait..." THUD!

MC: "Sensei! What is happening? Is Pumpkin out? What's going on there? Sensei???"

MPA: "Sorry Mancow! I dropped the phone! Pumpkin was out, but his mental toughness is clear and he is shaking it off! What a gladiator! Wait, there is a problem! With all the protective padding from the gear, Pumpkin can't get to his feet. He is just spinning in a circle! Like a upended turtle of war! Here comes the Turd! He's going in for the kill! He's leaping! Full Turd weight midair....ahhhhhhh SLAM! Oh, it's not looking good for the Pumpkin! He is clearly on the defense. Turd is punching! Over and over to the huge dwarf head! I've got to stop this Cow! Wait! Wait! Unbelievable! Pumpkin has somehow used the spinning back shell position to rock Turd with a surprise right hook to the head. Turd was way to close and his head gear has again spun backwards to blind him again! Turd's falling back and off the smaller man. Both rise in glory to their feet! I call this a draw! MATE! (Stop!) I mean STOP!!!

Mancow, both men are battered and bloodied but not defeated! There is no clear winner and the contest is a draw!" As the crowd explodes in a combination of cheers and a few boos from those that wanted the action to continue.

MC: "Sensei, thank you and your students at POWELLS WAY OF KENPO MARTIAL ARTS SCHOOL IN DOWNTOWN CHICAGO for hosting the Pumpkin-Turd Full Contact Karate Fight! We'll hear from our listeners after these messages."

As people started filing out of the Dojo to return to whatever it was they were doing pre-event, Mancow's Morning Mad House comes back on air after commercials and now the listeners would chime in. Time to know if what we had done would be a good thing for our tiny KENPO SCHOOL or did I make a mistake?

Again from memory:

MC: "Ok, Whoa…sounds like a hell of a fight at Powell's Karate School between Turd and Pumpkin. We'll hear from them later, probably from the hospital or a bar, but now let's hear as some listeners reflect on the action. Hello, you're on the air."

Listener One (LO): "Mancow! Love you! Love Your Show! Sounded like some heavy action! Turd may be bigger, but Pumpkin has a lower center of gravity…blah…blah…blah…great event! When is the rematch?"

MC: "Over at Powell's Karate, they teach Kenpo. Isn't that the stuff that Steven Seagal does to bust faces, snap arms and throw guys out windows?"

Here we go, I think, as martial arts is now the topic of conversation between unknown "authorities" and The Cow with millions of listeners out there across the country.

Listener Two (LT): "Mancow! Love you! Love Your Show! No, Steven Seagal does AIKIDO and Jeff Speakman in "The Perfect Weapon" does KENPO…which is mostly handstrikes. (TRUE) AIKIDO is mostly joint locks and throws (TRUE) They are totally different! (FALSE)

But good enough for me. The remaining conversations between Mancow and his listeners were benign. Not a negative comment about Kenpo, PWOK or the Martial Arts. Mancow was a man of his word. Thanks Mancow. Love you. Love your Show.

Martial Note/Business Note: Yes, even in this odd story there are lessons. The only two that you really need to glean here are:

1) Get in over your head. Then swim.
2) If you have an opportunity to get your business a fortune's worth of FREE advertising, do it.

THIS IS A PAINTING OF A HOUSE.

Story #2: DON'T BELIEVE EVERYTHING YOU ARE TOLD.

In an other clear example of the need to always REVEAL THAT WHICH IS HIDDEN, a

famous Tai Chi Teacher (not Kimball) came to Powell's Way of Kenpo in the late 1990's.

This Master was well known throughout the international martial arts in general and the Chicago

scene in particular. Master Waysun Lao (MWL) had come to Kenpo School to teach a seminar on

Tai Chi and Chinese weaponry.

MWL taught an amazing class on the LONG FORM of Tai Chi and the development of

INTERNAL POWER through its practice. The class was intense and enjoyed by all present..

But the lesson learned in this story came after the seminar was over. MWL and I were talking about the student reaction as he is scanning the various weapons and martial ornaments adorning the cool brick walls of Kenpo School. As his words continue to educate, he is looking at several Chinese worded scrolls that hung in a triangle formation on the dojo's northern wall.

Prior to opening the downtown School, I went over to Chinatown to purchase some items commonly seen in martial arts schools. Things like incense, porcelain Buddha statues, dragon and tiger paintings and, of course, the mandatory Chinese scrolls. As I went from store to store, they all had basically the same merchandise so price was more of a consideration than selection.

Unintentional Iron Arms Training, by way of the statue filled bags dangling from both arms that cut off blood circulation, was causing my fingers to go numb. Being a Warrior Shopper (WS) I push forward into the last store since it was the only Bushido thing to do. Upon entering and seeing the vast array of Chinese scrolls hanging from the walls, I am thrilled to say the least. But by looking past the doorway at the scrolls and not the slippery wet tile flooring, off I go into a feet first, near ass-skidding free fall. Bumbling and fumbling with the inner door exit bar and its "Hello, customer here" chimes that soon became entangled in the multitude of various sized bags twisting and strangling my Pin Arms of Death.

Pulling and spinning to get my head back over my feet; I dive into the store and nearly crash into a little old Chinese lady that's coming out. The resulting un-master-like entrance had the two store employees looking at me and each other like I was drunk, an idiot or both. Instead of calling the police or unleashing the exiting old lady's Kung Fu on me, they just say "hello" in unison. Finally untangled from the grappling hook chimes, I regain my balance and return the greeting with a red-faced smile. The female employee must have drawn the short straw and reluctantly came over to help me.

Telling her of my need for some positive, powerful and spiritual Chinese scrolls, she smiles (like

you sure do moron) and hand gestures to different ones while explaining the English translation..
I pick three that epitomized the values of Kenpo School; Strength, Power, Focus, Self Discipline,
Awareness, Honor etc. She smiles as I point to the three that met those themes the best. Another
bag for my now mummy-like, blood-starved arms and out the door I go a bit more majestically
than the entrance. The scrolls must work since the chimes did not attack me again on the way
out.

TAI CHI CHUAN'S LEGENDARY MASTER WAYSUN LAO IN CENTER.

So, now fast forward to PWOK and the Tai Chi Master that just finished the seminar and we are
talking as he is looking around the room at the walls. Paraphrasing the conversation:

MWL: So Sensei, you into Chinese politic?

MOI: Not really. Why do you ask?

MWL: Do you know what those scrolls say?

MOI: Yes. This one says "Power, Wisdom and Spirituality. The others basically say; Courage, Strength and Discipline. (Trying to remember the translations from the store lady)

MWL: No. The top one say 'Vote Ping Yi for Mayor of Hsing Ti village.' And the lower right scroll below say 'Re-elect Ying Tan to Council of Nang Po.' (Exact name recall and poling place sketchy on my part, but you get the idea)

I am just staring at MWL as his soft spoken words are pounding on my confused eardrums. This occurs while considering the weak position of any counter translation argument that could be made since the Master WAS Chinese, could read, write and speak Cantonese, Mandarin and other dialects of the language. On the other hand I get confused ordering from a Chinese take out menu. That's probably why they ask you to order by the numbers.

MOI: You are kidding me, right?

MWL: No.

Martial Note: Beware of believing everything you are told. Do the research, reveal falsehoods, find the Truth and embrace it. As well, try not to stumble into a store when buying unfamiliar items from ladies who drew the short straw.

DO THESE CHINESE CHARACTERS MEAN UNITY OF MIND, BODY AND SPIRIT OR YOU CAN ORDER CHINESE FOOD HERE? MAKE SURE BEFORE DISPLAYING...OR ORDERING TAKE OUT.

352

CHAPTER TWENTY NINE

The Importance of: OTHER INTERESTING STORIES…CONTINUED.

Story #3: WHEN FEAR NEUTRALIZES TRAINING-SPETSNAZ VS. GHOST

I met Sensei Boris at Gold Coast Martial Arts School in the mid 90's. Talk about "The Russian Bear" well this guy was it. We are talking about a 6'3'' 260 lbs behemoth that also happened to be a Russian Special Forces (Spetsnaz) combat veteran and a Master of Kyokushinkai Karate. This is the same powerful Karate style of the legendary Mas Oyama who killed a bull with a HAMMERFIST strike to the head. I did wonder how a man this size could be an Operator able to "Sneak and Peak" but then again, Hanshi was one of the biggest Navy SEALS of his era.

Anyway, Sensei Boris (SB) shared the first floor main section of the tri-level building at Gold Coast Martial Arts. (GCMA) At the time, Kenpo and Wing Tsun were taught on the top floor, Kyokushinkai and Shorei Ryu Karate in the middle with Aikido on the bottom floor. Depending on how much rain soaked through the porous roof, classes and Arts were moved about accordingly. We had more buckets than students at the time.

SB was the care-taker of the School during non-class time. Having a huge Spetsnaz Karate Master on premises rendered guard dogs obsolete. SB would sleep on the carpeted floor of the main locker room. By no means a 4 Star accommodation, it was probably much more comfortable than the rock hard streets of Prague that he slept on during the USSR's invasion of Czechoslovakia in 1968. Interestingly both Sensei Boris and Hanshi Shorty Mills were in SPECWAR combat at the same time on opposite ends of the globe in Vietnam and Prague.

One day, I arrived at the main entrance of the dojo and noticed that the entire hard steel door with reinforced glass was wide open. Not unusual you say? Well the fact that the locked door only opened inward was. The door that was supposed to open in, was now hanging on its hinges that were bent outward as it was forced at high impact from the inside. It looked like a fireless explosion of some type. It turns out to be the result of a hasty exit by Sensei Boris. What would make a 6'3' 260 lbs Spetsnaz-trained Karate Master run out through the in door without even unlocking it? The answer is a ghost.

It does not matter if you believe in ghosts or not, or whether Sensei Boris did. What he saw and shared with me caused him to run face first through the locked door and into the parking lot of GCMA. According to SB, who was still shaken in the daylight hours after his experience, here is what happened:

Sensei Boris was sleeping on the locker room floor after having locked up the School for the night. About 2 am, he hears unfamiliar noises inside the room. Staying quiet and using his Spetsnaz training, he listens for the direction of the noise. He closes his eyes momentarily to get the best possible night vision. Upon opening them, he is terrified to see a man "hovering" over him. Not next to, but hovering directly over him and parallel to the ground. As the fright overtakes the previously fearless combat veteran, he screams and runs out of the locker room and straight through the locked front door! He remained in the parking lot and unable to sleep, stared at the open front door until the sun rose in the morning. When reentering the building he found nothing and all other doors and windows were locked. Whether or not it was a real ghost or a nightmare is unimportant.

The fact that a well-trained, battle-tested Warrior could be so affected by either is the point.

Martial Note: Fear can render training useless and the mind ineffective. And that is bad.

Sensei Boris and I became friends after that incident. In fact, he gave me the Russian Hammer &

Sickle and Gold Anchor flashes from his Spetsnaz beret. I have them to this day in the case below.

THE MANY HONORED TREASURES GIVEN TO ME BY THE GREAT WARRIORS THAT I'VE MET ALONG THE WAY. THE BOTTOM CASE HOLDS THE SPETNAZ FLASHES AND OTHER GIFTS FROM COMBAT VETERANS WITH A GREEN BERET UP TOP . MY APPRECIATION OF THESE VERY IMPORTANT WARRIOR SYMBOLS AND WHAT THEY REPRESENT HAS NO BOUNDS.

2nd Martial Note: Sensei Boris trained in martial arts at a time when doing so was illegal in the USSR. Some of his fellow students were sent to gulag for years after getting caught practicing Karate. Martial Artists were deemed a threat to the State and stiff penalties were imposed on both teachers and students caught training.

Martial arts weaponry and practice were also outlawed in Okinawa by the invading Japanese. The advent of nunchuku (rice flail) kama (small wheat sickle) bo (water carrying long stick) and tonfa (grain churning handle) were designed as secret defensive weapons against the samurai sword. In addition, special "dances" were created that allowed for martial arts KATA (Forms) and techniques to be practiced by being hidden within the dance movements. In China, the birthplace of many martial arts, the Shaolin Temple, was burnt to the ground and the monks killed at a time when they were viewed as a threat to the ruling government. The suppression of martial arts practice and citizen weaponry by a fearful ruling class has occurred throughout history. The oppression suffered by our predecessors, the danger they faced and the penalties paid to pass the Arts forward can not be overstated. Thank them.

Here in America in the year 2013, you can practice martial arts in the open, legally own firearms and find a martial arts school in nearly every town. And most of the Great Masters are here. Be thankful for your time in history and practice, practice, practice.

Learn. Learn. Learn.

Teach. Teach. Teach.

Go Ahead And Compete With The Immortals.

It's your time.

TRAIN. TRAIN. TRAIN UNTIL YOU DIE.

"Who can wait for the dust to settle? Who can remain still until the moment of action?"-Tai Chi

CHAPTER THIRTY

The Importance of: WAITING.

Waiting.

In most cases the term is used as a negative pause in an anticipated action. You grab a product from a store shelf, walk up to the sales register and expect to pay for it immediately. Then you expect that you will leave the store and proceed uninterrupted with your daily routine. Waiting is an unscheduled interruption of your mental plan by a physical or situational occurrence. Too many people in line, too much traffic, the doctor is running late etc.

This is different from PATIENCE where you are doing one thing at a time and use the pause to do it well. While patience is considered a positive quality, waiting is not. And while waiting may not be considered a quality, the Ability To Wait (ATW) is. Especially in a Self Defense situation where ATW may be the difference between victory and defeat or life and death.

ATW Story #1: ZEN FLY

Arriving at Kimball's Crossroad's Academy to train one cold winter day, I was holding the door to let a young lady go in first. Not unusual since my Father taught me the importance of MANNERS from a young age. He used to tell me to treat everyone with respect and always mind my manners. I do so to this day and found that good manners, a smile and a sense of humor are the best defenses in combating the negative aspects of waiting.

While waiting for the woman to enter the doorway, I glanced down to the outside front window of the building and saw a fly. Wow you say! A fly! Karate Master sees a fly! Whoaahoo! You say that now, but won't after the end of the story. So entering the building and while waiting for the molasses-slow Tai Chi Elevator, I look outward from the elevator doorway which wasn't opening. So I am waiting. Waiting. Hit the button six more times. Door doesn't open. Getting irritated since being late for Kimball's class was a no-no. Feeling the tension build in my neck and the agitation tweak my nervous system, I start to sweat. The anxiety caused by waiting and the consequence of the delay was now mental, physical and emotional. The wait was making me a wreck and that is not conducive to a Tai Chi class preparation. The idea of Tai Chi for a martial artist is to increase internal power, not return a depleted human battery cell to normal strength. I know this and am now getting angry because of the self conscious state I have created while waiting.

Almost at full boil after ten minutes waiting for the elevator, I debate not going to class at all. In fact, I am now angry with Kimball for even having Tai Chi classes in a Tai Chi Elevator-equipped building! My eyes now watering and dry at the same time with my heart pounding at full thunder, the thought of heart attack crosses my mind. Newsflash: "Kenpo Warrior found dead at base of elevator in Chicago building of apparent heart attack. Now to sports…"

It was at the high point of the mental, physical and emotional clusterf*ck that I see it…the fly. Through my self-induced tunnel vision I see the fly still in the same place on the outside window as the wind-blown snow continues to blast its tiny wings. It just sits there. The strength of the wind gust sent a pizza box flying by and had people leaning forward to move against it. All this tumult and the fly did not move one inch. About to exit to see if the fly was dead, alive or somehow stuck to the outside window, the thought is interrupted by the opening of the elevator door. Finally, I enter and press the button for the year-long trek to the 5th floor and Crossroads

Academy. As the doors are closing, the last thing I see is the fly still there on the window.

Bad ass fly I thought.

Calming down slowly, I exit the elevator and move down the hall to the Academy door. Upon entering, Kimball is waiting for me. It turns out that since I was the only student to show up for that class, it hadn't even started yet. Kimball just looked at me and asked if I was ok. Saying yes but then unleashing a maniacal tirade about the elevator and being late blah...blah...blah. Kimball just listens and when I am out of fury, simply says "Let's practice." Amazed at the different states of being between Kimball and me we begin Tai Chi Long Form. How was he so calm? I was late for his class, knew that was unacceptable and had made him wait for me.

Beginning to relax as the serenity of the Academy and the soothing soundtrack of Kimball's voice over the Kyoto Monks CD chanting in the background, the focus is clearing my mind and body systems follow suit. After returning to a normal state of consciousness, I surpass it and now my power builds. Just as I am totally at ease and my mind is nowhere in particular, Kimball is leading the movements and while facing away says:

"Did you see the fly?"

"Yep" I reply.

"Been there all day. Pretty amazing considering the *bad weather and strong winds*."

'Not sure how its hanging on" says Kimball while creating Tai Chi Ball posture.

"Must be a Zen Fly." I chuckle without breaking concentration.

"Yeah. Or maybe he was just *waiting* with you for the elevator?"

"He handled the wait way cooler then me." I say.

"Yep... Zen Fly...I like that. Tee hee hee." Kimball whispers almost giggling.

Leaving class that night, with renewed energy, focus and power, I wondered how the fly could withstand the wind, freezing sleet and snow so well, whereas a wait for an elevator in a warm, enclosed building showed that I yet could not. After pondering this as the wait for the elevator going down was nonexistent, the ride down quick and the opening door instantaneous upon arrival at the ground floor.

I decided that it's best to practice waiting and using that time for better purpose.

When the elevator opened, the fly was gone.

ATW Story #2: AMBUSH IN VIETNAM.
Hanshi Shorty Mills (HSM) rarely if ever talks about his experiences in Indochina as a Navy SEAL with two combat tours in Vietnam. But since I had read as much as possible about the war and remembering the nightly television images as a child, my interest in the subject was intense.

I asked Hanshi why he didn't talk about the War and he replied that its over with. He said he did what he had to do and that it wasn't pretty. Inquiring whether he had flashbacks or not, he said no and that he was lucky since a lot of folks didn't make it back. Hanshi said he "left Vietnam in Vietnam." HSM said that he was just a "Better Warrior" than the enemy he faced in close up fashion and that's why he survived. HSM said that the only problem was when he came back on leave and was driving in San Francisco.

An overly aggressive cop had pulled Hanshi over for no apparent reason and began interrogating him on where he was going. HSM was just 24 hours removed from "The Bush" in the jungles of Vietnam where he was KILLING the Viet Cong and NVA up close and personal. His mindset was still in the bush with the thoughts of bringing Death to any adversary about to come out, when the police officer backed off and allowed Hanshi to go on his way. Lucky for all involved. I then asked HSM if he left Vietnam unscathed. He said almost and lifted his shirt to reveal shrapnel scars that ran up from his lower back up to shoulder blade. His massive back was testament that NO ONE left Vietnam unscathed.

While "lying in wait" for the enemy, elements of Hanshi's SEAL Team was deep in the bush alongside a trail frequented by the VC and the NVA. There mission was to assess enemy troop strength in the area where contact had been heavy of late. While totally concealed in the thick jungle, his team set up and waited. After many hours of silence and no movement by any member of The Team, Hanshi heard the sound of approaching steps in the form of mushy, squeaky footwear favored by the VC. The enemy was moving toward the SEALS and soon the foot sounds matched the outlines of triangle-hatted, black pajama-ed uniforms of the Viet Cong.

As they came within range, it seemed to be a small VC recon squad doing pretty much what the SEALS were trying to do. Assess the enemy strength undetected, ambush and kill as many as possible with then disappear back into the jungle. The VC appeared to be alone and small in number. Hanshi said the urge to open fire was almost uncontrollable. Almost. The SEALS let the small VC unit go by them without incident to make sure they were not the vanguard of a larger enemy force up the trail.

After waiting for a time, the SEALS thought that the VC unit was the extent of the force and hand signals exchanged between them debated whether they should have wasted them. Hanshi and the Team would wait some more before returning to base. It was not much longer after the hand signal exchange that Hanshi hears the sounds of combat boots, not tennis slippers, coming from the same direction as the VC. The Team lay prone and silent as first troops of a massive NVA force appeared. Hanshi remembers lying there head down weapon silent for hours as the first North Vietnamese Army soldiers passed by until they were all gone. Hours of wait. Had the SEALS not waited, and opened fire on the first small VC unit, they would have been chewed up by the massive NVA force that followed close behind. So from what Hanshi told me, in Vietnam, sometimes it was best to wait.

ATW Story #3: Mr. MIYAGI.

We all remember the scene from the original "Karate Kid" movie where Mr. Miyagi takes Daniel san to the bad guys Cobra Kai dojo to talk with the "No Mercy" Sensei . The tough guy teacher sees them standing inside the doorway and approaches them menacingly.

"Let's get out of here!" says Daniel san.

"Wait." says Mr. Miyagi.

You get to point. Waiting is hard. It takes practice. It may also be the difference in your overall health as waiting causes stress and many automatic human reactions that are not good for your well-being. Since I am not a doctor, you can better learn the negative aspects of stress elsewhere. This book is about Self Defense and previous stories demonstrate that your Ability To Take Action (ATTA) is directly related to your Ability To Wait (ATW). Wrong action at the wrong time can get you injured or killed.

Unless you have been in combat or another life and death situation you do not know how you will act. Everyone likes to think that they would be a "Rambo" or a "Mahatma Gandhi" in a real crisis. Without facing this "moment of truth" scenario, you think, but can't be sure what you will do. Will you panic and cower in fear of the mugger, home invader or the chance to save a person drowning? Or will you surge forward at the right time to take the right action? Only you know the answer. This unanswered question is at the heart of the matter for any would be Warrior.

Martial Note: The Ability To Take Action (ATTA) is only effective when the time is right. Diving into a river and waiting there in hopes of saving a future drowning person is noble but still a poor timing of action. Now, let's suppose you are confronted with a gunman in a hallway who approaches you with the weapon from a distance of 30 feet and you have nowhere else to go. If you were to take immediate action by charging the gun, odds are you would get shot dead reducing any further ATTA on your part. But if you have the courage to WAIT until the best opportunity to attack presents itself you may have a chance. How do you wait when you are about to be shot? Well, while no guarantee, if he didn't shoot you yet, maybe he doesn't want to shoot you at all. Perhaps the gun is a threat of violence and a tool to intimidate you. Bank robbers do it all the time with fake guns since ARMED robbery is much more severely penalized than robbery without weapons. Be sure to assume that all weapons are real and the assailant is prepared to use them. Using all your training in diplomacy, psychology, mental discipline and martial arts technique, you have a chance...If you can wait.

WAITING UNTIL THE MOMENT IS RIGHT CAN BE THE DIFFERENCE BETWEEN LIFE AND DEATH. WHAT WOULD YOU DO HERE? YOU WILL NOT KNOW FOR SURE UNTIL IT HAPPENS AND YOU MUST ACT OR NOT ACT WITHIN A SPLIT SECOND.

Waiting until you are actually in a position to do something is as important as knowing what to do once you get there. Your adrenaline will be pumping with the "fight or flight" mechanism at full throttle. Since you can't retreat or run forward, the only way to give you a chance to engage the assailant is by waiting. Kenpo Karate has some of the most effective gun attack defenses of any martial art, but racing up to a firing gunman to attempt Kenpo gun defense technique CIRCLING THE MOON won't be as effective when you are bleeding to death. If you can wait until the moment is right and the distance between you and the gunman is manageable, you have a chance. While the authorities recommend total submission in the face of a gun threat, I agree only to a point. In assessing the threat, and convinced that even if you give him the wallet he is going to shoot you anyway, resistance is the only option.

While on the topic of gun threat, NEVER let anyone tie you up or force you into the trunk of a car. That reduces your ATTA to thanking him for killing you quickly. It's also bad if you are not in favor of being tortured, dismembered and having your body parts spread over three states. If he is close enough to tie you up or close the trunk, he is close enough for you to act. Attack, gain control of the gun and keep the weapon pointed away from you or others. A gun itself doesn't kill you, it's the bullet that comes out of one end of it that does. Control that end at all cost.

Martial Note 2: If the weapon is a semi-automatic pistol, when controlling the gun make sure that you grab and hold the slide at the top. Keeping the slide from moving back and forth will prevent the gun from firing or chambering another round. When confronting a revolver, you must grab and hold the cylinder and keep it from revolving. If it can't revolve, it can't shoot the bullet. An additional option with a revolver is grabbing and holding the hammer at the back of the gun in either the closed or open position. This will prevent the hammer and firing pin from igniting the bullet charge. Remember to grab the weapon and hold its barrel away from you.. Approach any weapon defense by understanding how it works, ways it can hurt you and real techniques to avoid harm. And Practice Them As If You Life Depends On It. Because it does.

The most effective defense against any attack is best summed up by Mr. Miyagi's "No be there." But if you are "there" hopefully your training and poise will match the threat with right action.

Understand WAITING and its importance to your survival. Just Wait and See.

THIS IS MASTER VIC PRACTICING THE ART OF WAITING.

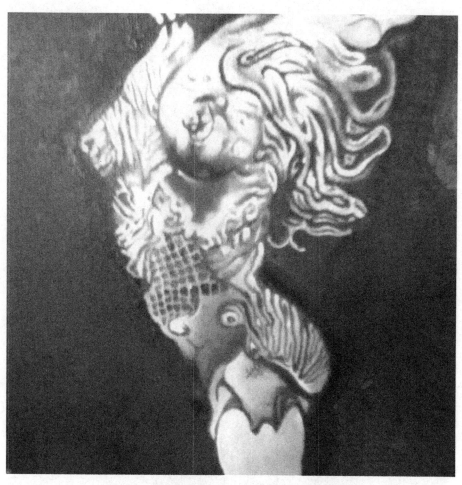

THIS IS KIM WARTHIGH. SHE WANTS YOU TO KNOW THAT THE LEG THAT IS ABOUT TO BREAK YOUR KNEE CAP WILL BE COMING FROM DARKNESS.

THIS IS MASTER KIMBALL COMING QUITE MENACINGLY FROM DARKNESS.

CHAPTER THIRTY ONE

The Importance of: COMING FROM DARKNESS.

dark: Middle English derk, from Old English deorc; akin to Old High German tarchannen to hide; secret-he kept his plans dark; not clear to the understanding; the quality or state of having a veiled or uncertain meaning; not explored because of remoteness; relating to grim or depressing circumstances; a time or place of little or no light-the raiding party snuck up under cover of darkness;

Quality or state of having a veiled or uncertain meaning; not explored because of remoteness.

That's one definition that describes the Kenpo principle of DARKNESS as it applies to Self Defense. There are other aspects involved as well. In the simplest sense, Darkness is somewhere in which you can not see well. An attacker is most successful when you are caught by surprise as he "Comes From Darkness". While this may mean it happens at night, where vision is compromised by lack of light and most violent crime occurs, it is not necessarily so. An attack in broad daylight can come from Darkness by an assailant hiding in a doorway, alley, from behind or any angle not covered by your sight. Of course, other senses play a role in your situational awareness and ability to quickly perceive and react to an attack from Darkness.

Other factors relating to an attack from Darkness are the speed of the approach from Darkness and the ability to recognize the threat and defend yourself accordingly. This is difficult and requires extensive training in the martial arts. We have all been startled at the movies when an imminent victim is searching through the house for some reason, the music is haunting and ominous, and are shocked when a cat jumps off the refrigerator. Now WE KNOW it's going to happen, are trained enough in life to realize it's a movie and we are in no real danger, yet most people will jump anyway.

Martial Note: A lesson can be learned from the above type movie scenario. While we are mentally and physically recovering from the shock of the leaping cat, the real attack usually follows shortly after. If you are startled by something or someone, stay alert until you are sure that you are safe.

So Darkness in this meaning is environmental and situational. The attacker may not even have touched you yet, but the surprise has already put you on the defensive. And while it may sound weird, being on the defense is not the best self defense. Training in this aspect of Darkness means learning about your surroundings by actually looking, listening, smelling and feeling what is really going on. This is harder than it seems. There is such an overwhelming rate of stimuli in any given life moment, knowing which are relevant to you and your safety are paramount. You can find many sources of training and instruction on this topic and its suggested you do so.

Martial Note 2: An example of a good training technique that we teach at Kenpo School is called REAR VIEW MIRROR. As you are walking down the street, observe the usual things that you normally do. People walking past, doors opening and closing as they enter and exit your forward line of sight. Extend you vision frame from ground to beginning sky and from side to other side. Not just from the building side to your right, to say, the street. But rather the building side to your right to building side to the left across the street. No need to swivel your head like "The Exorcist" just keep it level, with your sight line wide and your proximity to all you see sharp.

In other words look at what is going on around you and not at the sidewalk a few feet ahead.

While you are doing the above, begin working on REAR VIEW MIRROR. (RVM) As a person walks past you, keep you eyes forward and follow them as they pass WITH YOUR MIND. They continue to exist in your mind's eye even though they are now out of sight. They have moved into Darkness. If they have moved into Darkness, they can come back out of it as well.

Now, if you turned to see everyone that passes you on the street to make sure they don't attack, either you will look like a paranoid nut job or fall into the open sewer grate just past the orange warning cones gone by. Instead, keep that person in mind as you continue to walk forward. At any point, with any person, vehicle or storefront door you are training on, stop, turn around and look. Is the vision frame consistent with what your mind's eye tells you it should be?

While it is difficult to train to the point that you develop "360 Degrees of Awareness" it can be done. You want to have this RVM survival skill learned at your pace, not late night when the three guys that just passed you are not where they should be when you turn around.

Another training method is called I SEE YOU. In this exercise, make it a habit of seeing people you know before they see you. It happens almost daily so the training opportunity is abundant. If you are able to notice a familiar face first you "win" and if you are second to the "Hello" conversation you lose. You can figure why this ability might be important to your safety.

Another aspect of Darkness is what it tells you about the attacker who comes from behind and makes physical contact. As an example, if someone grabs you from behind with a right arm chokehold, its most likely that he doesn't have a weapon in that hand. It also screams to you "Where is the other hand and what's in it?" If the attack was a choke to make you unconscious, he would need BOTH hands. Why only the right hand attack? Is this really a Strong Arm Robbery? There is a reason for the one arm choke. But what is it? Does the attacker not know a proper choke technique? Or is there a knife or gun in the free hand? It's important to get this information immediately to know the right action to take. Your reaction will be different if the other hand holds a gun and is being poked into your lower back than if the free hand is just late in joining the other for a strangling choke.

In this scenario, the latter is what you find. The bigger attacker has come from Darkness, launches a two armed rear choke but has not locked it on due to the trailing hand. SHOWTIME. After ascertaining that there is no weapon employed (yet) it's just a fight. Hopefully, YOU ARE A TRAINED FIGHTER and know what to do based on that training. If not, you are in trouble.

Understanding Darkness also provides important additional information. How big is he? How strong is he and how determined is the attack? What is his fighting skill level? All these questions need quick answers to give you a chance at a successful self defense response. If the attacker is leaning down to choke me, I know he is bigger. If his one arm is strong enough to hold me in place, he is stronger. (at that given moment) If it's not that strong and the impact of our contact is weak, he may be unsure, nervous, not a fighter or just a bad mugger. In that case, the information gained will also tell me the direction of my counterattack. Being grabbed from behind, I know that a FRONT THRUST KICK is not the right technique to employ on my part.

You need a full repertoire of self defense techniques that work and you have practiced to REVEAL THAT WHICH IS HIDDEN under the veil of Darkness and defend against it.

As well, you Can Enter Darkness to render your opponent helpless by attacking regions of the body that are difficult to protect. The human body is designed to move, attack and defend forward. Doing these things backwards is much more difficult. Move Into Darkness and apply a choke or execute strikes or locks that will achieve victory.

Martial Note 3: In the Kenpo technique DARKNESS, an attack is made to your right side. Let's say a right stepping right punch to your head. Stepping right to HORSE STANCE you PARRY the attack with you left hand, quickly transition to left leg crossover to HIDDEN FOOT while executing a right hand BRUSH BLOCK. These movements have now put you behind the attacker as you Enter Darkness. With his back totally exposed, untwist from Hidden Foot to Horse Stance as your right hand plucks his eye while your left PALM HEEL strikes the kidney. Finish with a right BACKFIST to his head. You are in Darkness and in control of the fight.

Many other martial arts techniques Coming From Darkness make them nearly impossible to recognize and react to before they land. What you can't see CAN hurt you. And it does.

Realize DARKNESS and the lessons it can teach. You know, shed some light on Darkness.

Sorry, had to say that.

WE ALL FALL DOWN. MAKING MISTAKES ARE A LEARNING EXPERIENCE. MAKE THEM IN THE TRAINING HALL AND NOT ON THE STREET WHERE FALLING DOWN CAN MEAN DEATH.

CHAPTER THIRTY TWO

The Importance of: MAKING MISTAKES.

It's well known that we learn more from our mistakes than by our successes. Nobody likes to make a mistake, but everyone does. Its part of the human condition and no one is perfect. Making mistakes means you are learning. Often the bigger the boo-boo, the greater the lesson. Agreeing that Life is about learning, and mistakes are a part of learning, it's ok to make mistakes. Most of the time.

In a Life or Death situation, YOU CAN NOT MAKE A MISTAKE. Seems DEATH takes issue with our optimistic view of the value of mistakes and encourages our "learning" by happily escorting us to The Other Side. (TOS)

While it may be necessary to make mistakes in things we don't know, it IS NOT OK to make mistakes in things we do know. Its ok Doctor, I know you were doing your best when you took out my kidney instead of the bad appendix you were supposed to. Same applies to Self Defense situations, where the mistakes made in perception, reaction and action can get you killed. Oops! I know FLASH OF SILVER Kenpo knife defense, but mistakenly forgot to move out of the weapon's way before counterattacking. Try telling that one to Odin if they let you into Valhalla.

O-Sensei Phil Porter once told us that to move a martial arts technique into automatic execution through muscle memory and brain synapse building, it takes at least 5,000 repetitions of practice. And that's AFTER you have learned the technique and can do it properly. Mastery of technique and its potential for instantaneous application can take 10,000 or more reps of the same movement done "perfectly". That's a lot of time and effort in training to make that skill your own.

Have you trained enough in the technique you will need for the unknown attack to come?

That's why we say TRAIN. TRAIN. TRAIN UNTIL YOU DIE.

In a Serious Self Defense Situation remember this equation: mistakes = defeat and death.

MARTIAL ARTS MISTAKES ARE TO BE MADE IN THE DOJO NOT IN THE STREET.

In daily life, there is a big difference between mistake and failure. A mistake is a correctable action and a temporary setback with the added value of new knowledge, whereas failure has a more permanent quality. Failure can only be realized when you stop trying completely. Don't. We like to say that "I didn't fail, I just didn't succeed yet". Being unsuccessful at something at one point in time doesn't denote failure. It's just that you were not successful THEN. That doesn't mean that you couldn't have succeeded at the task ten minutes ago or an hour later or if conditions were different. Failure is not attempting further success. So keep at it, whatever it is.

Here is a funny story about **MAKING MISTAKES.**

I was heavily into TAMESHIWARI, which is the breaking of inanimate objects with flesh and bone. Many martial arts use Tameshiwari as a barometer of martial skill. The idea is that the force required to break a single board is the same needed to break a collar bone. (about 9 lbs of pressure) Adding additional boards to the stack equates to increased bone size density and the increase in power required to break it. Two boards could equal a wrist, four boards for forearm, a concrete slab for a femur etc. It's assumed that if you can break the inanimate one you can break the live body equivalent. Makes sense and I respect the Arts that utilize the ancient technique as long as it's real. Some find it necessary to exaggerate their power by using old brittle and cracked boards or repeatedly wetting and drying concrete slabs to make the break easier.

No true martial artist would do this.

Tameshiwari demonstrates power.

378

TAMESHIWARI IS A CLEAR DEMONSTRATION OF POWER.

Anyway, Kenpo School was invited to do a demonstration for the Boy Scouts at a Knights of Columbus facility in Westmont, IL. It wasn't included in the Chapter on Demonstrations since the lesson is more relevant here. After arriving at the club and walking to the third floor where the demo was to take place, a Black Belt came over to me. About to speak, he started bouncing up and down on the old wooden floor. While he was clearly in vertical motion maybe a half inch down and up, his feet never left the floor. At first I thought he was doing an optical illusion like the Bending Pencil trick. He started to speak while bouncing and asked how many concrete slabs that I was planning to break. Saying "7" he kept bouncing and suggested that I scale that number way back. The flexible floor was indeed a problem since it would absorb force applied diminishing the power of a downward HAMMER FIST. This meant that it would require MORE force to break LESS. The Black Belt was right, definitely should use less concrete.

Boneheaded, a Warrior and an idiot, I was having none of it.

Martial Note: In concrete slab breaking, or any Tameshiwari for that matter, you must use enough force to break the pile, Duh, you say? Let me tell you what happens if you don't. When flesh and bone meet concrete, normally you lose. But if you have enough power, force and focused energy behind your motion, you can smash through the matter without injury. Picture running face first into a brick wall. Wall wins. Hit the same brick wall while inside a moving tank. You (and tank) win. Same with breaking. As long as you hit with enough force to break ALL the slabs, your hand will not be injured. If you do not hit with enough power to break the objects, the force of your strike will move into the unbroken brick with energy returning hard back into your hand. That's not good since the small bones in a hand can not withstand the force, as well as that last unbroken slab did. The result is a broken hand and an unsuccessful breaking demonstration. Not sure which worse a broken hand or an unsuccessful attempt.

For the Boy Scouts demo I was going to break seven slabs of concrete for the first time in public. In each previous demonstration, I had successfully completed breaking one more slab than the previous demo. It was important to me to add a slab each time to be sure not to hold back any force when doing the break. Perhaps since I had already broken six successfully, any complacency could be rewarded with a trip to the emergency room. Not having ever broken seven slabs before, it kept me on edge and focused on smashing through the obstacle. It had worked so far and would work again. Oh yeah, the bouncing wooden floor? I didn't let the thought of the floor enter my mind while stacking seven concrete slabs with spacers on two upright rectangular cinder blocks in the center of the room. The place was packed and several parents were filming or taking pictures of the event. Big time Karate Expert in the House!

Lucky me.

Martial Note 2: The use of spacers between the concrete slabs is not meant to trick the audience. It's like this. The force needed to break one slab needs to be nearly doubled to strike through two. Three bricks spaced require 3x the force etc. The notion that "one slab just breaks the other in a downward domino effect" is not accurate. It's the energy that breaks the lower slabs not just the higher concrete. I learned this during a successful break where the technique was sufficient to cut through all the spaced concrete slabs. On film, you can see that the bottom three bricks cracked first, before the upper two slabs had broken. Energy focused is a powerful force. It's just as important that your martial arts technique has speed, power, and focused energy behind it, as it is to hit the proper targets in rapid fashion with the right weapon. (hand, foot, elbow, etc.)

Without the use of spacers, the force dynamic changes drastically. Putting a second slab directly on the first without spacers then requires an increase of applied force that is not double to break both but maybe 4X the energy. I've done it both ways and have a measuring system of force required to complete either challenge. But for demonstration sake, the audience does not care about physics and that four concrete slabs without spacers is the same strike force necessary to break ten slabs that are spaced. They want to be impressed and entertained. I mean, if all that mattered is the outcome and proof of martial arts power, I could just as easily walk into the audience and kill the biggest guy with a chop to the throat. All the audience will remember is that "the Karate guy broke four blocks of stone" or "the Karate guy broke ten blocks of stone" In demonstrations, we are going for effect and ten is better than four. Capish?"

So it's SHOWTIME. I kneel about 7 feet facing the pile of concrete as it stares ominously back at me. I had no doubt that 7 concrete slabs would break that evening. Just didn't see the extent of damage about to pay a visit via the bouncing baby blocks. Taking a few moments to meditate and get the whole being into focus of a trained Tameshiwari expert into smashing mode. It's time. The energy in the room is right. The energy of my Kenpo Warrior Brothers and Sisters is right. The energy in me is furiously focused on the task as hand. The energy situation with the floor, however, was not on board. In fact, the boards of the floor had their own wisdom and warning to teach, but tunnel vision made the information hidden from my mind. Even though I had been told by a friend, a physicist and a Black Belt about the floor, on I go headlong into the abyss of a painful lesson on energy and flex. Time for Reality to be Taught Here…to Me!

I stand and deliver. As my fist is making concrete contact with the top slab, the first three bricks break in submission of force. The last four were not as submissive and remained unbroken as the energy passed right through them into the vast expanse of power absorbing uber-floor. As the top three slabs lay in a near perfect "V" position resting on the stubborn four below, I am in shock and rage. Undeterred, I raise my fist way above head and begin a maniacal mashing of my hand into the bottom of the concrete V. Descending strike after strike, the bottom slabs break one by one as does my hand. After four consecutive blows, the V grows to six slabs and the defiant seventh with floor ally remains unbroken. At this point, I must have looked like a madman since the crowd became silent as my fellow Black Belts see the blood dripping from my broken hand and grab me by both arms and around my waist to stop the self abuse. I was not having any of it. Failure was not an option. With Vampire red-black eyes warning off my dear friends, I deliver one final downward strike which obliterates both brick and hand. With all seven patio slabs lying in defeat, I stared at the floor and it remained unfazed. If it was up to me, I would have continued the assault with an axe and chopped that floor to pieces. Instead, as my eyes and sense of reality return to normal, I stand and bow to a silent, wide-eyed audience. After looking at me and my broken hand that ballooned to Fred Flintstone-like proportions, they see the stone-faced Glory of a Determined Warrior. At least I'd like to think so.

Did I FAIL to break all seven slabs in one blow? No, I just didn't succeed then.

Were seven slabs finally smashed into pieces? Yes.

Was my hand busted up? Yes.

Did I care? No.

Martial Note 3: The floor absorbed the energy and like a big trampoline bounced it back into my hand shattering the small bones that God had put there for other purposes. If He had intended man to break concrete with his hand, He would have given us huge bone clubs at the end of our wrists. Its probably why construction workers use back hoes, pneumatic drills and sledge hammers to break up old concrete. Lesson learned? Listen to friends who know what they are talking about and don't let ego get in the way of insight and rational thinking. If you can.

Funny Story about **MAKING MISTAKES #2: POLYMER 2000**

Moving through K-Mart pushing a shopping cart with the standard, wrong direction rolling front squeaky wheel ahead of me, I enter the outdoor gardening supply/plant section of the store. You know, the canvass roof covered open air section of the place attached to the brick and mortar store. It's a seasonal addition where you pick up the peat moss and soon to die plants that should make your landscape the envy of the neighborhood. It's dead of winter as I leave the main store into the deserted, but accessible outdoor area. I head over to the concrete patio blocking area for some off-season deals on items to break. As I uncover the 2"H x 8"W x 16"D slabs from beneath the snow covered, ice glued plastic protection wrap, its now a matter of prying them apart and loading them into the crippled cart. At 16 lbs a piece, the 15 block order is really pissing off the wayward wheel as it screeches is agony as I begin the trek back to the indoor checkout cashier.

On my way in, a store clerk is exiting and asks if I have found everything I need. As he stares at the concrete blocks, he asks if I am involved in a mid-winter construction project. I answer that I am not and need these slabs to practice breaking them. He inquired from which stack these patio blocks were taken. As I point out the freshly recovered brick pile, he says ok and he is glad that I didn't get them from the adjoining stack which held the patio blocks made with the new Polymer 2000 additive.

In polymer concrete, thermosetting resins are used as the principal polymer component due to their high thermal stability and resistance...The adhesion properties of polymer concrete allow...for higher durability and higher strength. -Wikipedia

He explains that it's much "easier" to break the ones I have. Resisting the urge to test his theory by cracking one of each type of concrete over his head, I say thank you and push the annoying

384

Screechmobile into a line to check out. Still miffed at the store clerk's inadvertent insult, I leave the cart and race back to grab a single Polymer 2000 patio block. As the crooked wheel stared up at me in disbelief, I add the new block to the top of my purchase. When reaching the cashier, I ask for a black ink marker and draw an "X" on the polymer block to distinguish it from the similar looking "easier" blocks. Then away we go to the dojo.

I spend an hour practicing Tameshiwari and am pleased with my technique. About to call it a day, I look over to the lone Polymer 2000 block as it mocks me from the corner. Walking over, I pick it up and place it on the two upright cinder blocks that had witnessed the previous breaks. Should have known something was up, when pinching the outside skin of my pointer finger, the pain sent warning signal to any neuron that would listen. Any mental dissent was not ever allowed since brick breaking is all about the belief in your power to successfully break all the blocks. There can't be the slightest doubt, or the "not successful right now" theory can send you back to the hospital.

Years earlier, while teaching a class at the downtown School, I set up a standard Tameshiwari scenario with the two cinderblocks holding up a single concrete patio block. It stayed in the middle of the dojo throughout class as the students worked around it. Nothing was mentioned about it during the class and no one inquired why it was there. Near the end of class, I hop up onto the horizontal concrete slab and talk about Tameshiwari and its history. After about 5 minutes of jumping up and down on the brick while talking to show its strength, I ask:

"Who here would like to break this concrete slab and take a piece home with them?"

No one answered.

"Do you know that each and every one of you could break this block with no problem?"

Again, no volunteers.

"I would never ask you to do anything that you are not capable of doing. Everyone here can do this, but who will step up, face their fear and succeed in breaking through the unknown?" I could see that several students wanted to rise, but none did.

"Too bad. You had a chance to defeat a fear tonight, but you chose not too. That's Ok. The fear is still yours." I say then leap back off the slab and smash it to pieces with my fist.

"Let's bow out. Don't ever let a chance to face a fear go untaken. Because that fear will rise again in some form and you will have to deal with it then and not in the safety of the dojo."

Long time students still tell they remember that class vividly from nearly a quarter century ago.

This strong belief reinforced my determination to defeat the Polymer 2000 block 5 ft away.

I began the usual meditation and preparation for what was a laughably small amount of concrete to break. It was one measly concrete patio block. No problem as the quiet in the room matched the quiet in my mind. Then, like a cancer, doubt starts its spread through my mind. Trying to control it with every technique I know, it's a mental battle that takes several minutes to decide. With Warrior Spirit again eclipsing common sense, I stand and walk toward the single obstacle. Just as I raise my hand above my head and begin is rapid descent, the words "wooden floor" flash in my mind and causes me to abort the attempt as I slow then stop the strike 2 inches from the slab.

I was mortified at my cowardess. This painting is repeated from Spetznaz story for effect.

How can this happen after all my training? This picture used twice in book purposely. Where did all my fearless training go as self doubt somehow crept into my mind. I didn't even see a ghost!

How did the doubt thought of the wooden floor permeate my mind at the moment of truth. Unacceptable.

I sit there in utter despair at my mental weakness, thoughts of failure with the need to really reassess the previously unswerving belief in myself. This is really bothering me as I walk to the back of the dojo and grab an iron (might've been steel) heavy hand mallet from the supply cabinet. I wanted to get revenge by seeing how hard I would have had to hit the polymer block with my hand to break it by smashing it to bits with a tool.

387

Approaching in fury, I can't wait to smash that patio block to oblivion. Raising the hammer overhead, just like a readied hand strike, down comes the mallet toward the POLYMER 2000. As the iron mallet hits the polymer patio block its head breaks off and rolls off the slab an onto the floor a few feet ahead. Standing there with just the top splintered wood handle of the broken hammer still in my hand, I look down at the unbroken polymer brick that would have pulverized my hand had I hit it. Staring at it with a mixture of disbelief, belief and relief, I see that the mallet's heavy iron head had left only a crescent shape on the face of the concrete block. It resembled a bowl shape with the top left open. The polymer concrete patio block was smiling.

Two other slight markings at the top and the added impact shape made the Polymer 2000 into a big rectangular Smiley Face. I smiled back. My hand smiled up at me. My brain smiled down.

But I don't think the P2000 was taunting me. Rather it appeared to be offering some lessons:

1) Don't make the mistake of judging strength by size.
2) Sometimes it's ok to "not succeed right now".
3) No matter what happens or how hard you're hit, Keep Smiling.

Funny Story about **MAKING MISTAKES #3: INTERNAL POWER.**

As previously discussed, the use of spacers in Tameshiwari helps keep the force required to break all slabs calculable. Without spacers, the required force increase needed grows exponentially. But I thought it was an excellent way to test my level of Internal Power after many years of martial arts training with The Masters. This would not only be the first time that I attempted 4 concrete patio slabs without spacers, but would be the focus on the night's class. It would be a demonstrative lecture on the pursuit of Internal Power, pushing yourself beyond previous boundaries and not being afraid to "fail" temporarily in front of others.

The class began and there were several prospective new students attending for the first time. I had thought about postponing the Internal Power lesson to give the new folks a taste of what we normally do in class, but with the blocks already set up at the front of the dojo, decided to proceed. The set up was similar to the one at the Old Town Chicago School where I stood on the lone concrete slab while delivering my lecture on "Facing Fear".

Wearing a black Kung Fu top with the white end of sleeve cuffs and the thick string ties down the front, its Internal Power SHOWTIME for me. Beginning the lecture part of class by welcoming the new people and explaining that what's being attempted has not been done by me before. Not even one slab, never mind four! Another difference from previous breaks, besides the lack of spacers, would be that from a kneeling position and without raising a hand overhead, I would slap the top brick with my hand from 6" above. This would mean that the bottom concrete should break first since the energy had nowhere else to go as the top blocks remained undisturbed. Talk about setting yourself up to fail. I had never done any of this before, but I knew that it could be done… and just hoped that it would.

Kneeling directly in front of the four part block of concrete, I told the students that this is my first attempt to break concrete with a open hand slap from a distance of 6-8 inches away. This preparation included the " No Failure…Just Not Successful Right Now" lecture. As well, the monologue included the statement that they should not be embarrassed for me if the attempt is not successful since I would not be embarrassed myself.

Enough talk. Lesson time. For everyone.

With mind clear, chi humming and my hand hovering just above the block…SLAP!

The hand technique was good, the energy transfer fine, but the result not so good. The non-polymer block just sat there unfazed. Non-Success Now #1. I temporarily flashed back to the bouncing wooden floor as the thought that our School mat was stretched and bound canvass over tatami on a wooden base frame. We had hockey pucks scattered between floor and canvass-covered tatami where there was no frame. The resulting "Pro Wrestling" type mat sound made when thrown down SHOULD HAVE reminded me of the Boys Scout demo and the broken hand, but didn't. MISTAKE. At least it was in the dojo and not the street.

After looking down at the block and with the pain in my hand registering in a non-bone-breaking Way, I brush the top block off the pile leaving a three slab obstacle remaining. The dojo is dead silent.

Hand rises to same position above the pile of stone and again descends rapidly…SLAP!

Nothing. Well except for more open hand searing pain from the return energy courtesy of the laughing patio blocks. Non-Success Now #2. Again, another top brick is slid off to the mat with only two remaining. Raising my hand for the third time, it was trembling in a quietly violent way. Students later told me that it looked like gasoline fumes were rising above the hand. Again, I slap at the two slabs with no breaking whatsoever. Non-Success Now #3.

I say "Ok then" as I brush the third block from the stack and pause. The room had developed a tension as my apparent failures were concerning the students. I felt no embarrassment. Just a bit of disappointment that I couldn't do what was set out to be done at the time it should have been. Addressing the tension and concern, I explain the above to them. Since it had turned into a class about "Not succeeding right now" and less about the attributes of Internal Power, the teaching thought line was pretty clear. DO NOT BE AFRAID TO FAIL. FOREGO THE USELESS,

CONFIDENCE-STEALING FEELING OF EMBARRASSMENT AND GET BACK AT IT. TRY AGAIN UNTIL YOU SUCCEED. DON'T QUIT. EVER.

Looking at the near comically scattered 3 unbroken slabs on the mat and the lone brick still in place, it seems ridiculous to try again. I mean if that didn't break, that would be a drag. About to end the lesson and have the Tameshiwari set up put away, I add the following words from memory:

"Well, I am glad that you were here for the class on Resisting Embarrassment. Glad you were here to see that even masters fail...temporarily. Just because I was not successful right now, that doesn't mean that I wouldn't have succeeded a half hour ago or couldn't succeed in an hour. Even if I could never accomplish the feat, the mindset of not accepting failure is what's most important for a Warrior."

As the words are hanging in the air, I finish with:

"What should have happened, and will when I succeed, is a simple slap of my hand..."

I slap the last concrete slab lightly from about three inches and IT EXPLODES into 5 or 6 chunks with smaller bits strewn about and concrete dust on the stained white mat below. Quickly recovering from the unexpected "success" finish my ending statement with "...and the concrete WILL BREAK. JUMBO!"

I look at a Brown Belt who stares back in disbelief as if it was planned that way from the beginning. Of course it wasn't, but they didn't have to know that. The "Ancient Chinese Secret" remained mine until now and I can't tell you how hard it was that night to not leap up and scream

"Man, did you see that?!!!!!"

Martial Note: Success can occur at any time as long as you stay confident, learn from mistakes made and keep trying. The state of mind called failure should not be part of the martial artists thinking. Keep at it. Refuse to be denied. Success is bound to follow the bold and determined. As far as the exploding concrete slab, the energy that did not return to singe my hand must have been destroying the brick on the inside. When I barely touched it, it was overloaded with energy and it disintegrated dramatically. Internal Power...cool.

Another quick story about how to act when you have an unexpected success that seemed impossible to accomplish went like this:

While working as the Midwest Regional Sales Manager, responsible for advertising revenue at a national consumer magazine, it turns out I was quite good at it. Selling millions of dollars of advertising has a way of endearing you with your superiors. Anyway, the sales team had set a revenue record for a particular issue of the publication. The resulting sales contest goodies included an Omega Seamaster Professional watch (the one James Bond wears) an all expense paid trip to go marlin fishing at the resort of Cabos San Lucas, Mexico and $1500 in spending money. It was an amazing show of generosity by the company owner and a tremendous effort by the entire sales team.

Anyway, we were all at the airport awaiting our flight back to the US and were in the cocktail lounge talking about the amazing trip in all its glorious detail. My boss, a 6'7" man walks over to me as I am snacking on a travel size tube of Pringles potato chips that I bought at the news-stand next door. He says to me in a volume that made everyone else listen "So Powell, What's this Karate Chop Crap you do?" He said it in a funny way, was a great boss and friend, so he didn't get the usual response I give when approached like that. Laughing at the question while the sales team was watching, I sip my Corona and say:

"See this potato chip?" As I lean down and put the uniquely all same-shaped Pringles' style chip curve side down on the tip of my sock less loafer.

"Watch this. I will kick this chip into the air and catch it in my mouth."

Now there was no way this was possible, and I was doing the charade more as a joke than anything. I do a short quick rising knee SNAP KICK which coolly enough sends the lone chip flying about a foot over my head. Being a Warrior, I see things in action move in slow motion. Pleased that the chip flew at all, I was about to grab it with my hand as it stalled like a bi-plane at an air show. Just then, the chip starts its descent in the way those "helicopter" leaves spin fall from trees. It's heading down slowly toward my face and I simply stick out my tongue to see if I can at least hit it. Well, the odd contour of the Pringle had it land perfectly in concert with my outstretched oval tongue.

As it landed, I simply pull it into my mouth and start munching. Again, the tough part, like the final Internal Power exploding brick, was not flipping out in amazement at succeeding at something at a time its unexpected. For whatever reason, that chip was part explanation of Karate Crap to my boss. It was freak'n incredible. With chip now masticated and swallowed, I remain cool and say "That's what it's all about." in a dead-panned way. In shocked amazement, they begged me to do it again. Of course I declined. No showing off you know. It is said that "Luck is when Preparation meets Opportunity." Mmmm...could be. Love Luck.

Clearly no Martial Note here. Just a great story.

YOU CAN LEARN MANY INNOVATIVE TRAINING METHODS FROM SHAOLIN MONKS.

CHAPTER THIRTY THREE

The Importance of: INNOVATIVE TRAINING METHODS.

It is said that there is "Nothing new under the Sun".

That may be true to the extent that all the Knowledge that The Universe contains is already there. Everything there is to know has been knowable since the dawn of time. But what drove say, the Neanderthals, to make the first tools? The know-how had always been there. It was not until the NEED for that knowledge met with the INNOVATION and CAPABILITY to understand the need to CREATE it. As discussed in the Chapter on TEACHERS, any animate or inanimate can entity be a teacher.

Did the Neanderthals tire of trying to catch their dinner by running after it? They might think

"Umm. Ga Aaahnck, GaAaaa krunc, nohaunon-kuk. Caskuln-no-ak. "onok" With the assumed translation being: "AAhhh, slice hand with sharp stone! Hmm...should put on long stick, see if fly. Then throw at animal. See if it bleeds. Mm...pointed stick knife just kill moose! No run! Throw! Will make more moose-bleeding, food-getters "spear"! You get ...the point.

Its man's unrelenting quest to understand all that there is to know that releases the knowledge a bit at a time from the Universal Source. But only when man is ready for that which is being revealed. Revealing that which is hidden can only be realized when the time is right for that information to emerge and the circumstances right for that emergence. Why didn't the Neander-thal create an M-16 assault rifle instead of just a spear? It wasn't the right time in History for it.

Revealing knowledge is a process.

So is learning the martial arts. And the top modern Masters will teach you the skills, transmit the knowledge and create a Warrior in ways that have never been done before. Just as computer technology has changed how we do everything, modern teaching methods have changed the way the Arts are taught, learned and practiced.

But many of the new methods are just step forward refinements of that which has already been done. Nothing new under the Sun...just new ways of understanding, refining and transferring that which has always existed. Training that more effectively maximizes time on task and allows for faster dissemination of more and more martial information. It's like the ability to gather vast knowledge on most any subject can be found using the Internet. As new innovative methods are created to replace what is now cutting edge, the ability to learn anything, including martial arts will accelerate accordingly to become a short-lived state of the art.

To end the monologue here is an example.

In ancient times, martial arts training methods might mean working in the rice field from morning to night. Afterward, you would walk 12 miles to your Teacher's School, probably at his home. You would pay him for the lesson with a bag of rice or whatever you could afford and he would set you in a HORSE STANCE and leave you there standing in one position for three hours! Occasionally he might check on your progress. If he didn't come out and beat your legs with a bamboo stick, you were probably doing it ok. Then you'd leave on dead legs for the 12 mile trip home. Sleep if you have time, get up at dawn and back to the rice field. Repeat this training schedule for years until you are proficient. That's basically how the Arts were taught.

Nowadays, you pull up to your dojo in a motor vehicle and may have traveled fifty miles to train with a particular Master. You pay whatever monetary fee required, train with the Master, exit and return to vehicle and go home. So training has come along way as society and man evolved.

So which is better?

TRADITIONAL martial artists would say the Ancient Way. The training back then was much more difficult and that modern martial artists are not as tough. Wanna tell that to Shorty Mills?

MODERN martial artists would say that newer, more accelerated training methods offer much quicker results making them superior just as the assault rifle would be a better, more efficient killing method than the spear.

POWELL'S WAY OF KENPO says (borrowing a line from a great movie "Trading Places" when Eddie Murphy is on the beach with a cocktail and the former butler, now rich, asks about lunch. "Lobster or the cracked crab?" says the butler to his hot new girlfriend. "Can't we have both?" she asks. "Why not?" he replies.) YES WE CAN HAVE BOTH!

At PWOK we provide BOTH Ancient training methods for toughness and Modern methods for accelerated growth. Any dojo you attend should offer the same type of training regiment and philosophy.

Since the martial arts are about growth, the training needs to offer clear markers of progress in the student mentally, physically and spiritually. I don't mean spirituality with God. American martial arts reflect its society and that means diverse religions, ethnicities and nationalities. It is important that the dojo you attend, does not force any particular religion on you in training. There are group specific schools like Christian Tae Kwon Do Clubs, Jiu Jitsu for Jews, Atheist Academy of Aikido etc. Besides, you will be saying "oh God!" plenty during your training to proficiency in the Arts.

We are talking about spirit growth that comes as a bi-product of Unity between Mind and Body. The Arts will reveal whatever is needed deep down and develop the answer to those needs. If you are weak, you will get strong. If you are strong, you will learn limitations. If you are shy, you will become more outgoing. If you are arrogant, you will learn humility. And so on.

At PWOK, our training is based on UNITY between a clear, calm MIND and a strong, healthy BODY. To achieve this, The Ancients have taught us to imitate the creatures in Nature. You want to be Strong as a Bull, Fast as a Cheetah, Quick as a Pit Viper, Fearless as a Tiger, Skilled as a Praying Mantis and Deadly as a Black Momba. The older methods of training involved similar animals and reptiles by imitating the Tiger, Crane, Snake etc. We do this Way honor by transmitting the 1500+ year old Teachings, Techniques and Forms of Kenpo. The same forms that Ancient Warriors, our predecessors, practiced in the mountains of China over a thousand years ago! We add new technique that contribute to the growth of the Art and the strength and power of its practitioners.

Why create new techniques and training methods now? Because the times have changed and so must defenses and new training systems evolve. People are bigger and stronger than ever in Human History, so we too must be strong. Especially if we are not descendants of the tall, powerful, aggressive Norsemen/Northmen/Normans/Vikings. Technique, skill, endurance and courage often are enough to overcome Evil in a form that is bigger and stronger than you are.

That is the purpose of this book? TO MAKE YOU STRONG.

Gotta love that TV commercial from back in the day where a muscular, in shape, old man says "I am not strong for my age. I am strong." Or from the great movie "The 13th Warrior" when the Viking tosses the heavy sword from the ship down to "Ebin" who can't hold it from hitting the ground. "It's too heavy!" says Ebin. "Get Stronger!" replies the Viking.

So we too say GET STRONGER!

After living the Martial Way for 35+ years and having been trained in both traditional and modern fashion, I love both. That's why we train as hard as we do in the way that we do. Some of the more unique training methods employed over the years created a Reality-Based School that consistently turns out superior students that are great fun-loving, open-minded killers that do not kill. Some of these Relatively Unique Training Methods (RUTM) are as follows:

RUTM 1: PUSH THE JEEP.

You already know about this one.

RUTM 2: SAMURAI JUMPING JACKS.

You know this one as well. The key to the effort is to remain on the balls of your feet THE ENTIRE TIME no matter the speed or amount of the Jumping Jacks. As discussed, forearms and calves are the prime muscles for issuance of martial power. Thousands of Samurai JJS develop the core, legs and calves while strengthening your mind and self discipline. After the recent Holiday Season, in the first class of 2013, the students were welcomed back with 2013 SJJS. Happy New Year! Once again, not a surprised look on any face of the Kenpo Warriors.

RUTM 3: SPECTRAIN.

Special Training (SPECTRAIN) has been an annual event at Powell's Way of Kenpo for the past 15 years. We alternate between a cold weather month and a hot one to challenge the already challenging training. Black Belts lead students in a 12 hour marathon of martial arts training from 7 pm Friday night until 7 am Saturday morning. The schedule is twelve (12) fifty minute classes with ten minutes break between each to hydrate, urinate and eat. The sessions involve physically demanding distance and sprint running, weightlifting, calisthenics, contact sparring and groundfighting. In addition to intense BODY training, we focus on MIND-BODY work by teaching, practicing technique and running forms from a different Art each session throughout the night. The SPIRIT is tested and strengthened by a relentless pace (except for scheduled breaks) and the dogged effect of sleep deprivation.

There are also guest instructors from other disciplines that provide fresh insight, new knowledge and different training methods. All in all, it is a night best summed up with "NO LIMITS." And when a new obstacle is placed in front of the students, like continuing onto 2000 jumping jacks when they were told only 1000 would be done. (Expect the unexpected) THERE IS NEVER THE SLIGHTEST SIGH OR TELLING SMIRK OF DISAPPROVAL. No, these are KENPO WARRIORS and meet every task and challenge as OPPORTUNITY FOR GROWTH with a stone-faced, wooden doll face. As a Teacher, it is exhilarating to witness and be part of.

PWOK had a wooden sign that hung in the downtown Chicago dojo and read:

"THIS IS A WARRIOR HOUSE…A WAY PLACE.

A TRUE SCHOOL OF THE WAY.

THERE IS THE OPPORTUNITY FOR TREMENDOUS GROWTH.

THERE IS ALSO THE POSSIBILITY OF DEATH HERE.

STAY FOCUSED IN YOUR TRAINING.

AND WHEN YOU LEAVE THIS WORLD WE WILL WARN THE DEAD,

THAT A KENPO WARRIOR IS COMING!"

RUTM 4: TWO BUCKETS AND A GONG.

Borrowed from Navy SEAL training, we have workouts that can be "quit" only by striking the "Submission Gong" as the hardcore SEAL training leads most candidates to ring a bell to leave the program. No disgrace to "not succeed yet". Just have to refocus, reset limit bar and return. Many don't. But then again that's why the US Navy SEALS are the most feared Warriors on the planet. When they come for you, that's about it. Back at PWOK, after one particular class of unusual mediocrity and lack of effort, it was gut check time at Kenpo School as I then ordered a "who really wants to be here" pair down. Master Ron, then a Sifu, was tasked with a night of training so intense and a requirement that at least two students had to quit. If Sifu was unsuccessful, he would be held accountable. Sifu Ron never disappoints.

The School had been set up with a bucket at the front of the dojo and one by the door. The door bucket also had the submission gong next to it. Sifu Ron lead from the front and did all the training along with the students. Everyone was going to puke, the question was which bucket would you choose? The front bucket was for a temporary break, as you threw up in it AND RETURNED to class. The door bucket and gong was to be thrown up in and the gong banged if you WERE QUITTING. At the beginning of class, the reasons for and rules of were explained. In choosing the front bucket there is no shame. The door bucket meant dishonor. It showed that you gave up. Do that in the street when under attack and that makes you DEAD! That is not acceptable. Now while the students were told (don't believe everything that you are told) that if you banged the gong, that meant that you were leaving the dojo never to return. Of course, if they had returned to face their weakness, they would not have been turned away. That night three pieces of "dead wood" puked, gonged and left for good. Great job Master Ron. Those that stayed proved to themselves two things:

1) They were not quitters and were strong enough to confront adversity and triumph.

2) Perhaps training in a mediocre way was not the best idea while attending Kenpo School.

The Two Bucket System was never again needed at Kenpo School as the Legend of its existence continues as a reminder of what is expected of every Kenpo Warrior to this very day.

RUTM 5: THE REMINDER POLE.

While the extreme reprimand of the Two Bucket System was never again needed at PWOK, that doesn't mean that training intensity was always at expected levels. In instances were the students seemed distracted for some reason, I would call for The Reminder Pole. (TRP) While walking to PWOK one day, there was one of those steel sign posts lying on the ground near the dojo. Its sign-less top was opposite a huge, thick cone shape of concrete at the base. It looked so cool that I had to have it. Students brought it into Kenpo School were it was cleaned and taped. Two 45 lbs iron weightlifting plates were clamped in place at the non concrete end. It took 6-8 people to lift it and 10 or more to run with it around the block in Times of Mediocrity. (TOM) While not as disgusting as Two Bucket System, it was at least as effective. The cone shape of the jagged concrete, the added iron plates and the narrow but strong steel shaft made no part of TRP comfortable to carry let alone run with. Many a student running the pole for a long distance traded the painful round pole position that dug into their shoulder for sharp pointed concrete front that did the same in a different way.

One time while waiting for Hanshi to come to the new Brookfield School for the first time, I had a direction marker in the form of eight high ranking students stand with TRP at the corner of the block. Didn't want Hanshi to get lost. Turns out he was about twenty minutes late and The Reminder Pole was held aloft for about 45 minutes straight. Five of those students that did what was asked of them eventually became Black Belts and Kenpo School Instructors. Those same five have been with me for nearly two decades and are today great Masters in their own right.

As Hanshi Shorty Mills' Corvette arrived at the intersection, he was on the phone with one of his Black Belts. Upon seeing TRP direction marker waving and running back toward PWOK leading him to his reserved parking spot in front of the School, he just says over the cell phone "I'm at Billy's School. These guys are just Animals!" Gotta love that.

RUTM 6: GAUNTLET OF TERROR.

Maybe not that unusual as circuit training has become mainstream in gyms and health clubs across the country. But when we first started doing it some 20 years ago, it was not called circuit training, it was called the GAUNTLET OF TERROR. Why the catchy, scary name? The name was the least of the problem. PWOK ran a 10 station system of the most brutal physical tasks that only sick minds can create. There is a fine line between genius and madman, right? These will remain secret, lest they become known at some local gym and someone actually dies there. Suffice it to say that the entire 2 hour class from start to finish consisted of non-stop hardcore physical and mental training. Your only salvation, besides the Glory of completing the class, was the 1 minute resting station where you could have all the therapeutic massages, ice lattes and scones you could enjoy during that time.

RUTM 7: KNEES OF DEATH.

Partnering up, Student 1 (S1) holds the kicking shield as the Student 2 (S2) begins non-stop Muay Thai KNEE STRIKES to the midsection of the pad while clasping the back of the neck of the shield holder with two hands. The following is the method with no breaks in between:

S2 knees S1 for a warm up minute - S1 knees S2 for a warm up minute

S2 knees S1 at full strength for a minute - S1 knees S2 at full strength for a minute

S2 knees S1 continuously for 45 seconds - S1 knees S2 continuously for 45 seconds

S2 knees S1 rapidly for 30 seconds - S1 knees S2 rapidly for 30 seconds

S2 knees S1 quickly for 20 seconds - S1 knees S2 quickly for 20 seconds

S2 knees S1 19 times in 19 seconds - S1 knees S2 19 times in 19 seconds

S2 knees S1 18 times in 18 seconds - S1 knees S2 18 times in 18 seconds

S2 knees S1 17 times in 17 seconds – S1 knees S2 17 times in 17 seconds

This continues all the way down, back and forth, non stop until each person reaches 1 knee each. Then the last action is ONE FULL MINUTE of knees each for S1 and S2. Relentless.

Knees of Death. No Lie G.I.

RUTM 8: COLD FOOT.

We run barefoot about a mile when the snow is deep and the temperature is freezing. No reason other than mental discipline, physical toughness, ignoring simple pain and personal achievement. Wet and cold is the worse physical state for human beings. Ask a Navy SEAL.

RUTM 9: NOW THAT'S HOT.

We run barefoot about a mile when the day is hot and the temperature is searing. No reason other than mental discipline, physical toughness, ignoring simple pain and personal achievement. Hot and sweaty is the best physical state for human beings. Ask a Beach Bikini Model.

RUTM 10: MEDICINE CABINET.

Home training method whereby the usually annoying event of opening your medicine cabinet to watch items tumble to the ground becomes skill time. You must catch the falling item before it hits the sink. Every one that does is a "knife wound" or an "attack" that you failed to intercept. At the beginning, you will probably smack the aspirin bottle into the shower to the concern of family members. After practice, you will catch it regularly. After awhile, you can easily catch multiple falling items with no conscious effort. When you can snatch the mouthwash from the air…it will be time for you to leave…the bathroom. (Humor based on "When you can snatch the pebbles from my hand…" from the original Kung Fu movie with Kwai Chang.)

RUTM 11: FLICKERING TV.

While watching television at night use the randomly timed screen light changes to practice making your hand weapons quick and proper. When the light emanating from the TV changes, you form a new hand weapon. PWOK uses a twenty count of different hand techniques.

The first ten:

1) FIST. Make sure fist is tight with first 2 knuckles protruding from front of fist and middle finger segments are tucked back. Top of hand is in a straight line with forearm in a way that you could place a book atop and see no space between fist, arm and book. After checking arm and fist from the side, look down from above to make sure two lead striking knuckles are in direct alignment with the two bones of you forearm. Failure to do any of the above can leave you with a broken wrist, fist or knuckle when making contact rendering that weapon useless from then on.

2) CAPPED HAMMER. While the fist is a hard weapon meant to strike soft targets like stomach and face, Capped Hammer is a soft weapon used to hit hard targets like skull and elbow. Make sure that thumb is pinned hard to top of fist making the bottom striking area hard enough to break bones but soft enough to absorb energy without injury.

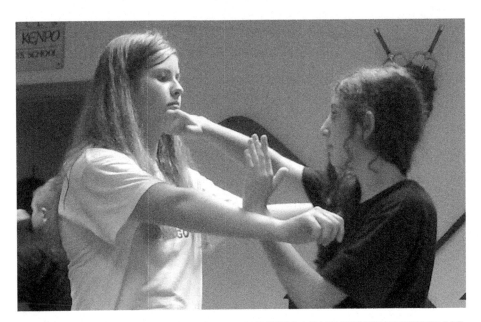

MASTER VIC'S DAUGHTER, ALICIA MEZERA, DELIVERS A HAMMERFIST TO DEIDRA LEE.

3) PHOENIX.   To make pointer finger knuckle strike strong and effective, move top finger from Capped Hammer fist forward so that top digit of finger (one with the nail) is aligned with the top of second digit of 3 folded fingers below. Make sure Hammer fist thumb helps reinforce striking knuckle by pressing down and forward to the back of folded, protruding top striking knuckle. Use primarily on soft targets like eyes, temple, solar plexus and nervous system strikes.

4) MID KNUCKLE. Best way to practice forming this strike properly is to look at your closed fist. Temporarily moved thumb from fist position so it looks like you are hitchhiking. Move middle knuckle up so that top of fingernail digit is aligned with top of middle digit knuckles of pointer and ring fingers. Here's the secret to structural integrity of the weapon. Allow pointer finger to unfold at top of second digit so that the bottom half of finger is now pointing into your palm. Use fatty part of hitchhiking thumb to press inward toward newly extended pointer finger

until both nails of pointer and ring fingers touch. This will form a strong seat for the striking mid knuckle. Cement the system by replacing the thumb to original fist position at the base of the seat. Squeeze hard to form a penetrating weapon used to hit muscular and nervous systems. While considered a hard weapon meant to strike soft targets, I have seen a properly formed mid knuckle break a slab of concrete.

5) HALF FIST. Also called a PANTHER or LEPOARD STRIKE, simply fold all fingers like a Capped Hammer fist. Then extend top of second digit knuckles on first three fingers (top of third digit knuckle on pinky) so all four are aligned. Reinforce strike with thumb as in Capped Hammer. Looking down at Half Fist, it should appear that your fingers have been cut off in a perfect line by a meat cleaver. Strike throat with chopped off surface area. This strike can Kill.

6) PALM. Hit with the palm heel when directing force and the palm center when transferring Chi with Internal Power.

7) CHOP. Hit with the Pisiform bone on the outside bottom of your chop. It's the outer nub where the wrist meets the hand. Expose it by pulling your chop's fingers and thumb back toward you. Like a snowboarder who stops sharply by turning the board and rooster tailing snow all over you. Focus you strike there for soft targets and use the meaty side of your hand when chopping hard ones.

8) DART. Hold your hand open as if you were showing the length of something. Then fold lower 3 fingers in a descending step pattern with the pointer finger extended outward from the top of the steps. Rest attacking finger on steps protruding only to the first digit bend line. Any farther out and the finger will not have the support and strength necessary to penetrate effectively and can be easily injured. Not sticking the pointer figure out enough will render it ineffective.

When studying the hand weapon from above, the pointer finger is not locked out straight as it can easily be broken that way. Rather provide a slight bending arch to the finger that will protect it during use. The striking tip of Dart, even when arching the finger, should realign with the center of hand, wrist and forearm providing back up mass and structural integrity of technique. The lone target of Dart is the opponent's eyes.

9) THUMB. I always think of the Sean Connery movie "The Presidio" where he beats a guy nearly to death with just his thumb. Cool. As in Dart, you want to protect the weapon from overextension and injury without compromising its effectiveness and penetration. Make a Capped Hammer then slide the thumb forward and curved up to only one half the top digit. This hand technique is used for over the shoulder thumbnail strikes to the eyes of attacker grabbing you from behind. It is also used to attack the femoral nerve near the groin to release a front Bear Hug when both your arms are pinned at your sides.

10) TWO HEADED SERPENT. Cool two finger strike to one or both eyes of attacker. Similar to a Kenpo Salutation prior to doing a form like BOOKSET or MASS ATTACK, the "Two Headed Serpent Guarding Pearl" the pointer and middle finger are arched in a near half circle with nails pointed straight at target. Thumb and ring finger meet with thumb directly over ring finger nail. Create tension in this loop which strengthens the venom of the two attacking serpent fingers. Pinky joins the finger loop from below with added upward pressure reinforcing the strength of all components of the Two Headed Serpent eye strike.

Ok, I said ten, but here is an important Bonus one to practice during "Flickering TV".

11) CLAW. There are many different types of claws with varied uses from different martial systems such as Tiger Claw and Eagle Claw. You can research the different techniques that suit

you best. I am more interested in talking about the integrity of the claw and ways to make it more effective and less painful to execute. Picture the basic claw with all fingers and thumb rounded like you are holding a grapefruit. All digits must be pointing at the target in this case the face of the opponent. As in other hand techniques, over extension of the fingers means they can be broken. Curling of the fingers too much will protect the claw but make your striking points dull as a cotton ear swab.

As well, while eyes and soft skin of the face are the target of the poking, ripping or tearing claw, that soft skin is pulled tightly over rock hard bone. So while your claw's middle and ring finger drive deep into the soft eye jelly, your pointer and pinky may break as they hit the forehead and cheekbone.

The way to avoid this is to train your fingers to be "educated". That means they have a mind of their own and while moving in unison with the claw, they function independently of it and each other. The fingers that find the soft targets continue applying force while the ones that meet hard surface resistance back off and bend.

There are many ways to educate your weapons. Learn how to avoid broken fingers and your claw will be a very fearsome weapon of self defense.

Martial Note: Educated Hands can also be explained in the way that a short right punch from 6 inches away can knock out a huge guy if you hit the facial nerve. This highly vulnerable facial nervous system runs throughout the face and is especially close to the surface at the non-fatty, skin on bone part known as the chin. The story of a World Champion Kickboxer doing a demonstration asked a little kid to hit him as hard as he could in the face. He bent over and while still talking to the audience, the kid hauls off and jacks him with a pin armed haymaker to the champion's chin knocking him out cold. Educated Hands...Learn about them soon at a School near you!

RUTM 12: KEEPING THE DOJO IMMACULATE.

Taking nearly as much time keeping the School clean, clear and maintained is as important as any physical or mental training we do. The sweeping of the mat before class and the sanitizing of it after. The cleaning of the mirrors before class and the taking out of the garbage after. A clean dojo equates to a clear mind. Clutter in either can affect your training and your health. These are just twelve of the Relatively Unique Training Methods employed at Kenpo School. We have many others that test the mettle of a person in all aspects of Mind, Body and Spirit. Character is built in the raging fires of adversity just as the sword of the Samurai was forged, pounded and honed to perfection by a master sword maker.

All that's left is for you to Polish Your Sword.

SIFU STEVE BANKE HAS TRAINED WITH ME SINCE AGE 10. HE IS CURRENTLY STUDYING MARTIAL SCIENCE IN COLLEGE. HIS INDETERMINABLE AMOUNT OF TIME TRAINING AT POWELL'S WAY OF KENPO WAS LONGER THAN MOST.

CHAPTER THIRTY FOUR

The Importance of: INDETERMINABLE AMOUNT OF TIME.

We all know that we are going to die.

Some say that time is already written and is a matter of Fate. Others would say that there is no Grand Scheme and the time and place of our Death has not been set. That it's a random thing. Whichever philosophy you believe, one thing is for sure, Death will put a crimp on your lifestyle. Since we don't know the exact moment of our personal death, that means we have an Indeterminable Amount Of Time (IAOT) to Live.

As Warriors, we try to gobble up Life and live in a Way that exemplifies that high ideal. Training in The Arts gives us a chance to do so with minimal fear by understanding pain and its relation to death. Those that are afraid of getting hit because it hurts are going to be in for a rude awakening when The Reaper comes a callin. How do you want to die? At the moment of death, do you want to be in a panicked, frenzied fearful state or do you want to meet death with a calm understanding that it is a part of Life and not to be afraid? Warriors will choose the latter. Life and Death philosophy has been debated for ages with no clear answer provided by much greater minds than mine. So I will tell you what I do know.

When you go to a martial arts school, you will have an indeterminable amount of time to train for an attack that has not yet occurred. There is no way to see the future, so there is no way to be sure your training will be sufficient for the moment it is needed. You must make every moment count in your training. Try to emulate your Teacher's movements and thinking when learning, practicing and training your techniques and making them your own. Wash. Rinse. Repeat. Realize that the very martial arts technique that you learned today, no matter how new to you, may be the very one you need to work that night when attacked by a mugger. You have to understand that you can't know everything there is to know about any and all possible attacks when you first start training. Maybe you will know enough, maybe not. But what choice do you have? Train. Train. Train until you die.

The Way of The Warrior Is Death. Life Ends In Death. No problem.

The Vikings exalt "Rush to meet Death before someone else takes you place!"
You have an Indeterminable Amount Of Time on Earth. Use every moment well.
As if what you do at this exact moment is your last act on Earth. And do it right.

SANTA CLAUS OR AN ELECTRIC MONKEY TEACHING KIDS CLASS?

CHAPTER THIRTY FIVE

The Importance of: TRAINING OUR CHILDREN.

There is no greater gift than being born in The United States of America. We are the most prosperous, wealthy and powerful nation on Earth. No outside enemy can invade and occupy us as our military is by far the strongest in the world. Yet every day innocent Americans die at the hands of one another. The reasons can be argued with the same ferocity as The Meaning of Life and Death. The question is how to protect the innocent, especially the children, which is the core future of our great country?

The answer is to train our children in the Way of Martial Arts while they are young. The ability to learn the proper values of Honor, Trust, Loyalty, Bravery and Kindness, among others, are imbued in our kids by the age of 12. Check with child psychologists for the specifics. Both of my children, Rachel Savannah and Nico Alexander, were trained as Warriors since birth. At the Lamaze Child birthing classes prior to Rachel's arrival on Planet Earth, the instructor asked what the parents were looking forward to most about the new baby. When it was my turn, I said that "We are looking forward to raising a martial artist from birth." Everyone just looked at me. During her actual birth some wild things happened that defy explanation. It is said that when a Warrior enters an electrically rich environment, odd anomalies occur. Kinda like when the Terminator first comes to Earth and all the lights flicker and horns sound etc. This is exactly what happened.

Rachel was born at Northwestern Hospital in downtown Chicago near the Great Lake Michigan. We had prepared the birthing room with soft chanting music from a new cassette tape in a brand new boom box. It was a pleasant setting, as pleasant as it can be while my wife was in back labor for 25 hours! In fact, before taking her over to the hospital, I asked if she could "hold on" while I taught kids class. She stayed at home, across the street from the dojo curled in a ball, until I returned and she suggested poignantly that we go "NOW!"

SHOWTIME.

My wife, Bonnie of the Washington DC purse snatcher fame, was finally ready to deliver Rachel and both Mom and Baby were hooked up to the latest state of the art fetal monitoring electronic systems available as Northwestern. There were four clocks on the wall showing different world times from New York, London, Tokyo and Sidney. The chanting tape was replaced in the new boom box with an melodic Native American Indian drums and chanting. Then it happened.

The boom box tape pops open and shredded cassette tape spews out as the music grinds to a halt. All for clocks on the wall start spinning backwards and then the lights go out in the room as emergency lighting clicks on. The fetal monitors go out completely then try clicking back on. The doctor can not see properly and asks that Bonnie and Fetal Warrior be moved to another room with "better light". I try to keep calm and say to the doctor "Wow. That's intense. Does this happen often?" trying to reassure myself that all was ok. "No never. Never before in my 30 years here." I thought about going to throw up. Thoughts of Rosemary's Baby invade.

Bonnie is wheeled down the hall and into a room at the end of a long corridor into a fully lit room. From what I remember, the hallway lights were illuminated, so it must have been a electrical problem in our room only. I was too freaked out to ask, because Rachel was coming. Rachel came into this world without further paranormal incident. After checking to make sure that no Omen-like "666" appeared on the back of her neck, and after a thorough clean up, I held her on my chest next to the hospital bed and we both fell asleep as Bonnie looked on. Now you can draw your own conclusions about what happened at Northwestern that day. I know what happened…a Kenpo Warrior was born. Taurus the Bull, incidentally.

Quick story about how martial arts training begun at an early age forms values of Self Confidence, Self Worth and Self Respect. Normally, I tell parents to wait until 5 years old to start their kids in the martial arts. Five years too late, but better late than never! Some children have been successful starting at 4 and I have had 3 year old siblings of other students practicing in the same class. But for the most part 5 years is best since the difference in cognitive and physical development between 4 ½ and 5 years old is both amazing and substantial.

Rachel was tucked in front of my gi top just days after her birth as I taught Kenpo classes in Old Town. Her little pink, hospital-issued skull cap hid the first synaptic connections being formed by watching the martial arts after entering the world just a few days prior. Her new world would consist of eating, drinking, diaper-changing, being loved and doing Kenpo. She crawled on the mat as an infant, started kicking and punching as a toddler, and won the Midwest Jiu Jitsu Championship by age 9. She "choked out" a radio celebrity live on the air as he described the sensation of being put to sleep while dropping the mike during a promotional stop at a Brookfield car show. Rachel was 10 when she submitted her first adult.

RACHEL SUMBITTING A BOY CHAMPION FROM A OHIO TEAM AT LEFT AS BROTHER NICO LOOKS ON AFTER WINNING HIS JIU JITSU CHAMPIONSHIP MATCH IN RT PIC.

When Rachel was 4 years old she was attending Apple School, a highly reputable pre-K institution on Wells Street just south of Old Town in Chicago. I received a phone call from the school's principal asking me to stop by her office when picking up Rachel that afternoon. Inquiring if anything was wrong, the principal replied "We don't know." Not good I thought.

Seems Rachel had gotten into a confrontation with the formidable classmate, Mathew. Upon greeting the principal with Rachel in tow, the following was basically what transpired:

Principal (PR): "Mr. Powell, thank you for coming. Rachel was involved in an incident today with a fellow student, Mathew R."

Me. Concerned Parent (M.CP): "Ok. What happened?"

PR: "Rachel was in free play time and was telling the other kids what to do as she was cooking dinner in the play oven. She has some kids setting the table, others washing dishes and so on"

M.CP: "Sounds like good leadership skills to me."

PR: "Maybe so. But I think Mathew took issue with being bossed around by Rachel."

M.CP: "Why, was he on dish patrol?" I say jokingly to uncomfortable silence.

PR: "Anyway, Rachel was issuing orders and Mathew went over to ask her to stop and they got into it."

M.CP: "A fight?"

PR: "We are not sure."

M.CP: "You are not sure? You don't know what a fight looks like?" I say getting a bit perturbed with the vagueness of the principal's answers.

So I ask Rachel what happened directly.

M.CP: "Rachel, what happened today in the kitchen?"

Rachel Savannah Powell (RSP): "I was making dinner with my friends, Daddy. And Mat-u came over and grabbed my arm."

M.CP: "Then what happened?"   RSP: "I said-Mat-u let go of my arm."

M.CP: "Did he let go?"   RSP: "No."

M.CP: "Then what happened?"   RSP: "I said again-Mat-u! Let go of my arm!"

Mat-u: "Or what?"   RSP: "Or I'll choke you out!"

PR: "That's it! That's what she said! What does she mean 'choke you out'?"

M.CP: "If Mathew didn't release her arm she was going to make him unconscious."

PR: "WHAT?" Ignoring the principal's dramatic confusion, I ask Rachel, "Did you try to choke him out?"   RSP: "No Daddy."

M.CP: "Why not?" RSP: "He let go of my arm."

M.CP to PR: "Please make sure Mathew nor any other student puts their hands on my daughter. If that happens again, I want to be contacted immediately. Thank you Principal for calling me."

Rachel and I walk out hand in hand.

There were no further incidents of anyone putting their hands on Rachel in Pre-School.
As Hanshi Shorty Mills says "No one has the right to put their hands on you. If they do, they
give up the right to be healthy!" Hanshi, your grand student Rachel, has the concept down pat.
When Rachel was nine years old, she had been training at Kenpo School for nine years. This is
what she wrote to help new students succeed in their martial arts training at our dojo.

A Warrior's First Time...by Rachel Powell

"When you first walk in, everything spins.
You watch and learn and you see what they do
They're training to save people. People like themselves.
Any person can be a hero...inside your spirit it dwells.
Once you understand what they do, everything will fall into place . A place for a warrior like you.
This place is real. It is no fake. When you first come in, your world will spin and shake,
Then it will become smooth, on a path only warriors take."

Additional stories about bringing up a female martial artist from birth could go on for awhile.
Suffice it to say that Rachel is driven to excel in everything she does in academics, athletics and
humanitarian endeavors. She has received numerous honors in all three. At this writing she is
attending the prestigious Rutgers University in New Jersey double majoring in Public Planning
and Policy and Pre-Law.

A definite winner and an impressive example of the power of Warriors.

THE FATHER DAUGHTER LOVE TRANSENDS MERE CONCEPTS LIKE ETERNITY.

RACHEL AND DADDY-O.

Now to the other side of the same coin. Training a male martial artist *even earlier* than birth.

Nico Alexander Powell's training began the moment that I found out my wife was pregnant with

a second child. While waiting until Rachel was actually breathing outside air to begin hearing a

lifetime martial arts dialog, Nico was receiving instruction while still in the womb, the so-called

"wojo". At 3 years old, Rachel already had three years of training on the mats at PWOK

watching, listening, learning and imitating the martial arts moves She spent the first few years crawling in and out of sparring Warriors, students practicing forms and techniques and hardcore physical training.. Dangerous you say? The danger was to any student or teacher that fell on or bumped into my daughter. PWOK teaches awareness and they were sure to be aware when Rachel was crawling around. Rachel also was skilled in "Don't Fall Off The Boat" balance games. Just like I learned on my Dad's USMC-issued "Infant Chest Gym".

Nico was born in Chicago during the 1996 Olympic Summer Games held in Atlanta. It was quite amusing to watch gymnasts working the parallel bars as Bonnie worked gripping the bars parallel to her hospital bed trying to hasten a baby's arrival into the world. I was clearly more amused than Bonnie as she didn't find my conveyed observation all that comforting versus the pain of labor during childbirth. Something about a bowling ball and my ass is all I could make out through the cheering Olympic fans and a mother's growling agony.

So while Nico's emergence onto the Earth-plane was a bit less dramatic than Rachel's clock-spinning, music-stopping light show, it was intense nonetheless. When the doctor said it was a boy, I jumped up and nearly KO'd myself on some overhanging baby delivery equipment. With adrenaline pumping, head hurting and heart pounding, I met Nico Alexander Powell for the first time. In a temporarily shocking time warp, Nico looked exactly like my Father with the original "Powell Scowl" that I saw as a kid when screwing something up. Confused as to why Nico could already be mad at me moments into outdoor Life, I remembered all the in utero training and teaching that he had to sit through for 9 months before being born. The scowl was like "So you're the one that's been keeping me up at night with all that Kung Fu stuff!" When I finally understood that it was not really a baby version of my Dad and actually just my newborn Son, everything became both calm and unbelievably thrilling.

We sent out a birth announcement that said "Rachel Savannah Powell announces the arrival of her new training partner Nico Alexander Powell" and they were both dressed in baby kung fu uniforms. Rachel in red and Nico in black. Nico's training at PWOK was similar to Rachel's and he picked up The Arts as quickly as she did. Again, it was eat, drink, diaper-changes, being loved and doing Kenpo! Standard lifestyle in a modern Warrior household. Jumbo!

Nico became a Recreation Wrestling Gold Medalist and a 3x Midwest Jiu Jitsu Champion before age 11. Just as with Rachel, I will provide a Nico story that exemplifies what martial arts training can do for a child in the development of a healthy sense of self worth and self respect. The coolest thing about watching Nico compete is the stoic yet intense attitude and demeanor he exhibits. During wrestling matches, he never seems nervous, is unconcerned that he may be outweighed quite a bit (in recreation wrestling, weight classes can be broad and have a 10 lbs swing from little to big.) or that the opponent looks meaner. He just goes out there, kicks ass and wins. But in the event of a loss, Nico understands sportsmanship, hops up and shakes hands afterward. I have a great picture taken from the back vantage point of a huge, muscular wrestler with Nico facing him, hand raised by the referee in victory, just looking upward and staring emotionless at the vanquished tough guy.

Very cool.

The story that I want to relate is about how training in the martial arts gives a child the will to persevere when facing adversity. This includes standing up to bullying, a tough school project or doing something that you don't really want to do. Nico won his first Midwest Jiu Jitsu Championship demonstrating the value of never quitting. In the finals, Nico was matched with the same excellent Judo player that had beaten him handily the year before. When Nico realized that he was to face the same boy for the championship, I thought I saw the slightest bit of doubt cross his mind. It cleared quickly enough as he looked at me for some last minute coaching. I simply told him that "You can beat him. Most important, win or lose give it 100% like you always do." He just nodded and went to the center of the mat. The Judo player and his coach remembered last years match and were quite confident of victory.

For the first two periods, it looked like a repeat of last year's contest. The score was 11-2 in favor of not-Nico. The final period, it was more of the same and the score rose to 14-2 with under 30 seconds left. I was preparing my "importance of learning from defeat" speech as Nico was still giving his all and the Judo player was coasting just a bit with the score so insurmountable.

With 19 seconds left in the match, I yell "Come on Champ! You've got to submit him!" Nico fought to his feet and as the Judo player threw him forward with a front trip, Nico stepped out and while spinning in the air executed a flying arm lock with both his legs wrapped tight. And before his head hit the ground, Nico was arching his back, pelvis forward going for the submission. With 10 seconds left, Nico is balancing on the top of his head on the mat, both feet pointing to the ceiling and both arms clamped tight at JP's wrist and forearm. Screaming "Break It!" and with Nico glancing at me in a "Dad, its just a tournament." kinda way, I look at the clock with 2 seconds left as Judo player yells "TAP! TAP!" as he is slapping his submission sign onto Nico's outstretched victorious leg.

Down 14-2 with 30 seconds left there was no quit. Just 100% Smashmouth Effort expected of all Powells and Warriors that are like us. Great job Champ! I couldn't think of a better story to illustrate the power of training at an early age and the value of never quitting. Not ever!
At the time of this writing, Nico is a Junior in High School, a three sport athlete, a scholar and involved in humanitarian causes like "Best Buddies" for the mentally handicapped and "Special Olympics" for those challenged physically. Like his sister, Nico is a Warrior and a great person.

At Powell's Way of Kenpo Martial Arts School and as many other top martial arts schools throughout America, we train the children intensely. Just like the adults, but in a miniature, less physically demanding way. Don't get me wrong, they train hard, but their bodies are growing and we let that occur naturally with muscle tone, weight control and flexibility the focus. But the mindset and the techniques taught are transferred with the same disciplined focus of purpose as the adults.

As an example: PWOK has a very intense training drill called "KIDNAP" and it's serious business. Kids 12 and under stand at the far end of the dojo mat facing the wall. Their backs are exposed as adult instructors approach silently to "interact". The adults may just tap the student on the shoulder as a relative or friend might. The kid is expected to turn quickly, assess the stranger's identity and intentions then take appropriate action. In the case of a family member, a "Hi. Aunt Edna!" with a smile is ok. For a friend, it might be a "Hey Mikey, you startled me. Don't do that!" stern warning. Any unknown adult is met with an automatic increase in distance and verbal and physical counter measures. These actions need to be automatic. They become so by learning, practicing and training in awareness that these types of situations are more prevalent than anyone cares to acknowledge.

If it is an attacker that grabs the kid from behind and attempts to drag them down the length of the mat and into "the trunk of a car" its SHOWTIME! And we are as serious as bat to the head. We tell the students that if the adult successfully drags them the full length of the mat, they are "in the trunk" and won't ever see their parents again. Harsh you say? They are just kids you say? Do you know what sick, psychotic pedophiles do to "just kids"? Read the f'n papers and the number of child abductions EVERY SINGLE DAY in the US from neighborhoods just like yours. Amber Alert may be a bit too late. Most kidnapped children are murdered in the first 24 hours of abduction. How are they are transported? Car trunk mostly. No time for niceties.

The kids can do almost anything to resist. Originally there were no restrictions on what they could do. Several adult instructors were bitten severely, had their eyes damaged from Kenpo eye pokes or their face ripped by Tiger Claws. After we tried padding for bites, goggles for eye protection and face shields for claws, we deemed it too unrealistic. As well, the kids were losing baby teeth early from chomping on the arm pads and jamming their tiny fingers attempting eye strikes into hard plastic goggles. The protective gear was removed and children were shown defensive tactics that would include these attacks if real, but altered in practice for the Kidnap training drill in the dojo.

You may say that a kid can not defeat an adult in a fight. And you would be right. But a trained child that automatically puts up determined resistance verbally and physically has a chance to escape. While way to rare, instances of children fighting back and getting free from an adult predator have been proven on video surveillance tapes available to view on the Internet. Defiance is better than reliance. Adults who are assaulted can not rely on the mercy of their attackers and neither can children facing abduction.

On the news today was the story of a 2nd grade girl in Ohio walking in the well-to-do neighbor hood to her home at the end of a quiet suburban cul-de-sac. She saw a strange man leaning on his beat up white van on her side of the street. Without saying a word he grabbed her by the forearm and tried to drag her into his vehicle. She remembered two things mother taught her:

1) Fight Back!
2) Hit as hard as you can and don't stop until you get away!

That "training" probably saved that little girl's life. During a TV news interview, which shielded her face, she explained what her mom had taught her and had a message for other kids:

"Stand up for Yourself and Fight Back!" A Warrior in the making for sure. Jumbo!

Train. Train. Train your children well if you want them to have a better chance of growing up.

Word.

DAUGHTER RACHEL AND ME WITH UFC STAR AND KENPO HALL OF FAMER KEITH HACKNEY, WHO DEFEATED THE 6'8" 600 LBS SUMO WRESTLER EMMANUEL YARBOROUGH AT UFC 3.

CHAPTER THIRTY SIX

The Importance of: REAL SELF DEFENSE EXPERIENCES.

While most normal human beings are not thrilled at the prospect of being forced to hurt some one, it is the natural byproduct of an attack on a trained Warrior. With proper training and mental, physical and spiritual strength, you can be confident that you are prepared for most confrontations. As a trained fighter, you have a responsibility under the law to use the least amount of force required to thwart the attack. Only if you are in fear for your life or serious bodily injury is overwhelming lethal force a legal option. And again, if you kill someone while defending yourself, be sure that you can prove self defense. Also hire a good attorney. Since you are a martial artist you will be held to a higher level of restraint by the courts. But as we have stated before, court and jail is better than death and dismemberment. Even if your Accidental Death and Dismemberment Insurance premium is paid up.

Now Real Self Defense Experiences (RSDE) need not always involve physical violence. You may render a fight moot with acute verbal skills, intelligence and self control. That too is RSDE. You can always resort to physical violence to protect yourself, but once you take that action, other less dangerous avenues of communication are closed. I like to adhere if possible to the famous philosophy of the Shaolin Temple in the original Kwai Chang Caine "Kung Fu" movie:

"Avoid rather than Check. Check rather than Hurt. Hurt rather than Maim. Maim rather than Kill. For all life is precious and none can be replaced."

But no matter how hard we try to be nice, sometimes it is necessary to not be nice. Here are a few of those times:

Story 1: ATLANTA MUGGER.

I was on business in Atlanta attending a trade show at a convention center near the stadium where the Hawks play professional basketball. For some reason, it seems every city has most of its pro sports arenas and stadium venues surrounded by less than safe neighborhoods. There was a shuttle bus that ferried business folk to and from the Convention Center and various hotels nearby. While the walk there would take ten minutes, the shuttle bus's many stops could take up to 30 minutes to get to and fro.

It was a sunny, warm day, so I decided to walk to the massive Convention Center. In total businessman attire with a conventioneer badge swinging from my neck and briefcase in hand, off I go on my merry way for a quick jaunt through "the hood".

While walking uphill and about halfway through the trek, I notice four miscreants standing in a tight circle either passing a bottle or smoking a joint. They see me and their demeanor changes as they are now discussing my future and their part in it. Maybe if they were not so drunk and high, they could see that I walked with purpose, clearly saw them and was proceeding on my way. In their boozed-infused brains, they must have thought it was their lucky day as an out of town businessman wandered into their concrete jungle. They probably saw an opportunity for more beer money in their future while I saw trips to the hospital and broken bones for all.

After their Yalta-type conference, their attack strategy was clear. One would saunter over to me and ask for money. If there was any resistance, the implied threat was that the other three would race over to assist Mugger 1. Seemed like a sound plan, and if I was anyone else, it might have been. I however felt my mood turn murderous. How dare they assume that I would cooperate?

As Mugger 1 is moving in a diagonal line toward me slicing the small, square shaped parking lot separating us into two equal triangles. In other words, he was moving from the upper left corner of the parking lot to the lower right corner and moi. His movement alters between threatening, welcoming and pitifully begging. I am not fooled as he gets within range. Here is what transpired:

Mugger: "Hey man! Do you have a smoke?"

Me: "No. I don't smoke."

Mugger: Wanna buy some pot?"

Me: "No. I don't get high?"

Mugger: "What about money?"

Me: "What about it?"

Mugger: "You got any?"

Me: "Yes. I have plenty. Why do you ask?"

Mugger: "Give me some of it."

Me: "Are you asking me or telling me?"

Mugger: "What do you think?"

Me: "I'll tell you what I think." As I surge up about a half inch from his face. I was so close that I could smell his bad breath and the stench of his unwashed beard. "Tell you what- GIVE ME all YOUR MONEY before I wrap this briefcase around your f'n head! Confused that his plan had somehow gotten away from him, he just looks into my now black eyes as if he accidentally picked a fight with a thirsty vampire.

Mugger: "Ahhh...what?" as he looks away from my gaze at the now long distance between him

432

and his friends. They are just staring back at him and do not move.

Me: "I am going to ask you again. Give me all your money RIGHT NOW! Before I snap your neck like a twig and ass rape your corpse before your homies can even get here! Now! Give me YOUR Money! NOW!"

Mugger: "Man, you crazy! I ain't giving you no money. Your one f'd up dude!"

Me: "No money? Then move the f**k out of my way so I can go make some!"

The would-be mugger let me pass. Wonder what he'll tell his friends when he gets back to them.

Probably something like "That crazy f**ker tried to ROB ME!"

I call that strategy "Mug the Mugger".

Bet that his buddies didn't share a joint with him after that failed expedition.

Story 2: KENTUCKY HOSS.

Again on business, I was meeting with one of my top customers while selling advertising space for a national consumer magazine. It was a great annual trip as there are only three big accounts in Louisville, KY to call on. The two early morning appointments were concluded then it was off to fun time with the main account. A business lunch in Louisville can start out with noon time shots of Woolford Reserve Kentucky Bourbon whiskey then playing 9 holes at a local golf club or spent watching horse racing at Churchill Downs-Home of The Kentucky Derby.

Since the client had just signed off on a $90K ad schedule, we were all in a festive mood. That translated to continuing "sipping" Woolford and me deciding to return to Chicago the following day.

As it were, that meant my Southern hosts felt the need to return the favor by taking me to nearly every cool bar that they new in the Greater Louisville area. I asked if we could go into the backwoods of Kentucky for some real moonshine. Thinking better of it when they replied "Sure if you want to go blind drinking "white lightning" get lost in the woods and don't mind reenacting a scene from the movie Deliverance." Ah…no thanks, I'll pass. We'll stay on the main roads.

We ended up at this great redneck bar bordering on the sticks of Deliverance-land. After awhile, I guess the remaining elements of my business suit (shoes, socks, slacks, white shirt and skivvies) seemed to irk a few of the locals. Probably was a fashion mishap to be too dressed up in this suspenders, overalls and oily jeans tavern. Bet it didn't help that the three of us were laughing so hard we were turning purple. Anyway, I feel the eye gaze energy of a few Yankee-haters and scan the bar to find the source. Turns out nearly everyone was looking at us, but I eventually found the main eyeballer in the usual form of a huge, belligerent redneck. "Surprise! Surprise! Surprise!" as Jim Neighbors/Gomer Pyle-USMC rang my inner ear.

Looking at him, he was sizable and glared hostility at me in traditional bar stare down fashion. After a few moments of "I see you too" I returned to my conversation and started laughing again from something one of my customers said. The laughter was totally unrelated to the Bubba stare down, but I guess that he saw it differently. He thought we were laughing at him and here he comes. As he is approaching the table, I stand up to let him know he wasn't arriving in stealth mode. While looking up at him, I realize that my diplomatic skills are at an all time low courtesy the Woolford Reserve and irked since I wasn't the one starting trouble. As well, even though we are friends, my group is still made up of customers from a business relationship that could be damaged if we ended up in jail. There wasn't that much talk, but what there was went like this:

Kentucky Hoss: "Man, who the f**k y'all think y'all are coming into MY bar and makin fuss?"

Me: "Makin fuss? Your bar? So your name is Trudy? 'Cause that's what it says on the blinking sign out front you f**king moron!" He didn't take the comment very well.

I am accustomed to more pre-confrontation dialog that usually defuses the situation. This was apparently not in vogue at "Trudy's". Without another word, Kentucky Hoss proceeds to push-chuck me hard over a few tables and I am grateful for the hard cement wall that stops the rapid backward flight while keeping me on my feet, albeit at a rakish angle.

SHOWTIME.

Proceeding to an upright position, I remove the tables and chairs with hands and feet toward big Kentucky Hoss. Catching the eyes of my seated customers, they appear unconcerned. Cool. Passing them mumbling that it was like a "Wild-West Saloon brawl, but in the South" I arrive at Kentucky Hoss. Leaning his head back and up a bit to execute Point #3 of the traditional 8-Point Redneck Calculation. Remember from the Preakness on how rednecks prepare to fight? Recap:

3) Use Grizzly Bear Technique of standing up straight to make self look bigger and more threatening.

The difference between both drunk redneck confrontations is this time the fight had already started via Kentucky Hoss' horizontal bench press of me over a few tables into a cement wall.

No, this time the calculation was mine and quite simple. Hurt rather than maim since the option to avoid and check had passed during my visit to the wall.

Perhaps Kentucky Hoss was a bit surprised since he appeared ready for me to push him back. I could tell he was momentarily confused as I climbed up him and smashed his Loovil face three times hard. Standard short lead left, crisp overhand right, tight left hook. I rode him down like a bronco on depressants as he hit the floor hard and my weight crunched his lower ribs. Not sure if he was out cold or just quitting, but while dismounting, I felt him twitch and cracked him in the puss again with a big right before hopping off.

As I get off him and look down from a safe distance, he does the Terminator thing and just won't stay down. Not sure if it was his Kentucky toughness or my "hurt rather than maim" philosophy. In any event, up stands Hoss with a closed right eye, puffy contused face and split lips. He spits out some blood like tobacco chewers do and it looked kinda cool. I was happy that no teeth followed as I respected his moxie. But now I had a job to finish. A right rear leg wheel kick was ordered up and sent on its way. For some reason that night, I thought myself taller than I am. The kick to the head was a poor technique choice courtesy of overconfidence, the whiskey or both. And Kentucky Hoss had enough Yankee pounding for the night. Dixie rises again!

With the kick in mid-flight, Hoss gets revenge for all the rednecks that fell victim to my Wrestling, by using my own favorite technique against me. Yep, Kentucky Hoss DOUBLE LEGS me! And being on one foot there is not a thing that I can do about it. So this is what it feels like experiencing impending doom. He lifts me up and up. Then slams me down HARD! In fact, being aware that skull to cement is not a good match, I tuck my chin and try to slow the takedown by grabbing any part of exposed Hoss. Not much to grab as I am counting the milliseconds until impact. Martial Note: Expect the Unexpected. Since the Unexpected Hurts. While waiting to hit the ground as soft as possible by keeping contact with him, the timing to protect my head while pulling him into a Guard was probably accurate. The concrete planter that my lower back and kidney landed on...not so much. We hit so hard that the thick sharp angled ledge of the stand alone stone structure broke into pieces. Yeah it hurt, and I was probably bleeding internally, but that is where I prefer to keep my blood...on the inside! Now with Hoss in my cement planter-delayed Guard, I say "Nice takedown man! That's f'n hurt!"

He says "Good! Look at my face ya lil sh*t!"

Finally, I say "Sorry man! Here's some more." while Leg Sweeping him and rising to Mount. With no anger, I hold him down by the throat and punch him in the face repeatedly until, like a hockey fight, the refs have had enough, and I am willingly pulled off downed Hoss. I return to the stunned silence of my table as my clients then toast me saying that was wild. They mention that the manager called the police and it was time to go. Agreed.

Martial Note: Anger has no place in a fight...on your part. Get the opponent as angry as possible, though, since anger leads to mistakes. Mistakes in combat lead to defeat. A slap across the face, instead of a punch is a great way to incite an opponent's anger. Just be prepared to handle the initial fury that this action causes. Wait for the clear opening and deliver the strike. A great Karate Master once said: *"The angry man will defeat himself in battle, as well as in life."*

Back to Trudy's. Walking up to the bar to get the bill and my credit card, the only open space is next to where Hoss is sitting drinking a beer. Our eyes meet and I ask him if he needs another brew. He answers "Yeah. Thanks man."

"No problem, I figured that I'd better get the bill and split before the cops get here. Maybe you should too." Hoss says "Nah, they know me. It's cool."

I order a beer for each of us and ask the staring bartender for the bill. When the beers get there, we clink bottles, take a swig and I say "Man, its going to be a painful night of pissing blood from that slam you put on me." He says "Got help from the flower pot!" We both crack up.

I sign the bill, leave a great tip so maybe she won't give my name off the cc receipt to the cops and slam the remaining beer. About to leave, I say "Hey man. Sorry that we had to meet that way. Next time I'm in town let's just cut to the beers!"

Hoss finishes with "Yeah, fer sure. Sorry about pushing you over the tables. You just remind me of my f'n Boss and he's a dick! And you guys were so frigg'n loud when you came in! Then when you called me a chick, I lost it. Now I gotta to go to work in the morning and explain what happened to my face".

"Tell them that you made a new friend.' I say while turning away and start walking to the parking lot and my waiting customers. Kenpo is an excellent tool for barroom clarification and alternative conflict resolution. That is how old fashion fighting is done. Both participants agree to engage and there is a winner and a loser. If both contestants are hurt, then both are losers. But at the end, when it's over its over. Remember in High School when a former enemy became a friend after a 3:05 pm fight? Kinda like that.

That is not how it's done nowadays. A bar fight or any confrontation in modern day is not always over when its over. If you have not thoroughly and convincingly defeated the opponent, chances are there will be further aggression. As an example, you are forced into fisticuffs and knock the guy out with one punch. You see it as over, he may see it as a lucky shot. Even worse, if the hostility has not abated, the vanquished may leave the bar, bring back a gun, pull

438

a knife or wait for you outside with friends or a baseball bat. Just because you think a conflict is resolved, unless you are sure, assume it is not and take measures to stay safe by being aware. Best advice: Don't fight. If you have to fight, win decisively and be aware that there may be repercussions to that action. It's said *"When two tigers fight, one is injured and the other dies."*

RESPECT IS PROBABLY THE SINGLE MOST IMPORTANT ASPECT OF A WARRIOR.

CHAPTER THIRTY SEVEN

The Importance of: RESPECT.

As human beings we are born of dignity as a pristine representation of God's Love on Earth.

But while growing we get bumped, banged and bruised by Life and then we learn, yearn and earn RESPECT.

*R*emember that

*E*veryone knows

*S*omething and

*P*erhaps can

*E*ven teach you

*C*ertain

*T*hings

It is absolutely amazing what people know. No matter what you are an expert in, there are infinite topics in which you are ignorant. I mean that in all due respect. Know it alls are not only idiots but can be quite annoying. No one knows everything about everything. You may know the genus and species of a South Australian Bizarre Looper Moth but couldn't tell the difference between the angle of a right hook to the chops and the right angle to hook a tuna in deep sea chop. So know what you know. Learn what you can. And then share all that you know with anyone that cares to know what you have learned.

In learning the martial arts, you can read books and magazines, watch DVDs and demonstrations, and listen to audio tapes and hear what experts say. But you must EXPERIENCE them in order to UNDERSTAND them. Once you have MASTERED whatever Art you have trained in, start on another as a BEGINNER. With this philosophy, you can learn more about the martial arts and more about The Way of Life. Enjoy the process since the only end to learning is Death. Then some say that the journey continues even after that.

Respect is a concept that should be instilled in our children early in life. Teaching the difference between respect and weakness is important as well. An essential element in teaching the idea of respect is that the child learns the importance of SELF RESPECT. If you do not respect your-self, you will not respect others…you will FEAR THEM. Again, this is not a book on child rearing, its is a treatise on self defense and that education and training starts with respect and self respect at the core.

Bullying is recognized as a major social problem that inhibits student growth and human social development through physical and mental fear. Stymieing creativity is the last thing we want for our children. Since the whole pre-college academic hierarchy is based on older, bigger and stronger students being educated in the same building as younger ones, it seems that bullying is just a part of growing up in the system. It is not. Bullying is wrong and is the direct result of PARENTAL FAILURE to instill the core values of respect and self respect in their children. Looking for the school bully? Look at his or her parents or parent. With my children being trained fighters, if I ever found out that they were bullying another child, there would be hell to pay. They know that because that is how they were raised.

The toll taken by bullying has never been greater. In previous times, when school let out and you got home, the torment ended. You had a sanctuary to recover from the damage of the day.

441

Now, with social media tied directly to your cell phone and computer, the bullying is 24/7. And this has lead to an increase in SUICIDES and SCHOOL SHOOTINGS tied directly to cyber-bullying. While we can not hope to shield our children from the technology of instant communication to a widespread audience, we can combat its effect by teaching our children the proper values, the difference between right and wrong, and how to develop the intestinal fortitude to stand up to bullying for themselves or in defense of others. It's not easy, but it can be done.

Respect others and respect yourself.

Martial Note: The martial arts teach these values from the get go.

I HAVE LIVED, LOVED, SUCCEEDED AND FLOPPED. IT'S AN AWESOME JOURNEY.

CHAPTER THIRTY EIGHT

The Importance of: FLOPS.

There is a difference between a mistake, a flop and failure.

As we discussed, a failure is a permanent state of not succeeding at something. A flop is the near catastrophic feeling that you failed…miserably. A flop can be temporary or permanent, has some elements of mistakes and failure but is not exactly the same. A mistake is a temporary action with little emotional content and can often be corrected. Flops contain a more personal component. As if a flop is tied directly to your very being. Using humor to ease the emotional pain of flops is as important as steeling your determination to continue on task until you achieve either success or at least a non-flop.

Some Epic Flops Experienced (SEFE):

SEFE 1: THREE WINDS JOURNAL.

In the early 1990's several of us came up with the brilliant idea to start a martial arts magazine. "Three Winds Journal "would be the definitive monthly text of all things martial. We had the vision. We had the determination. We had the talent. We just didn't have the money. Flop.

SEFE 2: THREE WINDS JOURNEY.

Fresh off the idea of launching a martial arts magazine with five people and no money, we would now focus on bringing our Warrior Life Way to the eager masses by way of the latest, greatest technology-cable television. Only problem was that nobody at the station was interested. None-the-less, with our determination not to flop in two types of media, we pressed forward until the cable station decided it was worth the set time cost just to shut us up. Ok. By any means necessary, we would save the world with our wisdom, skill and vision. We made a pretty cool "pilot" that had Sempai Nick Black (Six Flags/Gangi kickboxing demo fame) doing the on air introduction and voice over as Hanshi Shorty Mills, Masters Kimball Paul, Kelly Carter and I went through various self defense, meditative and sword scenarios. Some funny stuff happened while we were all totally serious since the budget to shut us up was valued at only one take:

1) Kimball sneezes so hard, as Sempai Nick is announcing the "stars" of the show, that his long Tai Chi robe wafts up like a concert pianist seating himself for a performance by flipping up his tuxedo tails. This kills the whole "masters" effect and sets the stage for more gaffs.

2) I start the show with a blistering display of Kenpo Karate totally unaware that my black and silver spiked hair and goatee surrounding my intensely focused stare has all the trappings of a mad demon dancing at some satanic ritual just before the human sacrifice. The TV camera angle and lighting didn't help. When watching the tape after we were turned down for a cable series, I scared myself in a most maniacal way with a harsh new view of self image.

3) Kimball's Tai Chi segment went well enough, but when describing the balance needed in Tai Chi, the phrase "you must cut the body in half" just hung in the air and only added to the weirdly demonic Kenpo beginning. This slightly macabre explanation of weight distribution was in odd contrast to the "Monopoly Monocle Man" comical movements Kimball made when he entered and exited the camera shot.

4) Hanshi was perfect…as all TENTH DANS are. Amusing though as the camera had a bit of

trouble following the huge man as he dropped from an upper body close up into a full split then popped back up so fast that the camera lost track of him as he just disappeared downward. Then, as Hanshi is having his students attack him in a realistic self defense scenario, I hear bones cracking sickly and folks flying off screen to an unknown demise. DISCLAIMER: No Humans Were Killed or Injured during the filming of Three Winds Journey…that we know of.

5) Last laugh track to the story is my performance of a 5 concrete slab Tameshiwari breaking demonstration. First of all, with only one take allowed and only one set of 5 bricks to break, the pressure was on. In addition, there were quite a few lines to be said after the successful break. With Master Kelly and Master Kimball finishing up a razor sharp sword fight, which happened to be the least violent part of the show, I am sitting in the background mediating in front of the pre-stacked concrete and awaiting Kimball's Monopoly Man exit stage left. As Sempai Nick sets the stage in dramatic fashion with "Now a special treat, Master Bill Powell will show the power of the martial arts by breaking five slabs…" When he is finished with the intro, he steps off camera and I obliterate the slabs as chunks of concrete of various size spew out across the stage. No time to relax, now the tough part, remembering my lines.

Again, so focused on the task at hand and still unaware of the disturbing demon face look that I was actually portraying, I step over the crushed concrete and directly toward Sempai. He steps back slightly and later told me that it looked like I was coming out of an ancient tomb to murder him. No hostility intended, he was just the next stop in the successful completion of my mission-Focus, Break, Focus, Talk. Focus and don't trip on the sharp chunks of rock strewn about while moving off camera. Almost made it. The last frame of my exit shows my left foot only. At the same moment the front weighted lead walking foot is impaled by a vengeful sliver-chunk of just defeated concrete. Not sure if off screen, I ignore the searing pain of the ball of my foot which seemed to scream up to my eyes and brain "Watch where the f**k you are walking oh great karate master!" Damn chunk-a-rock.

When all was said and done, we were proud of our one take performance and hoped that the station decision-makers would know that we could do better with more on air experience. They didn't. We were turned down in favor of a knitting and crocheting show that was deemed less menacing and more family friendly. Hope they can wield the "knit one pearl two" hand hook techniques when the home invaders come to disrupt their friendly family environment late one night.

So while Three Winds Journey joined Three Winds Journal into the flop section of this book, all was not lost in our effort. We got to meet the legendary Pulitzer Prize winning author and famous Chicago luminary Louis "Studs" Terkel when leaving the studio. His book "The Good War" is one of the greatest narratives of its time. Not all would-be cable television "stars" can say that they have had such an honor. Man that was so cool.

SEFE 3: MR. BUTLER.

Master Bob Wainwright and I were asked to do a martial arts demonstration at the Brookpark Elementary School in Oak Brook, IL. It was a long day as we taught every single period of a regular school day. It was fun and by no means a flop. The near flop/fopah came after we had completed the day's teaching and were leaving. The school administrator was thrilled and very thankful for our efforts as the kids said they really had a blast. As we return the courtesies, she asks if we would like to meet Mr. Butler. I said sure as usual when asked to do something that I have no idea what I've just committed to.

As Master Bob and I walk out the front door of the School, there stands a beautiful horse and the administrator leads us toward the introduction. She says "Sensei Bob and Sensei Bill, I would like to introduce you to Mister Butler!" After growing up watching the "Mr. Ed" talking horse

TV show, I am about to rub the nose and say "Well Hello there Mr. Butler!" Just then, Sensei Bob elbow shivs me in the back which painfully redirects my hand and focus to the man standing next to the horse. Taking the sharp hint and a 50/50 shot that I would address the correct Mr. Butler, I continue the hand to horse face motion bypassing the animal skull and into the waiting outstretched hand of Mr. Butler.

THIS IS NOT, HAS NEVER BEEN, NOR WILL EVER BE MR. BUTLER.

Being from the East Coast I did not realize this was one of the most wealthy, philanthropically generous men in the state. His family owns Butler National Golf Course, Butler Polo Grounds and large swaths of donated forest preserve land named in the family's honor. Every time I drive through Oak Brook, I chuckle when seeing the Butler name that is everywhere and thankful that the near flop was averted via a Sensei Bob elbow tip. Ignorance does hurt.

So, since flops do not necessarily mean failure and mistakes are means of learning and ok in life but not in self defense, there is only one thing to do.

Flop away.

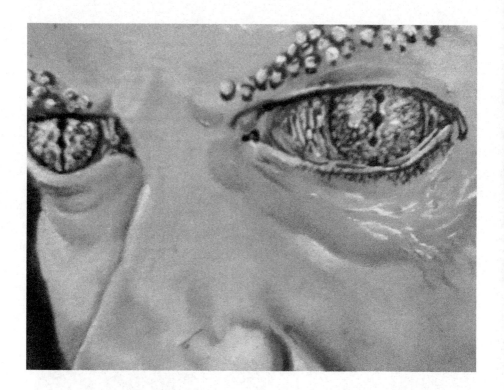

EVEN WHEN FLOPPING MAINTAIN PERSPECTIVE. KEEP A WARRIOR SENSE OF HUMOR AND EMIT AS MUCH GRACE AS YOU CAN MUSTER. VIEW THE EXPERIENCE AS AN EVOLUTION, REMEMBERING THAT LIFE TEACHES AND TRAINS YOU THROUGH CHALLENGE AND HARDSHIP. JUST LIKE A SNAKE YOUR MOLTING OF OLD SKIN TO NEWER TOUGHER VERSIONS CONTINUES ON UNTIL DEATH.

THE POWER OF FOCUS IN ANY ENDEAVOR CANNOT BE OVERSTATED.

CHAPTER THIRTY NINE

The Importance of: FOCUS.

Focus is one of the most important aspects of achievement.

Without mental, physical, emotional and spiritual focus, nothing GREAT can be achieved. Most folks spend their time on earth is a state of wandering numbness through the time-tested methods of alcohol, medication, ignorance and complacency. It is just easier to feel powerless to alter daily events by just "doing what we can" and "hoping for the best". Bullfritters!

This is your show. Your one and only opportunity to live your life to the fullest. With an indeterminable amount of time to live, you had better give it 100%. As Bull Meecham (Robert Duvall) says in 'The Great Santini' "Gobble up Life or it will gobble you up!" or "Get busy living or get busy dying!" from Stephen King's 'Shawshank Redemption'. There are many great quotes that give us an inkling on how we want to live…how we should live. But do we have the power and focus to actually live these ideal concepts? Martial arts training keys on FOCUS.

According to the definition in Wikipedia: Focus

Word: Fo-cus

Noun: The center of interest or activity.

Verb: Adapt to a prevailing level of light and become able to see clearly.

Noun Synonym: Center.

Verb Synonym: Concentrate.

In martial arts, as in most things, it takes focus to perceive reality, understand the situational material, separate truth from subterfuge, eliminate unrelated stimuli and execute proper action. There are other more subtle elements of focus, but these are the most easily explainable pieces. The lack of any of these parts of focus can render your action improper. Worst case scenario by missing all segments of focus:

You see a fire. You race to grab a bucket of water and race toward it. People are screaming. You glance up at the beautiful moon and stars then at a girl that looks like your sister. Why is she wearing a bikini? You trip in the sand and spill the water all over some folk's campfire. You are not welcomed to stay.

This time with focus.

You see a fire. (Perceive reality that it is a campfire not a wildfire)

No need to grab a bucket of water and race toward it. (Understand the situational material-its just a campfire on the beach and people are screaming because it's a party)

The fire is under control even though it has flared mightily when some idiot threw his grain alcohol drink on it. (Separate truth from subterfuge)

The moon and stars are beautiful but staring at them while running can cause you to trip over something or bump into someone walking in front of you. (Eliminate unrelated stimuli)

Cruise over to the bikini clad girl that is not your sister and say "Hi". (Execute proper action)

You are welcome to stay.

A quick funny story that has an absence of the important elements of focus just related:

Back at the University of Maryland in 1982, I needed to turn in a very late term paper to a fairly strict professor who would not be pleased to hear my story of poor academic focus. But being young, fearless and ignorant, I marched over to his office with the paper in my backpack and a pile of bullshit excuses in my head. Judging on his mood, I would select from the myriad of classic BS on why the paper was late, why he should accept it and why it was really not my fault that it was late. Like I said classic lack of focus led to the need for classic Bullashitta.

Arriving at the office, the obligatory "Be Back in 5 Minutes" torn notebook paper message greets me. Grrrr...now I am somehow indignant that he is making me wait. (I had not yet had enough martial arts training to understand "The Importance of: WAITING") So I sit down.

Seated directly across from the professor's glass office door, the kind where you can see your reflection but not directly inside unless the light is just right, I am running through my BS scenarios while glancing at the image in the glass and note, as all kids do, just how cool I look. With sunglasses, a tattered sleeveless Grateful Dead shirt and hanging hemp "Peace Sign" necklace on, my view of self was grand. So much so, that I stand and grab a pair of nunchucks from my backpack and start to whirl them adding to the oh-so-cool reflection. Why the Okinawan farm implement in my school bag you ask? Maybe the teacher wouldn't buy my BS story and I'd have to crack him. Just kidding, I had an Isshin Ryu Karate Club class after school that day. No matter. Back to my coolness.

As I am going through a traditional nunchucku set, which demands focus to keep the high speed cylinders of wood from moving off course and into your nuts or temple, thoughts of the BS re-enter my head. Just as I see the "Be Back in 5 Minutes" notice being pulled off the glass *from the inside,* the octagonal shaped weapon returns at blistering speed from between my legs to the exact center point of my sunglasses-adorned nose splitting them in half and cracking my forehead wide open.

As the pain registers, the office door opens and the professor stands there just staring at me as the remaining half of the sunglasses' twisted frame falls un-majestically to the floor joining the first half. With blood flowing, head spinning from the blow and embarrassment flushing over me, the professor asks stoically "Can I help you?"

"Ahhh yes professor, I uhhhhh…I need to talk to you about…ahhh medical attention."
I say for some reason trying to clear the cobwebs and focus.

"Yes. I was watching the whole thing through the glass from my desk. Forgot to take the sign down. So what it is you want to discuss besides your bleeding profusely all over my floor?"

"Can I sit down?" I inquire as nausea replaced embarrassment.

"Can you stop bleeding?" he says while handing me some napkins off the nearby coffee station.

"I think so." I say while trying to come up with the appropriate BS story for the situation. Guess there wasn't one. So holding my nose shut and with eyes still watering uncontrollably, I sit down and let him know that my paper is late.

He says he knows and that I could just have left a note. I think he was being funny like I didn't have to go through all the blood-letting to get his attention. Reaching with my free hand into the back pack I retrieve then hand him a manila folder with my name, paper title and bloody finger prints on the cover. The professor takes the paper and puts it on his desk without comment.

Getting up to leave I ask "Don't you want to know why it is late?"

"Not really. I have heard them all. Besides, I can tell that you have been pulling a few all-nighters getting caught up with school work." the professor states.
A bit confused, I am about to say something when the prof cuts me off with "Seems one of your friends drew eyeballs with a black marker on your eye lids. So as you were sitting here bleeding and with your eyes closed from the smack in the face, you were still staring at me. I figured that that was good enough for me. Thanks for not trying to sell me any BS!"

"No Sir." I end with while limping out the door still unbalanced from the sock to the sinus.

If you can't see that I violated every tenet of Focus in this story, I suggest you...ah focus.

Martial Arts masters have been writing and teaching the importance of focus for thousands of years. You can easily research the subject, apply what focus you do have and go train at a School that regularly preaches its importance in achieving martial arts power.

Here it is in a the proverbial nutshell:

Focus in the martial arts is an acquired ability to harness the most power, speed and transfer of energy generated by a specific technique and delivered with proper timing to the correct part of the opponents body. This focus is environmental, situational, transitional as well as, mental, physical, emotional and spiritual. All elements must come...well...into focus.

CHAPTER FORTY

The Importance of: EMRACING THE WEIRD.

In any great Life endeavor, it's pretty easy to act on and react to good things and bad things. The challenge comes in having the brass balls or steel breasts to Embrace The Weird. (ETW) To comprehend the complicated nature of understanding The Weird, just repeat the word several times. Weird. Weird. Weird. Weird isn't it? And that's just the word. Never mind the entity that includes the vast array of people, events, circumstances and situations that we face that are just plain weird. As a martial artist and a well-trained fighter, it is much easier to deal with the weird and experience where that strange entity takes you. Often you will have missed some great opportunities and experiences if you do not Embrace The Weird.

ETW 1: MEETING A GALLOPING GHOST.

I had just finished the breaking demonstration on the cover of this book. It was during an Octoberfest celebration in Brookfield, Il just down the street from Kenpo School. It was a glorious sunny day. The 10 slabs were pulverized to the Pink Floyd tune "Meddle" at full blast from huge speakers of the event's professional sound equipment. Man it felt intense as the only words in the song "One of These Days, I'm Gonna Cut You Into Little Pieces" blares out as I reign down a crushing Hammer of Thor strike accompanied by the pounding music. Cool, but not weird. Yet.

After finishing, and as students are cleaning up the concrete carnage, up walks a man dressed in all black. From his long black pony tail, full length black trench coat, black shoes and socks and black fingerless gloves to his black marble eyes, he was intense looking. It's only when he said he was "Looking for me" that it started getting a bit weird. WAITING for fangs to grow out of his pearl white teeth that matched the naturally white face skin of someone who attends daily meetings of The Undead or who knows the danger of sun-related skin cancers, I wondered how he was able to walk in the daytime.

In my usual "subtle as a hammer" inquiries, I ask plainly but seriously "Are you a vampire?" He chuckles "no" but didn't offer any explanation for the "Vampire Diaries" skin tone and attire.

Here is basically what was said next:

"My name is Doc Mack and I own a video game company called "Galloping Ghost". I'd like to talk to you about starring in a new video game that we are producing. Is it something that you'd be into?"

"Of course!" I say as usual before asking if it was an X-rated, testicle sucking vampire snuff film where everyone is killed while being filmed. Having just finished watching a similar video in the Nicolas Cage movie "8mm" but with families around, I keep the question for a later date. Doc thanks me for the time and says that he'd be in touch. When I start to explain where my dojo is down the street, he simply says "I know where to find you." Creepy if not yet weird. That was on a Saturday.

The following Tuesday, I am at Kenpo School feeding the snakes when Doc Mack appears, perhaps intending to feed.. There are wind chimes attached to the front door to alert me to a visitor. Seems Doc Mack has no need for chimed entry as he materializes in the doorway, with of course, a black briefcase. Asking him if he needed to "be invited in" I get a return stare that said enough with the vampire comments already.

As he rounds the circumference of the dojo mat, we shake hands and move into my office. He sits down and looks at me as in what appeared to be a final confirmation that I was indeed either the character for the video game or that I was the one to eat. Of course I keep this observation to myself. Doc reaches in a briefcase, which I thought might have had a stake and hammer within, but didn't know why he'd bring them to the meeting. Instead, he hands me a very detailed ink drawing of… me. Now it's off to Weird Town on a train with frequent stops in Bizarreville. I mean, did he sketch this from memory? Maybe take pictures like the spies on surveillance? When anyone that you met once appears 3 days later with a detailed drawing of you from memory, especially with Doc's all-black persona…well its weird. But such is life.

DOC MACK OF GALLOPING GHOST PRODUCTIONS AND LARGEST ARCADE IN US.

Replacing my initial "What the f**k?" reaction with "Wow. That's cool." I garnered a few more minutes of life. Putting out of my mind, at least temporarily, that he was a vampire, we got down to business. Doc explained that the recollection from the Octoberfest and his basic art skills (believe me they were not basic) rendered the image that I held in my hand. Man was it spooky accurate. He then handed me a second ink drawing that was labeled "Grant". Grant was basically me with an intense Viking-like outfit and a HUGE hammer. I immediately liked the Thor look and thought of several phallic jokes that I didn't share with Doc. To get a look at Grant go to www.conqueringlight.com, click on "Characters" and scroll down until you see the dude with the spiked hair and big hammer. Or just check out the black and white pic below. Conquering Light is the second installment and sequel to the "Dark Presence" arcade game series. It is based on a massive hand drawn comic book created by Doc. The guy is a genius. Then again, so were Jack The Ripper and Hannibal Lector. Stay focused Billy! Fo-cus.

ARCADE VIDEO GAME CHARACTER IN "CONQUERING LIGHT".

I spent the next 2 years shooting Conquering Light against the green screen. The ability to return to the exact same "foot print" outline placed on the floor at the beginning of a movement is unbelievably hard. With all my martial arts training and years spent doing KATA, where you are SUPPOSED to return to the exact spot where you started, it took many, many takes to get it right. It was so disconcerting to have completed a complex finishing move only to see my foot 1/4 inch out of the floor print. The slight "not quite" head shake of Doc Mack was as crushing as your Karate Teacher saying that you suck. It took awhile, but finally all Grant segments were filmed properly and post production continues. Maybe by the time you are reading this, you can go play Conquering Light and kick my ass repeatedly. I chew owl ass meat playing videogames. Probably why I don't write a book on the subject. But I can swing a big hammer for sure.

Doc Mack's Galloping Ghost Arcade is now the largest video game company of its kind in the US. Dark Presence and Conquering Light are technologically years ahead of the latest action fighting games available today. You'll see so when you play. I expect that when the much anticipated games are offered, I will gain a measure of financial benefit for all the hard work in bringing Grant to life. At the very least, I will be immortalized in some future kid's desk drawer by way of the Grant miniature that has been created as part of the game's promotional marketing. Or more likely blown to pieces like the nasty neighbor Sid in "toy Story". Either way. Cool.

MOLDING PROTOTYPE OF "GRANT" VIDEO GAME MINIATURE FIGURINE.

The point of this story?

If you don't have the guts to Embrace The Weird, you may not take the chance of working with a potential vampire genius or get to be a videogame superhero with your very own action figure. Well actually, it's not an action figure since it doesn't move, but you get the idea.

On the other hand, ETW can also lead you to be a vampire snack if things get really weird.

ETW 2: GAINING THE SECRET OF FIGHTING.

The sojourn to learn the best martial arts from the best Teachers was filled with ETW.

In allowing the Carlson Gracie Team move into the Downtown Kenpo School after their unexpected and unfair eviction from the health club space they rented, I realized that learning Brazilian Jiu Jitsu was an ongoing example of Embracing The Weird. We are talking about a totally different culture where Team members spoke mostly Portuguese and some of the BJJ Teachers didn't speak any English at all. At first the students were not very friendly and it made for many miscommunications as cultures clashed, but as Warriors that was ok. Some of the things that I had to get used to while hosting my Brothers from Brazil (BOB):

They never washed their gis. After a morning sweat drenched, exhaustive class, the Teachers would just take of the tops of their uniforms and stand them in the corner of the School. I didn't mis-speak. The gi tops were so crusty with non-washment that they would literally stand up by themselves as if on a storefront mannequin and dry that way. I tried to assimilate. Perhaps this was part of the training like the apparent need to have smashed up cauliflower ears to show BJJ prowess. I've wrestled since I was a pup and my ears still look fine. Thank you New Jersey state-mandated wrestling headgear for the current non-vegetable ear parts. Carlson Gracie Jr. once told me that some fighters in Brazil smash their ears intentionally to look tougher and more proficient. Who am I to dispute the ways of a country that gave us the "Girl from Iponema" and the bikini wax that we so admire? The American equivalent would be washing your Black Belt over and over again or tying it to the back bumper of a flatbed truck and dragging it down the street to look more experienced than you really are. There is only one way to get a properly tattered Black Belt. That is to put it on and tie it over and over again until it nearly disintegrates. Over the last 35 years, I have had three belts literally snap in my hands after the "10 millionth" time I donned it. Real is as real does.

Anyway, I, William J. Powell was the one person with the stones to explain to the top experts in BJJ that many students weren't quitting because they were pussies, but they couldn't stand the stench of being mounted and olfactory submitted by a death gi. This and the penchant for being late or not showing up to teach class are elements of which paying American students will not put up with. I held my tongue until after winning the 1999 East-West Submission Wrestling Championship in Peoria, IL in my first competition as a member of the vaunted Carlson Gracie Team. It was from that point that Carlson Gracie Jr. and I would spend a lot of time together outside the dojo and became great friends. At the time he lived in suburban Westchester and I would drive Jr. into Chicago to his School…in my School, nearly every day of the week. We would stop at a bagel shop for breakfast and coffee and talk about the Arts and America. He loved both.

During one such conversation, Jr. asked how he could keep more students and I mentioned the above "problems" with both the American view of acceptable hygiene and the need to be on time to teach class. CGJ was happy to hear the comments. At some point thereafter, the stench of Old School BJJ was replaced with the New School for America changes. Either way, you still went to sleep when the choke was set deep. You just had more pleasant dreams with the later.

In fact, more students did stay after these revelations.

Besides a non-stop embracing of new ideas and concepts, I learned The Secret of Brazilian Jiu Jitsu at a time when a "Don't ask. Don't tell." policy meant more than gays in the military. And it happened in a most weird way at the home opener of The Fighting Irish and the heated, longstanding Michigan-Notre Dame football rivalry. Go Ahead. Embrace The Weird.

As mentioned, CGJ and I had become friends and I invited him to join me and two other Warriors for the car ride down to South Bend, IN for the classic game. Not as familiar with the relevance of Notre Dame vs. Michigan in college football, I explained it would be the equivalent of questioning the importance of Carlson Gracie Jiu jitsu versus the other top academy in Brazil. He barked something in Portuguese and just stared out the window for a bit. After awhile, Jr. looked at me through the rear view mirror from the back seat and said. "Piraca, This will be a war then, Unh?" I replied with a smile and nodded a grin.

I was taking the great CGJ to a new first time experience and that was very cool indeed. Incidentally, "Piraca" means "penis" in Brazil. Often the Team would call me "Piracone" (Big Co*k of Brazil) You should have seen the many confused faces on the other Brazilian Jiu Jitsu teams as I was winning the 2001 Pan American Games in Orlando, FL while Jr. and Jeff Neal are coaching me screaming basically "Penis! You can do it! Yes Penis! Yes! Base yourself Penis! Penis watch the arm bar! Then you will win! Yes. Penis. Yes! You will win now Penis!"

And I did.

In fact, there is a new BJJ technique based on the previously heretical move of EZEKIAL choke when you are stuck in the HALF GUARD. After winning the Pan Ams, the technique "Piraca" is now taught in Brazil as an effective submission from the Half Guard. First a non-moving video game action figure and now a technique named after me. Groovy Unh? Ossssssssssssssss.

Ok. You have suffered long enough. How did I get the secret to a feared, secret martial art at a time when it was most feared and most secret? Alcohol. Here is what happened.

When we arrived in South Bend in record time courtesy of my fire red 1999 Pontiac Firebird Formula, we were stoked. Jr. seemed amused by all the drinking and hot young co-eds racing around the Notre Dame campus. I mentioned to him this was another reason for clean gis.

"No lie Piraca!" he said in return.

As we made our way to the stadium and finishing the last of a few tailgating beers that stowed nicely in the Formula's trunk, we get to the gate and are waiting in line to enter. One of the security guards recognizes CGJ and races over to introduce himself. After some indiscernible Portuguese dialog between them, Jr. says "Come Piraca, we will get good treatment."

And we did.

Not only were we allowed in for pre-pre game warm ups where the players aren't even in uniform yet, we were ushered to four "special seats" near the field that were way better than the nosebleeds that I had in my pocket. They didn't even take our tickets! So, as the security dude is calling on his radio and several more fans of CGJ arrive, we are told that we (he) is to be VIP guests of Notre Dame at midfield as the teams are racing onto the field at game time. National TV audience and we would be standing on the knuckles of The Fighting Irish symbol's lead fist in the middle of the field. Embracing The Weird or what?

So there we are. I don't think Jr. had any idea how rare this was. In Brazil it probably happens at soccer matches and surfer competitions all the time. Not here. Not Notre Dame-Michigan in the Heartland of America. This relatively small human with big time family legend and incredible skills and personality was at home even in the most odd, unfamiliar circumstances. Brazilian Jiu Jitsu had not only made its way to victory in the UFC's Octagon, but gained relevance on the Midwest's Grid Iron. Way to cool for words, but I am doing my best to relate the quintessence of the martial arts in life. This is when ordinary daily life events take on extraordinary meaning and mind blowing experience.

Before going down to the field for the teams entry from the tunnel, Jr. and I sat and talked about Brazilian Jiu Jitsu. After awhile, CGJ asked if we can get beer in the stadium and I said no since it was a college game. While not disappointed, I could see him scanning the crowd for a fellow Brazilian that he would probably ask to go find him some beer. No need I assured Jr. and then reached down my pants to retrieve two of four plastic sandwich bags with zip lock tops that were rolled up, tucked under my meat and held a total of a quart of vodka. While warm and slightly creepy on delivery, Jr. watched as I poured the contents of a single bag into his large ND plastic soda cup mixing it with the icy pop. He smiled as I did the same.

So we sat and drank vodka and coke for about 45 minutes during the pre-game warm ups. After awhile, CGJ asked if there were any more "Piraca piraca bags". I pulled out a fresh warm rolled up sack of booze and we repeated the exercise once again. By the time that we were asked by the security guys to follow them onto the field, we were feeling no pain. Out of the blue, I say to the legendary Carlson Gracie Jr. "So what is the secret of Gracie Jiu Jitsu?" He looked at me for a bit then put down his cup and crossed his hands, palm up at the wrists. He then made a soft pinching motion with both hands that simulated grabbing the sleeves of an opponent's gi. Then ever so slowly, he pulled his hands back to his sides uncrossing his arms as he did so. Jr. smiled as I understood when he said "Piraca, this is the secret of our Jiu Jitsu." Holy Sh*t I thought.

As the importance of what I just witnessed was sinking in, the Brazilian security guards asked us to follow them onto the field. They escorted us onto the hallowed turf of the Notre Dame field where legends like Knute Rockne, Johnny Lujack, George Gipp, Paul Hornung and Joe Montana once played. It was intense and the four of us just stood there on The Irishman's knuckles as the Michigan Wolverines, who that year would win the 1997 National Championship, came bursting out of the tunnel with the Big Blue "M" flag leading the way. We may be stampeded to death by the many tons of huge armored humans running directly at us. The flag tip cracks me in the face during the fly by and some Michigan players shout at me "Don't Touch The Flag!" It seems that it was considered bad luck to do so.

Wish that I could have predicted that it was there championship year and countered with a snappy comeback on luck. Then out rushes Notre Dame and the same potential to be squished arises. We survive and just take in the amazingly odd set of weird circumstances that led us to this very "once in a lifetime" moment. We took it all in and as the team captains were called to the center for the coin toss and we were escorted back to our seats.

Embrace The Weird. You will never know where it will take you, what you may learn and the incredible experience it may provide.

ETW 3: PIZZA DEATH THREATS.

One of my Teachers (name withheld for security reasons) was in town to watch a Full Contact Karate World Championship bout between then champion Don The Dragon Wilson and the challenger M. "The Punisher" P. "Punisher" was a well known fighter in his own right. But Don

Wilson was famous in movies and with numerous Karate titles, including then the Defending World Champion, and was the heavy favorite. Seems someone forgot to tell "The Punisher" though, as he soundly defeated "The Dragon" to take the title.

The post fight party took on a drastically different look as the "Congrats Dragon!" banners were taken down and wine bottles replaced by real Polish Vodka with non-English labels. There was a bottle spaced every 2 feet along the length of the 30 ft table. That's one bottle of vodka for every four seats. As a gentleman seated across from me said "In Poland, when we crack open a bottle it is to be finished." So you can imagine the incredible festivity surrounding the new champion's victory party. Well into the party and with the Champ seated at the far head of the table, my Teacher gets up and walks over, introduces himself to the Champ and sits down for a conversation. I am watching intently in between vodka shots with my new friend from Warsaw and then it happened.

As my Teacher is speaking, in walk three guys in black suits, cell phones hanging from their hips and "Jimmy The Greek" type bling in the form of large gold chains and pendants hanging from their necks. They appeared to interrupt the conversation I was watching from a distance as they ignored my Teacher and started talking directly to the Champ. Teacher leapt up out of his chair and in one simultaneous vertical and horizontal movement slapped the closest suited man across the face so hard that his gold pendant shot up to smash him in the head. He crumpled to the floor as his cell phone flew across the room and broke into pieces. I heard the slapped say "You are dead!" as the other two picked him up ushered him out of the room. Teacher sat back down and finished his talk with the Champ. Afterward he came down to where I was sitting and asked if I was ready to go. Guess Teacher had finished his business for the day.

When we got into the car and with no explanation offered, I asked:

"What the f*ck happened back there?"

"I was talking to the Champ and those guys just walked up and interrupted us." They apparently wanted to talk with him, but didn't wait their turn." he says.

"Then what happened?" as I glance over knowing what happened next.

"Then I say 'Excuse me, I am talking to the Champ." Teacher explains.

"Do you know who I am?" asks the biggest suited guy apparently in a threatening manner.

"Yes I do. You are the guy with the stinging right cheek!" and I cracked him says Teacher.

"Yeah, I saw that." As the conversation turns to a new subject I drive Teacher to his hotel.

If the story ended here, it would not have made the selective cut of stories explaining the Importance of Embracing The Weird. Since it is here, more happened. Much, much more. The next day, I was to pick up Teacher at his hotel since he was going to spend the last few days of his trip in my high rise condo in downtown Chicago. As I call his room to let him know that I was on my way, I get a personalized voicemail on the hotel message system:

"Hi. This is "Teacher" Sorry I missed your call. I have checked out but will be staying at my friend Billy Powell's place at 1636 North Wells Street in Chicago. You call me on his home phone 312-951-0771 until I fly back to New York on Friday night. Talk to you soon" Beep.

I hung up thinking that the information was a bit detailed but didn't know the trouble it was about to cause. Not long after Teacher arrived at my dwelling did the calls start. "We are looking for 'Teacher'. (Actually they mispronounced his name in every subsequent call) The calls came every half hour or so and became more and more threatening. Then came the start of the pizza deliveries. We had twenty different deliveries of various numbers of pizzas from a variety of restaurants in the City over the two days the Teacher stayed. Now being Italian, and not particularly afraid of pizzas, it was the calls from the downstairs doorman announcing the deliveries by different men in suits and bling that had me a bit concerned.

Kinda like the Greek tradition of showing up at your door in tuxedoes with baseball bats to let you know that you really pissed someone off. It appears that Teacher not only pissed someone off, but he brought the whole urinal trough to my home.

Obviously, my wife was concerned as she didn't order any pizza and had a bit of negative attitude regarding the Teacher since our past escapes usually ended up getting us all in trouble. Trying to shield her from the situation Teacher and I analyzed the threat and subsequent moves.

Teacher was unconcerned and he told me that if anyone is really going to kill you "They don't send pizzas first." It made sense to me. Then again I hadn't slapped anybody in a suit recently. So with my wife arguing that the best way to get rid of the problem was to get rid of the problem…i.e. Teacher, I am trying to think of an alternative. It was not feasible to boot my Teacher from the condo any more than it was possible to ignore the growing annoyance and fear building in my wife by keeping her in the dark. As the pizza deliveries, doorman calls and death threat phone messages continue and with Bonnie yelling at me for Teacher to leave. I needed some alone time to think. I went into the back bathroom in the master bedroom and sat on the toilet, lid shut. I turned on the radio and "Sweet Home Alabama" was playing on it. At the beginning they say "Turn it up!" so I did. As the tune progressed, I wondered what Rambo,

Terminator protector Kyle Reese or Dirty Harry would do. It's funny that when you don't have any actual experience in a particular situation, your mind will search any and all compartments to assist in a plan including movies, books and what friends have said.

I was a Warrior and needed a Warrior Plan. Movie scenes from "Cobra" "First Blood" and "Heartbreak Ridge" played non stop in my mind. As my wife opens the bathroom door, I am loading my Glock 45 pistol and have a fully prepped Mossberg Pump 12 gauge shotgun leaning against the toilet paper roller. Blue Oyster Cult's "Don't Fear The Reaper" has replaced Skynyrd as the War Song Of Choice. (WSOC) I was going to protect my family even if I was in over my head. No choice.

"Ah Honey...What's going on?" Bonnie asks with a look of concern.

I explain that the Teacher had slapped a man that was part of a larger group and perhaps he was pissed off and that is the reason for all the brew-ha-ha. She asks what we are going to do and I nod at the shotgun and say "Fight back!" She closes the door slowly while shaking her head and I know she was going to give Teacher an earful.

And she did.

Teacher finally left without incident, but what a pain in the ass it is to have to look under your car for a bomb or the rear view mirror to see who may be following you. I drove Bonnie to work every day after the bomb scan and insisted that she carried her "Lady Smith" .38 in her purse. I bolstered my confidence with a holstered Smith & Wesson 686 chambered in .357 magnum load for added intimidation value. Magnum force helped Dirty Harry and it would help me. Incidentally, that was the last time that the Teacher visited me in Chicago. Though we do talk on the phone, the topic of Chicago's legendary deep dish pizza never arises in those conversations. Martial Note: Sometimes Life leaves you in a desperate, fearful situation that you are not familiar with and asks you to make do. Either curl up in fear, surrender to the enemy and hope for mercy or prepare for Death and be ready to smash back hard.

So to conclude the chapter, while Embracing The Weird can seem treacherous and appear dangerous, for The Brave it is a path that just unfolds naturally. Simply follow it, be prepared for anything and enjoy the netherworld experiences and lessons that only come your way by Embracing The Weird.

EMBRACING THE WEIRD GUARANTEES YOU LIFE WILL BE A HECK OF A RIDE.

PAIN, DISCOMFORT, EMBARRASSMENT AND CLEAR DEFEAT LEAVE IMPRINTS.

CHAPTER FORTY ONE

The Importance of: LEAVING AN EMOTIONAL IMPRINT ON THE ENEMY.

An Emotional Imprint is the neurological component of a memory.

Similar to a feeling of euphoria and well being when you think of a pleasant experience or the dread, impending doom and physiological reactions when the thought attached to a memory is negative. It can manifest in any number of forms physically, mentally and emotionally.

In my case, when a strong past negative experience enters my consciousness, I involuntarily make a hand gesture in the form of a fist, chop or claw. The mental words that accompany the automatic hand gesture is "Ok. Then let's fight!" Don't ask me why, it's just the result of an Emotional Imprint that one or more past experiences have ingrained in me. That combined physical and mental reaction is usually the extent of the involuntary actions. Once I realize that negative thoughts are taking a shot at control, I counter with the powerful Hindu mantra "Neti. Neti. Neti." This translates to "I am not that thought. I am not this thought thinking about that thought. I am not thought." Usually that is enough to change mental direction and the return of physiological body systems to normal. If left unchecked, Emotional Imprints will dictate your mood, demeanor and view of Life. Don't let that happen. As the great Bruce Lee once said;

"Negative thoughts are the weeds that strangle confidence."

When involved in a fight, YOU MUST LEAVE AN EMOTIONAL IMPRINT ON THE ENEMY. That was written in BIG LETTERS to convey the importance of doing so. If you are in a confrontation and let's say you knock your adversary out with a big right hand to the face. Since you are a trained fighter, this is not all that hard to imagine. If you win a fight in this manner, you may have *prevailed in your mind.* I mean it seems pretty clear, two humans voluntarily engage in combat, one wins, one loses or it's a draw. So if you knock them out cold you win right? Maybe.

If the punch was sufficient to leave the Emotional Imprint of Defeat *in the opponent's mind,* then yes, the fight is over and you have won. The Emotional Imprint on the loser will be sufficient that he will remember his loss, have the mental and physiological reactions to that defeat and its association with you. There is a good chance that that is the end of it. Maybe. But, if the knock out was the result of a "lucky punch" in the mind of the foe, it did not leave the proper Emotional Imprint and the fight is not over. Every time you come in contact with that person, the animosity remains, the conflict is unresolved and the chance for a flare up probable. To leave the correct Emotional Imprint, the victory must be so decisive, so clear cut and so devastating to his mind, body and spirit that you have left no doubt about the outcome of this or any further encounters. Only in this manner can you achieve victory and hopefully a lasting peace.

Conflict resolution of this type also has an effect on any future would-be adversaries who are there at the time. Swift, effective and absolute defeat of another "equally matched" human also leaves a less painful, but no less significant Emotional Imprint on all those present.

From "The 48 Laws of Power"…

CRUSH YOUR ENEMY TOTALLY

"All Great Leaders Know That A Feared Enemy Must Be Crushed Completely.
Sometimes They Have Learned This The Hard Way.
If One Ember Is Left Alight, No Matter How Dimly It Smolders,
A Fire Will Eventually Break Out.
More Is Lost Through Stopping Half Way Than Through Total Annihilation:
The Enemy Will Recover, And Will Seek Revenge.
Crush Him, Not Only In Body But In Spirit."

You only need to stick a paperclip in a light socket once and you know what will happen.

EAGLES BEAK- MUSCULAR, SKELETAL AND NERVOUS SYSTEM STRIKES.

SIR... PLEASE STOP BOTHERING ME AND SIT DOWN.

CHAPTER FORTY TWO

The Importance of: FIGHTING ONE FIGHT PER FIGHT.

Fighting hurts.

The more times you fight, the more likely you are to get hurt. The only reason people fight is that think they have something to gain. This could be perceived as the need to gain respect, honor, revenge, money or more nobly to defend principle, yourself or others. Some say there's no reason to fight. This is said mostly by those who can not. Humans are born to fight. We are born into this world fighting for air, then food, then love, then security, then knowledge, then achievement, then health, then preparation for a fearless death. Americans are taught from the beginning "Fight for what's right!" "Go Trojans! Fight! Fight! Fight!" "You've got to fight off that cold!" "They fought back from 30 points down!" "Fight the Good Fight!" And so on.

The problem with this overemphasis on fighting as a good thing is that often it ends up being a bad thing. You give a whooping to a jerk that clearly deserves it and the crowd is cheering. Ok. Then the guy falls and cracks his head and he's dead or paralyzed. The cheering stops and you are now in deep sh*t. Hopefully it was in self defense and not just two guys in an agreed upon fight. In Illinois the law states that you do not have a Duty to Retreat but, as a trained fighter and martial artist, you had better have a good reason why you didn't. If not, you are in trouble. Now I know we covered the "Better tried by 12 than carried by 6" concept and its true. But be aware that the cost in legal fees, time spent in jail, where there are plenty of folks to fight with, means you gained nothing.

While it's tempting to seal the face of the drunken dickhead, resist fighting unless you are truly in danger. Then fighting in that case will be for a most important gain-your safety, continuing good health and well-being.

In terms of Fighting One Fight Per Fight think of it this way:

A fight is a physical, mental and spiritual conflict, in this case, between two people. It has a prelude, a beginning, a contested period, an end and an aftermath. You are facing off with an opponent and both are in a fighting posture. Diplomacy is over. (Prelude) Your foe throws a front kick toward your gut (Beginning) you step back out of the way, maybe intercept part of his foot with a downward block (Contested period) and you both reset to fighting posture. (Where is the End? Where is the Aftermath?) The battle is not over. That's one fight and it was a draw.

You reengage and start the fight and the process all over. No winner after the contested period? Reset to fighting posture and that's Fight Number 2. More engagements, more exchanges of blows and counter strikes, no winner...that's more fights. More chances to get hurt or killed.

We want to FIGHT ONE FIGHT PER FIGHT!

Let's revisit the first fight. You square off with your opponent. He attacks with a front kick to your gut. This time instead of moving backward, you sidestep forward to a 45 degree angle and use a looping downward block (SWEEPING SERVANT for Kenpo folks) to deflect the kick past as you move forward into Darkness. Your barrage of fast, effective, well placed, well timed strikes COMING FROM DARKNESS cuts the opponent down. You make sure he is completely crushed, and then you call off the dogs and assess the situation. (The End and the Aftermath) The fight is over and you did so in a single fight. That means there is less chance of getting hurt, injured or killed. Mission accomplished without a hospital visit.

An example that underscores the importance of this concept on a grand scale in terms of number of people that might have been injured if there had been more than one fight. Preakness Stakes again. During "Wrestle You for $10" college days, I mentioned the huge infield party at Pimilico Raceway in Baltimore, MD that hosts the 2nd leg of Horse Racings Triple Crown. Between the entrance to the track and the open space of the massive infield, there is a long concrete tunnel that party-goers need to travel through to enter and exit. Not that hard going in, but very scary coming out with nearly 100,000 others who are drunk, stoned, tripping or just spatially ignorant.

The tunnel is perhaps 200 feet long but seems a lot longer when packed with people smashed together so tight that its hard to breath. It's ok as long as you are moving in unison like a long snake, but any slowdown of the flow sends a wave of fear and panicked pushing through the masses inside. If someone were to fall, it is quite possible that they could be trampled to death. It is that dangerous and a real concern even for the incredibly wasted.

While walking with a few buddies toward the tunnel after an incredibly profitable day for CaPoop Enterprises, its starting to get tight. The tunnel entrance is a wall of people and we are about to be a part of it. You have to kinda Zen-out and just go with the flow as if it's no big thing. About 20 feet from the wall of waiting to enter waste-products, some redneck behind me thinks it appropriate to pour his beer down the funnel of my shoulder-draped, leather-slung, hand-made beer bong. The last of the unsold great "Unofficial Official CaPoop Beer Bongs-Get Yours For Only $35" that we sold there. Fortunately for me and for him, the beer was warm.

As I turned to look at the offender, it becomes apparent that he is hammered and has at least two equally drunk friends with him and they think that this is so funny. I however did not.

481

Martial Note: When situations like this arise, you have to look at the whole picture from above, like a GPS street map. In having this type of situational awareness, you have a better chance of right action. Wrong action, in this case "tunnel-vision" could have disastrous results. The main concern is the panic that would start if the fight carried on into the tunnel and people could get seriously hurt or killed. As well, if I turn and fight, my friends and the offender's friends will get involved and that would surely create an uncontrollable problem due to the conflagration's proximity to the tunnel entrance. 11 people had been trampled to death at The Who concert in Cincinnati just six months earlier. It poked my mind as a key factor in the coming conflict.

With all the up to the millisecond data programmed into a Warrior's Mind, I Take Action.

Quickly spinning in place to face Warm Beer Pourer (WBP) I simultaneously grab his trachea and groin with both hands and squeeze hard. (ATTACKING CIRCLE) I stare deep into his soul as his life and any future children's lives hang in the balance…of my hands. Squeezing his jeans so hard that I felt testicle meat squishing out between the fingers of my clenched fist, I was sure he would throw up. And of course he did. Good thing that I had him by the throat and twisted his head so the puke jet could be directed laterally onto his nearest friend who was walking slightly ahead of WBP. After the dual squeeze and vomit deflection, I immediately let go of both and spin back in place to begin my walk forward as if nothing had happened. This had several effects:

1) There was now a blockage of Homo sapiens BEHIND a redneck wall created by the WBP puke show going on just before the filing cow-to-slaughter-style into the tunnel started. The crowd flow behind them was still in a wide open area and the stoppage did not incite any panic.

2) The brief time it took to freeze Warm Beer Pourer and Friends in place that created the

Redneck Wall also allowed more space for the people directly in front of us to enter the tunnel without the pressure of folks pushing them from behind. Therefore, they were not pressing anyone in front of them helping the whole chunk of tunnel travelers to enjoy a more civilized procession out of the infield care of moi. There was less "moo-ing" than normal for the tunnel.

3) My friends are huge Maryland Rednecks and had they noticed me in a fight, they would have jumped in. That would only have added to the problem. As it were, they walked oblivious of the Real Death Moment (RDM) that had just occurred behind them a second earlier and walk care-free toward the tunnel. The return from vampire transport speed to regular human motion may have seemed to them like the "glitch" from the "Matrix", but their beer buzz quickly neutralized the anomaly.

4) The WBP group gave us a wide birth as we entered the tunnel. I'll bet there was at least 30 feet of space between the Redneck Wall and our group and another 20 foot gap between us and the last folks entering the tunnel ahead. We literally walked through the tunnel, the three of us, basically alone. When we got to the far side, my friends commented how easy it was to get out. I told them what happened and they were pissed at me for not letting them know about the WBP trouble. Of course, being huge grits, they wanted to wait for the warm beer pouring boys to exit. Since only I knew who the bad people were and while faking a search for the WBP crew, they walked without comment right past us and my "Deliverance" posse.

After saying "No, let's go!" they realized that no brawling would take place and jumped on me executing an old fashioned Charlie horse-infused, pile on "ass-beating". Point well taken. The next time I am faced with a situation that could get any of my friends hurt of a large group of people trampled, I'll be sure to yell "FIGHT!" so they can get some. Not.

Martial Note: The TRACHEA GRAB is one of the most psychologically disruptive, emotional imprint leaving self defense techniques there is. Here is why. When you aggressively, skillfully and purposely grab a person by the throat it does several things automatically.

It shows that you are not kidding. No human wants their throat touched by an aggressor. The fact that you did so with such unexpected ease is terrifying at the most primordial level. It is the way large cats have killed antelope in the Savannah since the dawn of time. There is a reason that hearing "You will be hung by the neck until dead" is such a pants pissing verdict from the court. I'd rather be shot by a firing squad or have a little taken off the top with the guillotine.

Since it is a basic human instinct to survive, you must let go as soon as the grab is secured and the slight energy transferred so that it vibrates the floating bone in the foe's throat. If you hold on to long, the opponent's natural instinct will be to fight back in any way possible to survive. Simultaneously, the neck and throat muscles tense up in a response to the attack in a delayed fashion restricting breathing. These reactions, combined with the sheer dread of having your life taken from you and given back in a microsecond, gives the technique such power. You want to leave the energy with him in the form of fear and not redirected to self preservation because you have him by the throat. You do not have to let go of the Trachea Grab if it is a life and death situation and your intent is to kill. Then again, if you want a quicker, less psychologically involved technique, you might as well use a HALF FIST strike to the windpipe and end it there.

So it is paramount to your health and safety that you refrain from fighting. If you have to fight, make it a one time thing and win decisively. Be sure his attack is thwarted, his anger and aggression nullified as his will to fight crushed. In other words...Fight One Fight Per Fight.

Capish?

FORGIVE YOURSELF YOUR HUMAN FAILINGS, SHORTCOMINGS, FAILURES AND FEARS. IF NECESSARY RAM A SHARP THREE PRONGED TIGER FORK UP THE ASS OF ANYONE THAT GETS IN THE WAY OF YOUR GOD-GIVEN RIGHT TO LIVE, LEARN AND GROW.

CHAPTER FORTY THREE

The Importance of: FORGIVING THE ENEMY AND YOURSELF.

It is important to forgive.

Great Warriors know to never underestimate the enemy by assuming away his/her capabilities. Regular folk should be aware of this too. Just like the classic comic book superheroes that we loved growing up and still do today, where each was imbued with certain powers and a few clear weaknesses. Wanna fist fight with Superman? Maybe if you had some Kryptonite bracelets on. Could you defeat Iron Man in anything? Sure if it's a swimming race and his feet couldn't touch bottom. No jet propulsion from his hand and feet of course. The Hulk? Only if you had a Doctorate or Masters Degree in Anger Management. Even then it's still a maybe. We are strong relative to a house cat, but weak compared to a gorilla. Get over it. There will always be some one stronger, faster, smarter and more skilled than you. Hopefully not all in the same person confronting you. Know that rarely do Warriors in peacetime ever get into confrontations of the deadly kind. Warriors know their kind and unless blinded by rage, alcohol or as a matter of honor will they engage.

Martial Note: Don't even take away the capabilities of a house cat. They may run across your face while you are sleeping and paw leap scratch your cornea without warning. Feed them, love them and keep the litter box clean. Seems like they are always planning some type of attack. As well, if happen upon a feral cat stuck in a bush and it growls at me while reaching in, I will retreat. Not because I can't take the cat. I am bigger, stronger, smarter and more skilled, but still don't want to deal with the fury of a hissing, clawing, biting cat.

Back to the strength and weakness paradigm and its inevitable need for forgiveness. The point is, even the most powerful superheroes in our minds or in mythology had innate strengths and defined weaknesses. Achilles' Heel anyone? I'll bet the Great Warrior Hector would have liked to have known that bit of information before being slain by the invincible Achilles and having his body dragged behind a chariot for miles.

Every one has strengths and weaknesses. Even you. Forgive your weakness and gain strength. So what do we strengthen? How do we eliminate weakness? How do we know our true strengths and weaknesses outside the confines of our own mind and image of self? Simply live. Live, learn, experience and the world will show you both. Then simply strengthen your strengths and limit or eliminate your weaknesses.

But to do this, you must first Forgive Yourself.

Forgive yourself for the human condition which is fraught with frailties and fallibility. Knowing that we are going to age, sicken and die is as important to the modern man as it was to the ancients. No matter what we do or how much we do it "Death For Us All!" Only when you truly grasp the absoluteness of this reality will you be ready to really live. Only then will getting stronger and less weak have any real meaning in your life. Reality Teaches Relativity. (RTR)

No matter how much weight you can lift, how many people you can defeat in a fight, how much education you have amassed or how healthy your lifestyle, it will not extend your life one bit longer than The Reaper dictates. Absorb this statement, understand it completely, and ingrain it into your very core and you will live a good life. Of course, we could build a bomb shelter with reinforced concrete and steel deep underground, with only one door and a .50 caliber machine gun pointed there while you sit in a chair directly behind it. Will you live any longer? No.

Is it really living at all? Will you be safe from the home intruder but succumb to the cancer growing in your stomach? What price your perceived safety while living the life of a ground hog versus the risks and joys of living life to the fullest keenly aware of your fate is already determined? It does not matter whether you believe in fate or not. I guarantee you that you will not live one moment longer when you die.

The Way of The Warrior Is Death. The Way of Love Is Life. Train Hard and You Can Find Both.

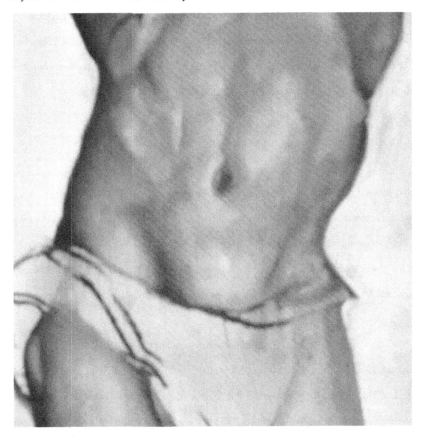

LOVE, FAITH AND THE BELIEF THAT THERE IS SOMETHING ON THE OTHER SIDE GIVES PEOPLE THE HOPE THAT BY BEING A GOOD PERSON YOU WILL GET THERE. BE A GOOD HUMAN BEING BECAUSE IT'S THE RIGHT THING TO DO AND LIVE IN LOVE.

The reason the Samurai were so effective in battle is that Bushido (Way of the Warrior) was an unshakeable core belief with the sword the extension of their very existence. They knew it was possible to meet a superior samurai in battle at any moment, so they had to BE PREPARED TO DIE in order to have the best chance of LIVING. No thought of victory and defeat, no regret or anxiety about the future. Just that one moment of truth where they could be all that they were trained to be and exercise the birthright of the samurai class; TO BE OF WAR! They were Warriors in the Moment and struck down the enemy without thought, self consciousness or fear of death. Or they were slain in that very same moment and were unconcerned. Jumbo.

As we acknowledge our inherent human failings and the incredible abilities to impact life during a short, minuscule existence, it is possible to Achieve Glory and Immortality by Creating Greatness. Some humans become immortalized by living a life that creates something great and transcends their personal death to live on. Inventors, Artists, Soldiers, Warriors, etc. do this.

How do we Create Greatness?

We start by Forgiving The Enemy.

It has been said that we are our own worst enemy. Probably true as Kenpo School is adorned with wise sayings and statements of power to strengthen us during times of trouble. Self help books make millions by talking to this concept and motivational speakers, preachers and religions also help us to "be strong". I like to say that the best self help is to help yourself.

"Dance with the Demons of Your Own Folly" written by moi hangs above the office at PWOK.

Now, the enemy that is not within lies outside of us in the form of other forces. For the scope of this book, we'll just discuss the human component as the enemy. That way, I am less likely to be blown up by a fanatical religious group that takes issue with my view of Theology.

Clearly, the most obvious human enemy is the one that physically attacks you. Be it a bar room fight, a mugger on the street or an intruder in your home at night. These enemies can be forgiven, but only after they are soundly defeated, successfully repulsed or shot dead.

Why forgive the vanquished?

Because if you don't, you will carry the negative emotional imprint of the enemy's pain and suffering with you long after the blows have ceased. Their defeat can reverberate in many ways in you. Did I have to fight? Why did he want to fight me? Didn't I look tough enough? Did I do something to provoke his anger? Did I use too much force? I feel guilty that I hurt him. Maybe he needed money for food. Was he was just drunk. Maybe his mom is sick. I should have been able to talk my way out of the situation. And so on. All these thoughts will eat at your soul, gnaw at your mind and drag on your heart. It may also affect how you react to the next confrontation and that moment of uncertainty could usher in your defeat, injury or death.

So forgive the enemy for his human frailties just as you have forgiven your own.
Then, with love in your heart and forgiveness in your mind, soundly bash, thrash and smash the enemy. Do so without anger, vindictiveness or malice. But leave no doubt that you are the victor, he the vanquished and then forgive both. Then move forward and away bereft the karma that this event in your life could have generated.

It takes great strength to forgive. Training provides great strength. So train to forgive.

SIFU STEVE BANKE WHO HAS TRAINED WITH ME SINCE HE WAS A KID PASSES THE KNOWLEDGE ON TO A YOUNG STUDENT THAT STARTED AT HIS AGE AND NOW PASSES ON WHAT HE HAS LEARNED TO OTHERS IN COLLEGE..

CHAPTER FORTY FOUR

The Importance of: NOT SAVING THE WORLD.

The world is a big place.

Most likely you alone will not be able to save it. Not even your little piece of it. Why? The world does not want to be saved and therefore its a waste of your limited time on Earth attempting to. Now that does not mean that we shouldn't want to AFFECT, IMPACT and INFLUENCE our world or any part of it. Truth is we can not do it alone. Most that have tried have been assassinated, ruined or otherwise silenced in their ambitious attempts at change. But we should be inspired by their grand ideals, empowered by their strength and not fearful of their ultimate sacrifice. Death for us all, so spend your time alive in a worthy manner. Worth.

"You are Worthy in as much as you are held Worthy by those you consider Worthy." -unknown

While this book is in no way as important as many others, it is relevant. The relevance is in the fact that training in the martial arts can affect, impact and influence life events through the learned ABILITY TO TAKE ACTION. (ATTA) Just as a pebble dropped in a still pond creates ripples that vibrate throughout the world, Right Action in the form of ATTA can save the life of a child who one day may invent the cure for all cancers. If you had not acted and he/she died, the ripple of non-invention would alter the course millions of people's lives. The ramifications of this truth are mind-bending.

In the martial arts as in any great endeavor, the ability to pass on any body of knowledge that is helpful to mankind is worthy of passing on. From the students that I taught as 5 year old children who grew strong, self confident and motivated to become stellar humans doing great things as adults, to the late life beginner who wants to stay healthy and learn a strength for death, it makes me worthy, relevant and a world changer. Not so much in what I alone have done but rather what those whom I've taught have done and will do. When they teach what I taught them to their children and it prevents them from being bullied 50 years from now, was my life not then Worthy? Did the thousands of students taught over the past 35 years that then influenced others, created new ideas, inventions or save other's lives mean that what I have done is immortalized? Will my life's ambition and the action it had wrought carry on long after I am corpse bones? Yes. I like to think that my life was a big f'n pebble in a large-ass pond. Weird pond however.

So, if what you do in the speck of time you are on Earth is worthy and those which you have influenced for the better continue the ripple, you will have changed the world if not saving it.

One of my Black Belts, Doug E. Doug joined the Peace Corps and traveled to Tonga on the other side of the globe. Tonga was the first place that the sun rose to usher in the new millennium. So on January 1st 2000, my Kenpo was being taught to the natives at sunrise on the sandy beach in Tonga. He yelled "Jumbo Sensei!" and I swear I heard it from half the world away.

Hey. Hey. Ripple me.

Sensei Al Fish is a Teacher at PWOK. During the September 11, 2001 attacks, his wife was a flight attendant on a plane that was in the air at the time, but not one of the hijacked aircraft. Shortly after her safe return to Chicago, Sensei Al informed me that he was going to take the fight to the enemy wherever they be. The US Army Rangers were happy to provide the training and the airplane ride. But he would have to get to the ground on his own as an elite Paratrooper. In his first jump, he took two of the silver coins with his unit's insignia in relief on them. One for him and one for me. I am honored and cherish it to this day. He also brought me back some sand as part of the lightening fast spearhead invasion force in Iraq.

SENSEI AL FISH AND SNIPER RIFLE WITH THE US ARMY ON THE ROAD TO BAGHDAD.

Sensei Al was one of the first combat veterans of Operation Iraqi Freedom to return home in our area. After introducing him to the Mayor of Brookfield, he rode in desert fatigues atop a truck during the PWOK procession at the annual July 4th parade. He received standing ovations from the masses of town folk that lined the streets for miles. PWOK was very proud of his valor in combat. We also took first place for our "Combat Float" in the parade. Sensei Al has several great stories about using our Way of Kenpo system to kick various ass, both enemy and allied in the deserts of Iraq and Kuwait. This included his victory in a 50 man "Toughest Soldier" tournament while stationed in Germany after his part in the War. The stories are great and usually start out with "My Teacher, this lil f*ck in Chicago is just..." I'll let him fill you in on the rest over a few beers someday when you are in town. He is currently a successful executive at amazon.com in Indianapolis.

SENSEI AL FISH AT THE TIGRIS RIVER OUTSIDE THE IRAQI CAPITAL OF BAGHDAD. PWOK IS VERY PROUD OF TRAINING THIS GREAT WARRIOR AND HONOR HIS GLORY.

Sensei Barbara Miller is the epitome of "The African Lion Head" given to me by a female student many years ago during the "Give this to your teacher as a gift from the Women of Africa" story. She is not only a tremendous Teacher, she is a Deadly Warrior. While beautiful, feminine, petite and nice, she will seal your face, eviscerate you with a blade, and then knit you a quilt with your own guts to keep you warm during your recovery. SBM also has attended nearly every single class since 2001 and that is while juggling her regular job, her family and her aerobics instructor obligations at a Chicago health club. She also is PWOK's Warrior Scribe documenting in writing every single thing that has been taught at Kenpo School from the very beginning. Empowering women?

You betcha. No problem there. Jumbo!

SENSEI BARB MILLER. MOTHER. BUSINESSWOMAN. TEACHER. KILLER.

THE EVER CHANGING FACE OF THE WARRIOR AS THE LOVE OF LIFE INFUSES ACTION CREATING KNOWLEDGE, EXPERIENCE AND IN SOME CASES WISDOM.

Master Sean Baker came to train at Kenpo School in a quite interesting way.

MASTER SEAN BAKER, COMBAT VETERAN AND SUBMARINER ABOARD THE USS SCRANTON SERVED DURING THE PERSIAN GULF WAR. DEATH AND WICKED DESTRUCTION FROM THE DEEP BLUE SEA. MASTER SEAN IS A GREAT WARRIOR.

When I first opened the Brookfield School while at the same time operating the Old Town Chicago Dojo, it was a bit challenging. At the time I taught nearly all the classes and couldn't be in two places at once. No matter that we are all made up of subatomic particles and should be able to walk through walls and access parallel universes. My training, however has not yet reached that magnitude. Maybe next life.

Anyway, to announce the Grand Opening of a War House in "downtown" Brookfield, I took out a 2 full page spread advertisement in the Suburban Life newspaper at a hefty expense. Since the School wasn't even open yet, there were no students and not enough Teachers, this went against the very simple and successful business model of the Chicago School. In this case, with the space rental, the need for mats, equipment, marketing and construction work, PWOK Brookfield STARTED IN THE RED. That is not the best business model, but it is the most common.

So after signing the contract for the ad space with the promise of money that I don't yet have, it wasn't long until the newspaper appeared at the doorstep of the nearly complete dojo. I had a bad feeling when I heard the ten or so complementary copies for advertisers plop down at the School entrance.

My ill at ease feeling was not un-clairvoyant.

As I blow sawdust from a just cut 2x4 off my hands, I open to the center spread and there she be.

BROOKFIELD GRAND OPENING!

POWELL'S WAY OF KENPO MARTIAL ARTS SCHOOL

REALTY TAUGHT HERE.

REALTY? REALLY? AM I OPENING A F'N REAL ESTATE SCHOOL? COME ON MAN.

I had been in publishing as an ad salesman for 20+ years and knew that a mistake like this was endangering the sales commission of my account rep and the advertisers get really pissed off. Never mind my as yet non-established Brookfield Karate School reputation.

Once it appears in print and is in the readers hands that's it. Print a retraction? Not for an advertisement. Maybe a make good or price reduction.

What would it say any way?

We apologize for mistaking a House of War for those that want to learn to sell a house?

After taking the time to meditate, realize we all have human error and erase thoughts of beheading the newspaper staff, I pick up the phone to express my dismay in a calm, mentally disciplined manner:

"Hello. Surburban Life! May we help you?" the as yet un-ear torched receptionist answers.

"You guys f**ked up my god-d**ned ad! A TWO PAGE SPREAD AD FOR MY NEW BUSINESS!!!!!! Put me through to my rep "Cheryl"! PLEASE!

I got voicemail which was probably for the best.

During the return call, Cheryl didn't see the problem and did what I would have done when confronting an enraged advertiser, she put a positive spin on it saying:

"It looks great! What exactly is the problem?"

I feel my face wrench in an unnatural manner as my brain chemicals are straining to keep up.

It looked kinda like this.

With stroke-like annunciation and a wildly twitching right eye, I stammer:

"Wwwaahuttt eexactlly is the PROBLEM!?"…Izzzzz that what you asked??????"

"We are a MARTIAL ARTS SCHOOL NOT A REAL ESTATE OFFICE!"

"REALITY IS TAUGHT HERE NOT REALTY! Capish?"

"Ohhhhhhhh…didn't even notice" She says in an honest sounding voice.

"Neither did your top notch copy editor. I mean, what are the letters…maybe 2" tall?"

"We will reprint it correctly Mr. Powell next Thursday."

"Thank you." I hang up and tend to the twitching eye by accidentally rubbing sawdust into it from the bit I missed before grabbing the phone. Grrrrrrr.

So what does this have to do with Master Sean Baker?

Of the two times the 2 full page spread advertisement ran in Suburban Life to the entire geographic region the paper reaches, I GOT one single student…his name was Sean Baker.

And I'll tell you what. It was well worth the investment.

MASTER SEAN (RT) AND SIFU TONY KRIVAK DOING BATTLE IN THE WAR TROLLEY. PAINFUL, TAR BURNING MEETINGS BETWEEN WARRIOR AND STREET TO COME.

Master Sean Baker has been instrumental in transporting the Warrior Ethos of the Chicago School to the suburban Brookfield Dojo. Without him, the transfer would have been extremely difficult. At a time when I was running both Schools, his effort made the transition to one War House smoother.

Again, since we have trained together for so long, the stories we could tell would fill an amazing, funny ass book.

Besides becoming a Kenpo Master, he has taken a serious liking to slamming people on the ground HARD keeping them there with his Rampone, Gracie Jiu Jitsu, Combat Do and Wrestling style.

In fact, Master Sean helped me restart the dormant Riverside-Brookfield Junior Bulldogs Recreation Wrestling Program. These types of feeder programs make sure that a wrestler has mat experience before reaching High School and improves the quality of the HS wrestling team.

After I retired from Head Coaching duties and returning full time to PWOK ground fighting education, Coach Baker stayed with the staff for years and was instrumental to their success.

That program continues to this day.

Besides still teaching at PWOK, Coach Baker coaches wrestling at the Illinois powerhouse "Vittum Cats" grappling club. Both his children Aidan (boy) and Annelis (girl) are Wrestling Champions in their own right. Master Sean is also a highly successful trader on the Chicago investment scene.

MASTER SEAN BAKER'S DAUGHTER ANNELIS ON RIGHT, WON THE "WAR OF THE ROSES MID AMERICAN OPEN" CHAMPIONSHIP. SHE RECEIVED A WRESTLING SCHOLARSHIP OFFER RIGHT AFTER. WOW. WOMEN WARRIORS OF WRESTLING.

Along with these accolades, Master Sean was the Head Coach of our highly successful "Hammers of Thor" MMA Team and inducted into the USMA International Hall of Fame.

One ad. One student. One Master.

Groovy.

"THE WARRIOR TRUTH IS THAT AS YOU ATTAIN MASTERY, YOU WILL FIND THAT TALISMANS ARE ABOUT AS IMPORTANT AS NEEDING A MAP FOR YOUR BONES TO FIND YOUR SKIN. YOUR TRUE POWER LIES NOT IN IMAGES, DEITIES OR SYMBOLS; BUT RATHER IN THE TRUTH THAT IS THE BIRTHRIGHT OF ALL WARRIORS. THAT YOU ARE THE VERY BLOOD OF THE UNIVERSE...INVINCIBLE AND IMMORTAL."

-WILLIAM POWELL DECEMBER 8, 1990

Master Jason Gose is the epitome of a Kenpo Warrior.

DON'T LET THE FRIENDLY SMILE FOOL YOU. KING COBRAS GRIN AS WELL.

He is dedicated, strong, intelligent and ferocious in battle.

And that's just when he is playing poker with friends.

He is very good at poker because of what I call his "War Face Façade" more visually akin to a "Guy Fawkes" mask used by "V" in "V for Vendetta" in the movie. You can look at Master Jason straight in the eye, and unless you trained him from White Belt to Black Belt Master, you could not be sure what he is REALLY thinking. Kinda scary actually.

When I see him driving home from work in a more than normal frequency, he looks like the

consummate businessman. Bespectacled with glasses and in office attire, one would think him

a normal guy in his conservative Honda Accord and the salt and pepper school boy haircut.

If there was an incident of road rage, you'd think that this guy wouldn't be that big a problem.

You would know you were wrong while gathering your teeth from the front grill of your nice

Escalade.

Master Jason is a "Killer that does not Kill". Damn laws against murdering idiots and scumbags.

After almost two decades of training together, he is what I call an "Important Piece of Popcorn".

To put that statement in perspective, I was asked once to grace a martial arts magazine cover of a

relatively small publication. Very honored, but the details were never finalized by the closing

date of that particular issue.

The designer wanted one of those leaping off a rock with a flying kick to nowhere covers.

I don't fly. I don't ski. And I don't do leaping bullshit.

When it became clear that that was the project, I said no.

Weird for someone who always commits to new adventures before hearing the details?

Maybe, but I prefer to crush human physical bodies and minds in a Loving and Caring Way with feet

planted firmly on the ground. Not from some ball sack slap to the opponents eyes while descending

from a useless flying kick. Probably leap from the rock, sail over the attacker and sprain my ankle

on landing courtesy of a pissed off hermit crab flipping me the bird.

When asked how I would do the cover, I said immediately that it would be a bit unusual. I would be at a table in a bar (with or without gi) and have students sitting around me. After taking a small basket of popcorn from the bar, I would dump it in a single pile on the table directly in front of me. Looking at the photographer, I would have him prepare to snap the photo on my mark. When he was ready, I would stand and with both hands shove the popcorn so that it moved all over. "NOW!" I'd bark as the popcorn shoots in all directions with most landing at various ranges on the table and floor. So the picture would be me, stern faced in the background and the popcorn in mid air toward the photographer. Then I would explain.

"You will notice that I pushed the pile of popcorn at the same time and yet all did not go in the same direction. Some landed far down the table, some in the center, a bunch at the beginning and many on the floor. These kernels all started in the same place with one Teacher ushering them along The Way. But since they are individual kernels and not one is the same as another, they moved different lengths and in varied directions. I continue to use my hands together and individually to usher the tabled popcorn to the far edge which represents Mastery. The problem is that the ones closest to the far edge may not have the patience to wait until I get to them as I am focused on the stationary or slow rolling popcorn pieces right in front of me.

It's a quandary in that if I just focus on pushing those closest to success at the expense of attending to the slow kernels, they will become frustrated and quit. On the other hand, if I focus on the slow moving beginners, the well down the table corn will get bored and quit. And what about the folks is varying positions between the beginning and end edges of the table? Who do I focus on? Where to direct my efforts? Now that's the challenge in training human beings.

Never mind those that have fallen off the table completely. Which ones do I try to save? The kernels that scurried off the table at the far edge of the table, the ones that fell from the very beginning? The middle? Who to "save" and at what cost by missing someone who needed the training the most and is now lost and bitter. Do I pick up one kernel because I like it more than another?

That is what martial arts teaching is all about. Helping as much popcorn of all shapes, sizes and abilities down the table as far as their will drives them. That is the story of martial instruction. A more relevant a visual representation of what I do than a sandy flying kick with accompanying scrotum to forehead scraping Ball of Groin Sack Strike."

The magazine designer just looked at me deciding whether I was a genius or a madman.

Probably both.

He thanked me saying they'd be in touch which I knew wasn't going to happen. And that's OK.

So back to Master Jason as an "Important Piece of Popcorn" statement. Following his popcorn journey from Beginner to Master, it would look something like this:

First push of popcorn and Jason flies easily to the far end of the table about ¾ of the way down. (White Belt through Purple Belt) I thought he had the most talent and potential to be someone in the martial arts so I spent time focusing on him. This usually took the form of threatening to kick his ass if he didn't start using more control and stop hurting classmates with his aggressive style. He did cut down on the broken noses, sore ribs and the double leg Death Slams that usually left his sparring partner unconscious or with an injured back from being pile driven into the mat.

Purple Belt-Popcorn at Full Stop. Getting married. More responsibility at work and children in the offing has Jason questioning his commitment to Kenpo and the extraordinary time he spends training at PWOK. Bottom line. My main popcorn quits Kenpo School and I don't see him again for several years. Bad kernel choice on my part? How many pieces of corn did not get the training they needed because I was sure this popcorn was worth the time. Was I totally wrong? No. I was not wrong. Master Dave Saboe, a friend of Jason's mentioned to me that Jason had been asking about Kenpo School and might be interested in coming back. I looked at Dave (not yet a Black Belt) with "Are you f'n kidding me?" Jason was one of my most powerful students and he just quits? I don't know.

After thinking it over for awhile, I acquiesce, swallowing my anger and send Jason an email inviting him to the annual SPECIAL TRAINING (SPECTRAIN) that would bring him immediately back into the fold by sharing 12 hours of sweat and blood with the Warriors he abandoned. The email exchange went something like this.

My email to him: "Jason: Special Training is this Thursday at 7 pm sharp. Be there."
-Sensei.

Jason's reply: "No thank you. I CHOOSE to not attend."
-Jason.

I went ballistic. F*ck Zen and mental discipline, I wanted heads on my Tiger Fork. Jason's would have to wait but Dave's was available for repositioning that same Tuesday. After relaying the story to Dave with a tone of a land walking piranha looking for a head to chomp off, he just say's "Hmmm…That's weird". I just stared at Dave for a while. Fast forward years hence to the Brookfield School and the group was changed into street clothes after a brutal class. Sitting up front, we cracked open a fine bottle of top shelf tequila that a student had brought me back from Mexico. We all imbibed and celebrated the successful growth of the Brookfield Kenpo School with a few non-gringo caliber shots.

Just then, I see someone in a jogging outfit with a hat pulled down over his ears peering through the sweat clouded condensation of the front door with hands up by his eyes to focus inside. I tell the closest student to invite the traveler in for a shot and a welcome. The figure that entered was clearly out of shape with a sickly green-yellow complexion and hesitancy in his gait. As we lock eyes, I realize its Jason. Not sure if he would be hugged or beaten, I rise with outstretched arms in lieu of a handshake or a claw to the face.

He said he moved just down the street in Brookfield and when he saw the "coming soon" sign for PWOK, he would jog by every day hoping to find a way in. And he did.

Master Jason is now well beyond the need for my popcorn ushering and has never let me down again. MJG is an honored member of The United States Martial Arts International Hall of Fame and Powell's Way of Kenpo's main "sparring" Instructor.

MASTER JASON WITH WIFE STEPHANIE AT THE USMA HALL OF FAME INDUCTION CEREMONY.

So maybe my Popcorn Choosing was not that far off. JUMBO!

NEVER LEAVE BEHIND FORMER STUDENTS WHO QUIT FOR WHATEVER REASON AND WANT TO REJOIN THE DOJO. NO ONE IS BEYOND REDEMPTION. WITH A THREE STRIKE POLICY, THE FIRST TWO ARE FORGIVEN. BUT ON THE THIRD YOU ARE OUT FOR GOOD.

Master Vic Mezera is a lifelong Boxer and earned his feared reputation being raised in a tough part of Chicago. He became the neighborhood and area champion with unmatched speed, accuracy and power with an unblemished record. As well, Master Vic is an Excellent Karoke Singer, an Inspiring and Dynamic Instructor and A Warrior's Warrior. He is ALWAYS there when you need him and goes out of his way to help no matter the inconvenience to himself. Not many people are like Master Vic. He works hard and expects his students to do the same. Practice!

MASTER VIC SNAPPING AN ELBOW AS HE PREPARES TO LOWER THE "BOOM!"

Master Vic, like Master Sean Baker has developed an affinity for ground fighting. It's great to watch the men and women that I have trained for so long realize and pass on the integral component of ground work in real self defense. Master Vic teaches the Monday Jiu Jitsu classes is in great physical shape and LOVES fighting on the ground. It was not always this way.

When I first met Vic many years ago, he came to the Brookfield School in a quiet and humble manner. After explaining that he was a Boxer and a Smoker, I told him that only one could stay. Not that you weren't allowed to join Kenpo School if you were a smoker, you just wouldn't be able to keep up with the demanding work outs if you smoke. Vic said he was going to quit smoking and I mentioned that Kenpo will help him out by giving him no choice. Become a Karate Expert or a Emphysema Patient. Easy pick. Vic was off his minimum pack a day, 20+ year smoking habit within a few months of beginning his martial arts training. Ah fresh air.

Back to Vic and ground fighting.

After a bit of get acquainted chatter, Vic told me that his Dad was a Judo Champion and then added a personal secret. While he was an accomplished Boxer, he was very uncomfortable with being touched, held or the idea of grappling on the mat with other people. I said that I understood and that we will take care of it. Pronto.

So I grabbed Vic, chucked him to the mat hard and kicked the crap out of him with Wrestling, Judo, Jiu Jitsu and Rampone for about three minutes. I mean intense violence without injury. After I made my point, we stood and I said "How do you feel now?"

Vic just looked at me and said something like "Feel fine Sir. Thank you."

"You're welcome." I smiled.

No other words were necessary as Vic not only became a skilled fighter on the ground, but totally embraced the Ground Fighting Arts and developed into an Expert Instructor in them. In the same manner as Master Sean's children are being trained in the Warrior Art of Wrestling and have achieved great success already in their young careers, Master Vic is doing the same. But make no mistake Master Sean is not training them for medals, trophies or plaques, but so they can handle themselves growing up and in life.

MASTER VIC MEZERA, MASTER SEAN BAKER, MOI AND THE GREAT SHORTY MILLS.

Master Vic has a similar philosophy and in keeping with the 1500+ year old tradition, passes Kenpo Knowledge down to his children just as his Father taught him Boxing and I passed down the Other War Time Arts to him. Both his children are excellent martial artists, academics and great human. Master Vic's son Tory (Victor Jr.) has trained with me since childhood, became a Midwest Jiu Jitsu Champion, is currently a Shodan (1st Degree Black Belt) in Kenpo and will be attending Florida State University this Fall.

Master Vic's daughter, Alicia is a beautiful, charming young lady with the infectious spirit of a winner. Kenpo has helped her overcome a wee bit of shyness. This does occur naturally when your training allows you to quietly "speak your mind" through martial technique by throwing a bigger, stronger opponent to the ground with ease. Following in her Father's footsteps, Alicia is also a talented Karaoke singer and joined me on stage for a tune or two. We were cracking up so hard that our lyrics were undecipherable and I was replaced as a back up singer, by her big brother Tory.

MASTER VIC COVERING THE RIGHT FLANK OF THE WAR TROLLEY.

MASTER VIC DEMONSTRATING KEEN AWARENESS AS OTHER MASTERS, ARMY RANGERS AND UNSUSPECTING CHILD WARRIORS REMAIN DISTRACTED.

Great Master. Great Kids. Great Work Ethic. Great Teacher.

Great Friend.

So-so deer hunter.

JUMBO! Master Vic!

BESIDES BEING A TOP NOTCH BOXER, AN INDUCTEE INTO THE USMA INTERNATIONAL HALL OF FAME, MASTER VIC IS A RESPECTED COACH OF THE HAMMERS OF THOR MMA TEAM. HERE HE OFFERS PRE-FIGHT STRATEGIES TO THOR CAPTAIN JASON "SUPERMAN" SCOTT. KNOWING MASTER VIC, IT WAS PROBABLY ALONG THE LINES OF "NOW LOOK! GET IN THERE, BOW, THEN BOOM! KNOCK HIM OUT."

Master Dave Saboe is a Master's Master.

Ever since surviving the third prong on my "What the f**k is with Jason and him telling me to kiss off on SPECTRAIN?!" Tiger Fork incident, things have progressed nicely. Master Dave Saboe of the Fifth Dan is one of the greatest martial arts minds that I have ever met. He took what I showed him, meshed it with his brilliant vision and took the whole thing to another level in his own way.

There is no greater honor for a Warrior Educator than to watch a beginner student absorb, understand and adapt to emerge into one of the top Teachers in the entire country. He is that amazing.

Oh yeah. He does all this from a wheelchair.

Let's take a step back to when I met Dave. Actually, Master Jason Gose of the "I choose not to come to Special Training" and the "Shihan, Please remind me later to tell you how cool that looked." cartwheeling Indiana Hick Moron fame was the one who brought Dave to Kenpo School.

As mentioned in Master Dave's Foreword to this book, he first became interested in our Kenpo School when seeing another student with bruises on forearms and legs and inquired what had happened. Jason simply stated "Kenpo School" and dropped the subject. After repeated new artistic type bruises on his friend, Dave asked to get involved. Jason finally brought him to his first class. At first, I thought Dave seemed quite normal, but that was not accurate. He is a unique human in many different aspects.

Dave arrives to the locker room in a beautiful full business suit looking sharp. We greet and he disrobes meticulously piece by piece of attire and carefully places or hangs the items accordingly.

Not that weird, I just noticed it. No it was weird.

Class begins and I put on what is now called a "Sensei Smorgasbord" where I mind blow new students with a vast array of technique from all aspects of our system sure to interest the newcomer. It has never failed. I thought that it might have that night.

Glancing at Dave throughout the night to gauge which things peaked his interest. His stone faced revealed nothing the entire class. He worked out hard, sweated profusely but had no emotional expression that would show what he was thinking. Not used to this reaction to my classes, I turn up the intensity.

Again nothing.

Convinced that he was not getting what he wanted, I figured him an odd, quiet piece of popcorn and brought the level back to normal and refocus on the rest of the School as the students looked like they had just returned from a trip to Mars. I should have looked at their faces during class instead.

After bowing out, we return to the locker room, towel off (no showers at PWOK) and start getting dressed. When Dave ascends the stairs, our eyes meet and he says nothing.
He had just removed his work out stuff and was putting on a single black sock standing on one leg like a flamingo. Finally, I say "So Dave, what did you think of class?"

He thinks for the proper words, which I had no idea what they would be and says verbatim "It was the single greatest experience of my life" in a stoic, emotionless way that made me think he was making fun of me. Clearly that was not going to work.
I say "What?" with a glare that probably didn't match the friendly greeting that was offered up when we met earlier that night.

Dave simply repeated the exact same words.

Come to find out from Jason later that night that Dave LOVED class and was being honest. It WAS one of his great experiences and his face and smile muscles just seem to be detached from the brain emotion impulses. Glad I waited for the scoop before choking Dave out with his own $75 neck tie. As a final note on the first meeting, Dave dressed back into the full business suit and left the School looking exactly the way he entered. Yeah…weird.

At that point, I had no idea that this odd fellow would eventually become a great Hall of Fame Karate Master, a lifelong friend and my partner in the ownership of the Brookfield PWOK some twenty years later.

More than most, Master Dave was at many of the events include in the book, but the stories that we could tell would really make up another 400 page book. No lie.

Let's fast forward twenty years and Master Dave Saboe of the Fifth Dan basically runs Kenpo School in every aspect. Since this book has taken years to write, MDS has been the main force in keeping Teaching Quality High and Student Training Brutal. (TQHASTB) Being a bit more philosophical in my old age, Master Dave remains committed to the beautifully barbaric tenets that Kenpo School was built on. Hardcore or there's the door. The Machine still generates the best students, Black Belts and Masters because of the intense commitment of my brother Dave.

My appreciation has no limit.

You can learn more about Master Dave's evolutionary theories on martial arts and personal self defense through either his "Way of Self Defense" Academy or from his #1 selling book

"GET REAL! A Practical Approach to Personal Safety" available on Kindle at www.amazon.com. Of all the amazing things about Master Dave, his mind is well…mind blowing. With the quiet unassuming demeanor, you STILL can't figure out what he is thinking until he says it. Then in 99.9% of the time he is right. See something that you think is interesting? Send it to Master Dave and he will agree, want time to get the facts, or simply destroy the issue with facts, figures and resources that would make snopes.com jealous.

One time I thought I had him. He was about to start class and I mentioned that we had a martial arts event coming up next month on the Saturday May 23rd . Master Dave replies that it must be the 22nd since the 23rd is a Sunday. AHAH!!!!!! GOT EM!

I am staring at the calendar perched on the wall right above my desk at the School.
I jump up in a glorious tirade of victory and run around the mat like a jamoke screaming "YES! YES! Finally I am right and Master Dave is wrong! JUMBOOOOOOO!!!!!!!!...AHHHHHHHH!"

Master Dave just sat there watching me present the tirade of the century and says nothing.

Finally, exhausted that I can't get the slightest rise out of him, I say with scorn in tone
"SO WHAT DO YOU THINK OF THAT MASTER DAVE, KNOW EVERYTHING DUDE?"

He raises his left eyebrow only and simply says "That is last year's calendar Sir."

I say "FFFAAAAAAAAAAAAAAAAAAAAAAAACCCCCCCCCCCCCCCCCCCCCCCCCCCK!"

And walk silently back to my office, shaking my head and throw the old calendar away.

Anyway, Master Dave is a real life example of "Professor Xavier" leader of The X-Men.

He motors around in a fast as sh*t wheelchair that makes me think we need to have a Kenpo Chariot technique for "Ben-Hur" equipped wheelchair assaults that can cut you up or run you down. I am sure there is a weapon in every part of his machine. And the knobby all terrain wheels are a bitch on the toes.

Anyway he teaches mostly by explanation using two demonstrating students that show what he wants the class to practice. All this unbelievable information and knowledge TRANSMITTED DIRECTLY from Master to Student BY WAY OF OTHER STUDENTS. It is this amazing skill that had me nominate Master David J. Saboe for induction into The Kenpo Karate International Hall of Fame this June 29th 2013. A rare honor that is only meant for the highest achievers in The Art that we love so much. Master Dave is intrepid, and a go getter. He is successful in all he does and is humble at the same time. He has a beautiful home, a great wife an former student, Suzanne and a new son Greyson.

MASTER DAVE'S SON GREYSON AND I SHARE A SOMBER MOMENT.

MASTER DAVE AND ME IN ST LOUIS AT HIS INDUCTION INTO THE UNITED STATES MARTIAL ARTS INTERNATIONAL HALL OF FAME IN 2007.

Master Dave's book "GET REAL! A Practical Approach To Personal Safety" is a top seller.

THE NAME OF THIS BOOK IS GROWING TIGERS. BUT AS STATED IN AN EARLIER CHAPTER THAT WHILE SNAKES ARE A MOLTING EXAMPLE OF CHANGING SKINS INTO EVEN BIGGER, STRONGER MORE FIERCE CREATURES, THE SAME HAPPENS TO HUMANS. TIGERS SEEM TO BETTER VISUALLY REPRESENT THE GROWTH OF HUMANS INTO WARRIORS. BUT WE WILL…

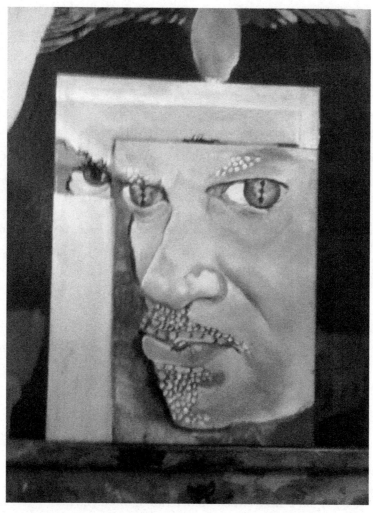

…NEVER FORGET THE MOLTING OF THE SNAKE AND ITS LINK TO STRENGTH.

When I first started A Reality Based Dojo that was designed to teach The War Time Arts in a most realistic way, I had to go through ten tough guys Marines, Wrestlers, Fighters, Street Thugs, Bouncers etc. to find one student that would stay. Now every student that comes into the Brookfield School seems to want what I wanted to teach 35 years ago... The Way. It has to be taught in the fire of "practice" battle but needs to be as close to the edge of reality as legally, physically and morally possible. After all this time, and with Master Dave at the helm, backed by the other Masters that I trained from white belts, this has become a reality. We are well known, respected and to a certain degree feared. They say that its better to be feared than respected. I say we can have both?

Fear for the fools that doubt martial arts and respect from those that want to learn, already know or wish to improve their understanding of an entity that has no beginning, no middle and no conclusion. Seek out all you can learn from anyone who knows anything about whatever it is you care about.

I want to acknowledge a couple of the great Teachers at PWOK, that because of space constraints and the "confidential nature" of what they do for a living, the stories are not for public airing.

SIFU JAKE CACCAVALO, LAW ENFORCEMENT.

SIFU OMER HOUSTON, LAW ENFORCEMENT.

SECURITY EXPERT AND KENPO BLACK BELT, SIFU ADAM WEINTRAUB

MASTER KEVIN DILLON, RETIRED POLICE OFFICER AND CREATOR OF THE INTERNATIONALLY FAMOUS L.O.C.K.U.P. LAW ENFORCEMENT COMBAT SYSTEMS. TRULY A BROTHER FROM ANOTHER MOTHER. A MEMBER OF THE USMA INTERNATIONAL HALL OF FAME AS WELL.

WWW.POLICECOMBAT.COM

CHAPTER FORTY FIVE

The Importance of: NEVER GIVING UP.

I have thought of giving up many times.

At the time, it seemed to be the right thing to do. I mean tapping out is an important part of Brazilian Jiu Jitsu and Japanese Judo. If you don't tap, you will go to sleep or at the worst, have one of your limbs snapped in half or at least hyper extended. It's about as much fun tapping out as having a cold. Defeat sucks. But just as a cold will pass, so will the pain of defeat. The key here, WHEN NOT IN A LIFE OR DEATH SITUATION, is that temporarily giving up because you know that you made a mistake, are caught and resistance is futile, tapping is the smart thing to do. Then again, tapping out is the Gentlemen Warriors way of saying "great technique" with out having to offer up a severed appendage.

As we alluded to before, this is not Defeat. You simply didn't Win right now. Not that you couldn't have escaped the choke or arm bar a minute ago or in twenty minutes, you just couldn't now. When in training this is OK. In the street it is not. Defeat and submission in the street can mean death.

Quick story.

I was with my great friend John Corlett who called to tell me that he was at O'Hare and had a 4 hour layover and would I like to meet him for a beer at the airport. With a 5.0 liter fuel injected 5 speed Firebird Formula, I told him I'd scoop him up, bring him back downtown for some real fun and get him back for his flight.

Mistake.

Well, not knowing that the trip downtown would entail a $240 credit card drinking bill and that was just mine. John must have spent way more in cash. Short story long, we drank way too much in 4 hours while reminiscing over our storied life chock full of ...stories.. So that should tell you about the upcoming events.

Last bar before hitting the airport and we should have not stopped there.
The bar had great food, but a unique policy.
Any woman that was standing, was to be offered a seat by a gentleman. Sounds like chivalry.
Normally, I would have been the first one up like Sir Galahad. Not today however.

The problem was that we were so inebriated that we needed the seats. So we sat, unaware of the policy until the bouncers asked us to move. We could not and that was the problem. After being asked several times to remove our hineys from the stool, we refused and were asked to leave.

We didn't want to.

Problem.

After heated debate and with the 8 bouncers vs. 2 idiots odds, we said ok and were about to leave.

Then it happened.

Walking with armed escort (they didn't have guns) but did have us by the arms as we were moving toward the door peacefully, one of the bouncers smacks me with an open hand slap in the back of the head. Now, there are not many things that push my buttons. This happens to be one of them.

Just like Chuck Norris can't stand his cowboy hat messed with, the head slap is my thing.

When I felt the unnecessary slap, I turned to the group and expressed my dismay by punching the Slapper in the puss. Guess that is not normally what he was used to, but now he was. He fell back into his bouncer gang holding his nose and the cracking walnut sound that told me it was broken.

Now the point of the story.
His cronies attempted to tackle me in what looked like an untrained bowling pin formation. Unfortunately for the strategy. The head pin was on the ground with a smashed nose. So the spare sides move in a flanking motion and grab my arms and legs. OK fine. I was wrong and ready to leave…relatively peacefully. Besides John had to get to the airport. Seemed to me that we were even. Slapper smacked Reaper in the back of head, Reaper benevolently makes sure Slapper learns the importance of a nose when breathing. Apparently my conflict arithmetic was not accurate.

Then Head Pin gets up and tackles my already held body and all 5 of the bouncers that could grab me as we end in an X pattern on the floor. One on each leg and arm with bleeding Head Pin on my chest. I am not fighting back, knowing that I am in the wrong and trying to "give up". Then bleeding nose Head Pin puts his sharp edged forearm bone shiv across my windpipe and is pushing down hard. I feel the pressure on my throat and start tapping him to say…"YOU GOT ME!" He keeps the pressure full force and I am now in danger. After several taps and what words I can speak "Ok! I quit.! Stop!" Head Pin does neither.

So, in a technique that would cost me attorney fees, an over night stay in jail and court ordered mandatory social service meetings, I bite his nose clean off. Now, without exaggerating, the nose didn't end up in my mouth or on the floor, but did flap on his face from left to right and back as blood spewed a Rooster Tail over the whole pile of us. Needless to say that Head pin now had a

533

much bigger medical problem that his broken nose since he basically had none.

During this melee that was again moving in slow motion, I scan for my huge Grit friend John who I can't locate. Turns out he was at the back of the pack and the blood splat just missed him. He later said, from his view, it looked like a zombie movie with all these corpses piling on and eating the victim. That's until he saw Reverse Flying Head Pin sail past and realized that I was the zombie.

Well, needless to say, the patty wagon and several large cops took control and placed me in the back of the cruiser while they took statements. Bottom line. "Yes Sir! I did bite his nose off in self defense." The trooper just looked at me as my calm assessment was different than most bar brawls he had written reports on.

After a bit of time, I finally see Grit and he is coming to my defense. The cop courtesy rolls down the front passenger window so we can communicate. John is screaming in a redneck wasted monologue "Those guys attacked my friend!" Nice try John as the sitting cop asks "Do you want to go to jail too?" Grit looks at me and says "I have a plane to catch." As the officer rolls up the window, I ask one more favor. Sir, may I please say something to John?" He smiles as if he knows its going to be humorous and rolls the window down.

John comes closer as the window descends figuring I wanted him to call my wife or a lawyer. Instead I say calmly "Welcome to Chicago. Don't ever f'n come back!"

Wooooot Woooot! Away I go in the patty wagon, handcuffed and thinking that this didn't work out so well.

Martial Note: No matter how much you like Houdini, are a yoga teacher or just a flexible person.

YOU CANNOT GET OUT OF TIGHT HANDCUFFS PLACED HIGH UP ON YOU BACK. Even with all the police movies, magic shows and TV tricks I had seen it all went for not. Besides, lets say I do yoga my ass out and rhino my way out the locked cop doors and tumble to the street. Where am I going to go? I'm still cuffed and in a bloody tee shirt. As well, the police have my jacket with ID and everyone at that bar knows me. Best bet be polite. Just sit my jail breaking-ass down and cooperate respectfully with police.

When John got to the airport, he had trouble seeing the flight information. He asked a older gentleman to assist since he had "eye trouble" One smell of Grit's breath and the man said "Just take any one of them. It will get you somewhere." John was a bit lost but eventually found the plane. He was awakened and asked to leave the plane after it arrived in Baltimore after everyone had departed and the maintenance crew was finished. It took the crew a few tries to revive him.

THIS IS THE LEGENDARY REDNECK FRIEND JOHN C. FROM COLLEGE

JOHN NORMAN CORLETT AKA GRIT- GREAT FRIEND WHO IS FUNNY AND SUCCESSFUL AS A HUMAN BEING TEETERING ON GENIUS AND TOTAL MADMAN. LOVE THIS DUDE AND HIS MARYLAND WAYS.

I was going to entertain you with another of the many stories on Not Giving Up.

But if you are a human being with any kind of motivation, you have plenty of you own stories.

Some funny. Some not. So for once I will get to the point:

DON'T EVER GIVE UP. EVEN AS THE LAST DROP OF LIFE BLOOD LEAVES YOU AND YOUR EYES STARE INTO THE GLORY OF OBLIVION, THRUST OUT WITH YOUR SWORD. AND UNTIL THAT VERY LAST INSTANT YOUR LIFE NEVER, EVER, GIVE UP.

CHAPTER FORTY SIX

The Importance of: LIVING THE WAY.

If you have read this far, you have either been entertained, waiting for the bull crap, or enjoyed the read and are interested in some of the things written here. I wanted this book to be as entertaining to a Grandmaster of 60 years in the Arts as to the new student that has never stepped in a dojo to those that are afraid that they cannot adequately protect their family in these challenging times.
You can. You will. You must.

Hope I achieved that goal.

This chapter will deal with a favorite student of mine Tony Krivak. I have trained Sifu Tony for many years and like Master Vic is always there in a jam. Any kind of jam. One time I mentioned to Sifu that I had a leak in the roof of my house and asked, quite innocently, does he recommend anyone that he trusts to do me right. That was Saturday evening about 7 pm.

At 6:15 am on the next day, Sunday morning, I hear noise on the roof above my 3rd floor bedroom. I grab my Glock, always at bedside, and try to figure out how a raccoon could have such loud steps. I walk downstairs naked, gun in hand and grab a LARGE dishtowel from the kitchen to cover my privates and exit with my Doberman Zeus out the back door. Another unskilled Ninja?

No, it was Tony (not yet a Black Belt so no "Sifu" title yet) as he hangs his huge head over the drain pipe gutters 3 stories up.

"Hey Bro" I say. What's up?"

"I fixed the leak in you flashing by the chimney so you shouldn't have any more trouble."

"How did you get up there?" I query.

"Ladder in the front, I didn't want to wake you, or startle you and be tossed to my death."

"Hmmm. Ok "How much we owe you?"

He just stared at me and I got the message.

"Thank you. I am going back to bed." I say.

"No problem, Thank you for not shooting me…and wearing the…ahhh…towel." Tony replies.

"JUMBO!" I bellow.

"JUMBO!" he returns.

This early example of the friendship, helpfulness and willingness to go clearly out of his way to come to someone's assistance continues unabated until this very day. The instances are beyond count and surely started well before he saved that boy in the jungle by freeing him with his knife.

SIFU TONY KRIVAK LEADING OUR PARADE PROCESSION. BESIDES BEING A MASTER MASON, HE IS A MARTIAL ARTS EXPERT, A GREAT FATHER AND A FELLOW BIKER. HE CAN MATCH ME STORY FOR STORY IN ANY CONVERSATION. TWO TO FOLLOW.

TYPICAL SIFU TONY LIVING THE WAY STORY #1: MAN OF THE KANKAKEE.

Sifu Tony (ST) had ridden his Harley Davidson to "The Helmet Roast" which is the classic no holds

barred kinda event that you'd expect of bikers to enjoy. Ask him of the sordidly glorious details.

Anyway, ST and some fellow attendees had some beers and decided to test their mettle against the

formidable combination of inebriation and the mighty Kankakee River in Illinois. There was an old

defunct railroad trestle that used to span the river when Chicago was more of a industry train

spanning hub in the past. Well, there was very little of the remaining track above, but there were

still the five cement pylons that spanned the river equidistantly in support of the now ghost like

upper structure. The concept seemed feasible and had been accomplished ON THE FIRST PYLON

whereby said biker/drunk would get in the water and immediately swim hard at a 45 degree angle up

river against the current and then ride the flow headlong into the first cement pillar and grab on.

Then the "victor" would swim his bloody scraped face and arms back to shore via the calmer waters between Pier 1 and the shoreline launch point.

Sifu Tony lives The Way.

He announced after slamming a cold beer that he would do ALL FIVE PYLONS and end up on the far banks of the Kankakee river. And off he went.

I was not there and can not guarantee that I am not missing even more important parts of the story, but will try. Here is what happened as Sifu explained it to me. I have been with him enough on such other "Embracing The Weird" adventures (we rode our Harley's 18 hours straight over 1,000 miles between Sturgis South Dakota and Chicago, in which I had to speed up to 80 mph to kick the side of another bike whose rider fell asleep and was veering off the road to his death) Do you believe that story couldn't even make the cut of the chapter on the importance of "Coming to the Defense of Others"? So, point being, Sifu Tony's accounts of stories are beyond reproach as we have both witnessed each other do the extraordinary. So here is me telling the tale of ST Living The Way:

"So, after slamming the beer, I swim out to the point which would allow the current to take me back to Pylon 1. Then I do the same thing and swim out on a 45 degree angle and return same way to Pylon 2. I did notice that the current was stronger by the speed with which I shot back to the second pylon. On I go, same technique out and even quicker ride to Pylon 3. With two left and the technique sound, off I go in pursuit of Pylon 4. But just as many romantic type relationships will tell...just because I wanted Pylon 4 didn't mean she wanted me.

I miss it and away I go, 200 lbs of non-dolphin racing IN THE CENTER of a very dangerous body of water. SWOOOOOOOOOOOOOOOOOOOOOOOOOOOOOOOOOOOOOOOSSSSSSSSSSSSSHHH!

This was not good. But I am a Warrior and did not panic.

As I am sailing full speed down the center of a furious water current, I see a bend coming and plan to use my 45 degree angle theory to begin my geometric swim toward the bend point. Using the current and my calculations, I should hit land. Another Lady in Waiting says "NO!"

Just as I near the land insertion point and within 30 feet of shore, the river takes a quick unexpected bend and the water flow sends me back out into the middle again! This happened two more times where the Kankakee twisted sharply creating new undertows and now thoughts of panic are drowned out by the real possibility of death. I also realize that I am getting exhausted. I float on my back like an inverted beer tick and try to calm my breathing and my now primordial racing mind.

Then, I glance over my shoulder just as I get a full nasal douche of Kankakee's non-quality H2O. Thankful for the extra pre-death insult, I see it. There she is in all her glorious beauty...a rotten broken down pier jutting out into the water and seemingly in the direction of my flow. Before the river got another chance to end my life, I swim "Balls out!" toward the most beautiful sight I could think of at the time. Just as I reach it, totally exhausted, The Grim Reaper in the form of some dickhead River-Neptune god, grabs my ankle and starts pulling me away from shore again.
Just as I feel the creepily tender hand bones of Death telling me in a soothing voice "come with me Tony...Its going to be alright....come..." F*CK THAT! I reach out and bury my fingers knuckle deep into the rotten wood pillar. Surprised it didn't make a deal with Death, the pier leg holds. I float there as the water rushes past me and I begin to slow my heart and my mind. Breathe.

Now, though temporarily immobile by way of my death grip on the pier post, I am not safe yet. The Reaper is sitting in a flotation tube drinking a pina colada about 6 ft away and is offering to help. Looking up, I see that there are old wooden planks that I could reach up and with time, pull my way into the dock and hopefully safety. Only trouble was, as I looked up to the greenish-black scum that was the bottom of the deck, there was every kind of spider, roach, ant and the always hideous "unknown dark reach into areas" I knew that I had no choice. I slammed my hand into the funky unknown and broke through to life like a f'n zombie-coming-outta-the-ground flick. After a few breaks, I pulled my self up an through the wooden deck, walked about 10 ft and collapsed face up on the sandy beach of some rich person's home.

Not sure how long I laid there.

Finally, I remembered that Helmet Roast was having a brat and burger BBQ when the sun went down and that motivated me to action. I got up and started a long, controlled run along the river banks. Fortunately at the time, I was working on cardio and running every day. At my normal pace, I ran a 10 minute mile. By the time I reached the Helmet Roast, I had run 30 minutes straight meaning the river took me 3 miles down.

When I first reached the festival, I instinctively grabbed a beer and asked where the brats were.

Guys just looked at me as if I were a ghost.

I slammed a beer, ate a brat and said simply "River took me about 3 miles down."

"Three miles down?" A biker asked with the follow up statement.

"Do you know that at about the 4th mile is the falls where those kayakers died!"

"I didn't know that." I said. But I was sure that the pina colada grim reaper did.

LIVING THE WAY MEANS MEETING CHALLENGES HEAD ON. AND IF SOMETHING GOES WRONG, DON'T PANIC, DON'T GIVE UP AND DON'T DIE.

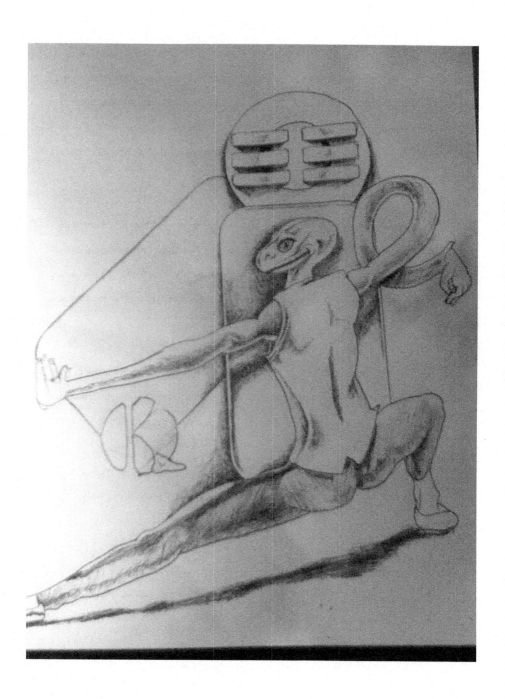

543

TYPICAL SIFU TONY LIVING THE WAY STORY #2: PAIN IN THE GLASS.

While attending a gathering of friends, I was sitting at the edge of a large glass table talking with others and enjoying the conversation. Then…oh yeah…it was a bachelor party, the talent arrives and a young lady put her huge boom box (I'm referring to her sound system) on the edge of the table where I was sitting. I started to get up to make room for her box, but when it was unnecessary, I sat back down. Should have stuck with my manners.

As I sit back, the table of glass shatters and there is no where for me to go but right through the center. Since there was no middle support piece the entire 4 x 4 ft circular piece of glass just imploded. I tried to brace myself against the outer rim, but that only helped a bit. Kinda like "Quint" the shark hunter as he is about to be swallowed whole by the 10,000 teeth Great White in the movie "Jaws" kicking the beast in the chin.

As a few friends helped me out they ask if I am ok to which I reply that I am sorry about the table. Then the blood starts soaking through my clothes in varied sizes and speeds through various sized holes, punctures and gashes. I realize that a hospital visit is in order when a friend lifts my shirt and pulls a shard of glass from my back. There were others, but he left them be.

Asking if anyone can take me to the hospital, everyone froze like ice sculptures of ghosts.

I knew that I was on my own.

Finally, as I am losing lucidity from losing blood, I TELL a friend I was with that HE WILL take to the hospital NOW. He replies that there is no way he was taking me in his Cutlass with all the blood threatening his pristine interior.

Martial Note: There is a big difference between acquaintances and friends. Friends will die for you, or at least come unhesitant to your aid. Acquaintances worry about the cost of interior blood removal.

After telling my friend that I will ride on the hood of his Cutlass for the couple mile trip to the closest hospital, he reluctantly agrees.

So there I am, on the front of his white Cutlass, blue interior incidentally, that I notice while lying on my stomach spread eagle like an X with my fingers holding on to the windshield wiper ridge.
I felt like an action hero in a detective chase scene as he is flying down the road, I am bleeding out and the lack of total blood volume began to affect my extremities and my grip. I thought how harsh it would be to almost get to the hospital when my blood starved hand muscles give way and I slip off the hood and get run over by my acquaintance's Cutlass.

I REMEMBERED THE KANKAKEE RIVER INCIDENT and the iron grip on that rotten pier that saved my life. And I willed myself to hold on.

I thought that I saw The Reaper again, now riding on a Vespa along side the car looking at me in disbelief.

Turns out it was just an old man, near death but not Death itself.

Finally getting to the hospital entrance, I slide off the hood easily due to the car wax/my blood mixture and the quick stop of the Cutlass. As I walk like a mummy into the Emergency Room's sliding door, my buddy is still staring at the mess I made on his hood. Note to Self: Acquaintance.

As I gimp on over to the reception desk, the nurse asks my situation and I reach down and pull the closest glass dagger from the back of my right thigh. The lucky draw was about 5 inches and in the shape of an arrow head. Not my best effort, I am sure, but enough to turn the receptionists face white as she scrambles for the PA system and orders emergency gurney STAT.

Short story long, the nurse orders the assistants to cut my pants off.

I said hell no, I just bought them and they were at my ankles when the ER Doctor entered moments later. The look on his face said "What the F**k happened to you?" while his professional bedside manner said "Mr. Krivak, have you been in an accident?"

I just looked at him, snake eyes and all.

I didn't have insurance at the time, so I asked how much to fix me up. He said with the ER visit, wound cleansing, staples, stitches, bandages, and antibiotics at least $350.

I asked how much to just remove the glass, clean the wound and tape me up.

Doctor said "Less than $150".

"Let's do that." As I handed him my credit card.

They bandaged me up, stuffed some fresh gauze and bandages in my hand and released me.

With no phone or anyone to call, I walked the six miles home.

Next day I was at work until my Dad saw the blood from a stubborn gash on my back blot through the company tee shirt. He had the same look as the doctor the night before and sent me home.

As I climbed down from the ladder leaning 50 feet up against the chimney that I was repairing, I heard the distinct whine of a Vespa zipping down the quiet suburban street. Not wanting to slip from a missed ladder rung, I looked down for proper foot placement. When I looked back up at the passing scooter and as the whine started to become more distant, I swear that I saw a boney white middle finger flipping me the bird.

No Death F**K YOU!

LIVING THE WAY IS NOT EASY BUT IT IS SIMPLE:

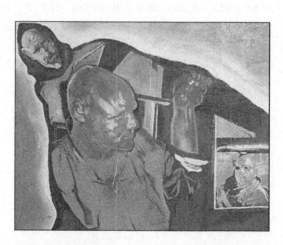

"LIVE EACH AND EVERY DAY AS IF A FIRE RAGES IN YOU HAIR!" -TAKUAN

THIS IS WHAT YOU GET WHEN TIGERS ARE GROWN PROPERLY. HAPPY DEADLY FOLK.

AND THEY START OUT JUST LIKE THIS.

THE IMPORTANCE OF GROWING TIGERS WHO CAN TAKE ACTION IS A KEY FACTOR IN RETURNING OUR SOCIETY TO A MORE CIVILIZED, CARING AND BENEVOLENT ONE.

CHAPTER FORTY SEVEN

The Importance of: GROWING TIGERS.

As stated in the beginning of this book, society as we call it needs to improve. There have always been bad guys and good guys. Loving people and hateful people. Those that have and those that have not. It will probably always be that way. But unless we get a grip on the reality that we are all intertwined and connected at the very core by our common humanity, things will only get worse. There have always been serial killers, rapists, robbers and bullies. Maybe it just seems that through instant mass media streaming worldwide, these cowardly deeds get more attention.

I don't know about all that.

Sometimes its hard to differentiate between "The Good Old Days" and the "Nowadays".

I mean, while you probably never heard of a mass shooting at "Rydell High School" in the 1950's movie "Grease" we have all heard of Al Capone's "St. Valentine's Day Massacre" in Chicago 30 years earlier. While we hear daily news about war, world food shortages, natural resource depletion, genetically altered food dangers, have you read the history of the "Dust Bowl" that starved the Great Plains and nearly caused another Civil War with California? These farmers were called "Okies" as a derogatory term that could get you arrested if you were considered a drain on society. Was that the "Good Old Days"? You get my point, it seems that the current inhabitants of this globe at any particular time in history always have it bad and yearn for the past.

Would you prefer to go to a modern hospital even though they may be getting kickbacks from pharmaceutical companies or would you rather go back to surgical procedures common during the American Civil War where amputation was done with a saw in a filthy tent without anesthesia?

Everything in Life depends on your perception.

Once again, I don't know about all that.

What I do know is that no one will hurt my family, my friends or me without a fight. Some contemporary Warrior friends of mine tell me that I was born at the wrong time and would be more at home on the bloody battlefield's of The Crusades.

Don't know about that either.

I do know that I am here, now, and have the Ability To Take Action. Or not.

And as long as I breathe air, I will teach others to do the same.

The writing of this book, the creation of the Warrior House known as Powell's Way of Kenpo and the knowledge being passed on from my students, now Masters has already made my life worth living and in a sense making me eternal. Whether this book will have relevance in 6 months or 600 years is unimportant. It was not written for financial gain, and while that would be nice, it was meant to help that one person out there on the edge of giving up, feeling powerless or frozen with fear of events to come.

And as long as people try to hurt other weaker individuals, I or one of my students, or one of their students or others of our ilk will be there to take or not take action. Society is unraveling. Things tend to do that.

But maybe that is why sewing was invented.

SO GROW TIGERS GROW. GET STRONG & BE KIND AS YOU REACH FOR THE PEAK.

CHAPTER FORTY EIGHT

The Importance of: GROWN TIGERS.

While we all view ourselves, or are taught that we are unique individuals, that is a bit misleading.

We at this moment in time are the latest evolution of the DNA of all our ancestors before us.

From the first creation of man by either God or a newly spawned walking fish, we are a part of life, not apart from it. No matter how hard I meditate, train, alter my consciousness, I am still and will always be William Joseph Powell, only son of Robert Joseph Powell and Rosemarie Ann Casciari. My parents' ancestral DNA is the result of their parents, my grandparents William Powell and Sally O'Houlihan pictured on the opposite page with Joseph Casciari and Helen Coccodrilli.

I can no more change who I am now in the evolutionary process than go backwards up the chain and back into a monkey jumping tree to tree. Or as some distant offspring of Adam and Eve.

This knowledge and its true realization is that you will become who you are destined to be.

As they say "It's in your DNA."

Now just because I am parts of all my family before me, I do have a very unique set of DNA strands that make me a short, stocky, intelligent and powerful man. This genetic code is unique to me and to a large extent unchangeable. I mean, I can lift weights to get more muscular or go to school to become more intelligent, but I could never grow to be 6 feet 6" tall even with my 1970's platform shoes or stilts.

The point of this last chapter is to make clear that your ability to Grow As A Tiger is both limited by your DNA and limitless by your capacity to grow in Mind, Body and Spirit. Wow. HWS.

So while I am only here for An Indeterminable Amount of Time on Earth, I CHOOSE TO LIVE AS A WARRIOR. I CAN AND WILL TAKE ACTION IF NECESSARY IN DEFENSE OF MYSELF OR OTHERS WITH NO CONCERN FOR MY WELLBEING WHATSOEVER.

It is my hope that something in this book of my Life made you want to take steps to assure that your time here is worthwhile and you can pass your knowledge onto Young Tigers as you evolve into an Older One.

TRAIN. TRAIN. TRAIN UNTIL YOU DIE.

Do something that has meaning so another person of the next generation has something to improve upon.

In the meantime, get training for you and your family and live the life you are destined to.

Then maybe you will have some stories to tell that will make even Thor chuckle.

JUMBO!

William Powell, Shihan

A Man Of The Sixth Dan

William Powell - Founder and Head Instructor of Powell's Way of Kenpo Martial Arts School

- **6th Degree Black Belt, Chinese Kenpo Karate**

- **4th Degree Black Belt Okinawan Karate Do**

- **1st Degree Black Belt Japanese Aikido**

- **1st Degree Black Belt American Judo**

- **Expert level in Carlson Gracie Brazilian Jiu Jitsu, Thai Boxing/Muay Thai, Occidental Tai Chi Chuan, Chinese Kung Fu, Knife and Blade, American Freestyle and Greco Roman Wrestling**

- **2007 Charter Member of Kenpo Karate International Hall of Fame**

- **2003 and 2004 United States Martial Arts International Hall of Fame Inductee**

- **2001 Pan American Games International Jiu Jitsu Gold Medalist**

- **2000 Pan American Games International Jiu Jitsu Bronze Medalist**

- **1999 East-West Submission Wrestling Champion, Peoria IL**

- **1996 World Martial Arts Hall of Fame Inductee**

- **Founder of The Hammers of Thor Mixed Martial Arts Team**

WARRIORS AROUND THE WORLD HOPE FOR A SPEEDY RECOVERY FOR KENPO MASTER AND STAR OF "THE PERFECT WEAPON" JEFF SPEAKMAN WHO IS BATTLING CANCER.

PICTURED HERE BETWEEN MASTER TERRY O'SHEA AND MOI.

AND SO YOU KNOW THAT I PRACTICE WHAT I PREACH, AFTER RECOVERING FROM TRIPLE HERNIA SURGERY A FEW MONTHS AGO, I AM BACK ON THE MAT WITH THE CARLSON GRACIE TEAM FOR THE FIRST TIME SINCE I WON THE PAN AMS IN 2001. ME IN THE CENTER BOTTOM ROW WITH CARLSON GRACIE TO THE LEFT.

AND YEP I GOT MY ASS KICKED AGAIN…FOR THE FIRST TWO CLASSES THAT IS.

ALL ARTWORK AND ILLUSTRATIONS IN THIS BOOK CREATED BY KIMBALL PAUL. ORIGINAL FULL COLOR CANVAS PAINTINGS AVAILABLE FOR SALE AND NEW ART PIECES CAN BE COMMISSIONED AT KIMBALLMASTER@YAHOO.COM. SEE THEM ON KIMBALL'S FACEBOOK PAGE, OR SEARCH "MY MASTER'S VOICE"-PAINTINGS BY KP.

MY WARRIOR BROOD ALONG WITH RACHEL'S BOYFRIEND JOE MAHONEY WISH YOU PEACE.